THE ECONOMICS OF FRANCHISING

This book describes in much detail both how and why franchising works. It also analyzes the economic tensions that contribute to conflict in the franchisor–franchisee relationship. The treatment includes a great deal of empirical evidence on franchising, its importance in various segments of the economy, the terms of franchise contracts, and what we know about how all of these have evolved over time, especially in the U.S. market. A good many myths are dispelled in the process. The economic analysis of the franchisor–franchisee relationship begins with the observation that for franchisors, franchising is a contractual alternative to vertical integration. Subsequently, the tensions that arise between a franchisor and its franchisees, who in fact are owners of independent businesses, are examined in turn. In particular, the authors discuss issues related to product quality control, tying arrangements, pricing, location and territories, advertising, and termination and renewals.

Roger D. Blair is Huber Hurst Professor in the Department of Economics at the University of Florida, where he has served on the faculty since 1970. He teaches courses in antitrust economics, law and economics, and the economics of sports. Professor Blair has published 165 articles, primarily in economics journals and law reviews, and has contributed numerous chapters to books. He has served as an antitrust consultant to the U.S. Department of Justice; the Federal Trade Commission; the attorneys general of Arizona, California, Florida, Missouri, Oregon, and Washington; and numerous corporations. The books he has coauthored include *Antitrust Economics, Law and Economics of Vertical Integration and Control, Monopsony: Antitrust Law and Economics*, and forthcoming from Cambridge University Press, *Intellectual Property: Economics and Legal Dimensions of Rights and Remedies*, with Thomas F. Cotter.

Francine Lafontaine is Professor of Business Economics and Public Policy at the Stephen M. Ross School of Business at the University of Michigan and Professor of Economics, Department of Economics, University of Michigan. Since joining the faculty at Michigan in 1991, Professor Lafontaine has primarily taught applied microeconomics to MBA students, along with elective courses on firm strategy and antitrust and on the economics of franchising. She has published numerous scholarly articles on franchising in top journals in her field, including the *Journal of Political Economy*, the *RAND Journal of Economics*, the *Journal of Law and Economics*, the *Journal of Law, Economics and Organization*, and the *Journal of Industrial Economics*, as well as in marketing and entrepreneurship journals. Professor Lafontaine is widely recognized as a world expert on the subject of franchising and, as such, has acted as consultant to various companies and Federal Trade Commission.

The Economics of Franchising

ROGER D. BLAIR
University of Florida

FRANCINE LAFONTAINE
University of Michigan

CAMBRIDGE UNIVERSITY PRESS
Cambridge, New York, Melbourne, Madrid, Cape Town, Singapore, São Paulo

Cambridge University Press
40 West 20th Street, New York, NY 10011-4211, USA

www.cambridge.org
Information on this title: www.cambridge.org/9780521772525

First published 2005

Printed in the United States of America

A catalog record for this publication is available from the British Library.

Library of Congress Cataloging in Publication Data
Blair, Roger D.
The economics of franchising / Roger D. Blair, Francine Lafontaine.
p.   cm.
Includes bibliographical references and index.
ISBN 0-521-77252-4 (alk. paper)
1. Franchises (Retail trade)   I. Lafontaine, Francine.   II. Title.
HF5429.23.B53   2004
381′.13 – dc22   2004055147

ISBN-13 978-0-521-77252-5 hardback
ISBN-10 0-521-77252-4 hardback

To my parents, Jacques and Thérèse, who would have been proud,
and my family, Robert and Colette, for always being there for me.

To the memory of my parents, Duncan and Eleanor Blair,
who gave me so much.

Contents

Preface

Franchising has become a very visible part of the economic landscape in the United States. Its role in distributing products to customers in the rest of the world has also grown considerably over the last several decades. In this book, we describe what franchising is and how it works. In most situations, franchising works very well for franchisors, franchisees, and consumers alike, which is why it has grown to the extent that it has. Because it works well most of the time, we expect that franchising will continue to flourish in the world economy. At the same time, however, we know from economic principles that franchise relationships are by their very nature fraught with many difficulties arising essentially from differences between the needs and goals of the franchisors and those of the franchisees. Economists and management researchers have made significant progress in the last twenty or so years toward increasing our understanding of the sources of these problems. We highlight much of their work in this book.

We had many goals in writing this book. First, from a managerial perspective, we hope that an improved understanding of the basic sources of friction in franchise relationships will allow franchisors and franchisees alike to develop better ways of dealing with each other's concerns, either through the franchise contract itself or through other means of their choosing. Second, from a public policy perspective, we hope that jurisdictions considering various forms of regulation and control of franchise relationships will be better able to assess the validity and merit of the claims made by interested parties, and thus the cost and benefit of various forms of intervention. In particular, we explore the not-so-obvious consequences of many types of public policies. Finally, from an academic perspective, we want to provide researchers with a clearer understanding of franchising as an institutional framework. By doing so, we hope to foster more interest in the study of franchising itself and of contracts and organizations more generally.

For past and continuing collaboration, we thank our colleagues, Sugato Bhattacharyya, Amanda K. Esquibel, James Fesmire, Jill Boylston Herndon, Arturs Kalnins, David L. Kaserman, Patrick J. Kaufmann, Scott E. Masten, Emmanuel Raynaud, Richard E. Romano, Kathryn L. Shaw, and Margaret E. Slade. We also thank Robert Picard for his expert data management and assistance throughout this project. We are also grateful to Anne Parmigiani for her careful proofing of the manuscript and to Colette Picard for proofing the tables. Our editor at Cambridge University Press, Scott Parris, also deserves a special thanks for his patience and continuing encouragement. Finally, we are grateful to the National Science Foundation (NSF), under grant SBR-9312083, and our respective institutions for their support.

1

Introduction

Franchising has become a part of everyday life for most consumers in the United States today – it is everywhere. Numerous firms in a variety of industries have adopted franchising as a method of doing business. As a result, consumers now often purchase meals and hotel services along with car repairs, clothing, specialty foods, and many other types of goods and services through franchised companies. Why have so many firms involved in such different activities all chosen to organize themselves as franchised companies? We know that a combination of factors makes franchising desirable. On the one hand, the increased reliance of consumers on brand names, due in part to increased consumer mobility and greater time constraints, has played an important role in the development of retail and other chains.[1] In addition, chains can benefit from lower costs through bulk purchasing programs and by realizing economies of scale in production, new product development, and advertising. These benefits, however, really explain why *chains* have become more prevalent in the economy, not why *franchising* has become so ubiquitous. After all, the stores in these chains could all be corporately owned, as is the case in many chains. Why then do we see so many other chains organized as franchises? The answer apparently lies in the capacity of franchising to combine the chain's comparative advantages in creating brand recognition and capturing economies of scale with the

---

[1] The increased time constraints, in turn, can be traced to the increased participation of women in the labor force, and the resulting "out-sourcing" by households, as well as the increasing complexity of products available for consumption. The result is that households must now make a greater number of more complex consumption decisions. Known brands that reduce uncertainty and thus save time become particularly valuable to customers in this context. Moreover, the cost of creating and maintaining national or internationally known brands has gone down dramatically over time.

local entrepreneur's local knowledge and drive.[2] In other words, in the ideal franchise relationship, each party is able to specialize in what each does best and yet benefit from the efforts of the other. In fact, as we will see in more detail later, most franchise contracts are written such that both parties share in the sales revenues of the franchised outlet. The contract thus ensures that both parties have incentives to put forth effort to increase those revenues. Such joint incentives are more difficult to achieve in a corporate environment and therein lies the main long-term advantage of franchising over corporate organization.

The capacity of franchising contracts to harness the effort of a central entity, the franchisor, and of a number of local entrepreneurs, the franchisees, explains in our view much of its current prevalence and popularity as a way of organizing certain economic activities. In particular, franchising is well suited to retailing and service businesses as firms in these sectors need to establish a large number of geographically dispersed outlets to reach customers. In that context, both suppliers of franchises, namely the firms who organize themselves as franchised chains, and the demanders of franchises, that is those individuals eager to develop a small local business, benefit from the interconnection that franchising affords them. Franchisors and their franchisees thus cooperate with one another in a kind of partnership. In many regards, the interests of the franchisor and its franchisees are mutually compatible. Their cooperation increases value for both parties: both earn more profit than they would absent this cooperation.

In an economic sense, we know that franchising must be efficient as an organizational form since it continues to thrive in competition with other organizational structures.[3] In this book, we summarize much of what is known about the economics of franchising. We examine the economic principles that help explain its popularity as a method of distribution, but also highlight how economic principles can shed light on many ways in which franchisor and franchisee needs diverge. These divergent interests create conflict between the franchisor and its franchisees, conflict that undermines the value that cooperation creates. For continued success, this conflict must be minimized. We believe that clearly laying out the sources of conflict is a good first step toward that goal. We therefore devote a substantial portion of this book to the analysis of conflict in franchising. We also devote significant attention to describing

---

[2] Caves and Murphy (1976) first made this point and developed the argument.

[3] This follows from the survivor principle. For more on this principle and its origins, see Stigler (1968).

franchising and analyzing how it works. In the process, we report data on various aspects of the franchise relationship wherever available and relevant, complementing existing data with new empirical information we derive from a data set on U.S. franchisors that we have built over time from directories. Because our data and our knowledge of applicable law are particular to U.S. franchising, much of our discussion is focused on the way franchising works in this country. This, however, is not as much of a shortcoming as one might suppose. First, we present non-U.S. information whenever we can. More importantly, the general economic principles that we highlight are relevant in all countries and, as will be clear from available data, franchising practices do not differ markedly between countries. Thus, our hope is that the content of this book will prove relevant to anyone with an interest in franchising regardless of where he or she lives and works.

Before launching into an economic analysis of franchising as an organizational form, we explore a few basics to frame our subsequent analysis. We begin by defining the franchise relationship, distinguishing between *traditional* and *business-format* franchising, and identifying the locus and extent of franchising in the U.S. economy. We then describe our data on franchisors, data that we rely on throughout the book. We conclude this introductory chapter by laying out a road map for the remainder of the book.

1.1 What Is a Franchise?

According to the *American Heritage Dictionary of the English Language*, the word franchise comes from the old French word *franche*, which means free or exempt. In medieval times, a franchise was a right or privilege granted by a sovereign power – king, church, or local government. Sovereigns granted *franchises* for various activities, such as building roads, holding fairs, organizing markets, or for the right to maintain civil order and collect taxes. In essence, the sovereign gave an individual or group of individuals the monopoly rights over a particular activity in a particular location for a certain period of time. In most cases, the grantee was required to make a payment to the sovereign power for this right or privilege, usually in the form of a share of the product or profit. That payment was called a *royalty*, a term still in use to this day.

Today, a franchise agreement is most often understood as a contractual arrangement between two legally independent firms in which one firm, the franchisee, pays the other firm, the franchisor, for the right to sell the franchisor's product and/or the right to use its trademarks and business format in a given location for a specified period of time. But this use of the term franchising in the English language only goes back to the late 1950s: according to Dicke (1992: 2), the word franchise – understood as a method of doing business or distributing goods and services – entered the English business lexicon in 1959. Moreover, governments still grant franchises in certain industries. This occurs, for example, in the cable TV industry in the United States where the rights to be the sole provider of cable services in a given market for a certain time period are sold by local governments to firms usually through what is called a "franchise bidding" process.[4] In addition, the word franchise is used in the sports industry to refer to the right to operate a team in a particular locale.[5] In this book, however, we focus on the type of franchising that represents an ongoing business relationship between legally independent commercial firms, and accordingly we use the term to mean only such arrangements.

According to the Federal Trade Commission (FTC), the body that has jurisdiction in the United States over federal disclosure rules for franchisors, three elements must be present for a business relationship to be deemed a franchise.[6] First, the franchisor must license a trade name and trademark that the franchisee operates under, or the franchisee must sell products or services identified by this trademark. Second, the franchisor must exert significant control over the operation of the franchisee or provide significant assistance to the franchisee. Third, the franchisee must pay at least $500 to the franchisor at any time before or within the first six months of operation.[7] Note that though this definition of franchising is specific to the U.S., most definitions used by authorities outside of the U.S., including Australia, Canada, and the European

---

[4] For more on "franchise bidding" in the U.S. cable industry, see for example Zupan (1989a, 1989b) and Prager (1990) and the references therein. For an analysis of contemporary highway construction franchise contracts granted by a government, see Engel et al. (2001).

[5] For examples of this use of the term franchise, see Noll and Zimbalist (1997) and the history of the NFL at http://www.football.com/history/index.shtml.

[6] For a detailed account of different definitions of commercial franchises used in the academic literature across a variety of fields, see Stanworth and Curran (1999). For a review of the legal elements of franchises as per the text of various state franchise laws, see for example Pitegoff (1989).

[7] See Federal Trade Commission (1979). See http://www.ftc.gov/bcp/franchise/netrule.htm for a guide to this rule. Note that in its interpretive guide, the FTC specifies that payments for inventory at bona fide wholesale prices for resale are not considered a "minimum payment" for the purposes of this last requirement. See Final Interpretive Guides, 44 Fed. Reg. at 49967.

Union (EU), rely on a similar set of criteria.[8] In their implementation, however, foreign definitions are often less inclusive. We come back to this briefly below.

1.2 Traditional and Business-Format Franchising

In the U.S., the Department of Commerce (USDOC) historically has distinguished two separate types of franchised relationships: *traditional* (or *product and trade name*) franchising and *business-format* franchising. The former is characterized by franchised dealers who "concentrate on one company's product line and to some extent identify their business with that company" (USDOC 1988: 1). Thus, the Ford dealer, for example, is identified as a distributor of Ford automobiles. As the name suggests, traditional franchising is the oldest form of modern franchising. By most accounts, it can be traced back in the U.S. at least to the mid-1800s when the McCormick Harvesting Machine Company and the Singer Sewing Machines Company sold their products through sales agents who were given exclusive sales territories.[9] Initially, these firms, like others who used such agents at the time, imposed few restrictions or qualifications on their agents and exerted very little control over them. Over time, however, both companies found they needed more control over these sales agents if they were to protect their respective reputations and brands. The McCormick Company responded by establishing company-owned branch houses throughout the U.S. and Canada. These branch houses were given oversight responsibilities for the sales agents in their territories. As a result, McCormick was able to systematize procedures and communications with its agents, thereby transforming them into what one would now call "dealers." As for the Singer Company, it addressed the need for control by converting many of the independent agencies into company outlets. More importantly, it devised a series of recommendations for the remaining agents as to how the offices should be run and, for the first time, required detailed

---

[8] See the *Franchising Code of Conduct*, Commonwealth of Australia, 1998; the *Arthur Wishart Act in Ontario*, Canada; and the *EEC Block Exemption for Vertical Restraints*. Note that a definition of franchising is no longer included directly in the *EEC Block Exemption for Vertical Restraints*, but a description of the contents of franchise agreements is found in the attached guidelines (text fig. 35, 36, 189ff.) and the know-how definition has remained the same as in the old *EEC Block Exemption for Franchise Agreements*.

[9] See Dicke (1992) on the history of franchising in the United States, including a detailed account of its evolution at these two companies. See also Marx (1985) on the development of franchising in automobile retailing in the U.S.

financial reporting from these agents. The contracts and methods of control that Singer developed at the time are largely recognized as the forerunners of the modern franchise agreement.[10]

Traditional franchising today is comprised largely of automobile dealerships, gasoline service stations, and soft-drink bottlers.[11] In all of these businesses, the franchisor is a manufacturer who sells finished or semi-finished products to its dealers/franchisees. In turn, the franchisees resell these products to consumers or other firms in the distribution chain. Because the franchisor's product is sold to its franchisees, the franchisor's profits from its dealer network flow from the markups it earns on these products. In contrast to what occurs in business-format franchising, as described below, traditional franchisees do not pay running royalties on their sales.

Traditional franchising accounted for 72.7 percent of all sales by franchised chains in 1986, the last year in which the U.S. government collected and published statistics on franchising.[12] The remaining 27.3 percent of all franchised sales were generated by business-format franchising firms in which the franchisor primarily sells a way of doing business (i.e., a business format) to its franchisees. A business-format franchise thus "includes not only the product, service, and trademark, but the entire business format itself – a marketing strategy and plan, operating manuals and standards, quality control, and continuing two-way communication" (USDOC 1988: 3).

The first true business-format franchise system was created by Martha Mathilda Harper (Plitt 2000). This entrepreneur developed her network of Harper Beauty Shops from the early 1890s onward using a business model

---

[10] In England, the development of franchising is usually traced back to the development of the "tied house system," namely the ownership of licensed beer retailers by brewers. See especially Knox (1958) on the reasons behind the growth of this system in London.

[11] William E. Metzger is said to have been the first franchisee in automotive retailing; he obtained a franchise to sell steam automobiles from General Motors Corporation in 1898 (Justis and Judd 1998: 1–9). Coca-Cola sold its first bottling franchise in 1899.

[12] The USDOC cancelled its publication of *Franchising in the Economy* in 1988 as part of its privatization program. This publication was the only source of Census-type data on franchising in the United States. Efforts by the International Franchise Association (IFA) to take over the publication of this annual report on a permanent basis were unsuccessful. However, in cooperation with Frandata Inc., the IFA Educational Foundation recently produced *The Profile of Franchising, Volumes I, II, and III*. These profiles report summary data per sector based on information contained in the disclosure documents of all franchisors that had to file such documents in at least one of the twelve filing U.S. states. Though the resulting set of franchisors covered in the profiles is not the whole population of franchisors in the U.S., these publications provide some very useful information that we rely on when appropriate in the remainder of this book.

that included all of the components of a business format as described by the USDOC, and more. But though she grew her network to more than 500 shops in the U.S., Canada, and Europe by the mid-1920s, Mathilda Harper unfortunately did not leave a lasting mark on franchising. Other firms, such as the supermarket chain Piggly Wiggly, Hertz Car Rentals, IGA (Independent Grocers Association), A&W Restaurants, Ben Franklin Retailers, Maid Rite (a hamburger restaurant chain), and Terminix Termite and Pest Control all started franchising in the 1920s and are still franchising today. According to the French Franchise Federation, Jean Prouvost, owner of the Lainière de Roubais, launched his network of Pingouin stores also in the 1920s, thereby initiating the concept of franchised distribution in France.[13] These early entrants were followed in the 1930s by companies like Howard Johnson Restaurants, Stewart's Drive-In, Arthur Murray Schools of Dancing, and Culligan in the U.S., and by the Canadian Tire retail chain and its Associate Store program, Merle Norman Cosmetics, and Le Groupe RONA among others in Canada.[14] But it was not until the 1950s, with the advent of chains such as Burger King and McDonald's, and the economic boom of the post–World War II era, that business-format franchising fully came into its own in the U.S. and Canada, and, even more recently, throughout much of the rest of the world.[15]

Business-format franchising today encompasses a very large number of firms that provide a wide array of goods and services: automotive products and services, computer sales, business aids and services, construction and maintenance, legal, domestic, and childcare services, and non-food retailing as well as the more visible hotel, fast-food, and car rental franchises. In exchange for the business format, franchisees typically pay a relatively small lump-sum fixed fee at the beginning of the contract period and pay running royalties that are usually calculated as a fixed percentage of the

[13] See Fédération Française de la Franchise (2003: 12). Though this source indicates that the network of stores was developed in the 1930s, the French National Archives states that it was started in 1923. See http://www.archivesnationales.culture.gouv.fr/camt/fr/egf/lettrel.html.

[14] Some networks, such as IGA, le Groupe RONA, and Best Western International, are organized as cooperatives whose role it is to provide their franchisees (members) with purchasing power and name recognition. The development and organization of these cooperatives is interesting in light of Caves and Murphy's (1976: 576) view of franchising as a mechanism by which "franchisees hire out the collective and large-scale production of goodwill." See also Lafontaine and Raynaud (2002) for an analysis that draws an analogy between food production cooperatives and franchises.

[15] See Arthur Andersen & Co. (1995) for an overview of the number of franchisors and franchisees in 36 countries around the world.

franchisee's sales revenues.[16] Business-format franchisees also often contribute an additional fraction of their sales or revenues toward an advertising fund for the chain as a whole. Presumably, the advertising carried out
with these funds benefits all franchisees and thereby benefits the franchisor
as well.

In the end, the distinction between traditional and business-format franchising is somewhat arbitrary and basically a matter of degree. Dnes (1992a)
and Klein (1995), for example, both argue that there is little economic difference between the two, in terms of either the type of agreements they rely on
or the type of support provided or control exerted by franchisors. And when
it comes to theoretical analyses of franchise relationships, the distinction between these two types of franchising indeed is largely irrelevant: researchers
have considered both types simultaneously in many studies. But while in
theory the distinction may not be so meaningful, it is important from a descriptive standpoint for two main reasons. First, in many countries outside
the U.S., traditional franchising is not included in franchising statistics. As a
result, the franchising sector appears artificially large in the U.S. relative to
these other countries. Second, in the U.S., authors often refer to all franchising when they emphasize its economic importance: after all, sales of goods
and services through traditional and business-format franchising together
amounted to almost 13 percent of real gross domestic product (GDP) (see
Chapter 2), or 34 percent of retail sales, in 1986 according to the USDOC
(1988: 14). When presenting data about the growth in franchising in the U.S.,
however, the data more often measure business-format franchising only. This
is because business-format franchising has grown much faster than traditional
franchising over the last few decades. Thus, the separation of franchising into
two different types has allowed the trade press to mostly emphasize those franchising figures that show franchising in its most favorable light. We return to
the issue of franchising growth in the next chapter.

1.3 In Which Industries Do We Find Franchising?

As noted by the USDOC (1988: 14), "[r]etailing dominates franchising, accounting for 87 percent of all franchising receipts in 1987. The retail sales
of all firms associated with franchising reached about $522 billion in 1987,

---

[16] There are exceptions to royalties calculated as a percentage of total revenue. These include
minimum payment provisions, increasing and decreasing scales, and royalties defined
as a percentage of profits. These alternatives, however, are observed far less frequently
than constant rate sales revenue royalties. See Chapter 3 for details.

or 34 percent of all U.S. retail sales, which are estimated at $1.5 trillion."[17] Table 1-1 shows the sectoral breakdown for sales, the number of establishments, and employment for franchised firms in the U.S. in 1986 as per the USDOC (1988). It also shows average sales per establishment in each sector.

Table 1-1 first confirms that sales through traditional franchising are almost three times the level of sales of business-format franchisors. In contrast, the bulk of the establishments and employment are in business-format franchising. The number of establishments is twice as large and the number of employees is almost three times larger in business-format than in traditional franchising. This implies that sales per unit and sales per employee are much larger in traditional than in business-format franchising. This is shown in the last column of Table 1-1, in which sales per establishment for car dealerships and soft-drink bottlers completely overwhelm those of gasoline stations as well as those of every type of business-format franchise. While the government data above all pertain to 1986, a recent report on the economic impact of franchising in the U.S. economy suggests that business-format franchising in 2001 encompassed 4.3 times as many establishments and employed four times as many workers as traditional franchising did.[18]

Table 1-1 also illustrates that franchising occurs in a wide variety of retail and service industries in the U.S. economy. Within business-format franchising, the bulk of sales, units, and employees in 1986 were found in the restaurant sector, which includes such well-known chains as Burger King, KFC, Little Caesar's, McDonald's, and Subway, among many others. The next largest sector from a sales perspective was the non-food retailing sector, which includes chains such as The Athlete's Foot, The Body Shop, Decorating Den, and General Nutrition Centers. From an establishment and an employment perspective, however, the second largest business-format franchising sector was the business aids and services sectors, with firms such as Money Mailer, SignFast, and Snelling Personnel Services.

The data in Table 1-1, however, reflect the sector distribution of franchising activities as it existed in 1986. Unfortunately, since *Franchising in the Economy* is no longer published by the U.S. government, updated figures corresponding to those in Table 1-1 are unavailable. This lack of data has made it quite difficult

---

[17] Retail sales in the U.S. reached $3.5 trillion in nominal terms in 2001 (U.S. Census Bureau, "Monthly Retail Trade Survey," *Historical Retail Trade Data*). Assuming that the proportion of retail trade accounted for by franchised companies has remained at about one-third of all retailing, franchising would now account for more than $1 trillion in retail business in the U.S. (in 2001 dollars). We address the issue of franchising growth in Chapter 2.

[18] See IFA Educational Foundation and Price Waterhouse Coopers, 2004.

Table 1-1: *Sales, establishments, and employment in franchising in the U.S. in 1986*

Sector	Sales ($ thousands)	Number of establishments	Number of employees*	Sales per establishment ($ thousands)
Automobile and Truck Dealers	307,256,000	27,600	947,400	11,132
Gasoline Service Stations	86,618,000	120,510	596,400	719
Soft-Drink Bottlers	19,662,000	1,203	126,200	16,344
All Traditional Franchising	413,536,000	149,313	1,670,000	2,770
Automotive Products and Services[a]	11,300,863	36,763	186,182	307
Business Aids and Services[b]	13,288,254	52,718	669,522	252
Construction, Home Improvement, Maintenance, and Cleaning Services[c]	4,615,360	18,900	118,991	244
Convenience Stores	11,278,895	15,524	152,688	726
Educational Products and Services[d]	935,166	8,625	41,210	108
Hotels, Motels, and Campgrounds	15,983,990	8,203	555,674	1,949
Laundry and Drycleaning Services	291,802	2,297	9,891	127
Recreation, Entertainment, and Travel[e]	3,549,025	7,901	27,732	449
Rental Services (Auto–Truck)[f]	6,155,006	9,528	66,423	646
Rental Services (Equipment)[g]	716,019	2,718	14,926	263
Restaurants	52,273,863	78,203	2,453,621	668
Retailing (Food Non-Convenience)[h]	10,746,011	19,852	214,768	541
Retailing (Non-Food)[i]	23,102,779	45,456	274,663	508
Miscellaneous[j]	1,305,715	6,122	44,486	213
All Business-Format Franchising	155,542,748	312,810	4,830,777	497
Total Franchising	569,078,748	462,123	6,500,777	1,231

Note: * Includes part-time and working proprietors.

[a] Includes Tire, Battery, and Accessory Stores; Auto and Truck Wash Services; Brake and Muffler Repair and Services; and some establishments with significant sales of non-automotive products such as Household Appliances, Garden Supplies, and others.

[b] Includes Computer Services, Business Consultants and Brokers, Security, Dentists, Insurance, and Others.

[c] Includes Furniture Repairs, Water Conditioning, Lawn Care, Sewer Cleaning, and Carpet Cleaning.

[d] Includes Day-Care Centers and Health and Diet Services.

[e] Includes Travel Agencies, Miniature Golf Courses, and Dance Studios.

[f] Includes Leasing.

[g] Includes Formal Wear.

[h] Includes Retail Specialty Food Shops, Donut Shops, Ice Cream Stores, Coffee Services, Candy Stores, Bakeries and Supermarkets.

[i] Includes General Merchandise, Drugs and Cosmetics, Gift Shops, Shoes and Apparel, Hardware, Paints and Floor Covering, Furniture, Draperies and Bedding, Consumer Electronics, and Vending.

[j] Includes Beauty Salons, Fitness Centers, Wholesale Services, and Others.

Source: USDOC (1988) (with calculations for rows involving "all traditional" and "all business format").

to accurately assess how franchising has evolved since the mid-1980s in the United States.[19]

In this book, we rely on a database on franchisors that we have constructed from franchisor directories to shed some light on the evolution of franchising and the franchise relationship since the mid-1980s, and to provide a more accurate description of current data patterns. Our database covers all the franchisors that appear at least once in the 1981 to 1993 *Entrepreneur's* "Franchise 500" surveys or in the 1994 to 2002 editions of Bond's *Source Book of Franchise Opportunities*, now called the *Bond's Franchise Guide*.[20] Each year, these publications give detailed profiles for about 1,000 franchising companies and, hence, cover a very significant portion of the industry. In each case, the data for a given year are obtained from the next year's survey or directory as these are all published early in the calendar year. In other words, our 2001 data are from the 2002 *Bond's Franchise Guide*. After 1994, we chose to use the *Bond's Franchise Guide* because *Entrepreneur's* 1994 survey covered fewer chains than usual and, from 1995 onward, *Entrepreneur* stopped reporting advertising fee data. Furthermore, the *Bond's Franchise Guide*, which has the advantage of providing more details on each of the franchisors it profiles, had become an annual publication by then.[21] Together, these sources provide information from 1980 through 2001 (except for 1999, as the 2000 *Bond's Franchise Guide* was never published) and cover more than 5,000 franchisors in total, 12 percent of which on average are Canadian.

Table 1-2 displays the specific number of franchisors included in our data each year. For the years when this information was available, namely the early 1980s, the table also shows the total number of U.S. franchisors according to the USDOC. It is clear from this information that our data are not of census quality, meaning that not all U.S. franchisors are included in our sources. In fact, the number of U.S. franchisors in the data is slightly below the numbers

---

[19] The 2001 snapshot provided by the IFA Educational Foundation and Price Waterhouse Coopers (2004) does not use the same sector classification as the USDOC. Moreover, it only provides aggregate information on total establishments, jobs, payroll, and value added in each sector and does not allow us to follow franchising activities over time. Of course, we still rely on it whenever it provides additional insights into franchising activity.

[20] We exclude from our data the few chains that are in these sources but yet report either no outlet at all (that is, no company nor franchised outlet) or report absolutely no fees (that is, no royalty rate, franchise fee, advertising rate, or ongoing fixed payments) in the survey year.

[21] The *Bond's Franchise Guides* were also published in 1985, 1989, and then in 1990–91 and 1991–92, and in 1993. Since then, they have been published yearly, except for the 2000 edition (with the 1999 data) that was skipped.

Table 1-2: *The coverage of our data set*

Year	Number of franchisors – USDOC data*	Number of franchisors – our data	Number of units of these franchisors – USDOC data*	Number of units of these franchisors – our data
1980	1584	1089	252,548	164,483
1981	1673	1100	260,555	175,907
1982	1770	1220	268,306	189,259
1983	1877	1169	276,195	196,090
1984	1942	880	283,576	199,373
1985	2090	926	301,689	206,146
1986	2177	1075	312,810	211,991
1987		1075		217,261
1988		1023		217,038
1989		1059		230,059
1990		1096		238,284
1991		1018		238,545
1992		992		240,505
1993		1100		223,554
1994		1100		223,234
1995		1104		251,108
1996		1103		273,283
1997		1033		283,769
1998		995		303,168
2000		984		344,585
2001		1158		382,061

Source: The source for the data in columns 2 and 4 is USDOC (1988). We compiled the other data.

shown in column 2 of the table given the proportion of Canadian firms in our data. The implication is that we cannot easily make inferences on the extent of franchising or its growth over time from our data. Moreover, Table 1-2 shows that the extent of coverage of franchised companies by the directories that are the source of our data has changed over time, with an especially important decrease in coverage in 1984 and 1985 relative to surrounding years. Finally, by the mid 1980s, the proportion of franchisors included in our data was around one-half, while the proportion of units covered by these franchisors was around two-thirds. In other words, Table 1-2 also shows that the average franchisor that appears in our data tends to be somewhat larger, in terms of units, than the average franchisor that does not.

In sum, while we make no claim that our data reflect the whole population of franchisors, they still cover a substantial portion of franchising activity, and thus help us shed light on what has occurred in this important sector of the economy since the mid-1980s in the United States in a way that no other source can achieve.

It is important to recognize that there is significant turnover in the set of franchisors included in our data each year. This explains why 5,052 different franchisors appear at least once in our data, even though most estimates put the current population of franchisors in the U.S. somewhere around 2,500.[22] Our data contains many more largely because of the significant amount of entry into and exit from franchising that has occurred during the 1980s and 1990s. We come back to this issue in Chapter 2. For the purposes of describing our data, Table 1-3 simply details the number of franchisors that appear once, two times, or three times, and so on in our data, and the average year when these different sets of franchisors started in business and in franchising. The information on the average year they started franchising confirms that franchisors that appear only a few times in our data tend to be those that got involved in franchising relatively late in our sample period.

For each franchisor in each year, our data sources specifically provide information on (1) the number of company-owned and franchised outlets; (2) the years of business and franchising experience; (3) the royalty rate, advertising fee, and franchise fee charged by the franchisor; and (4) a set of variables describing, for example, the amount of capital required to open an outlet, whether the chain is Canadian or not, and the type of business in which it is involved. For those years when our data are extracted from the *Bond's Franchise Guide*, we also know other characteristics such as the number of states the chain has outlets in, the amount of initial training provided by the franchisor, the typical number of employees in a unit, the average square footage needed, the number of outlets outside the U.S., the duration of the contract, and so on.[23]

We have described the data that we will use throughout this book to document patterns in franchising in the U.S. and address various issues related to contract terms and practices; we can now return to the question of the sectoral distribution of business-format franchising as it now stands.

---

[22] As shown in Table 1-2, in 1986 the USDOC estimated the number of U.S. franchisors to be 2,177. Since then, estimates of the number of U.S. franchisors have varied widely in the trade press, but listings from directories suggest that 2,500 to 3,000 is a reasonable estimate. In their production of the *Profile of Franchising Volume III*, the IFA and Frandata examined all franchisors that had filed a Uniform Franchise Offering Circular (UFOC) in one of the twelve states requiring such filing in 1998. They obtained information for a total of 1,226 franchised companies. As the authors acknowledge (see p. 13), this figure cannot be used as an estimate of the population of franchisors in the U.S., as franchisors that do not operate in any of the twelve states requiring such filing do not appear in their data.

[23] For the years prior to 1993, and for about half of the chains in our data set, we were also able to obtain data on the number of states in which the chain has units and on the amount of training provided from the USDOC's *Franchise Opportunities Handbook*.

Table 1-3: *Sample characteristics*

Observed	Number of firms	Number of observations	Started in business in (mean)	Started franchising in (mean)
Only once	1,429	1,429	1977.8	1984.3
Twice	946	1,892	1978.5	1984.7
3 times	591	1,773	1976.8	1983.4
4 times	460	1,840	1974.4	1982.4
5 times	278	1,390	1976.8	1983.0
6 times	254	1,524	1974.5	1982.2
7 times	204	1,428	1974.8	1981.9
8 times	165	1,320	1971.8	1980.6
9 times	97	873	1971.6	1980.6
10 times	110	1,100	1971.2	1979.4
11 times	86	946	1973.2	1978.5
12 times	72	864	1972.7	1979.9
13 times	70	910	1969.4	1977.1
14 times	48	672	1970.6	1976.9
15 times	36	540	1971.1	1978.1
16 times	37	592	1966.1	1973.2
17 times	37	629	1966.2	1972.5
18 times	37	666	1968.5	1974.4
19 times	25	475	1965.0	1969.9
20 times	34	680	1964.3	1969.9
21 times	36	756	1961.8	1965.5
Total	5,052	22,299		

Note: Although our data covers a period of 22 years, from 1980 to 2001, we can observe a given chain a maximum of 21 times since we have no data for the year 1999.

Using the sector definitions of the USDOC, Table 1-4 shows this distribution for the 1,074 franchisors that appear in our data set in 1986 and compares it to the number of franchisors per sector in 1986 according to the USDOC (1988). This exercise required that we classify each of the franchisors in our data among the sectors used by the USDOC. Since their sector definitions are not very detailed, there is room for classification error.[24] Still, we can see

---

[24] For example, while the distinction between food retailing and restaurant is generally easy to make, it is not so obvious when it comes to donut or bagel shops. The sector definitions are made somewhat clearer in a series of footnotes in *Franchising in the Economy* that we reproduce under Table 1-1. From these, we see that the USDOC considers donut shops to be part of food retailing, not the restaurant sector. We followed their lead on these and on bakeries where we suspected that the bulk of the business was in retail. We classified as restaurants those chains where the bulk of the business is for prepared food consumed on the premises or for take out.

Table 1-4: *The sectoral distribution of business-format franchisors*

Sector	Number of franchisors in 1986 per USDOC	Number of franchisors in data set in 1986	Proportion of population sampled in 1986	Number of franchisors in data in 1996	Number of franchisors in data in 2001
Automotive Products and Services	174	95	54.6	73	80
Business Aids and Services	436	189	43.3	173	180
Construction, Home Improvement, Maintenance, and Cleaning Services	184	100	54.3	130	167
Convenience Stores	27	14	51.9	8	10
Educational Products and Services	68	34	50.0	56	62
Hotels, Motels, and Campgrounds	50	21	42.0	14	21
Laundry and Dry-Cleaning Services	19	9	47.4	10	12
Recreation, Entertainment, and Travel	45	24	53.3	40	29
Rental Services, Auto–Truck	27	17	63.0	13	18
Rental Services, Equipment	36	21	58.3	13	8
Restaurants	488	209	42.8	243	245
Retailing (Food Non-Convenience)	198	100	50.5	89	103
Retailing (Non-Food)	339	176	51.9	174	159
Miscellaneous	86	66	76.7	67	64
Total Number of Business-Format Franchisors	2,177	1,075	49.4	1,103	1,158

Source: The source for the data in the first column is USDOC (1988). We compiled the others.

15

from Table 1-4 that our best effort at classifying all the franchisors suggests that our data covers between 42 and 77 percent of the franchisors in each of the USDOC sectors in 1986.

Table 1-4 also shows the number of franchisors in our data set, per USDOC sector, ten years later in 1996, and then again in 2001. It is difficult to disentangle from these figures how much of the change in numbers of franchisors per sector between 1986 and 1996 or 2001 is due to sampling changes, and how much is due to real growth in some sectors compared to others. Assuming that there has not been a major change over time in the survey sampling procedures used by our sources, the data in Table 1-4 suggest that there has been some decline since the mid-1980s in the number of automotive products and services franchisors and equipment rental franchisors. On the other hand, the data indicate that there are now more franchisors in the construction, maintenance and cleaning services industry, in the educational products and services sector, and in the restaurant sector. We expect the latter reflects the relative growth in the number of sandwich and bagel shops as well as the newer quick-casual segment of this industry. These patterns are confirmed generally by corresponding data from the IFA Educational and Price Waterhouse Coopers (2004) report which show a significant decrease, relative to the 1986 USDOC data, in the number of establishments in the automotive sector in the U.S. (from the 36,763 shown in Table 1-1 to 28,755 in 2001 according to the IFA report) and a substantial increase in the number of restaurants (from 78,203 in Table 1-1 to 183,318 in the IFA report). Unfortunately, differences in sector definitions between the sources prevent us from making further comparisons.

As we discuss in some detail in Chapter 2, our data set offers a good approximation of the overall population of new franchisors except for the last few years of our data. To provide a better sense of where entry has been most prevalent in the 1980s and early 1990s, we rely on the number of new franchisors in our data per USDOC sector. Specifically, we present in Table 1-5 the number of franchisors that started franchising in every three-year period, starting in 1980 and ending in 1997. We end with 1997 because we only have a few years of data to identify the new entrants at the end of our sample period and, hence, we do not capture them all. But from our earlier data, more than 90 percent of the franchisors appear in our data within five to six years of when they start franchising. Thus, the number of new franchisors in 1995 and 1996 may still be underestimated in Table 1-5; for all the years prior to that, however, we have a reasonable estimate of the number of new entrants.

The data in Table 1-5 first show a sizable reduction in the number of new franchisors in the early 1990s relative to the 1980s, even ignoring the 1995 to

Table 1-5: *The sectoral distribution of new business-format franchisors*

Sector	Number of franchisors in data set that started franchising in:							Total
	1980–82	1983–85	1986–88	1989–91	1992–94	1995–97		
Automotive Products and Services	50	55	50	30	19	12		216
Business Aids and Services	143	102	131	114	70	35		595
Construction, Home Improvement, Maintenance, and Cleaning Services	73	58	68	71	48	39		357
Convenience Stores	5	4	4	3	5	3		24
Educational Products and Services	32	28	34	24	32	9		159
Hotels, Motels, and Campgrounds	8	8	11	7	4	7		45
Laundry and Dry-Cleaning Services	2	8	11	4	4	3		32
Recreation, Entertainment, and Travel	26	26	20	22	26	8		128
Rental Services, Auto–Truck	13	8	4	3	3	2		33
Rental Services, Equipment	19	32	13	18	3	2		87
Restaurants	139	107	134	120	84	27		611
Retailing (Food Non-Convenience)	64	69	66	32	35	19		285
Retailing (Non-Food)	130	105	143	90	90	52		610
Miscellaneous	73	51	52	58	31	24		289
Total Business-Format Franchising	777	661	741	596	454	242		3471

Source: Compiled by the authors.

1997 data. On average, for the three 3-year periods in the 1980s, there were more than 700 new entrants; for the two 3-year periods in the early 1990s, the average declined to 525. Consistent with Table 1-4, Table 1-5 also shows fewer new franchisors in the automotive products and services sector and in the equipment rental sector in the early 1990s than in earlier periods. Other sectors, such as the educational products and services sector and, to a lesser extent, the construction and maintenance and restaurant sectors, show a fairly constant number of new entrants over the 1980 to 1994 period despite the fairly large decline in total entry at the end of this time period. In other words, in proportion to total entry, these sectors are more than holding their own. This further supports the data in Table 1-4 in which we found significant growth in these sectors.[25]

According to the USDOC data and industry sources, the growth in business-format franchising was tied to the fast-food industry in the 1960s and to the business aids and services and the automotive products and services in the 1970s. Our data suggest that in the 1980s and early 1990s, it has been tied mostly to the personal service sector (such as maid services, day-care facilities, lawn maintenance, and health and fitness services) and to the diversification and continued growth of franchising within the restaurant industry.

1.4 Plan of Study

Our goal in *The Economics of Franchising* is to both describe how franchising works and highlight the economic tensions that contribute to conflict in the franchisor–franchisee relationship. To this end, we begin in Chapter 2 with an examination of four popular misconceptions regarding franchising. These misconceptions involve the extent of growth, the financial security afforded by franchising, the size of franchised chains, and the extent of single-unit ownership by franchisees.

In Chapter 3, we highlight some of the main components of franchise contracts, paying particular attention to the financial components of the contract, namely royalty rates, franchise fees, and advertising fees. For each of these, we examine in particular their levels and how they vary across chains and industries. We also investigate how the tendency to use these different fees and the levels at which they are set have evolved between 1980 and 2001.

---

[25] Of course, growth really depends not only on entry, but also on how many firms exit the sector. We return to this issue in Chapter 2.

We conclude, among other things, by pointing out the similarity between the fees structures and levels charged by U.S. and non-U.S. franchisors.

In Chapter 4, we explore franchising as a contractual alternative to vertical integration for franchisors. We show how firms involved in franchising typically use a mix of franchised and vertically integrated, or company-owned, outlets. We then present a more detailed examination of a set of vertical restraints that can be used to replicate the vertically integrated outcome, at least in theory, and evaluate their performance under various circumstances. Finally, we discuss agency–theoretic arguments that have been used to explain variation in the main financial contract terms used in franchise contracts, and show how these arguments also can shed light on why different franchisors choose different levels of vertical integration.

From that point on, each of the remaining chapters of this book is dedicated to a detailed examination of a specific conflict area between franchisors and franchisees. We begin each of these chapters with the economic motivation for the problem, followed by an examination of the relevant court cases and legislation, if applicable. We conclude each chapter by examining the likely effect of this source of conflict on franchisors, franchisees, and franchising as a method of distribution. Specifically, we explore quality control and quality decisions in Chapter 5. We review input purchase requirements in Chapter 6. Chapter 7 focuses on pricing decisions and price constraints. In Chapter 8, we examine outlet location decisions and the encroachment problem. We discuss inherent conflicts of interest related to advertising and promotion in Chapter 9 and terminations, renewals and transfers of franchised units in Chapter 10. Chapter 11 concludes by returning to the idea that despite all these sources of conflict, franchising is a robust organizational form that has withstood the test of time and will continue to play a major role in the U.S. and global economies.

2

Four Popular Misconceptions about Franchising

There are many misconceptions surrounding franchising in the United States and abroad. In our view, these misconceptions result from relying on casual impressions rather than a careful evaluation of the empirical evidence. In this chapter, we focus our attention on four such misconceptions. By summarizing the existing data, we hope to disabuse the reader of these misconceptions and thereby generate a more realistic appreciation of franchising.

We begin with the notion that franchising has been growing at a phenomenal rate in the U.S. for several decades. As we shall show, this impression is misleading: for the last two decades at least, our best estimates indicate that franchising in the U.S. has grown, at most, at rates commensurate with the rest of the economy. Interestingly, research conducted in the United Kingdom suggests that similar claims of tremendous growth in franchising in that country in the 1990s are also ill-founded. Second, we examine the extent of entry and exit for franchisors, and then also for franchisees. The data show that many firms indeed become new franchisors each year, a fact that is well-publicized in the trade press. But many firms also exit franchising or fail, and this generally receives much less attention. As for franchisees, we find that the notion that franchising poses substantially fewer business risks for franchisees than starting an independent business is not supported by the data. Third, we consider the size of franchised chains. Contrary to the impression created by the pervasive presence of very large franchised chains with household names such as Dunkin' Donuts, H&R Block, and McDonald's, we show that the majority of franchised chains are quite small and, thus, not well-established contrary to what people expect. Fourth, and finally, there is an impression that franchisees' businesses are necessarily small, "mom-and-pop" ventures, with each of them operating a single unit. This is also not true: multi-unit franchising is pervasive, and a number of multi-unit franchisees are large enough to rival the size of their own or other franchisors.

2.1 Growth: Fact and Fancy

In this section, we explore how franchising has grown relative to the economy as a whole since the early 1970s. These facts are then compared to the impression of tremendous growth found in the trade press. Our point here is not to deny the importance of franchising as an organizational form, nor the role that it has played in the growth of the economy over the last few decades. On the contrary, it should be clear from the preceding chapter that franchising is a very important method of doing business in the U.S. and elsewhere. But many of the reports of its growth in the last two decades have been grossly exaggerated and must be put in proper perspective.

We begin our assessment with the period 1972 to 1986, when census-type data on the number of franchisors, the number of units, and sales by franchised chains are available from the USDOC.[26] Table 2-1 contains the sales data, in real 2000 U.S dollars, and the growth rates in these real sales levels for traditional and business-format franchising, separately and overall (all franchising), between 1972 and 1986. For comparison purposes, the table also includes data on real GDP and its growth over the same period.

The data in this table imply that business-format franchising indeed has outperformed the economy as a whole over most of this period. Specifically, in real terms, business-format franchising sales have grown by 106.9 percent between 1972 and 1986 while GDP grew by 52.6 percent over the same period. Traditional franchising, however, has grown less than the rest of the economy, by 36.9 percent during this time. The result is that the sum of all franchising has grown at a rate that is basically the same as the rate of growth of the economy as a whole. This growth rate is nowhere near the double-digit growth rates suggested by the popular press. For example, the *Franchise Times*, April 1996, reports that "Franchising growth should increase in 1996, with total unit expansion projected between 12% and 14%, up from 1995's 10% to 12%." Equivalent and even higher growth figures appeared regularly in the trade press throughout the late 1970s and 1980s. We further examine the genesis of some of these very optimistic growth figures below. For now, we simply conclude that even business-format franchising did not grow at these

---

[26] This source, which was first published in 1969, was modified significantly in 1972 such that only the data from that year onward are comparable.

Table 2-1: *Franchising and GDP growth – 1972 to 1986*

Year	Traditional franchising Real sales (2000 $ billions)	Growth in real sales (%)	Business format franchising Real sales (2000 $ billions)	Growth in real sales (%)	All franchising Real sales (2000 $ billions)	Growth in real sales (%)	GDP Real GDP (chained 2000 $ billions)	Growth in real GDP (%)
1972	474.4		118.1		592.8		4,105.0	
1973	508.1	7.0	127.0	7.5	635.0	7.1	4,341.5	5.8
1974	458.5	−9.8	130.2	2.5	588.7	−7.3	4,319.6	−0.5
1975	463.8	1.2	130.9	0.5	594.7	1.0	4,311.2	−0.2
1976	518.4	11.8	141.0	7.7	659.4	10.9	4,540.9	5.3
1977†	556.7	7.4	157.6	11.8	714.3	8.3	4,750.5	4.6
1978	575.5	3.4	169.9	7.8	745.4	4.4	5,015.0	5.6
1979	571.6	−0.7	171.6	1.0	743.2	−0.3	5,173.4	3.2
1980	524.2	−8.3	174.6	1.7	698.8	−6.0	5,161.7	−0.2
1981	522.3	−0.4	168.7	−3.4	691.0	−1.1	5,291.7	2.5
1982	494.2	−5.4	176.7	4.7	670.9	−2.9	5,189.3	−1.9
1983	540.0	9.3	191.1	8.1	731.0	9.0	5,423.8	4.5
1984	612.8	13.5	202.7	6.1	815.6	11.6	5,813.6	7.2
1985	642.8	4.9	226.2	11.6	869.0	6.5	6,053.7	4.1
1986	649.7	1.1	244.4	8.0	894.1	2.9	6,263.6	3.5
1972–86		36.9		106.9		50.8		52.6

† Figures for 1977 for business-format franchising were interpolated from data for adjoining years in current dollars as the published data were not credible. The data for all franchising that year are taken as the sum of this interpolated figure and the data for traditional franchising.
Source: Data on franchising are from the USDOC's (1988) *Franchising in the Economy*. The GDP data are from the Bureau of Economic Analysis, National Economic Accounts (http://www.bea.doc.gov/bea/dn1.htm). The CPI which we use as our deflator is from the Bureau of Labor Statistics.

rates during this period: 106.9 percent over a 14-year period amounts to about 7.6 percent per year.

Figures 2-1 and 2-2 show the data on franchising growth relative to GDP growth in two additional ways. Figure 2-1 presents information on the evolution of the number of units of business-format and traditional franchised chains, along with data on the evolution of real GDP, from 1972 to 1986. We use the number of units instead of sales as an alternative way to capture real rather than nominal growth in franchising. Figure 2-2 jointly addresses the issue of same-unit growth along with growth in number of units by depicting the value of goods sold through franchising as a proportion of real GDP between 1972 and 1986. Such a ratio gives a "unit free" measure of the extent of franchising, eliminating the need to distinguish between nominal and real figures.[27] In both figures, the franchising data again are from the USDOC (1988).

Figure 2-1 first shows the dramatic *decrease* in the number of units in traditional franchising over this period, mostly due to the closing of a large number of smaller gasoline stations that were replaced by the new "pumper" stations that could handle much larger sales volumes. It also shows that the number of units in business-format franchising has grown steadily over this period. But, of course, GDP also has grown during this time. As the time trends in the two series are quite similar, it appears that in terms of units, business-format franchising was growing at a rate similar to that of the economy as a whole even back in the 1970s and early 1980s. Perhaps most importantly, Figure 2-1 addresses directly one type of claim about franchising growth that is currently found in the trade press: "With a new franchise business opening somewhere in the U.S. every 17 minutes, franchising is indeed the success story of the 1980s and 1990s" (IFA, Winter 1992 *Franchise Opportunities Guide*, 10). In the Winter 1995 edition, this figure had become "a new franchise business every 8 minutes" (12). But a new franchise business every 17 minutes is equivalent to 85 new franchises per day, or more than 30,000 new franchises per year. A new franchise every 8 minutes amounts to more than 65,000 new franchises a year. The data in the graph suggest a much more modest growth than either of these startling claims, even if we focus on business-format franchising and even if the period covered by the graph is seen by many as the prime period of growth for this form of franchising. On average, between 1972 and 1986, business-format franchising grew by about 9,000 units per year. This is noteworthy growth, but nothing close

---

[27] For meaningful comparisons, both franchising sales and GDP need to be measured in the same units, either both in real dollars or both in nominal dollars.

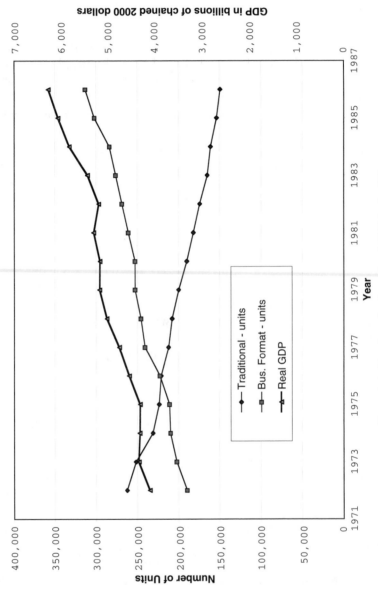

Figure 2-1: Number of units and real GDP in the U.S.

24

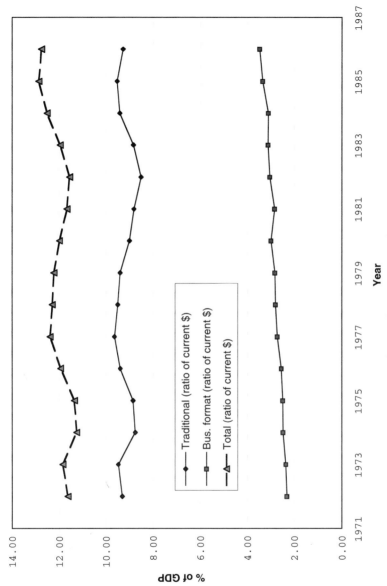

Figure 2-2: Franchising sales as a percent of GDP 1972–1986.

to the claims above. Further, if we extrapolate from the data in the graph, there is nothing there to suggest that this growth should be expected to increase dramatically later and thus justify the claims made in the early 1990s. Finally, the number of traditional franchised units actually decreased between 1972 and 1986, and again there is nothing in the data and nothing going on in the industry to suggest this would reverse itself. Indeed, the retail gasoline industry at the time was replacing its large number of older stations, each with just a few pumps, service bays and full service, with a smaller number of large self-serve multi-pump stations with attending convenience stores instead of service bays (see, e.g., Marvel 1995). And in fact, according to the U.S. census of retailing, the number of establishments within the traditional franchising sectors of gasoline retailing, car retailing and soft-drink bottling was down from 149,313 in 1986 to 130,640 in 1992, and by 1997, it had decreased further to 125,509.

Figure 2-1, however, and the discussion above focus solely on changes in the number of franchising establishments. This is an important variable to consider as most of the growth in franchising, especially in business-format franchising, is achieved through new units. Yet, sales revenues in franchising can increase independently from higher numbers of units if per unit sales volumes are increasing in real terms, as happened for example in traditional franchising. In fact, for traditional franchising, the only way to reconcile the data in Table 2-1 – where traditional franchising sales increased on average throughout the period in real terms – with the decrease in number of outlets shown in Figure 2-1 is to recognize that real sales per outlet have grown in traditional franchise businesses.

Figure 2-2 simultaneously captures growth in the number of units and in sales per unit relative to GDP growth by showing the ratio of franchising sales to GDP. From this figure, it is clear that the value of goods sold through traditional franchising outlets has fluctuated somewhat, but it has remained fairly stable overall as a percent of GDP between 1972 and 1986. The value of goods sold in outlets of business-format franchisors, on the other hand, has risen from 2.3 to 3.5 percent of GDP. Combined then, the value of goods sold through outlets of franchised firms increased from 11.6 percent in 1972 to 12.8 percent of GDP in 1986. Extrapolating from this trend, one would expect franchising sales to represent about 13.6 percent of nominal GDP in 2001, or 1.37 trillion dollars.[28]

---

[28] Nominal GDP in 2001 in the U.S. was $10.08 trillion. Note that under the assumption that franchise retail sales have remained at about one-third of all retailing (as they were in 1986, per the USDOC – see Chapter 1), and with retail sales in 2001 at close

Unfortunately, with the demise of the USDOC's *Franchising in the Economy*, it is quite difficult to assess how franchising as a whole in fact has grown in the U.S. since 1986. Efforts by the IFA and various partners to take over the publication of this report on a permanent basis have not been successful, mainly because the response rates achieved by the IFA and its collaborators have been too low.[29] Thus, from the perspective of assessing the extent and growth of franchising in the U.S., the loss of *Franchising in the Economy* has been a major setback.

In particular, it is the growth in business-format franchising since 1986 that is difficult to assess given the loss of this publication. This is because business-format franchising is not an industry but a way of doing business that is used in a number of different retail and service sectors. As a result, the standard source of industry data, namely the Census, is not useful for our purposes. Specifically, as the U.S. Census Bureau does not request information from retailers and service firms about how they are organized, one cannot find information relevant to business-format franchising in the data published by the Census Bureau.[30]

In contrast, traditional franchising encompasses all businesses involved in only a few sectors of economic activity. Hence, relevant data on this franchising segment are available directly from the U.S. Census Bureau. Table 2-2 displays the evolution of sales revenues in current dollars for car dealers and

---

to $3.5 trillion, franchise retail sales would amount to about $1.15 trillion. Assuming retailing still constitutes about 87% of franchising sales, as the USDOC indicates it did in 1986, then total franchising would amount to $1.33 trillion. Because this estimate is very similar to the one we obtained above using GDP data, it is reasonable to conclude that the retail portion of franchising indeed still represents about one-third of all retailing. This conclusion, however, contradicts the oft-quoted forecast that franchising would account for half of retail sales in 2000. This forecast, much too often quoted today as fact, can be traced back to the Naisbitt Group (1989), a study commissioned by the IFA. We chose to focus our analyses on the importance of franchising vis-à-vis GDP rather than retail sales because an important part of business-format franchising occurs outside of retailing.

[29] See, e.g., Lafontaine (1995a), Bond (1996), and IFA Educational Foundation and Frandate Corp. (2000) for discussions of the problems with issues of *Franchising in the Economy* that were published by the IFA Educational Foundation along with various partners. The last issue published by the USDOC was the 1986–88 issue, with 1986 data.

[30] Two exceptions are the "1997 Accommodation and Foodservices Series" and the "Characteristics of Business Owners (CBO) Survey" carried out in 1992 by the U.S. Census Bureau, which included some information about franchising. However, the former was limited to the lodging and restaurant sectors. The CBO survey was not designed to allow inferences on the extent of franchising and has not yet been repeated. Going forward, we will refer to some studies that have relied on some of these data for other purposes.

Table 2-2: *Traditional franchising and GDP – 1972 to 2001 (current $ billions)*

Year	New car dealerships Sales ($ billions)	% of GDP	Gasoline stations Sales ($ billions)	% of GDP	Soft-drink bottling Sales ($ billions)	% of GDP	All traditional franchising Sales ($ billions)	% of GDP
1972	75.4	6.1	33.1	2.7	5.5	0.4	113.9	9.2
1973	85.0	6.1	36.9	2.7	5.7	0.4	127.6	9.2
1974	77.2	5.1	43.1	2.9	6.7	0.4	127.0	8.5
1975	84.9	5.2	47.6	2.9	8.6	0.5	141.1	8.6
1976	105.6	5.8	52.0	2.9	8.8	0.5	166.5	9.1
1977	121.8	6.0	56.6	2.8	10.0	0.5	188.5	9.3
1978	136.4	5.9	59.9	2.6	11.4	0.5	207.7	9.1
1979	142.9	5.6	73.5	2.9	12.5	0.5	228.9	8.9
1980	130.5	4.7	94.1	3.4	13.9	0.5	238.5	8.5
1981	144.5	4.6	103.1	3.3	15.3	0.5	262.8	8.4
1982	154.7	4.8	97.4	3.0	16.8	0.5	269.0	8.3
1983	187.7	5.3	102.9	2.9	17.3	0.5	307.9	8.7
1984	225.9	5.7	107.6	2.7	18.1	0.5	351.5	8.9
1985	251.6	6.0	113.3	2.7	19.4	0.5	384.3	9.1
1986	270.4	6.1	102.1	2.3	20.7	0.5	393.2	8.8
1987	280.5	5.9	104.8	2.2	22.0	0.5	407.3	8.6
1988	303.3	5.9	110.3	2.2	23.3	0.5	436.9	8.6
1989	311.6	5.7	122.9	2.2	23.0	0.4	457.5	8.3
1990	316.0	5.4	138.5	2.4	23.8	0.4	478.3	8.2
1991	301.3	5.0	137.3	2.3	25.2	0.4	463.7	7.7
1992	333.8	5.3	156.6	2.5	25.4	0.4	515.8	8.1
1993	379.5	5.7	162.6	2.4	26.0	0.4	568.1	8.5
1994	435.7	6.2	171.4	2.4	28.3	0.4	635.4	9.0
1995	464.6	6.3	181.3	2.5	30.2	0.4	676.1	9.1
1996	502.3	6.4	194.6	2.5	32.0	0.4	729.0	9.3
1997	519.0	6.2	199.9	2.4	31.4	0.4	750.2	9.0
1998	545.1	6.2	191.7	2.2	32.3	0.4	769.1	8.8
1999	611.9	6.6	209.4	2.3	32.3	0.3	853.6	9.2
2000	638.0	6.5	244.5	2.5	33.0	0.3	915.4	9.3
2001	669.6	6.6	237.7	2.3	34.4	0.3	941.6	9.3

Source: U.S. Census Bureau: Car and Gasoline Retailing data are from the *"Historical Retail Trade Data"* series; data for Soft-Drink Bottling are from the *"Annual Survey of Manufacturers."*

gasoline stations and soft-drink bottlers from 1972 to 2001 per the "Historical Retail Trade Data" from the U.S. Census Bureau (for car dealerships and gasoline stations) and the "Annual Survey of Manufacturers" (for soft-drink bottling). The table also shows the proportion of nominal GDP that these represent.

The data in this table first confirm what we found earlier, namely that sales growth in traditional franchising between 1972 and 1986, although sizable in nominal terms, has more or less followed the growth of the economy as a whole in real terms over this period. But this table also shows that this pattern has persisted after the mid-1980s, so that sales via traditional franchising have continued to represent a fairly stable 8 to 9 percent of GDP all along. This is an important fact given that traditional franchising represents the bulk of all franchising sales. Consequently, its growth is a main driver of overall franchising growth in the economy.

As for business-format franchising, one can obtain estimates of the number of franchisors over recent years using various franchisor directories, and calculate the growth in these figures. This exercise, of course, only makes sense if the number of franchisors closely tracks changes in the number of units and sales revenues of franchised chains. Table 2-3 shows the growth in the number of franchisors, total sales of franchised chains, and the number of establishments over the 1972 to 1986 period, when all three measures were available. The correlation between the number of franchisors and real sales revenues is 0.93 and the correlation between the number of franchisors and the number of units is 0.99. Moreover, in every one of those years except 1976, the growth in the number of franchisors is greater than the growth in the number of units. We conclude that data on the number of business-format franchisors can give a good indication of the overall evolution of business-format franchising.[31]

Having determined that the growth in the number of business-format franchisors provides a reasonable approximation for the growth in sales and units when we can measure all three, we now turn to data on the number of franchisors after 1986 to assess growth since then. We focus on two main

---

[31] One might interpret the data presented in Chapter 1 in Table 1-2 as evidence against this conclusion. Indeed, the number of outlets of the franchisors in our data is clearly increasing over time despite the constancy of the number of franchisors surveyed. In other words, the growth in the number of franchisors in the U.S. cannot follow the growth in business-format franchising in the U.S. well if we see growth in the number of outlets and not in the number of franchisors in this table. However, the data in Table 1-2 are from a different source, and they include foreign as well as U.S. units. As the proportion of foreign units in these chains is increasing over time (from an average of 20% in 1993 to 28% in 2001), much of the growth in the size of the chains is unrelated to the growth in business-format franchising in the U.S. Furthermore, the increasing average size of the chains in our data sources also reflects the incentives of growing franchisors to participate regularly in the surveys, whereas franchisors that are declining in size choose to participate less frequently in such surveys.

Table 2-3: *Growth in business-format franchising – 1972 to 1986*

Year	Number of franchisors	Growth in number of franchisors	Nominal sales ($ billions)	Growth in nominal sales (%)	Real sales (2000 $ billions)	Growth in real sales (%)	Number of units	Growth in number of units
1972	909	na	28.7	na	118.2	na	189,640	na
1973	1,005	10.6	32.7	13.9	126.8	7.3	202,237	6.6
1974	1,051	4.6	37.3	14.1	130.3	2.7	209,727	3.7
1975	1,115	6.1	40.9	9.7	130.9	0.5	210,814	0.5
1976	1,161	4.1	46.6	13.9	141.0	7.7	222,317	5.5
1977†	1,281	10.3	55.5	19.1	157.6	11.7	240,524	8.2
1978	1,394	8.8	64.3	15.9	169.8	7.8	245,694	2.1
1979	1,459	4.7	72.4	12.6	171.7	1.1	252,702	2.9
1980	1,584	8.6	83.5	15.3	174.5	1.6	252,548	−0.1
1981	1,673	5.6	89.1	6.7	168.8	−3.3	260,555	3.2
1982	1,770	5.8	99.0	11.1	176.7	4.7	268,306	3.0
1983	1,877	6.0	110.5	11.6	191.0	8.1	276,195	2.9
1984	1,942	3.5	122.3	10.7	202.7	6.1	283,576	2.7
1985	2,090	7.6	141.3	15.5	226.1	11.6	301,689	6.4
1986	2,177	4.2	155.5	10.0	244.3	8.0	312,810	3.7

† Sales figures for 1977 for business-format franchising are interpolated from data for adjoining years in current dollars as the data in USDOC were not credible. The data for all franchising that year are calculated as the sum of this interpolated figure and the data for traditional franchising.

Source: USDOC, *Franchising in the Economy*, various years and Bureau of Labor Statistics (BLS).

franchisor listings, the Info Press's *Franchise Annual* and *Bond's Franchise Guide*, earlier known as the *Source Book of Franchise Opportunities*.[32]

Compared to the *Bond's Franchise Guide*, the *Franchise Annual* lists a larger number of businesses each year. In the 1995 and later editions, the *Bond's Franchise Guide* contains a note indicating that while the author aimed to cover the universe of potential franchisors in earlier editions, he now only includes a franchisor in his listing if a company representative can be reached by phone to confirm that the company is still franchising. From conversations with the publisher of the *Franchise Annual*, we learned that in editions prior to 1996, franchisors were left in that listing for some time even if they did not respond to requests for information. For the 1996 and later editions, franchisors that did not respond to such requests were excluded from the listing. This led to improved data quality for both of these directories, along with a dramatic decrease in the number of businesses listed in these publications from the year they implemented these changes. Moreover, in the 1996 edition, the publisher of the *Franchise Annual* indicated that his listing includes 129 distributors and 240 franchise consultants along with 2,338 actual U.S. franchisors. As such firms apparently were also present in prior years, the number of franchisors in this publication before 1996 was overestimated by roughly 15 percent. For all these reasons, we report the data on the number of U.S. franchisors in Table 2-4 starting with the 1996 editions of both publications. We take the number of franchisors in each edition to be an estimate of the population for the prior year because the directories are published early in each calendar year. Consequently, the data in Table 2-4 begin with 1995.

As we saw in Table 2-3, the USDOC estimated the population of franchisors in 1986 to be 2,177. From Table 2-4, it is clear that according to either of our sources, the population of business-format franchisors has grown on average more slowly than real GDP over the 1995 to 2001 period. Perhaps most importantly, the population of U.S. franchisors has grown little relative to the 1986 figures. Even using the higher *Franchise Annual* figures, the total growth in the number of franchisors from 1986 to 2001 has been only 24.6 percent, well below the 57.9 percent average growth in real GDP over the same period. As we have argued that the growth in the number of franchisors can

---

[32] Several franchisor listings are excluded from this table. First, we do not include the *Entrepreneur*'s "Franchise 500" survey. This survey is not meant to represent the whole population of franchisors at a point in time, but simply presents information on franchisors that choose to respond. Thus, it should not be used to assess the total size of the franchisor population. Other franchisor listings not included here for similar reasons are the *Franchise Opportunities Handbook*, published by the U.S. Department of Commerce, and the IFA's periodical *Franchise Opportunities Guide*.

Table 2-4: *The number of business-format franchisors in the U.S.*

Year	Franchise Annual Number of U.S. business-format franchisors*	Growth in number of U.S. franchisors (%)	Bond's Franchise Guide Number of U.S. business-format franchisors**	Growth in number of U.S. franchisors (%)	GDP Growth in real GDP (%)
1995	2,338	na	1,955	na	2.5
1996	2,164	−7.4	2,129	8.9	3.7
1997	2,021	−6.6	1,803	−15.3	4.5
1998	2,218	9.7	1,719	−4.7	4.2
1999	2,359	6.4	na	6.8	4.5
2000	2,545	7.9	1,954	6.8	3.7
2001	2,712	6.6	2,202	12.7	0.8
1995–2001		16.0		12.6	23.1
1986–2001[†]		24.6		1.1	57.9

* Figures reflect the number of U.S. franchisors (total U.S. entries minus number of distributors and consultants).
** Figures are from Exhibit 3 in the 1996 and later editions. For 1995, we use 85% of the rough number of franchisors (2,300) given the author's estimate that 15% of the franchisors in each edition are Canadian.
[†] Based on the USDOC figure of 2,177 franchisors in 1986.
Source: Bond's Franchise Guide, various years, and *Franchise Annual*, various years. Data on the number of franchisors is for the year prior to the edition year as the listings are published early in each calendar year.

be used to estimate the growth in business-format franchising, we are led to the conclusion that business-format franchising has become a more stable and mature form of business whose growth now lags behind the growth in the overall economy.

Our conclusion that the growth rate in business-format franchising has lagged behind overall growth in the economy since the mid 1980s is further supported by data on the number of units of franchised chains reported in the *Bond's Franchise Guide*. According to Bond (2002), the 2,522 U.S. and Canadian franchisors in his listing operated a total of 561,346 units.[33] From the detailed profiles, we were able to ascertain that on average 28 percent of these units were non-U.S. units in 2001. Assuming that this proportion of non-U.S. units applies to all chains in his listing, the number of U.S. units in 2001 would be 72 percent of 561,346, or 404,169. Comparing this to the 312,810 units of franchised chains in 1986 reported by the USDOC, we would estimate that business-format franchising has grown by 29.2 percent between

[33] This includes both company-owned and franchised units of franchised chains as this is the customary way to measure the importance of franchising in the economy.

1986 and 2001. If we assumed instead that the number of non-U.S. units of non-profiled firms in Bond (2002) was much lower than for profiled firms, we would obtain a larger estimate of growth. For example, if we thought non-profiled firms are likely to be small and operate only in the U.S., we could assume at the limit that all non-profiled firms have zero units outside the U.S. Under this assumption, the number of U.S. outlets in 2001 would be 561,346 less 28 percent of the units of profiled chains (382,061 from Table 1-2), or 454,369, leading to a total growth in number of units of 45.3 percent over the same period. This estimate is probably a good upper bound estimate on unit growth as it is likely that non-profiled firms operate some units outside the U.S. Note, that by comparison, real GDP grew by 57.9 percent over this period. Hence, we conclude once again that business-format franchising growth has at best mirrored and, in fact, seems to have lagged behind the growth in the overall economy between 1986 and 2001.[34]

The analyses above have pointed toward a number of reasons why the forecasts in the trade press of franchising growth often have been incorrect. When discussing the extent of franchising, most often both traditional and business-format franchising are included in the statistics presented. But when discussing growth, commentators invariably focus on business-format franchising. This ignores the reality that traditional franchising as a proportion of GDP has remained stable over time, and that it has declined in terms of number of outlets. Furthermore, growth forecasts typically have ignored the difference between nominal and real growth, and between franchisors' forecasted and realized growth. On the latter, it is clear from the forecast data published in *Franchising in the Economy* that franchisors invariably are overly optimistic when forecasting their own growth.[35] Finally,

---

[34] The recent IFA Educational Foundation and Price Waterhouse Coopers (2004) report suggests somewhat greater growth in business-format franchising as their estimate of the number of outlets in 2001 is 622,272. Taking this at face value, it implies total growth of 98.9 percent, much above GDP growth over the same period, but still not sufficient to justify the claims made in the trade press. Moreover, we believe that this figure overestimates the number of business-format franchise establishments. Though the report describes its methodology in some detail, it is not possible to assess the effect of various transformations used to derive the final estimate. In particular, the report indicates that the data on franchising are derived from Dun & Bradstreet's *MarketPlace* CD-ROM and from franchisor surveys, but these data and their validity are not discussed in any detail and the report does not provide any sensitivity analyses using different assumptions to derive final estimates.

[35] This is easily ascertained by comparing the forecast in earlier editions of this publication to the actual figures published later. Similarly, Seid (1988: 3) notes "Many new prospective franchisors I meet are certain they will sell far more franchises than can be reasonably expected."

estimates of franchising growth after the USDOC stopped publishing the relevant data typically have been based on data for small subsets of firms, often the most successful ones. For example, the *Franchise Times* (April 1996) article mentioned earlier was entitled "Growth forecast for 1996" and began with a statement that "Franchising growth should increase in 1996, with total unit expansion projected between 12% to 14%, up from 1995's 10% to 12%." It then went on to mention that this projection comes from Franchise Recruiters Ltd., in its "Annual Franchise Business Development Survey." This survey represents opinions and executive outlook for growth for the 100 franchising corporations in the U.S. with the *highest* projected growth rates. Not surprisingly, the estimates derived from such surveys cannot be applied to all franchising or even all business-format franchising. Yet, throughout the 1990s, articles in the trade and popular press have touted the figures obtained in this yearly survey as forecasts of overall franchising growth for the year, thereby suggesting double-digit growth each year. Together, all these biases have contributed to highly unrealistic forecasts of the future role of franchising in the U.S. economy, and by extension, its position in the global economy.

We conclude that there is no evidence to support the phenomenal growth rates in franchising as claimed by much of the industry and trade press. At best, the growth in business-format franchising has mirrored that of the U.S. economy since the mid-1980s. Interestingly, research by Purdy, Stanworth, and Hatcliffe (1996: 2–3) shows a similar pattern in the United Kingdom (UK). These authors examine total sales through franchised companies and conclude that after the rapid growth of the 1980s, " . . . franchising in Britain is currently going through a period of 'consolidation' in the 1990's, having grown by a modest 12 percent [in total] in the period 1990–95 [. . .]. If the figures were to be adjusted to allow for the effects of inflation, then we should see British franchise turnover even having contracted modestly during this period. . . . " Thus, the British franchising experience in the 1990s has been similar to that of the U.S.

2.2 Entry and Exit

We now turn our attention to the extent of entry and exit by both franchisors and franchisees. There is a perception that opportunities for franchisors and franchisees are burgeoning. There is some truth to this as many new firms get involved in franchising each year. But there is also a perception that franchising is *safe*, especially for franchisees as compared to independent business start-ups. The data we present below show that, in reality, substantial business risks exist for individuals who choose to invest in a franchise. In fact, franchising is no safer on average than independent business ownership, and in some cases is actually more risky. Similarly, franchising is risky for franchisors. Firms must invest significant amounts of money and resources to set up franchise systems. These investments are mostly lost when the firm ceases franchising. The strain associated with developing a franchise system simultaneously with a new business concept easily can increase the likelihood of failure. Of course, business failure is a fact of life. Our point is that this is just as true for franchisors and franchisees as it is for other players in the economy. We see this as no cause for alarm, but as a fact that should be more widely known and recognized in the franchise community. Ultimately, a false sense of security can only lead to hardship and disappointment.

2.2.1 Franchisor Entry and Exit

Reports that many new franchise opportunities become available each year as new firms start franchising certainly have contributed to the perception that franchising is growing rapidly. For example, *Entrepreneur*'s annual survey of *new* franchises has listed more than or close to 200 companies each year throughout much of the late 1980s and early 1990s. In 1996, the report mentioned "Last year, hundreds of small businesses entered the franchise arena. . . . " In this section, we examine the extent to which firms actually do get involved in franchising, but also consider the other side of the coin, the extent to which franchisors exit franchising.

When it still collected and disseminated data on franchising, the USDOC did not directly report the number of new franchisors each year in *Franchising in the Economy*, but it did report the number of franchisors as well as the number of "franchisor failures and departures" each year. We show these figures in columns 2 and 3 of Table 2-5. By definition, the number of franchisors at time t, or N_t, is equal to the number of franchisors in the previous year, N_{t-1}, plus the number of entrants, E_t, minus the number of exits, X_t. In other words, $N_t = N_{t-1} + E_t - X_t$ so $E_t = (N_t - N_{t-1}) + X_t$. Thus, we can calculate the number of entrants in column 4 of Table 2-5 as the sum of the figures shown in columns 2 and 3.

Because the data from the USDOC are not available after 1986, we turn to our data set to obtain information on the extent of entry and exit since then. Note that while these data do not contain all franchisors in any given year, the surveys from which they are obtained tend to be biased toward those

Table 2-5: *Entry and exit of franchisors*

| | USDOC, *Franchising in the Economy* | | | All franchisors in our 1980 to 2001 data | |
Year	Net change in the number of franchisors $(N_t - N_{t-1})$	EXIT: Number of departures and failures of franchisors (X_t)	ENTRY: Number of new franchisors (sum of columns 2 and 3)	ENTRY	EXIT
1980	125	116	241	288	80*
1981	89	125	214	240	47*
1982	97	120	217	249	122
1983	107	141	248	216	174
1984	65	119	184	219	133
1985	148	125	273	226	128
1986	87	183	270	270	125
1987				253	195
1988				218	50
1989				221	113
1990				199	307
1991				176	208
1992				173	127
1993				147	115
1994				134	536
1995				118	214
1996				83*	204*
1997				41*	70*
1998				52*	28*
1999				30*	15*
2000				17*	8*
2001				6*	na
Total	718	929	1,647	3,576*	2,999*

Note: Stars indicate the data cannot be used as estimates of the number of franchisors entering or exiting in the population of franchisors as the coverage of such firms in our sample is too incomplete during these years.

firms that are intent on growing, which means both established firms trying to recruit new franchisees and new franchisors. The strong presence of the latter group implies that our data should give a reasonable assessment of the amount of entry into franchising.

In column 5 of Table 2-5, we show how many of the 5,052 franchisors in our data indicate that they started franchising in each of the years from 1980 to 2001. We find that 3,576 or our franchisors began franchising in one of those years – with the remainder starting earlier than this. As noted in Chapter 1, firms that start franchising relatively late in our sample period, for example in 1998, are less likely to have appeared in these data than firms that started earlier due to the small number of post-1998 surveys we can rely on to generate our sample. Thus, the number of franchisors that we find entering franchising from 1995 or so underestimates the total population of new firms.[36] For the 1980s and early 1990s, however, we believe that our entry estimates are quite reliable. This is confirmed by the data in Table 2-5 as our figures on the number of entrants are very similar to the USDOC figures for all years when the two overlap.

The data in column 5 of Table 2-5 clearly show that the number of new franchisors has been quite high, and relatively stable, between about 220 and 280 each year, throughout the 1980s.[37] This number has gone down, however, in the early 1990s, to an average of about 150 each year. As just noted, we cannot rely on the figures shown for the years 1995 onward and so do not draw any inferences from them.

Finally, Table 2-5 contains information on the number of franchisor exits, first from the USDOC, in column 3, and then as per our data in column 6. To identify the year in which franchisors in our data exit franchising, we find the last year in which each firm appears in our main sources. We then establish whether it appears in the *Franchise Annual* in subsequent years.[38] When a firm is no longer found in the *Entrepreneur* surveys, *Bond's Franchise Guide*, or the *Franchise Annual* in any subsequent year, it is deemed to have exited franchising in the year in which it first disappeared from all these listings.[39] Note that exiting here means either ceasing to franchise (departures

---

[36] This is known as a right-censoring problem. As noted in Chapter 1, from the data in the early 1980s, we can ascertain that it takes about 5 to 6 future surveys to identify more than 90% of the set of firms that started franchising in any given year.

[37] The publisher of the *Franchise Annual* notes that he encounters an average of 400 to 800 new franchisors each year, a number that is much larger than our estimate of new franchisors. However, his figure includes not only new U.S. franchisors, but also new Canadian and other foreign franchisors, and also new distributors and consultants.

[38] We relied on the various internet sites, including individual franchisor and franchisee sites, to resolve a number of ambiguous cases, especially toward the end of our sample period.

[39] See Shane (1996) and Lafontaine and Shaw (1998, 1999) who also used this approach. We, like these authors, believe that these sources are comprehensive enough when combined over time to provide an accurate assessment of whether a firm is still franchising. In fact, from conversations with the author of the *Franchise Annual*, we concluded that this listing had a systematic bias pre-1996 toward including firms that may no longer have been franchising. The result is that we may systematically overestimate the duration or longevity of firms in franchising. This bias would make it harder to find the result that many firms leave franchising shortly after becoming involved in it.

in the USDOC nomenclature) or ceasing to exist altogether (failures for the USDOC).[40] According to the USDOC (1988: 12–13), among firms that exit franchising, roughly half simply leave franchising while the other half fail as businesses. Thus, we expect about half of the exits in our data to be failures of firms while the other half would be cases where firms decided that franchising was not right for them.[41]

In generating our information on the number of firms exiting, a selection issue occurs at the beginning and end of our sample period. For example, the numbers of franchisors we find exiting in 1981 is small because only a small set of firms, namely the firms included in the 1980 and the 1981 surveys, can make it into our sample and thus possibly be reported as having stopped franchising by 1981. Since the 1980 survey does not include all franchising firms in existence at that point in time, it is not possible for the sample to reflect all the firms that stopped franchising in 1981. As more firms are included in subsequent years, the coverage of the population of franchisors becomes more complete. Consequently, we are more likely to measure accurately the total number of exits in later periods. As noted earlier, however, toward the end of our sample period, our coverage of the population is reduced again, and so we once more lose the ability to capture the total number of exits.

Using the USDOC data as a benchmark for the early years of our data and our understanding that we need six to seven future survey years to capture

---

[40] A small portion of the exits observed here reflect cases where a chain is bought by another firm that then consolidates all its holdings in a single listing. If this is done while continuing to support and develop the chain separately, it is not really an exit. Unfortunately, it is not possible to identify these cases and eliminate them from the exit data. However, this type of takeover is fairly infrequent: More typically, chains that are purchased but continue to be developed separately are also listed separately in the surveys. In a few more cases, the buyer decides to discontinue the use of the trade name. The latter should count as exits: franchisees are unlikely to receive much support for their old brand from the new owner in such cases, making this type of exit quite similar to a failure, at least from the franchisee's perspective. Note that Shane (1996) contacted the founders of the 138 firms in his sample and verified that none had been acquired or had changed names, confirming that such events are quite rare.

[41] To our knowledge, only two studies have examined why franchisors that continued to operate chose to stop franchising. These studies were based on fairly small samples, one conducted in the UK construction industry (Kirby and Watson 1999) and the other in Australia with a convenience subsample of franchisors (Frazer 2001). These studies suggest that firms mainly discontinue franchising due to difficulties in recruiting and monitoring franchisees to ensure performance. Frazer (2001) also finds that the economic climate affected firms' decisions. Much more work is needed on franchisors' motives to discontinue franchising and on the effect this has on their franchisees.

most of the franchisors in operation at a point in time, we conclude that our estimates of franchisor exits are quite good from 1982 to 1995. But our point estimate each year depends both on publishers' decisions to clean up their databases and on actual exits. In drawing inferences below, we therefore focus on averages over several years rather than yearly exit rates.

In general, we find that the average exit rates are quite different before and after 1990. Between 1982 and 1989, the average number of franchisor exits per year is 130, whereas an average of 250 franchisors exit yearly between 1990 and 1995 mostly due to the large exit figures for 1990 and 1994. The overall tendency in the data thus suggests larger numbers of exits in the early 1990s than in the 1980s. The high rates of exits in the 1990s in particular are consistent with statements by Bond (2001: 25), for example, to the effect that "Over a 12-month period between annual publications, 10–15% of the addresses and/or telephone numbers [in his mailing list of approximately 2,000 franchisors] become obsolete for various reasons."

Most importantly, the data in Table 2-5 show that large numbers of franchisors enter franchising each year, but many also stop operating or choose to stop franchising. Over the whole sample period, for example, 3,576 new firms begin franchising, but 2,999 firms stop franchising, for a net increase of only 577 firms over two decades. Between 1982 and 1995, when the data are more complete, the net increase in number of franchisors is only 272 (2,819 entrants and 2,547 exits). It is quite clear that focusing on entry alone, as some of the trade literature tends to do, provides a very biased sense of the dynamics of franchising.

Table 2-6 explores the issue of the timing of exit relative to entry by extending the work of Lafontaine and Shaw (1998) to our longer sample period. Specifically, we show in this table the number of franchisors that begin franchising each year between 1980 and 2001 and of these, the number that are still franchising at the end of that year, and then at the end of the following year, and so on through 2000.[42] Again, this table shows that franchisor exits are sizable: of the firms that begin franchising in a given year, only 40 percent on average are still franchising after 10 years; after 15 years, only about 30 to 35 percent of the firms are still franchising.[43] Finally, the attrition shown in Table 2-6, though more rapid early on in a firm's franchising history, continues steadily over the life of the franchised companies in our data.

---

[42] We end with 2000 as firms that have not exited by the end of 2000 are simply still operating at the end of our sample period.

[43] Note that this occurs despite the fact that our methodology tends to overestimate the time that firms stay in franchising.

Table 2-6: *Number (N) of franchisors starting to franchise each year and percentage still franchising at the end of each year*

Year	N	1980	1981	1982	1983	1984	1985	1986	1987	1988	1989	
1980	288	88.9	84.4	78.1	67.0	61.1	55.6	51.4	44.8	44.1	41.0	
1981	240		95.8	88.3	78.3	71.3	62.9	57.9	51.2	50.8	49.2	
1982	249			94.4	87.1	79.5	73.9	69.1	61.0	59.4	56.2	
1983	216				92.1	86.6	83.8	75.0	67.1	65.3	62.0	
1984	219					95.9	92.2	88.6	82.6	82.2	78.5	
1985	226						95.1	93.8	88.9	87.6	84.1	
1986	270							98.5	95.9	93.3	87.0	
1987	253								94.9	92.1	87.4	
1988	218									97.7	93.6	
1989	221										97.3	

Year	N	1990	1991	1992	1993	1994	1995	1996	1997	1998	1999	2000
1980	288	36.8	33.7	32.3	29.9	23.6	21.2	19.1	18.8	18.8	18.8	18.8
1981	240	39.2	38.3	37.1	35.8	28.3	27.1	24.6	22.9	22.9	22.1	22.1
1982	249	50.2	47.4	44.6	44.2	35.7	32.1	28.9	27.3	27.3	26.9	26.9
1983	216	51.4	46.8	45.4	44.4	35.6	33.3	30.1	30.1	30.1	30.1	30.1
1984	219	68.5	61.6	59.4	57.1	42.9	39.3	35.6	34.2	34.2	34.2	34.2
1985	226	71.2	61.5	61.1	59.7	43.8	41.2	37.6	37.2	37.2	37.2	37.2
1986	270	75.6	70.4	66.7	65.2	46.7	40.0	36.7	34.8	34.1	33.7	33.7
1987	253	76.3	70.0	66.8	62.8	46.6	41.5	38.3	36.0	35.2	34.4	34.4
1988	218	86.2	77.1	73.4	70.6	54.6	49.5	44.0	42.7	42.7	42.7	42.7
1989	221	92.8	85.5	79.2	75.1	56.1	48.4	43.4	42.5	42.1	42.1	41.2
1990	199	95.0	89.9	85.9	79.9	61.8	55.8	49.2	46.7	46.2	46.2	46.2
1991	176		92.6	88.1	81.8	61.4	54.5	48.3	47.2	46.0	45.5	44.9
1992	173			96.5	92.5	79.8	71.7	65.3	63.6	61.8	61.8	61.3
1993	147				93.2	85.0	76.2	66.7	61.2	61.2	60.5	59.9
1994	134					94.8	79.1	70.9	69.4	68.7	67.9	67.2
1995	118						94.1	78.8	77.1	75.4	74.6	74.6
1996	83							94.0	91.6	88.0	88.0	88.0
1997	41								95.1	92.7	92.7	92.7
1998	52									100.0	100.0	98.1
1999	30										100.0	100.0
2000	17											100.0

Our results on franchisor exits are not only consistent with those of Lafontaine and Shaw (1998), but also with those of Shane (1996), who examined the rate of exit of 138 franchisors that started franchising in 1983, and with Stanworth's (1996) survey results in the UK. The latter asked eight industry experts to assess the success of a set of 74 UK franchisors known to be in existence in 1984. The interviewees evaluated the firms on a scale from

A to E, where A meant that the company was still franchising and growing and B meant it had reached maturity – either way it was a success; C indicated that a firm was still franchising but not considered a success; D meant the company still existed but was no longer franchising for lack of success at it; and E indicated that the firm had ceased to exist. Stanworth concludes: "At best, one franchise company in four could be described as an unqualified success story (categories A and B) over a ten-year period. . . . Around half the sample was judged to have failed completely and utterly (category E)" (27). Thus, exits are also not uncommon in the UK franchise community.[44]

From the perspective of franchisors, these high exit rates imply two main things: first, many firms try franchising but later decide not to pursue it. In most cases, these firms invest – and subsequently lose – substantial sums in the process. In his work, *The Complete Handbook of Franchising*, Seltz (1981) concluded his assessment of franchisor capital requirements with this statement: "As a general rule, then, franchisor initial capital requirements will fall into the range of $150,000 to $1,000,000, plus a properly capitalized functioning prototype operation" (58). In 2001 dollars, this would amount to capital requirements of $320,000 to $2,100,000. More recently, in a study commissioned by the U.S. Small Business Administration (SBA), Trutko, Trutko and Kostecka (1993) estimated that initial franchise development costs could exceed $500,000, or $630,000 in 2001 dollars.[45] This amount includes expenses incurred to develop clear and complete operating manuals, contracts, disclosure documents, and so on, as well as franchise sales staff development and training. Of course, how much a franchisor spends depends on the type of business and on the amount of care a franchisor puts into developing its franchise program. The point remains that substantial investments are needed, and that the bulk of these is lost upon exiting franchising.

Second, assuming that the USDOC data are still relevant today, about half of the exits documented above represent cases where the firm fails altogether. In other words, franchising is not a guarantee of success for franchisors. In fact, when firms must simultaneously invest resources to develop their franchise system along with their business concept, the strain can easily lead to failure. It is important that would-be franchisors understand the commitment of resources involved in developing a franchise program before they engage in it and that they spend time developing a viable business concept before they start investing in a franchise program. In fact, in their study of franchisors' survival in franchising, Lafontaine and Shaw (1998) found that the number

---

[44] Perrigot (2004) finds similar exit patterns among franchisors in France as well.
[45] See Stanworth et al. (1998) for further data and discussion.

of years in business before franchising was one of the very few factors that increased the likelihood of success in franchising.

In the end, the entry and exit figures shown here explain much of the perception of rapid growth found in the trade press. This perception is based on the correct observation that many new firms enter franchising each year. But this reality must be tempered by the knowledge that many firms also exit franchising each year. In the end, the reality is that business-format franchising in the U.S. has become a relatively mature industry, one that grows along with the rest of the economy.

2.2.2 Franchised Units Entry and Exit

For decades, the International Franchise Association (IFA) and the trade press have suggested that the failure rate of individual franchised units was very low compared to much higher rates of failure for independent firms. For example, in its Fall/Winter 1990–1991 *Franchise Opportunities Guide*, on p. 24, the IFA states that "In 1989, for example, less than 3 percent of business-format franchisee-owned outlets were discontinued – many for reasons other than business failure. By contrast, the SBA has reported that 65 percent of business start-ups fail within five years." Similarly, in their survey report, the IFA Educational Foundation and Arthur Andersen & Co. (1992: 16) note that "96.9 percent of the franchised units opened within the last five years are still in operation today."[46]

There are a number of problems with these statements. First, they often compare yearly rates of franchise failures to multi-year failure rates for non-franchised businesses, per the IFA quote above. In other cases, the reported failure rates for franchised businesses are based on self-reported data from small sets of franchisors. The failure rate reported in the Arthur Andersen quote above, for example, is based on self-reported data by a set of 366 franchised chains. Even if franchisors in this sample truthfully reported the data, the probability that mainly successful firms with low failure rates chose to participate in this survey makes it highly unlikely that the reported failure rate is a good estimate of franchised unit failure generally.

When one examines the failure rates of blue-chip franchises, the probability of failure is in fact relatively small. Using data from disclosure documents,[47]

---

[46] See Bates (1998) for references to several other such claims. The author contradicts these claims with his data. See also Bond (2001) for a pragmatic summary of existing evidence on this issue.

[47] Though the FTC does not require the filing of disclosure documents, nor does it review the information contained in these documents, the contents are reviewed in a

Kolton (1992) found that 4.4 percent of all franchised units were cancelled, terminated, not renewed, or reacquired each year in the 584 leading franchise systems in the U.S. Even this rate of failure, however, is much larger than those touted above. In particular, over five years, these failure rates for established franchisors still amount to one out of every five outlets failing, a rate that is lower than the five-year failure rate attributed by the IFA to independent businesses, but still not low in absolute terms.

Not surprisingly, when one considers all franchised chains, the failure rates are even larger. Bates (1995a, 1995b), in particular, used the Characteristics of Business Owners (CBO) database produced in 1992 by the U.S. Census Bureau to assess the rate of failure among a representative sample of small businesses, both franchised and non-franchised. He found that failure rates of franchised small businesses were greater than those of independent businesses, though not significantly so. Specifically, he observed that 34.7 percent of franchised businesses failed as opposed to 28.0 percent for independents over a five-year period. In other words, his data show that franchised unit failure rates are underestimated in the trade press *while at the same time* the rates of failure quoted for independent businesses are exaggerated. This makes franchising look less risky, when in reality it is at least as risky as independent business ownership. Finally, IFA and Frandata Corp. (2000) dedicate a whole section of the *Profile of Franchising* to what they call turnover rates. They find that for the sample of 834 franchisors for which they have data on this, 11.33 percent of franchised units in operation at the end of 1996, on average, had their contract canceled, or were not renewed by the franchisor, or were reacquired by the franchisor, or otherwise ceased to do business during 1997. The median turnover rate in these chains was 5.5 percent. Since we do not know the age of these units at the time they stopped franchising, the figures are not directly comparable to those from Bates (1995a), but they still clearly support the high failure rates he found in the CBO data. Moreover, the difference between the mean and the median failure rates confirms the existence of a group of well-established and relatively low-failure franchised systems (those below the median rate) that coexists with a number of franchise systems with very high rates of failure. Those latter firms are responsible for raising the average failure rate of franchised businesses in the economy much above the median rate.

---

number of cases by state franchise examiners, and franchisors are subject to both civil and criminal penalties if they misrepresent the information in these documents. Consequently, the data contained therein are much more objective than data obtained from surveys.

To our knowledge, there has been no systematic study of the effect of franchisor exit, whether it be a departure from franchising or a business failure, on the survival or growth of the franchised units that were tied to it. Frazer (2001) interviewed a set of franchisors that had stopped franchising in Australia between 1996 and 1998. Though she does not indicate the number of units or chains on which the statistics are based, she reports that immediately following the cessation of franchising by their franchisor, 37 percent of franchise units were converted to new employment relationships and later disbanded, 19 percent continued operating as independent businesses under new names, 18 percent were sold to an external party, 9 percent closed outright, 8 percent continued to work with their ex-franchisor under a distributor or license agreement, 5 percent continued operating under the original name, and 3 percent were purchased by the ex-franchisor and became company units. Thus, her data clearly show that the fate of one's franchisor and its decision to continue to franchise have a major impact on the future of any franchised unit.

Anecdotal accounts of individual cases confirm that success for a franchised unit is intimately tied to its franchisor's success in franchising. In that context, the high rates of franchisor exit documented above are quite troubling. In fact, the high rate of franchisor exit surely explains the remaining difference between the rates of failures quoted in Kolton (1992) and those found in Bates (1995a, 1995b). The latter examined failure rates of a random set of small businesses, so the sample would include units of chains that are not as established and where the franchisor is more likely to fail or stop franchising. These outlets, thus, are themselves more likely to fail.

We conclude that the data contradict the notion that investing in a franchised business is a risk-free or very low-risk endeavor. In fact, high franchisor failure rates suggest that joining a young or new franchised system is probably *more* risky than starting one's own business. Success in this case depends not only on one's own good ideas, resourcefulness, and dedication, but also on the capacity of the franchisor and the other franchisees to pull things together. The upside of joining a new franchise system also is potentially very high. Those who joined McDonald's when it was a fledgling chain have profited handsomely from this decision. When one joins an established chain, the probability of failure is lower but so is the probability that the venture will be hugely profitable.[48]

Three more points deserve attention. First, Bates (1998) further pursued his analyses of franchise failures using the same database, but this time distinguished which units were sold to new franchisees and which were sold

---

[48] This is an illustration of the usual trade-off between risk and expected returns.

to existing franchisees. He found that "franchise units have better survival prospects than independents, . . . (while) young firms formed without the benefit of a franchisor parent are more likely to remain in operation than franchised start-ups" (113). He explains these seemingly contradictory results by using the fact that the vast majority (84 percent) of new franchised units are opened by existing multi-unit operators. These units benefit from the multi-unit owner's experience in the business and are, not surprisingly, very likely to survive. In fact, they are much more likely to survive than independent businesses, and as they represent the vast majority of new franchised businesses, their high survival prospect gives rise to the first conclusion above. New units opened by new franchisees, which Bates called "franchise start-ups," however, were less likely to survive than independents in his data, giving rise to his second finding. He concluded that it matters greatly, when assessing survival, whether one considers firm-level or outlet-level data. In fact, he notes that "[t]he potential franchisee needs to know how start-up *firms* have performed, and data describing new *establishment's* performance cannot provide this information" (127). We return to the issue of multi-unit franchising in Section 2.4.

Second, it is important to recognize that in the majority of studies, the definition of a failure is that the firm ceases to exist. But failure in franchising is not really that simple. For example, in *Franchising in the Economy*, the USDOC supplied data on franchised unit discontinuations but also on (1) contract terminations by franchisors, by franchisees, and by mutual agreement; (2) non-renewals by franchisors, franchisees, and by mutual agreement; and (3) the number of franchised units repurchased by the company.[49] Holmberg and Boe Morgan (1996) discuss how all of these figures relate in some way to "failure" in a franchising context. The IFA Educational Foundation and Frandata (2000) study further describes different concepts of success and failure for franchised units and note how different indicators relate to each of these. In the end, the definition of turnover they adopt is guided as much by data availability as by their desire to limit double counting and define failure properly. Though these issues of definition make it difficult to arrive at a final simple "failure" rate, it remains true that all the studies suggest a much higher incidence of failure than that claimed traditionally by the popular and the trade press.

Finally, having established that franchising is not a panacea, we now return to our earlier statement that franchising is a useful way to organize certain

---

[49] In addition, for terminations by franchisors, the USDOC data further described whether the termination resulted from a financial default, a quality control violation, or "other." We return to some of these data in Chapter 10.

types of businesses and to the reasons why we expect it to continue to thrive. Franchising does not guarantee success to franchisees, but it gives them a way to develop a business locally as part of a larger system. That system, if well-established, provides access to products and suppliers, to a set of business methods, to managerial support, to a recognized brand, and so on. These are particularly valuable to individuals who do not possess the level of human capital needed to start a business from scratch. Again, early empirical evidence suggests that franchising attracts people who would not have chosen to open a business by themselves. Hunt (1972) in the U.S. and Stanworth (1977) in the UK both found that a large proportion of the franchisees in their samples – 52 percent and about one-third, respectively – would not have gone into business by themselves. Williams' (1999) work, which also relies on the CBO database, documents differences in human capital, such as formal training, business experience, and so on, between individuals who choose to purchase a franchise and those who go in business for themselves. He finds that on average those who opt for franchising have higher education and work experience, but lower levels of business experience. His analyses further show that those who choose franchising are substantially better off as franchisees than they would have been if they had tried to start their business on their own.

The conclusion to be drawn from this body of work is that while franchising is not risk-free, it does make it possible for people who might otherwise not have this opportunity to develop a business locally and, with some luck, thrive as part of a larger business entity.

2.3 The Size Distribution of Franchised Chains

In this section, we focus on another misconception about franchising: the idea that all franchisors are large chains. Most people think about large fast-food chains, or hotel or car rental chains, or even large gasoline station or car dealership networks when they think about franchising. But the reality is that while traditional franchising is fairly concentrated, with very large networks operating under just a few brand names, the vast majority of the 2,500 or so business-format franchisors in the U.S. operate small numbers of outlets. As in the preceding sections, we begin with information available from the USDOC's franchising data and then consider more recent data.

Table 2-7 shows data on the size distribution of U.S. franchisors in 1986, where size is measured by the total number of franchised and company outlets in each chain.[50] Of the 2,177 franchisors in the U.S. in 1986, only 56 operated

---

[50] We address the issue of dual distribution, namely the tendency chains have to operate both franchised and company units, in Chapter 4.

Table 2-7: *The size distribution of U.S. franchisors in 1986*

Size	Franchisors Number	% of total	Units Number	% of total	Sales $000	% of total
0–10	739	33.9	3,713	1.2	1,369,896	0.9
11–50	764	35.1	19,415	6.2	9,802,357	6.3
51–150	343	15.8	30,039	9.6	14,173,986	9.1
151–500	204	9.4	56,212	18.0	29,057,874	18.7
501–1,000	71	3.3	49,103	15.7	27,024,267	17.4
1,001 +	56	2.6	154,328	49.3	74,114,368	47.6
Total	2,177	100.0	312,810	100.0	155,542,748	100.0

Source: USDOC (1988).

more than 1,001 units. In total, these firms accounted for 154,328 units, nearly 50 percent of the units of all franchisors at the time. At the other extreme, 739 franchisors, or more than one-third of the franchisor population, had 10 or fewer units each, for a total of 3,713, or only 1.2 percent of all the outlets of franchised companies.

For comparison purposes, Table 2-8 first shows the size distribution of the franchisors in our data in 1986, followed by the same distribution in 1996 and 2001. Note that franchisor size here is measured by the worldwide number of franchised and company units in a chain.

This table first shows that our data set is biased toward larger franchised chains. In the USDOC data, 1,503 of the 2,177 franchisors, i.e., more than two-thirds of them, had less than 50 outlets in 1986 whereas 625 of the 1,075 franchisors covered in our data in the same year, or 58 percent of them, had less than 50 outlets. Still, the overall distribution illustrates that the same basic facts found above with the USDOC data still apply today: a large number of business-format franchised chains – the majority of them – are quite small contrary to the widespread perception that these chains are all large and national in scope. The median size of franchised companies historically has been below 50 units, and though the data in Table 2-8 suggest that it may be higher than this in 2001, given the bias in our data, we believe this median size is still below 50 units.[51] It is also still true today, however, that the majority of units (245,460 out of 382,061 in 2001) are associated with the small minority of very large franchise systems.

---

[51] See also Bond (2002: 13) on the size distribution of the 2,522 franchisors in his database (15 percent of which are Canadian) and IFA Educational Foundation and Frandata (2000) for further data. In both sources, the median franchisor has less than 50 units even though the latter source excludes a disproportionate number of small firms.

Table 2-8: *The size distribution of franchisors (F) in our data*

Size	1986				1996				2001			
	No. of F	% of F	No. of units	% of units	No. of F	% F	No. of units	% of units	No. of F	% of F	No. of units	% of units
1–10	280	26.0	1,404	0.7	210	19.0	1,051	0.4	171	14.8	974	0.3
11–50	345	32.1	9,132	4.3	379	34.4	10,195	3.7	350	30.2	9,557	2.5
51–150	212	19.7	17,619	8.3	256	23.2	22,693	8.3	302	26.1	27,261	7.1
151–500	151	14.0	41,685	19.7	171	15.5	46,706	17.1	211	18.2	57,275	15.0
501–1,000	49	4.6	34,308	16.2	45	4.1	29,827	10.9	64	5.5	41,534	10.9
1,001 +	38	3.5	107,843	50.9	42	3.8	162,811	59.6	60	5.2	245,460	64.2
Total	1,075	100.0	211,991	100.0	1,103	100.0	273,283	100.0	1,158	100.0	382,061	100.0

Note: F stands for Franchisors.

2.4 Multi-Unit Franchisees

In theoretical as well as empirical analyses, the franchised chain is typically described as a combination of franchisor-owned and franchisee-owned units, with the presumption that the latter are all individually owned and operated. In other words, franchisees all operate small mom-and-pop ventures, and are inexperienced and unsophisticated in business matters. The result has been a perception of imbalance of power between franchisors and franchisees, a perception that motivates many calls for regulation.

While many franchisees are indeed small business owners with just one outlet, it is important to realize that most franchised chains also include a number of franchisee-owned "mini chains" (Bradach 1995). For example, McDonald's franchisees own an average of three franchised restaurants.[52] In their study of multi-unit ownership and its effect on franchisor growth, Kaufmann and Dant (1996) found that 88 percent of the 152 franchised fast-food chains they surveyed included multi-unit owners. They note: " . . . multi-unit franchising is the modal form of franchising" (355). Kalnins and Lafontaine (2004), moreover, found that multi-unit owners accounted for 84 percent of all the franchised restaurants in seven large national chains in Texas in 1995. In terms of owners, however, franchisees with a single unit were still the majority in two of the seven chains (Dairy Queen and Subway). Finally, the IFA Educational Foundation (2002) documents that 20 percent of franchisees, each owning 4.3 units on average, were responsible for the majority (53 percent) of the units in the 145 franchised systems that responded to their survey. The remaining 47 percent of units were owned by the other 80 percent of franchisees, all of whom owned a single unit.[53]

The figures above imply that franchisees tend to be small, and indeed most are. But there is huge variance in the size of franchisees. Each year, the *Franchise Times* publishes a list of the largest 200 restaurant franchisees in the U.S., where size is measured by total revenue.[54] According to this source, the top 200 franchisees in the U.S. in 2001 operated 16,544 restaurants, or an average of more than eighty restaurants each. The top 100 operated 12,472 restaurants, or more than 120 each. The sales revenue of the top

---

[52] See Kaufmann and Lafontaine (1994).

[53] See also Kaufmann and Kim (1995) and Bradach (2000) for more data on multi-unit ownership.

[54] This list is produced by its sister publication, the *Restaurant Finance Monitor*, and is entitled The Monitor 200. It usually appears in the August issue of the *Franchise Times*. It has been produced yearly since 1993.

200 reached \$16.7 billion, or 12.2 percent of the \$136.5 billion sales revenue of the largest 100 restaurant chains in the U.S. Many of these franchisees are publicly traded companies. Moreover, these franchisees often are associated with more than one chain, operating different types of restaurants under various brands. In fact, several of them also are franchisors for other concepts.[55]

The main conclusions to draw from the data are that a very large number of franchisees, most likely the majority of them, to this day are single-unit owners, but multi-unit ownership is present at least to some degree in almost all franchised chains, and a large proportion of franchised units belong to multi-unit franchisees. Moreover, many multi-unit franchisees are large and sophisticated companies. In fact, the data imply that the largest 200 franchisees are larger on average than the typical (median) franchisor.

There are two main ways for franchisees to become multiple-unit owners. The most common is through the sequential acquisition of franchised units. Franchisors typically grant the right to buy additional units to franchisees once they have demonstrated that they can operate their current unit or set of units and that they can do so within the constraints imposed by the franchisor. In that sense, franchisors who allow franchisees to grow use the granting of additional units as a reward for high-performing franchisees and, hence, an incentive mechanism as well.[56] Note that most of the time franchisees are assessed the then current franchise fee and royalty rate for each additional

---

[55] For example, the largest franchisee in 2001 was RTM Restaurant Group in Atlanta, Georgia, the largest Arby's franchisee with 775 Arby's and 17 Sbarro units at the end of 2001. Through Winners International, an affiliate of RTM, it is also the franchisor of Mrs. Winner's Chicken & Biscuits and Lee's Famous Recipe Chicken restaurants. NPC International, the largest Pizza Hut franchisee in the world, was the second largest restaurant franchisee in the U.S. in 2001. At the end of that year, it operated 835 Pizza Hut restaurants. This franchisee was a publicly traded company from 1984 to 2001. Finally, rounding out the top three is Carrols Corp. in New York, a firm that operated 359 Burger King restaurants at the end of 2001. This Burger King franchisee is also a franchisor for Pollo Tropical, a regional chain of 70 restaurants, and Taco Cabana, a chain of 130 restaurants, that it acquired in 2000. The fourth largest franchisee in 2001 was AmeriKing, which operated 373 Burger King restaurants at that time. This firm filed for Chapter 11 bankruptcy protection in 2002.

[56] See Kaufmann and Lafontaine (1994) on this, and for evidence that McDonald's expressly recognizes the granting of additional units as an important mechanism to control franchisee behavior and give them incentives to perform. In the IFA Educational Foundation (2002) survey, 15.1 percent of franchisors indicated that they use multi-unit franchising as a way to reward good franchisees, and another 14.1 percent said they use it in response to franchisee requests (which presumably came from good franchisees, otherwise franchisors would have no reason to go along).

unit they buy, paying whatever new franchisees joining the chain at that time are required to pay.[57]

The other way to become a multiple-unit owner is with an area development agreement, in which the area developer is granted the right to establish a pre-specified number of units in an exclusive territory over a prescribed time table.[58] In the 2002 *Bond's Franchise Guide*, just over half of the franchisors that provided information on this (595 out of 1,128) used area development agreements. The standard practice in these cases is for the area developer to be the franchisee for the units, to own and operate them directly or through a local partnership in which the area developer maintains equity. The area developer usually is assessed a fixed fee for the right to develop the territory and then pays the then current franchise fee and royalty rate for each unit as it becomes operational. Bond (2002), however, indicates that both the franchise fee and the royalty rate are sometimes reduced under this type of agreement.[59]

While multi-unit franchising is pervasive, only a few studies have explicitly focused on it. In particular, Kaufmann and Kim (1995) have examined empirically the relationship between the use of area development agreements (and subfranchising agreements) and system growth rates (in number of units). They find that the use of these agreements correlates positively with chain growth. Bradach (1995) considers more generally the reasons why firms use multi-unit franchising. Using in-depth interviews, he finds that chain executives perceive multi-unit franchisees to be better than single-unit franchisees in terms of adding units, of maintaining uniformity within the chain, and of system-wide adaptation to changes in the firm's competitive environment. This suggests that franchisors do not really want unsophisticated mom-and-pop operations. But multi-unit operations also come at a price: executives also noted that owners of mini-chains may not adapt to local conditions as well as single-unit owners. Moreover, Brickley (1999) relates the extent to which

---

[57] Franchisees buying additional units may pay a lower franchise fee for these units; see Chapter 3 on this and on typical fees in franchising.

[58] Area development agreements should not be confused with subfranchising agreements, where the subfranchisor is granted the right to find the franchisees to develop a territory and to contract with them. Under an area development agreement, the grantee establishes and operates the units, whereas under a subfranchising agreement the grantee is given the right "to grant to others the right to establish and operate units" in the territory (Lowell 1991: 22). Note that both types of agreements are sometimes called master franchising. See Lowell (1991), Kaufmann and Kim (1995), and Bond (2002) for more on this.

[59] Bhattacharyya and Lafontaine (1995) document the existence of reduced franchise fees but not reductions in royalty rates for area development agreements among the 54 franchisors in their sample. See Chapter 3.

firms use area development agreements to the degree of repeat business they generate. Consistent with his argument that area development agreements are used to reduce free-riding problems – expected to be particularly acute in non-repeat businesses – he finds that area development agreements are significantly more likely to be used by franchisors involved in non-repeat customer industries.[60] Finally, Kalnins and Lafontaine (2004) use data on all outlets of seven major fast-food chains in the State of Texas to examine how franchisors allocate the ownership of new outlets between new and existing franchisees and, if the unit goes to an existing franchisee, what characteristics of an owner or of its units affect the likelihood that they are chosen as the owner of the new unit. They find that franchisors, even those that do not use area development agreements, are most likely to allocate units to franchisees in ways that generate clusters of geographically close and adjacent units belonging to the same owner. Their results imply that franchisors do not shy away from decisions that may result in a franchisee obtaining significant control over a particular market. Instead, the decisions that franchisors make suggest that their goal is to minimize unit control costs, as multi-unit owners are given control over sets of units that are close to each other so they are easy to travel between and oversee, but at the same time minimize competition and conflict among franchisees.

According to most sources, the extent of multi-unit franchising has grown significantly over the last decade. In examining the different needs and goals of franchisors and franchisees in the remainder of this book, we will consider the extent to which multi-unit and single-unit franchisees' goals and behavior also might differ.

2.5 Conclusion

Franchising clearly plays an important role in the U.S. economy and has proved to be a very successful method of doing business. Sales through franchised chains represent more than 13 percent of U.S. GDP. Given its economic importance, it is crucial to have a realistic assessment of franchising's current growth and the security it offers. The data suggest that franchising is growing in real terms at best at a rate similar to that of the economy as a whole. This is inconsistent with the extravagant claims made by the trade press throughout the 1980s and 1990s. The data also contradict the trade press claims and general perception of the financial safety that franchising offers investors.

---

[60] We come back to the issue of free riding on several occasions throughout this book, but see in particular Chapter 5.

Franchising turns out to be no safer than investing in other new businesses: the failure rates observed in franchising, for franchisors and for franchisees, are very similar to those of non-franchised businesses. What this means is that an investment in a franchised system should be investigated and assessed in much the same way as an investment in any other type of business venture.

We also examined two other misconceptions about franchising: (1) that franchised chains are all large, well-established companies; and (2) that franchisees are small, mostly single-unit owners. In spite of the impression created by the omnipresence of large fast-food systems and gasoline station and automobile dealership networks, we have shown that the majority of franchised systems are quite small, with less than fifty units. For a franchisee seeking the support of a tested business format and of a recognized brand – the main advantages usually associated with buying a franchise rather than starting an independent business – our data show that most franchised systems are too small to offer these. Franchisees that invest in small franchised systems must be buying in the hopes that the chain will grow and develop further. This is a fairly risky endeavor and must be recognized as such. Finally, it is also important to recognize that franchisees are not all single-unit operations. Several multi-unit operators own and operate very large chains within and even across other chains. Indeed, many of those multi-unit owners are larger than most franchised chains.

3

Franchise Contracts

3.1 Introduction

Franchise contracts stipulate the conditions under which a franchised outlet is to be operated and, in particular, the rights and obligations of both parties. In this chapter, we examine the terms of franchise contracts, with special emphasis on the monetary contract terms, namely franchise fees, royalty rates, ongoing fixed payments, and advertising fees. These fees, as mentioned in Chapter 1, are not used in traditional franchising and, therefore, this chapter is really about monetary contract terms in business-format franchising.[61]

As we will see in more detail in Chapter 4, if the franchisor is to maximize its profit, economic theory generally suggests that it should tailor its franchise contract terms for each unit and franchisee in a chain. In practice, however, contracts are remarkably uniform within chains and thus insensitive to variations in individual, outlet, and specific market conditions. Indeed, a business-format franchisor most often uses a single business-format franchising contract – a single royalty rate and franchise fee combination – for all of its franchised operations that join the chain at a given point in time. In her survey of 130 business-format franchised chains, for example, Lafontaine (1992b) found that 42 percent of her respondents offered their contracts on a take-it-or-leave-it basis with another 38 percent allowing some negotiations, but only for non-monetary terms. Thus, uniformity, especially for monetary terms, is the norm. Moreover, Lafontaine and Oxley (2004) show that American franchisors that have outlets in Mexico also typically use the exact same monetary contract terms with their Mexican franchisees as with their domestic franchisees. Thus, to a large degree, contract uniformity extends even across borders.

---

[61] In traditional franchising, the franchisor earns its profit through its own markups over cost when it sells its product to the franchisee.

Within the U.S., the Robinson-Patman Act encourages upstream firms to set uniform wholesale prices.[62] This law, however, cannot explain contract uniformity in business-format franchising as the law applies to the sale of commodities, and that does not include franchising rights. Various state level disclosure rules also increase the cost of using different contract terms with franchisees, as franchisors must file new versions of these documents in some states when they modify the terms of their contract for an individual franchisee. Yet, these constraints do not appear to be the main reason for the degree of uniformity in monetary contract terms that is observed in practice. First, legal constraints cannot explain the cross-border uniformity identified by Lafontaine and Oxley (2004). Second, disclosure requirements do not increase the cost of specifying fees using formulas, such as making the franchise fee or royalty rate a function of local population levels, specifying minimum and maximum levels of fees, and so on. In fact, as we describe below, franchisors do use formulaic fees, but only to a limited extent. Finally, and most interestingly, franchisors themselves point to other main reasons for uniformity. When asked why they use a uniform contract, only 22 percent of the 130 business-format franchisors in Lafontaine's (1992b) survey mentioned legal considerations as a factor despite the fact that franchisors could give several answers. Most, 73 percent of them, indicated that contract uniformity was desirable because of the resulting consistency and fairness toward franchisees, and another 27 percent of the respondents cited transaction costs as a main factor driving uniformity, stating that such uniformity makes it easier to administer and enforce the contract.[63]

The main disadvantage of contract uniformity that franchisors identified was the chain's inability to deal with special circumstances and the lost franchise sales that resulted. The existence of this drawback was mentioned, however, by only about half of the franchisors – the other half stated either that they saw no disadvantage at all in the use of uniform contracts or they did not identify any disadvantage when asked to do so.[64]

---

[62] The Robinson-Patman Act, 15 U.S.C. 13, forbids price discrimination by manufacturers or distributors toward resellers where the effect is to reduce competition or tend to create a monopoly.

[63] See McAfee and Schwartz (1994) for an opportunism-based explanation for contract uniformity, and Bhattacharyya and Lafontaine (1995) for a model that suggests that the benefit from contract customization may not be large enough to warrant even low customization costs. We come back to these explanations for contract uniformity in the next chapter.

[64] While franchise contract terms offered to potential franchisees at a point in time tend to be uniform, in the course of the franchise relationship a franchisor may adjust the terms

The uniformity of the monetary contract terms offered by a franchisor at a given point in time is useful from our perspective in that it allows us to detail those contracts. If each firm used a large number of contracts with varying terms, it would be much more difficult to describe franchise contracting. We come back to the issue of why the contracts are uniform in the next chapter, after establishing some of their main features in the present one. In the remainder of this chapter, we focus on the most typical monetary terms in franchise contracts, namely franchise fees, royalty rates, and advertising fees, and examine the frequency with which they are used and the typical amounts involved.[65] We discuss non-monetary contract terms, such as contract duration, termination clauses, input purchase requirements and territorial exclusivity, only briefly in the last section as we postpone to the relevant chapter any detailed description of those aspects of the contracts that relate specifically to each of the issues we address later in this book.

3.2 Franchise Fees

The vast majority of franchisors require that their franchisees pay an initial lump-sum fee called a franchise fee. This fee is paid only once at the beginning of the contract period. Of the various financial contract terms, this one varies the most across franchisees in a given chain. Table 3-1 reproduces data from Bhattacharyya and Lafontaine (1995), which they obtained from a careful review of the disclosure documents provided by 54 franchisors. This table shows that the variation in franchise fees flows from three main causes. First, some franchisors set this fee in a formulaic way, most often based on the size of the territory that a franchisee is awarded or on its market potential. Second, some franchisors require different fees for different types of franchised units, that is, different franchise options such as a free-standing fast-food operation versus a food-court version of the same business. Third, franchisors may require different fees for additional units sold to existing franchisees, or for

of the contract temporarily to give struggling franchisees a chance to survive. In other words, given that franchisee failure is damaging for the system, franchisors sometimes grant rent relief or reduce required royalties for struggling but otherwise promising franchisees in spite of specific contract terms.

[65] Franchisors also may require franchisees to pay a renewal fee at the end of the contract period in consideration for a new contract, and/or a fee to process ownership transfer when one franchisee sells his or her unit to a new or existing franchisee. We discuss these fees briefly along with other issues related to contract renewal and transfers in Chapter 10.

Table 3-1: *Variation in franchise fees*

Single Fee (including two firms for which the fee is zero):		19
Multiple Fees:		35
As a Function of Market Potential:	10	
Special Fee for Area Development Agreements:	10	
For Different Franchise Options:	6	
Discounts for Additional Units:	6	
Conversion Discounts:	2	
No Explanation for range of fee:	1	
Total:		54

Source: Bhattacharyya and Lafontaine (1995).

area developers, or set their fee differently for a "conversion" franchise, that is, when an existing business joins a chain.

The use of different fees for different types of transactions is not surprising – these are very often very different products, after all. Moreover, franchise fees are often understood in the franchise community as "payment to reimburse the franchisor for the incurred costs of setting the franchisee up in business – from recruiting through training and manuals" (Bond 2001: 29). As the franchisor incurs lower costs when selling a new unit to an existing franchisee, or when an existing business converts to become part of a chain, it makes sense that the franchise fees be lower in these cases. In fact, given that costs and franchisees' willingness to pay must vary across a variety of options and circumstances, what is more puzzling in Table 3-1 is that a full third of the franchisors in the survey indicated that their franchise fee does not vary at all.

Figure 3-1 displays the distribution of franchise fees charged by the 1,125 franchisors in our data that provided information on the level of these fees in 2001.[66] Note that when conveying information on the size of the fees, in this and in other figures and tables in this chapter, we use the average of a fee whenever a range is given in the data source.[67]

---

[66] What we refer to as 2001 data are obtained from the *2002 Source Book* and thus reflect contracting practices in 2001. Also, we use the end of 2001 exchange rate for Canadian dollars to transform the franchise fees of Canadian firms into U.S. dollars.

[67] When only a lower bound was given, as in "$30,000 and up," we use twice the lower bound as an estimate for the upper bound, and then calculate the mean between these two values. This amounts to using 1.5 times the lower bound as our measure of average franchise fee. When only an upper bound is given, as in "up to $40,000," we use half the upper bound as an estimate for the lower bound, and again calculate the mean. This amounts to using 0.75 times the upper bound as our estimate of the mean franchise fee.

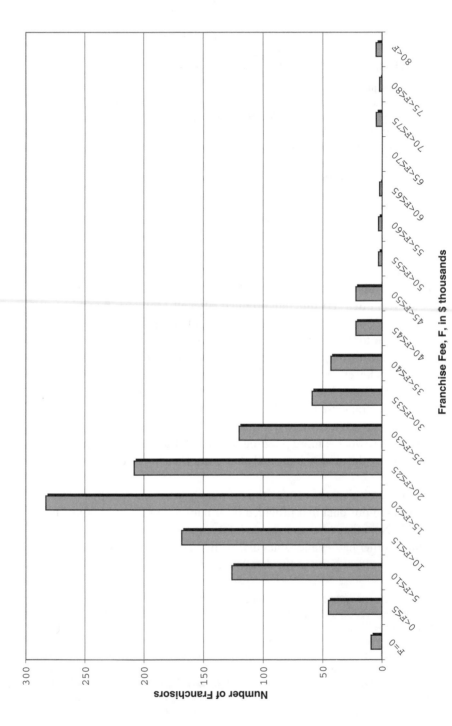

Franchise Fee, F, in $ thousands

Figure 3-1: The distribution of franchise fees in 2001.

Figure 3-1 shows that the vast majority of franchisors charge an initial franchise fee somewhere between $5,000 and $30,000, and most commonly between $15,000 and $25,000. The median fee is $20,000. Very few franchisors, only 9 out of 1,125, charge no such fee. At the other extreme, only 20 of the franchisors, or less than 2 percent of them, request a franchise fee above $50,000. In the 1998 *Profile of Franchising*, a slightly higher proportion, 7 percent of the 1,209 franchisors in the study, charged a franchise fee above $50,000. The difference might be due to a disproportionate number of firms with low franchise fees choosing to appear in franchise directories, and hence in our data, as such directories may be more useful franchisee recruiting tools for such firms. In any case, the main point of this figure is that it illustrates how small franchise fees really are, especially relative to the total payments made by franchisees to franchisors. Over the life of these contracts, franchise fees represent in most cases only 5 to 10 percent of the revenues that a franchisor obtains from a franchised unit, with the remainder coming from sales-based royalties or advertising fees.[68]

Figure 3-1 also shows the variance in franchise fees across firms. Table 3-2 explores this further by showing the distribution of franchise fees across sectors. The set of franchisors included in this table is lower, at 980 rather than 1,125, because we restrict the sample to those firms for which we have data on all the fees we describe in this chapter.[69] This makes it possible to compare the distribution of the different fees across a constant set of firms. Also, the sector definitions that we use in this and other sections of this book, when referring to our own data set, are not those of the USDOC. Those sectors definitions are based on old data and we have limited information as to what these sectors really contained. We therefore generated our own set of sectors to better describe the types of firms found in our data.

Table 3-2 shows a tendency for franchise fees to be higher on average in some sectors than others. Franchisors in the sit-down restaurant industry (Restaurants), for example, charge relatively high franchise fees, as represented by Bennigan's $65K franchise fee. Franchisors in the Contractors and

---

[68] For example, for a firm charging the median franchise fee of $20,000 and the median royalty rate of 5 percent, and assuming relatively low sales revenues of $500,000 per year in real terms over a fifteen-year contract (the average contract duration according to the USDOC data), total royalty revenues would be $375,000. Thus, the franchise fee would be just slightly above 5 percent of the total payments from the franchisee to the franchisor over the life of the contract (assuming no advertising fee).

[69] We also exclude the few firms that require royalty rates above 25 percent of sales to be paid to the franchisor, on the notion that such percentages must be applied to something else beside sales revenues (e.g., gross margins).

Table 3-2: *The distribution of initial franchise fees in 2001, per sector*

Sector	$0 < x \leq 10$	$10 < x \leq 20$	$20 < x \leq 30$	$30 < x \leq 40$	$40 < x \leq 50$	$50 < x$	Total
Automotive	10	17	36	4	2	1	70
Business	21	27	25	12	3	5	93
Contractors	4	18	12	4			38
Cosmetic	2	14	4			1	21
Education	6	8	10	5	5		34
Fast Food	18	110	73	14	7	3	225
Health and Fitness	3	9	9		1		22
Home Furnishings	3	7	9	1	3		23
Hotels and Motels	1		4	9	2		16
Maintenance	25	35	16		4	3	83
Personal Services	12	30	16	4	3		65
Real Estate	8	13	6		1		28
Recreation		4	7	3	1	1	16
Rental	3	6	5	1		2	17
Restaurants	1	12	23	22	8	3	69
Retail Food	2	13	24	2			41
Retail Other	6	35	56	14	7	1	119
Total	125	358	335	95	47	20	980

Personal Services sectors charge lower fees on average. But this table also shows that even within sectors there remains significant variance in franchise fees. In most sectors, we find firms that charge very low fees and firms that charge relatively high fees. Note that some franchisors try to attract franchisees by being "low-cost," defined typically as having a low initial fee. Firms that are interested in appearing in listings of "low-cost" franchises thus have an incentive to keep their upfront fee relatively low.

Finally, Table 3-3 describes how initial franchise fees have changed since 1980. Column 3 shows that the proportion of firms requesting an initial franchise fee has increased during the 1980s, to the point where almost all franchisors now request such payments. But these fees have always been quite popular: only about 10 percent of the chains did not request such fees in 1980. The last four columns provide information on the average and maximum franchise fee observed in the data each year since 1980, in nominal and then in real (2001) U.S. dollars.[70] Not surprisingly, in nominal terms, these initial fees

---

[70] We do not display minima as these are always zero.

Table 3-3: *The evolution of initial franchise fees, 1980 to 2001*

Year	Number of franchisors	% of franchisors with an upfront franchise fee	Mean fee, nominal ($ thousands)	Mean fee, real ($ 2001 thousands)	Max. fee nominal ($ thousands)	Max. fee real ($ 2001 thousands)
1980	952	89.8	13.0	27.9	300.0	644.8
1981	1,017	92.0	14.7	28.7	450.0	876.7
1982	1,136	93.0	15.1	27.8	250.0	458.8
1983	1,102	94.6	15.4	27.5	82.5	146.7
1984	843	95.3	16.7	28.5	100.0	170.5
1985	887	96.7	17.8	29.3	112.5	185.2
1986	1,032	97.0	18.2	29.4	250.0	404.0
1987	1,036	97.5	19.0	29.6	150.0	233.8
1988	1,005	98.5	20.0	29.9	120.0	179.6
1989	1,041	98.8	20.6	29.4	127.5	182.1
1990	1,082	98.7	20.7	28.0	110.0	149.1
1991	1,008	98.8	20.6	26.8	125.0	162.5
1992	981	99.1	21.0	26.5	128.0	161.6
1993	1,075	99.1	20.0	24.5	125.0	153.2
1994	1,071	98.8	20.0	23.9	128.0	153.0
1995	1,090	99.2	20.2	23.5	131.3	152.5
1996	1,079	99.2	20.8	23.5	128.0	144.5
1997	1,015	99.1	20.9	23.1	128.0	141.2
1998	971	99.2	21.6	23.5	300.0	326.0
2000	959	99.2	22.3	23.0	300.0	308.5
2001	1,125	99.2	22.2	22.2	300.0	300.0

Note: We do not display minima as these are always zero. Data for 1999 are unavailable as the *Bond Franchise Guide* was not published in 2000.

on average have increased over this period. In constant 2001 dollars, however, franchise fees increased over most of the 1980s, but have been decreasing since. In other words, nominal franchise fees did not keep up with the rate of inflation in the 1990s. Consequently, the average franchise fee in 2001 is more than $5,000 lower than its 1980 counterpart when both are expressed in 2001 dollars. Much of this decline, and the large reduction in the variance of these initial fees (not shown), can be traced to a reduction in the use of very high initial fees by just a few firms (see in particular the very high maximum values in the early 1980s).[71]

---

[71] The high maximum franchise fee in the last few years in Table 3-3 is for the U.S. Basketball League, which considers itself a business-format franchisor and offers contracts that qualify as such according to the FTC rule.

3.3 Royalty Rates

In addition to collecting an initial franchise fee, franchisors typically require franchisees to make ongoing payments throughout the life of their contracts. In most, but not all, franchise systems, these payments are calculated as a percentage of sales revenues. In their *Profile of Franchising*, the IFA Educational Foundation and Frandata (2000) reported that 1,006 franchisors, or 82 percent of their sample, requested some form of percentage royalties. They found that 61 franchisors, or 5 percent of their sample, instead charged a flat dollar amount per time period on an ongoing basis, and 22 of them, or 2 percent, required a fee per unit sold or per transaction (such as a fee per audit for an accounting firm, or per room rented for a hotel). Finally, 62 franchisors, or 5 percent of the firms in their sample, charged no royalties at all. Among the 1,006 franchise systems that operated under a percentage royalty, the report goes on to mention that this fee was based on sales revenues for 932 franchisors, while it was based on gross margins for another six franchisors.[72] The remaining 52 franchisors, almost all from the personnel, real estate, travel agency, and business services sectors, used some other basis that the authors do not describe.[73]

A number of franchisors that charge a percentage rate also specify some minimum level of royalty payments. Such minimum payments are the norm in other industries that use percentage fees, such as retail leasing, for example.[74] It is, however, difficult to ascertain the extent to which minimum royalty payments are used in franchising. To our knowledge, the only source of such information is Lafontaine's (1992b) survey, where 40 of the 123 franchisors that levied royalties said that franchisees are subject to some minimum dollar amount in royalty when their sales are too low.

Finally, a few franchisors that charge percentage fees rely on an increasing or decreasing scale, making the percentage rate itself a function of sales levels. Of the 118 franchisors that levied percentage royalties in Lafontaine (1992b), 93 charged a constant royalty rate no matter what level of sales or profits or margins franchisees achieve, while 18 franchisors used a decreasing scale

---

[72] Consistent with these figures, Lafontaine (1992b) also reports that 112 of the 123 respondents that levied royalties used a percentage of sales royalty. Two respondents used a percentage of profits royalty, four used a percentage of gross margins, and another four levied a fixed ongoing fee per month or week.

[73] One could speculate that this alternative basis for royalties would be some form of net revenues to the franchisee as these sectors are ones where sales revenues to the franchise are different from total outlet receipts.

[74] See, e.g., Pashigian and Gould (1998) and Wheaton (2000) on the structure of retail leases.

for royalties, that is a royalty rate that declines as outlet sales reach certain target levels, and two used an increasing scale. Both the use of minimum royalty payments and of royalty rates that change as outcomes reach given targets suggest that a number of franchisors find it useful to introduce some non-linearity in their contracts. Our data suggest moreover that the use of varying rates may be on the rise: in 1980, only 49 of the 938 franchisors for which we have royalty rate data indicated a range of possible rates, whereas 114 franchisors (out of 1,023) gave a range in 1990, and 149 franchisors (out of 1,085) gave one in 2001. Bhattacharyya and Lafontaine's (1995) detailed look at 54 disclosure documents suggests that most royalty rate ranges reflect either decreasing or increasing scales, or a policy of granting lower royalty rates for the first few years of the franchisee's business.

For all those cases where franchisors use percentage of sales rates, we can rely on our data to see in more detail the kinds of rates found in franchise contracts.[75] Figure 3-2 presents this distribution for the 1,085 franchisors for which we have this information for 2001.[76] This figure shows that royalty rates typically vary between 3 and 6 percent, and that 26 percent of the franchisors charged the modal royalty rate of 5 percent, which in this case is also the median rate. Interestingly, 8 percent of business-format franchisors do not require the payment of any royalties at all. Examples include Fantastic Sam's, Snap-on Tools, Ben and Jerry's Ice Cream, and I Can't Believe It's Yogurt. Some such franchisors, like Fantastic Sam's, instead require franchisees to pay a fixed amount per week or month for the duration of the contract – we explore this further below. Others, such as Ben & Jerry's, obtain revenues from sales of goods to their franchisees, just like traditional franchisors do. We return to the issue of input purchase requirements in Chapter 6.[77]

---

[75] As noted earlier, we exclude from our sample the few franchisors whose royalty rate is above 25 percent. Our data source does not specifically indicate whether the rates are applied to sales revenue, to gross margins, or to profits. As we just saw, for the vast majority of franchisors, the rates are a percentage of sales. But percentage rates above 25 percent suggest the use of an alternative basis, and thus we want to preclude comparing these with our sales-based rates or including them in our reported averages and so on.

[76] Again we use the mean value whenever a range of royalty rates was given in our data source. We also impute minima and maxima when these are not stated using the methodology described earlier for franchise fees.

[77] Rao and Srinivasan (1995) argue that retail franchised chains charge lower royalty rates than those in service industries because the former have an alternative mechanism at their disposal to extract revenues from their franchisees, namely they can sell inputs to franchisees at a markup. See also Lafontaine (1992a) for some discussion and related evidence.

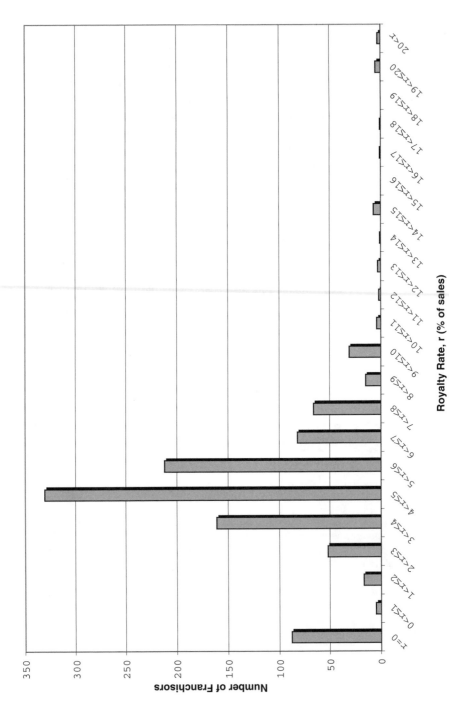

Royalty Rate, r (% of sales)

Figure 3-2: The distribution of royalty rates in 2001.

At the other extreme, a few franchisors do charge as much as 25 percent in royalties. As noted earlier, we eliminated from our sample those franchisors that charged even higher royalty rates on the presumption that these likely were levied on gross margins or profits rather than sales. Unfortunately, our data source does not specifically indicate whether the rates are applied to sales revenue, to gross margins, or to profits. Thus, firms with royalty rates of 15, 20, or 25 percent in our data may also be extracting a proportion of profit or gross margins rather than sales. Having communicated with some of these franchisors, however, we know that these high rates also can be percentages of sales royalties as well. Thus, we chose to include them in our analyses as long as their rates were not above 25 percent. We simply note that such high rates, when taken out of sales, leave little for franchisees to pay expenses and still earn normal profits. These businesses then tend to be concentrated in home-based, low overhead types of activities.[78]

We explore the variance in royalty rates further by looking at the sectoral distribution of these rates in Table 3-4. Again, we focus on those 980 franchisors for which we have full information on all fees. Table 3-4 shows first that royalty rates, just like franchise fees earlier, vary a lot within sectors. High royalty rates, however, are found disproportionately in the education and, to a lesser degree, the personal services and maintenance sectors. Indeed, examples of firms with high royalty rates in our data include Unishippers, Jackson Hewitt Tax Services, and Uniclean System. That firms in these sectors would require high royalty percentage rates is consistent, of course, with the notion that such rates are used more frequently in industries with low overhead. Yet, we also find more than 10 percent of franchisors charging no percentage royalties in these same sectors.

As noted above, low royalty rates are most frequent in the retail sectors: home furnishings, cosmetics, food retail, and other retail. This is what one would predict if franchisors that sell products to franchisees operate relatively high overhead businesses *and* can obtain much of their revenues from the markups they charge on their products. As just mentioned, we return to these issues in Chapter 6.

Table 3-5 shows how the usage of sales royalty and the average rate charged have evolved from 1980 to 2001. Of course, the proportion of franchisors using sales royalties was quite high even in 1980. Nonetheless, it has increased steadily throughout the 1980s and 1990s so that in 2001, 92 percent of

---

[78] As such businesses tend to be service rather than retail based, the high royalty rates that arise in low overhead businesses also explain part of the pattern noted by Rao and Srinivasan (1995).

Table 3-4: *The distribution of royalty rates in 2001, per sector*

Sector	$x=0$	$0<x\leq2$	$2<x\leq4$	$4<x\leq6$	$6<x\leq8$	$8<x\leq10$	$10<x$	Total
Automotive	5	2	9	35	19			70
Business	11	2	8	39	17	13	3	93
Contractors	1		6	26	4	1	0	38
Cosmetic	3	1	5	12				21
Education	3	1		6	11	8	5	34
Fast Food	6	2	52	151	13		1	225
Health and Fitness	3		3	9	6	1		22
Home Furnishings	2	3	8	10				23
Hotels and Motels			6	10				16
Maintenance	9		7	34	16	13	4	83
Personal Services	7	2	8	28	13	3	4	65
Real Estate	1		1	17	8	1		28
Recreation	1	1	1	7	6			16
Rental		1	2	8	5	1		17
Restaurants		1	42	25	1			69
Retail Food	5	1	7	22	5	1		41
Retail Other	15	3	31	66	4			119
Total	72	20	196	505	128	42	17	980

franchisors requested such fees.[79] The average royalty rate has increased slightly, from about 4.5 percent in 1980 to 5.2 percent in 2001, largely because fewer firms now have zero royalty rates (see column 6). Finally, of those franchisors that do not request any percentage royalty, we show in column 7 the number that charge ongoing fixed fees. In the *Profile of Franchising*, we saw that 61 out of 1,226 franchisors charged ongoing fixed fees instead of percentage royalties in 1998. Our data indicate that in the early 1980s only about one out of every four franchisors that did not request a percent royalty payment charged ongoing fixed fees. By 2001, however, one out of every two

---

[79] Udell (1972) found that 76 percent of the fast-food firms in his sample required the payment of percentage royalties, usually between 2 to 5 percent of sales. This suggests that the reliance on percentage fees increased in the 1970s as well. As we mention in Chapter 6, an important decision by the U.S. Supreme Court, *Siegel v. Chicken Delight* (1971), made it more difficult for business-format franchisors to earn revenues from sales of goods to franchisees at a markup. This likely encouraged a switch toward more royalty fees from the early 1970s onward.

Table 3-5: *Descriptive statistics for the royalty rates, 1980 to 2001*

Year	Number of franchisors in the data	% of franchisors with non-zero sales royalty	Mean royalty rate	Maximum royalty rate	Number of franchisors with zero royalty rate	Number of franchisors with no royalty but positive ongoing payments
1980	938	85.7	4.5	22.5	134	28
1981	1,016	87.1	4.6	22.5	131	30
1982	1,141	87.9	4.7	25	138	37
1983	1,093	88.9	4.7	25	121	46
1984	821	87.3	4.8	25	104	37
1985	853	90.6	5	22	80	29
1986	988	90.4	4.9	25	95	31
1987	1,006	90.4	4.9	25	97	39
1988	963	91.7	5	22	80	37
1989	993	91.2	5	22	87	46
1990	1,023	90.8	5	22	94	49
1991	948	91.4	5	22	82	44
1992	928	90.9	5	22	84	40
1993	1,035	90.4	5	25	99	52
1994	1,035	89.9	5	22.4	105	55
1995	1,045	90.7	5	22.4	97	54
1996	1,045	91.2	5.1	22	92	47
1997	982	91.6	5	22	82	44
1998	942	91.3	5.1	22	82	44
2000	927	92.0	5.2	22	74	37
2001	1,085	91.9	5.2	22	88	48

such firms, including, for example, Fantastic Sam's, used ongoing fixed fees instead of sales-based fees. Combined with the increased frequency in the use of percentage royalties, by 2001 we find that 96 percent of franchisors charged some form of royalty, either a percentage fee or ongoing fixed fees, whereas 89 percent of franchisors did one or the other back in 1980.

We provide more details on the amount of ongoing fixed fees in Table 3-6. Specifically, this table shows the evolution in the frequency with which such fees are used, and in the amounts requested, between 1980 and 2001. Column 3 shows the total number of firms requesting such fees, and the proportion of the sample they represent, regardless of what other fees the franchisor may charge. The data in this column confirm that such fees are the exception rather than the rule: The proportion of firms that rely on ongoing fixed payments is

Table 3-6: *The frequency and amounts of ongoing fixed payments (per month,
in U.S. dollars)*

Year	Number of franchisors	Number of franchisors (and %) with ongoing fixed payments	Mean fixed fee, all franchisors (nominal)	Mean fixed fee, all franchisors (real, 2001$)	Mean fixed fee when used (nominal)	Mean fixed fee when used (real, 2001$)
1980	1,089	40 (3.7)	17.7	38.0	481.2	1034.2
1981	1,100	46 (4.2)	17.0	33.2	407.5	793.9
1982	1,220	58 (4.8)	19.9	36.5	418.7	768.4
1983	1,169	75 (6.4)	36.4	64.8	567.7	1009.4
1984	880	63 (7.2)	39.2	66.9	548.2	934.4
1985	926	55 (5.9)	33.4	54.9	562.1	925.2
1986	1,075	60 (5.6)	38.6	62.4	692.4	1118.9
1987	1,075	69 (6.4)	33.0	51.5	514.4	801.9
1988	1,023	61 (6.0)	32.3	48.4	542.5	812.2
1989	1,059	64 (6.0)	29.3	41.9	485.2	692.9
1990	1,096	71 (6.5)	35.5	48.0	547.4	741.7
1991	1,017	64 (6.2)	37.3	48.5	601.9	782.7
1992	992	61 (6.1)	33.5	42.3	545.3	688.3
1993	1,088	86 (6.8)	33.5	41.1	493.2	604.5
1994	1,090	90 (7.3)	35.7	42.6	486.0	580.8
1995	1,096	93 (7.8)	41.2	47.9	531.7	617.9
1996	1,092	84 (6.7)	31.4	35.4	469.3	529.7
1997	1,022	82 (6.9)	29.3	32.3	421.5	465.1
1998	995	76 (7.6)	36.0	39.1	470.8	511.5
2000	984	67 (6.8)	33.5	34.5	492.4	506.4
2001	1,158	82 (7.1)	34.1	34.1	481.6	481.6

relatively low, and it has remained quite stable, around 6 to 7 percent, since
at least the mid-1980s. Moreover, a comparison of the number of franchisors
that use fixed payments with the number of franchisors with zero royalty that
use such fees, as per column 7 of Table 3-5, reveals that one-third to one-half
of the franchisors that rely on ongoing fixed payments collect those along
with positive royalty payments.

The next four columns of data in Table 3-6 show the average amounts
involved, per month, both in nominal and in real (2001) U.S. dollars, first
across all firms in the data (columns 4 and 5) and then for those firms that
use these types of fees only (columns 6 and 7). Focusing on the latter two
columns for now, we see that the average fee charged by firms that use these
fees has remained about the same in nominal terms over this period. But in

real terms, there has been a steady and important reduction in the amount of fixed ongoing payments from an average of about $900 per month to only about $500 in 2001. This, it turns out, is mostly due to the disappearance of a few franchisors that charged very high ongoing fees. When one considers the importance of these fees for franchising as a whole (that is, on average across all firms in the data as per columns 4 and 5), one finds that in real terms the average monthly amounts collected went up slightly in the mid-1980s and then started to go down again. By 2001, these fees were back to about the same level, on average, as they were in the early 1980s.

3.4 Advertising Fees

In addition to charging an initial franchise fee and running royalties, many franchisors also stipulate in their contracts that the franchisee must make contributions to support national, regional, and/or local advertising. For local advertising, the contributions are often stated as minima: the franchisor requires that the franchisee spend at least X percent of its sales revenues, or at least $X, on local advertising. For advertising fees generally, franchisors often state in their disclosure documents that the rates may be changed later, or, for those that do not require an advertising contribution, that an advertising fund may be instituted later, at the discretion of the franchisor. Franchisors thus leave themselves much leeway in this part of their financial dealings with franchisees. Contrary to franchise fees, which often vary across franchisees in a chain, this leeway relates to the ability to make changes over time, not to treat different franchisees differently. Of course, raising the amount that franchisees must devote to advertising at any point in time is apt to cause some conflict in a franchise system. We return to this potential problem in Chapter 9, which focuses specifically on advertising issues.

Like royalty payments, advertising fees are most often stipulated as a constant proportion of the franchisees' sales revenues. But again like royalty payments, advertising fees are also sometimes specified as a fixed monthly or weekly amount, or calculated as a function of the number of transactions, and so on. In Volume III of the *Profile of Franchising*, the IFA and Frandata found that 634 (or 52 percent) of the 1,221 franchisors for which they had advertising fee data required that franchisees pay a percentage of their sales toward advertising. The remaining franchisors either required no contribution at all (340, or 28 percent), or contributions only to local or regional advertising funds (149, or 12 percent), or a flat fee (66, or 5 percent of them), or a per transaction fee (13, or 1 percent of the sample). The remaining few firms used some other unspecified basis to calculate the advertising requirement.

Table 3-7: *Variation in advertising fees (excluding initial opening promotional fees)*

Single Rate:	44
Single Rate (% of Sales)	16
None Listed (= 0)	8
Single Rate Stated as a Minimum Requirement	13
Single Rate with Minimum Dollar Amount	5
Single Rate Stated as a Maximum Requirement	1
Single Rate with Maximum Dollar Amount	1
Multiple Rates:	3
Different Rates in Different Markets	1
Fee is a Function of Sales and Unit Size	1
Minimum and Maximum Rates Stated	1
Other Type of Fees:	7
Form of Advertising Specified (instead of amount)	4
Fixed Monthly Payments (with built-in increases)	2
Payment Set by Local Franchisee Group	1
Total:	54

Source: Bhattacharyya and Lafontaine (1995).

We provide additional information on the types of advertising fees that franchisors use in Table 3-7, which details the sum of the requirements for local, regional, and national advertising for the 54 franchisors whose disclosure documents were examined by Bhattacharyya and Lafontaine (1995). The information contained in this table once again confirms the prevalence of single percent-of-sales advertising fees, with an important number of cases where this fee is in fact zero. Note, however, that an even larger number of franchisors indicate that this fee is to be understood as a minimum. Similarly to what occurred with royalty rates, some franchisors (5 of the 44 with a single rate) require that franchisees contribute a minimum dollar amount to advertising if their sales do not reach the level required to justify this level of expenditures based on the stated rate. Only one franchisor caps the advertising contribution at some maximum dollar value.

Having established that most firms use a percent advertising fee (including many with no fee at all), we again use our data to examine in more detail the level and distribution of these fees. Note that as was the case for royalty rates, a steadily increasing number of franchisors report a range of advertising fees rather than a single value. The number of such occurrences is lower, however, than for royalty rates: in the early 1980s, only 20 out of our sample of about 1,000 franchisors gave a range for advertising fees. By the end of our sample period, this number was up to about 50 per year. As we did for the other fees, we rely on the average rate in those cases where a range is given.[80]

Figure 3-3 shows the distribution of the advertising fees as a percent of sales for the 1,028 firms with advertising fee information in our data in 2001. This distribution first confirms what was reported in the *Profile of Franchising*, namely that many franchisors (289, or 28 percent of our sample) do not charge any advertising fee. Advertising fees also are rather low relative to royalty rates. Of the firms that charge an advertising fee, the majority (466 out of 739, or 63 percent) set it at a level of 2 percent or less. Almost all firms set this fee below 5 percent, our modal (and median) royalty rate. These patterns are very consistent with those reported in the *Profile of Franchising*, where 68 percent of the firms that used a percentage of sales advertising fee charged 2 percent or less, while 98 percent of them requested fees of less than 5 percent.

We show the sectoral distribution of advertising rates in Table 3-8, restricting our data to those franchisors for which we observe all fees. This table mostly illustrates that relatively high advertising fees are found only in a few sectors, most strikingly the automotive and health and fitness sectors. A relatively small number of firms from the personal services and from the fast-food industries also charge high advertising rates. In many other sectors, no firm requires more than a 4 percent contribution.

Table 3-9 provides information on how the frequency and amounts of advertising fees have changed between 1980 and 2001. This table clearly shows that the mean percent advertising fee has gone up over this period, but this is entirely due to the increasing number of firms that request such fees. In other words, the average advertising fee charged by users of such fees has not changed on average over this period, but more franchisors now stipulate an advertising fee separately from royalties. In addition, the last two columns of this table show that the number of franchisors that charge ongoing fixed payments represents an increasing proportion of all franchisors with a zero advertising rate. This occurs because the number of franchisors requesting ongoing fixed payments has remained quite stable while the number that do not specify a separate advertising percentage fee has decreased substantially over the period of our data.

Finally, while percent advertising fees are often specified and administered separately from royalty payments, from a franchisee's perspective it is the sum of these rates that really matters – this sum determines the portion of each dollar of sales revenue that must be sent back to the franchisor. It is also the sum

---

[80] Here also we impute minima and maxima when these are not stated explicitly, as we did for franchise fees (see earlier footnote).

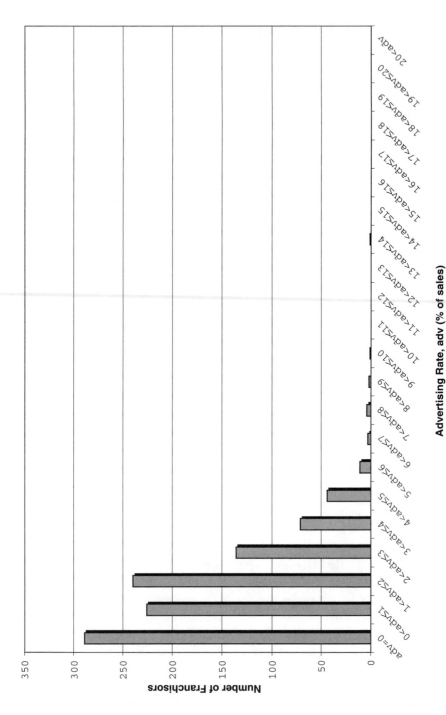

Advertising Rate, adv (% of sales)

Figure 3-3: The distribution of percent of sales advertising fees in 2001.

Table 3-8: *The distribution of advertising rates in 2001, per sector*

Sector	$x = 0$	$0 < x \leq 1\%$	$1\% < x \leq 2\%$	$2\% < x \leq 3\%$	$3\% < x \leq 4\%$	$4\% < x \leq 5\%$	$5\% < x$	Total
Automotive	17	13	8	10	4	9	9	70
Business	41	26	17	8		1		93
Contractors	14	6	12	6				38
Cosmetic	8	1	3	3	1	5		21
Education	13	4	10	5		2		34
Fast Food	17	47	63	41	36	18		225
Health and Fitness	6	5	3		2	1	3	22
Home Furnishings	7	6	7	1	1	1	5	23
Hotels and Motels		1	5	6	4			16
Maintenance	45	15	16	3	2		2	83
Personal Services	20	14	16	6	4	3	2	65
Real Estate	6	7	8	6	1			28
Recreation	6	4	2	2	2			16
Rental	5	1	4	6	1			17
Restaurants	7	20	16	18	6	2		69
Retail Food	14	13	11	2	1			41
Retail Other	37	36	29	10	4	2	1	119
Total	263	219	230	133	69	44	22	980

Table 3-9: *Descriptive statistics for advertising percentage rates, 1980 to 2001*

Year	N	% franchisors with > 0 advertising rate	Mean (users and non users)	Maximum	Number of franchisors with advertising rate = 0	Number of franchisors with advertising rate = 0, but positive fixed payments
1980	925	44.2	1.1	13.0	516	37
1981	1,026	48.5	1.2	16.3	528	46
1982	1,167	52.5	1.3	16.3	554	55
1983	1,114	54.9	1.3	16.3	502	71
1984	830	58.3	1.4	13.0	346	59
1985	873	60.1	1.5	10.0	348	48
1986	1,024	64.7	1.6	13.0	361	53
1987	1,043	65.2	1.6	12.0	363	65
1988	986	68.4	1.7	13.0	312	55
1989	1,018	67.6	1.6	15.0	330	56
1990	1,046	68.9	1.6	15.0	325	61
1991	972	68.2	1.6	14.0	309	57
1992	952	66.7	1.5	10.0	317	55
1993	1,038	68.1	1.6	10.0	331	67
1994	1,021	67.0	1.5	10.0	337	74
1995	1,007	67.9	1.5	10.0	323	76
1996	979	71.2	1.6	10.0	282	65
1997	926	70.5	1.6	10.0	273	61
1998	894	71.9	1.7	10.0	251	66
2000	876	72.7	1.7	10.0	239	59
2001	1,028	71.9	1.7	14.0	289	69

of these percentage-of-sales fees then that affects the franchisee's decisions at the margin. From the franchisor's perspective also, advertising expenditures are not bound by the amount collected specifically for this purpose. In chains that do not specify such a fee, franchisors still spend money on advertising. In other words, not all franchisors necessarily draw a clear distinction between royalty revenue and advertising related funds, especially early in our sample period.[81] For these reasons, in Figure 3-4 and Table 3-10 we present the distribution of the sum of royalty and advertising rates, overall and per sector respectively, in 2001.

Figure 3-4 shows that most franchisees paid somewhere between 4 and 9 cents out of every dollar of sales in the form of royalties and/or advertising fees to their franchisor in 2001, with a median (equal to modal) total rate of 7 percent. Only 65 franchisors (6.5 percent) do not charge any royalty or advertising fee based on sales. As described above, this includes of course Fantastic Sam's and Snap-on Tool. On the other hand, only a few franchisors (16 out of 1,000) require contributions that can add up to more than 15 percent of a franchisee's sales revenues, including again some well-known firms such as Pearle Vision and Jackson Hewitt Tax Service, a subsidiary of Cendant Corporation that had over 4,000 locations in 2002.

The data in Table 3-10 generally confirm that high total rates are used relatively more frequently in service industries such as education, health and fitness, personal services, automotive, and maintenance sectors. Franchisors in retail businesses, in contrast, tend to rely on relatively lower total rates. This is consistent with the conclusion we reached upon observing royalty rates by themselves. Thus, our data suggest that franchisors that choose a low royalty rate do not "make it up" by choosing a comparatively high advertising rate, or vice versa: in fact, high royalty and advertising rates generally go hand in hand. We confirmed this tendency by calculating the correlation between royalty rates and advertising fees. For the 980 firms present in our data in 2001, this correlation is 0.13 and highly statistically significant. But even within sectors, the correlation between these fees tends to be positive. Specifically, the correlation is positive in 13 of our 17 sectors, and significantly so (at the 0.10 level) in 8 cases. For the other sectors, the correlations are negative but not statistically different from 0. Note that we find the highest positive correlation between these fees (0.38 and 0.35, both significantly different from 0 at the 0.05 level) in the other retail and in the personal services sectors, respectively.

---

[81] See Stassen and Mittelstaedt (2001) and Chapter 9 of this book for more on advertising fees and advertising in franchising.

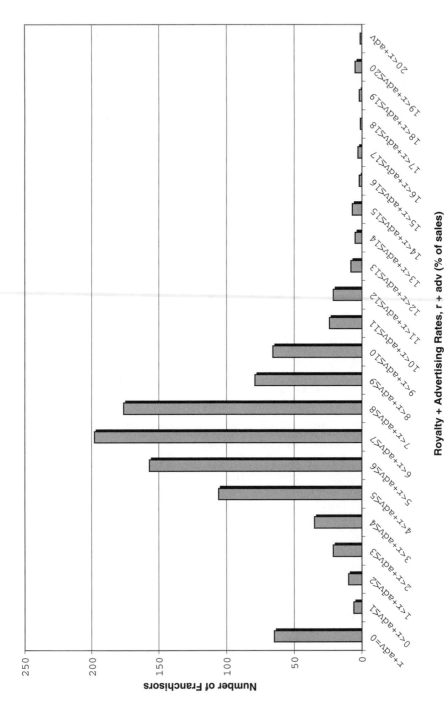

Royalty + Advertising Rates, r + adv (% of sales)

Figure 3-4: The distribution of royalty plus advertising percentage rates, 2001.

Table 3-10: *The distribution of royalty plus advertising percentage rates in 2001, per sector*

Sector	$x = 0$	$0 < x \leq 2\%$	$2\% < x \leq 4\%$	$4\% < x \leq 6\%$	$6\% < x \leq 8\%$	$8\% < x \leq 10\%$	$10\% < x$	Total
Automotive	3	3	2	13	24	12	13	70
Business	11	1	4	26	31	10	10	93
Contractors	1		4	12	15	5	1	38
Cosmetic	3	1		7	4	4	2	21
Education	3			2	9	9	11	34
Fast Food	3		8	53	107	46	8	225
Health and Fitness	3			4	7	1	7	22
Home Furnishings	1	4	1	9	6	2		23
Hotels and Motels				3	12	1		16
Maintenance	9		5	18	30	9	12	83
Personal Services	6		3	19	20	8	9	65
Real Estate			2	7	10	9		28
Recreation	1			3	6	4	1	16
Rental		1	1	1	8	6		17
Restaurants		1	9	27	28	5		69
Retail Food	4	2	1	18	12	3	1	41
Retail Other	13	3	15	39	37	9	3	119
Total	61	16	55	261	366	143	78	980

Table 3-11: *Descriptive statistics for the sum of royalty and advertising percentage rates, 1980 to 2001*

Year	N	% zors with non-zero % fee	Mean	Max	# of zors at zero	% of zors at zero with fixed payments
1980	875	88.2	5.7	22.5	103	26
1981	976	89.3	5.9	27	104	30
1982	1111	90.5	6.0	27	106	34
1983	1063	91.1	6.0	27	95	43
1984	797	90.3	6.3	30	77	35
1985	824	93.2	6.5	25.8	56	23
1986	954	93	6.5	27	67	24
1987	988	92.1	6.5	27	78	35
1988	942	93.1	6.8	27	65	31
1989	971	92.9	6.7	27	69	38
1990	995	93	6.7	27	70	39
1991	928	92.5	6.7	22	70	38
1992	906	92.3	6.6	23	70	34
1993	1007	92	6.6	25	81	45
1994	989	91.5	6.5	25	84	49
1995	982	91.6	6.5	25	82	46
1996	956	92.4	6.6	23	73	39
1997	910	92.6	6.6	20	67	35
1998	869	92.5	6.8	22	65	35
2000	855	93.2	6.8	23	58	30
2001	998	93.5	6.8	21	65	36

Finally, we present data on the evolution of the sum of royalty and advertising rates in Table 3-11. Not surprisingly, given the data presented earlier, the proportion of franchisors in our data that use some percentage fee has risen by about five percentage points. By 2001, a full 93.5 percent of the franchisors charge a percentage-of-sales fee to their franchisees, leaving only the same 65 franchisors mentioned above with no such fee. Moreover, mostly due to this increased participation, the sum of the average percentage fees has increased by a full percentage point between 1980 and 2001, from 5.8 to 6.8 percent. Finally, about half of the franchisors with no percentage fee request some type of ongoing payment from their franchisees. The remaining few business-format franchisors – less than 4 percent of the sample – must extract most of their revenues from franchise fees or, more likely, from markups on items that they sell to their franchisees just like traditional franchisors do.[82]

---

[82] Of course, firms that stated in the survey that they do not collect any franchise fee, or any royalty or advertising fee, were excluded from our analyses on the basis that these are not franchisors. See Chapter 1, Section 1.3, where we first describe our data.

3.5 Non-Monetary Contract Clauses

Aside from the set of financial contract terms reviewed in this chapter, franchise contracts contain numerous clauses governing the obligations of both parties during and after the contract period. These include statements about how the franchisee is expected to run the franchise, whether or not the franchisee has an exclusive territory, who owns or leases the property, the duration of the agreement and the circumstances under which the franchisor or franchisee may terminate it, when and where the franchisee may open another business, and so on. We describe many of these contractual obligations and clauses in the remainder of this book, as they relate to the issues we focus on in each chapter. For example, we discuss in Chapter 5 how franchisors may use a combination of contract clauses to monitor the behavior of, and provide incentives to, their franchisees in an effort to control the quality of the products and services offered by the franchisees and ensure a consistent experience for customers. In Chapter 6, which focuses on tying, we describe the extent to which franchisors require franchisees to purchase particular inputs directly from them or rely on approved suppliers. In our discussion of encroachment issues, in Chapter 8, we present data on the extent to which franchisors grant exclusive territories to franchisees; and in Chapter 10, on termination and non-renewals, we present data on contract length, termination, transfers, and non-compete clauses.[83]

3.6 Some Final Thoughts and Comments

In this chapter, we have described the main monetary contract terms found in franchise contracts in the U.S. In particular, we have shown the type and level of fees collected by franchisors, the variance of these fees, and how the fees have evolved since 1980. Before moving on to discuss dual distribution and vertical restraints in Chapter 4, a few final points should be made in relation to these fees. First, using our data but only up to 1992, Lafontaine and Shaw (1999) have shown that while franchise fees and royalty rates vary across franchisors, they remain quite stable over time within franchised chains. In fact, franchisors do not systematically increase or decrease their royalty rates or franchise fees as they become better established, whether this is measured

---

[83] A few franchise contract clauses, such as choice of law or mandatory arbitration clauses, relate to interpretation and enforcement rather than defining the franchise relationship itself or its economic underpinnings. Readers interested in learning more about such contract clauses, or about franchise law, would do well to consult a legal treatise such as Garner (2002). For an overview of laws that affect franchising in a number of different countries, see Zeidman (1989) and, more recently, Mendelsohn (2003).

in number of years in franchising or in terms of total outlets. The tendency instead is to keep the fees, especially the percentage of sales fees, relatively constant. Thus, the uniformity in fees described earlier across franchisees within a chain, and across borders, also applies over time within a chain.

Second, we have explored somewhat in this chapter the relationship between royalty and advertising rates on the one hand, and ongoing fixed payments on the other hand. Sometimes franchisors use both sales-based percentage fees and ongoing fixed payments. But in other cases, franchisors rely on fixed payments in lieu of a percentage royalty or advertising fee, in which case the use of fixed payments and percentage fees is negatively correlated. The theoretical literature on franchising implies that sales-based fees and initial franchise fees should be negatively correlated everything else being the same and, in particular, if the value of the franchise is held constant. After all, if a franchisee is asked to pay more in initial fees, this must be made up by a reduction in ongoing payments later on and vice versa. Empirically, this negative relationship has been quite elusive. For example, Lafontaine (1992a) and Sen (1993) found no negative relationship between the sum of royalty and advertising rates and the initial franchise fee for the sets of U.S. franchisors they studied, even after controlling for variables that proxy the value of the franchise. More recently, Kaufmann and Dant (2001) even find a positive relationship between royalty rates and franchise fees after controlling for unit sales. One could argue that the lack of observed negative relationship arises from differences in contract terms that affect both fees in similar ways and are not controlled for in these analyses. Along these lines, Sen (1993) finds that both fees decline if the franchisor imposes input purchase requirements on its franchisees, a requirement that allows the franchisor to collect markup dollars from their franchisees as discussed earlier. Any correlation analysis for royalty rates and franchise fees that would not account for such a clause might yield a positive or zero correlation simply because differences in the input purchase requirements make franchisors adjust both fees similarly. If firms do not modify their other contracting practices frequently, however, one can account for them possibly by examining the relationship between changes in the fees of individual chains over time. Lafontaine and Shaw (1999) perform this type of test and again find no relationship between total percentage fees and initial franchise fees. Of course, it may be that not all relevant factors are held constant in these analyses either. At this point, however, the empirical evidence suggests that franchise fees are set quite independently from sales-based fees. The absence of a negative relationship between the two types of fees implies that the franchise fee may not be set at a level to extract all of the economic rent that franchisees earn.[84] This would occur, for example, if franchisors mostly set their initial franchise fee to compensate for the costs they incur in setting up the outlet, as Bond (2001) suggests they do.

Finally, although fewer data are available on contract terms used by non-U.S. franchisors, studies of franchise practices outside the U.S. suggest that the basic types of fees, the extent to which they are used, and their levels are fairly similar to those described here for the U.S. Canadian franchisors included in our data, for example, use the same types of fees and set them at levels that are quite similar to those chosen by U.S. franchisors. Pénard, Raynaud and Saussier (2003) examined the fees used by more than 200 franchisors in France, and found that most of them also use percentage of sales royalties and initial franchise fees, though the latter appear to be slightly lower in France.[85] Frazer (1998) shows that while the same types and levels of fees are used by franchisors in Australia, there is a greater reliance on ongoing fixed payments as 17 percent of the firms in her sample of 262 franchisors rely on such payments compared to just 7 percent of franchisors doing the same in our data. Finally, Seaton's (2003) data show that the fees of 161 franchisors in the UK in 1998 are very similar on average, and follow the same general distribution, as the ones found here for U.S. and Canadian franchisors.[86] Moreover, the conclusions about the lack of correlation between the fees and their stability over time also apply to non-U.S. franchisors. Specifically, Gagné et al. (1998) establish a lack of negative correlation in fees for franchisors operating in Québec, Canada, while Seaton's (2003) analyses indicate that the fees used by franchisors in the UK also are not negatively correlated and do not change much over time either.

---

[84] See Kaufmann and Lafontaine (1994) and Michael and Moore (1995) for evidence that franchisees earn economic profit at least in some franchised systems and for discussion of the reasons why franchisors many choose to leave profit with their franchisees. Lafontaine and Raynaud (2002) argue that downstream profit (combined with monitoring and termination rights) and residual claims are complementary incentive mechanisms in franchised chains, i.e., they are used to reinforce one another.

[85] The authors do not mention advertising fees, but a report from the Fédération Française de la Franchise (French Federation of Franchising) (2003) contains data on such fees.

[86] Many other descriptive studies also have found similar fees in other countries.

4

Franchising, Vertical Integration, and Vertical Restraints

4.1 Introduction

This chapter covers a lot of ground, focusing as it does on the relationships among franchising, vertical integration, and various types of vertical restraints in both theory and practice. We begin with a description of the extent of company ownership in franchised chains. The vast majority of franchised firms operate at least some of their units themselves while franchising the rest. Thus, they choose some degree of vertical integration and then use contractual devices to organize the other units in the chain. There is considerable variation across franchised chains in the extent of company ownership, which in itself is worth exploring. In fact, why firms choose different proportions of company-owned units is a question that has received significant attention in the empirical literature on franchising.

Next, we describe a set of vertical restraints, many of which appear in franchise contracts. We show how, in combination or individually, these vertical restraints in theory allow franchisors to achieve the same results as vertical integration would permit. In particular, we examine the use of simple lump-sum fees, sales royalties, output royalties, input purchase requirements, resale price controls, and output quotas. We introduce these here, and then return to many of them in later chapters as we explore the sources of conflict between franchisors and franchisees. Finally, in the last section of this chapter, we review agency-theoretic arguments that have been used to explain variation in royalty rates across franchised chains. We then return to the issue of why firms use different proportions of company-owned and franchised units and show how the same arguments used to explain royalty rate variation can yield insights into why the extent of vertical integration also varies across franchised chains.

4.2 Dual Distribution or Partial Vertical Integration in Franchising

Firms involved in franchising typically engage in dual distribution, i.e., they operate some units directly and franchise the rest. For example, at the end of 2001, McDonald's had 30,093 restaurants worldwide. Some 8,378, or almost 28 percent of them, were company-owned and operated. The majority of franchisors, however, operate a smaller proportion of their outlets directly. In this section, we explore systematically the extent of dual distribution in franchising in the United States. We begin with the 1986 census-type data from the USDOC as it includes information on sales and employment levels that cannot be replicated today. We then move on to describe the current extent of dual distribution according to our data.

4.2.1 The Extent of Dual Distribution: 1986 and Now

Table 4-1 shows how total sales, establishments, and employees were distributed between company-owned and franchised units across sectors in 1986 according to the USDOC. Table 4-2 further shows average sales and number of employees per establishment, as well as sales per employee, for company-owned and franchised units in the various sectors. These tables establish that (1) the majority of the activity in franchised chains, or about 75 percent of sales, takes place in franchised outlets; (2) company-owned units achieve higher per unit sales, on average, than franchised units in almost all of the business-format franchising sectors defined by the USDOC; (3) the average number of employees is also larger in company-owned units than in franchised units; and (4) sales per employee, which can be interpreted as a measure of labor productivity, are not systematically greater in one type of unit or the other.

In Table 4-3, we explore how the average number of company-owned and franchised units per chain has changed since 1980, both in the USDOC and our data.

This table shows again that the average size of the franchised chains included in our data set has increased especially during the early 1980s and then again in the late 1990s. The latter growth in part reflects the increased international expansion of the chains in our data, as we find that the proportion of non-U.S. to total outlets has grown from 20 percent in 1993 to 28 percent by 2001. In the early 1980s, we find growth in our data, but not in the USDOC data. Assuming that the average size of franchised chains did not change during the early 1980s (as per the USDOC), the growth in our sample must be due to an

Table 4-1: *Total sales, establishments, and employment in company-owned and franchised units in the U.S. in 1986*

Sector	Total sales ($ thousands)		Total establishments		Total number of employees*	
	Company-owned	Franchised	Company-owned	Franchised	Company-owned	Franchised
Automobile and Truck Dealers	0	307,256,000	0	27,600	na	na
Gasoline Service Stations	15,591,000	71,027,000	21,692	98,818	na	na
Soft-Drink Bottlers	16,516,000	3,146,000	662	541	na	na
All Traditional Franchising	32,107,000	381,429,000	22,354	126,959	na	na
Automotive Products and Services	3,800,495	7,500,368	4,851	31,912	40,662	145,520
Business Aids and Services	2,338,187	10,950,067	6,676	46,042	255,907	413,615
Construction, Home Improvement, Maintenance, and Cleaning Services	1,351,950	3,263,410	748	18,152	15,371	103,620
Convenience Stores	6,732,322	4,546,573	8,974	6,550	94,393	58,295
Educational Products and Services	208,037	727,129	537	8,088	13,238	27,972
Hotels, Motels, and Campgrounds	5,061,835	10,922,155	1,147	7,056	135,292	420,383
Laundry and Dry-Cleaning Services	26,016	265,786	103	2,194	897	8,994
Recreation, Entertainment, and Travel	727,095	2,821,930	419	7,482	3,075	24,657
Rental Services (Auto–Truck)	3,523,889	2,631,117	2,449	7,079	33,372	33,051
Rental Services (Equipment)	306,096	409,923	665	2,053	5,040	9,886
Restaurants	18,803,699	33,470,164	24,364	53,839	847,760	1,605,861
Retailing (Food Non-Convenience)	2,781,204	7,964,807	3,509	16,343	45,308	169,460
Retailing (Non-Food)	7,324,902	15,777,877	11,228	34,228	67,999	206,664
Miscellaneous	279,272	1,026,443	476	5,646	5,536	38,950
All Business-Format Franchising	53,264,999	102,277,749	66,146	246,664	1,563,850	3,267,378
All Franchising	85,371,999	483,706,749	88,500	373,623	na	na

Note: *Includes part-time and working proprietors.
Source: USDOC (1988).

84

Table 4-2: *Sales and employment per establishment and sales per employee, company-owned and franchised units in the U.S. in 1986*

Sector	Sales per establishment ($ thousands)		Employees per establishment*		Sales per employee	
	Company-owned	Franchised	Company-owned	Franchised	Company-owned	Franchised
Automobile and Truck Dealers	na	11,132	na	na	na	na
Gasoline Service Stations	719	719	na	na	na	na
Soft-Drink Bottlers	24,949	5,815	na	na	na	na
All Traditional Franchising	1,436	3,004	na	na	na	na
Automotive Products and Services	783	235	8.38	4.56	93,466	51,542
Business Aids and Services	350	238	38.33	8.98	9,137	26,474
Construction, Home Improvement, Maintenance, and Cleaning Service	1,807	180	20.55	5.71	87,955	31,494
Convenience Stores	750	694	10.52	8.90	71,322	77,993
Educational Products and Services	387	90	24.65	3.46	15,715	25,995
Hotels, Motels, and Campgrounds	4,413	1,548	117.95	59.58	37,414	25,981
Laundry and Dry-Cleaning Services	253	121	8.71	4.10	29,003	29,551
Recreation, Entertainment, and Travel	1,735	377	7.34	3.30	236,454	114,448
Rental Services (Auto–Truck)	1,439	372	13.63	4.67	105,594	79,608
Rental Services (Equipment)	460	200	7.58	4.82	60,733	41,465
Restaurants	772	621	34.80	29.83	22,180	20,843
Retailing (Food Non-Convenience)	793	487				
Retailing (Non-Food)	652	461	6.06	6.04	107,721	76,345
Miscellaneous	587	182	11.63	6.90	50,446	26,353
All Business-Format Franchising	805	415	23.64	13.25	34,060	31,303
All Franchising	965	1,295	na	na	na	na

Note: *Includes part-time and working proprietors.
Source: USDOC (1988).

Table 4-3: *Average number of outlets per chain, franchised, and company-owned*

	USDOC, *Franchising in the Economy*			Our data set			
Year	Company-owned	Franchised	Total	Number of franchisors	Company-owned	Franchised	Total
1980	35.80	123.63	159.44	1,089	31	120	151
1981	35.00	120.74	155.74	1,100	31	129	160
1982	34.30	117.29	151.59	1,220	29	126	155
1983	32.56	114.58	147.15	1,169	31	137	168
1984	32.49	113.53	146.02	880	43	184	227
1985	30.58	113.78	144.36	926	44	178	223
1986	30.38	113.30	143.69	1,075	39	158	197
1987	na	na	na	1,075	37	165	202
1988	na	na	na	1,023	38	174	212
1989	na	na	na	1,059	36	181	217
1990	na	na	na	1,096	35	182	217
1991	na	na	na	1,018	38	196	234
1992	na	na	na	992	37	205	242
1993	na	na	na	1,100	32	171	203
1994	na	na	na	1,100	27	176	203
1995	na	na	na	1,104	33	194	227
1996	na	na	na	1,103	36	212	248
1997	na	na	na	1,033	37	237	275
1998	na	na	na	995	42	263	305
2000	na	na	na	984	52	298	350
2001	na	na	na	1,158	46	284	330

Note: The ratio of the average number of company-owned outlets to the average number of outlets is not a measure of the proportion of company-owned outlets in these data as the ratio of two means need not bear any relationship with the mean of the ratios of the original variables. See tables and figures on the extent of company ownership within chains.

increased tendency to include larger and faster-growing franchised systems in the surveys during the early 1980s.

Despite these potential biases towards larger and growing franchised chains, the data in Table 4-3 make it clear that franchisors have continued to operate at least some proportion of their units and to franchise the rest throughout the 1980s and 1990s, thereby confirming that dual distribution is an equilibrium strategy in franchising.

We explore the extent of dual distribution further in Table 4-4 by showing the ratio of total number of company-owned units to total units each year in the USDOC data (column 2) and the corresponding ratio in our data (column 4). We find first that the total number of outlets that are corporately owned across all the firms in our data, as a proportion of all outlets for these chains, is lower than it is for the population of franchisors per the USDOC data for all the years when the two data sets overlap. The difference in the ratios, however, is quite small, only one to two percentage points.

In column 5 of Table 4-4, we show the average proportion of company-owned units in the set of firms included in our data. If all the chains in the data operated about the same proportion of outlets corporately, the ratio in column 4 and the mean proportion of company outlets across chains in column 5 would be about the same.[87] The fact that the mean proportion in column 5 is systematically larger than the ratio in column 4 implies that larger franchisors on average have a lower proportion of company units than do smaller franchisors. We argue below that this is because many small (or young) franchisors are still in their adjustment phase after starting to franchise. That adjustment phase necessarily begins at 100-percent company-owned at the time they start franchising. This proportion decreases dramatically as new outlets are added under a franchise mode of operation, but remains relatively high until they become established.[88]

For now, going back to the data in Table 4-4, we note that, on average, firms in our data operated about 23 percent of their units directly throughout the 1980s. This proportion decreased, however, during the 1990s so that by 2001, the average franchisor in our data operated only 16 to 17 percent of its outlets directly. It is not possible to tell whether this decrease is due to changes in the composition of the sample over time, or whether it reflects real changes in the extent of company ownership by firms involved in franchising. We address this further below.

The extent of company ownership varies considerably across franchised companies, with the proportion of company-owned units ranging from 0 to 100 percent every year in our data (see Table 4-4, where a positive number of franchisors appears each year in the last two columns). Figure 4-1 illustrates the full cross-firm variation in the proportion of company-owned outlets for the chains in our data in 2001.

In addition to confirming the heterogeneity in the choices that firms make with respect to their proportion of company-owned units, Figure 4-1 establishes that most franchising firms directly operate only a small

---

[87] The difference between the figures shown in columns 4 and 5 arises because a ratio of means generally is different from a mean of ratios. Specifically, in column 5, each franchisor is given the same weight regardless of its total number of outlets, whereas in column 4, franchised units are all given the same weight, regardless of whether they belong to a large or a small franchised chain.

[88] The reduction in the average proportion of company-owned units over time in our sample of franchisors (see column 5) is driven largely by a reduction in the number of fully corporate chains in the sample, from over 50 in the early years to only about 20 in the last few years of the data (see last column).

Table 4-4: *The extent of dual distribution in franchising*

Year	USDOC Total company-owned units/ total units	USDOC Number of franchisors	Our data set Total company-owned units/ total units	Our data set Mean percent company-owned	Our data set Number of franchisors with no company units	Our data set Number of franchisors with only company units
1980	22.46	1,089	20.6	23.2	285	41
1981	22.47	1,100	19.5	23.0	273	51
1982	22.63	1,220	18.9	25.5	293	65
1983	22.13	1,169	18.3	25.0	294	65
1984	22.25	880	18.8	22.8	221	48
1985	21.18	926	19.9	23.1	216	48
1986	21.15	1,075	19.8	24.0	231	66
1987	na	1,075	18.4	22.3	243	54
1988	na	1,023	18	22.4	250	50
1989	na	1,059	16.6	22.4	260	58
1990	na	1,096	16.1	22.2	251	56
1991	na	1,018	16.2	22.8	259	68
1992	na	992	15.3	21.8	237	55
1993	na	1,100	15.9	21.4	268	54
1994	na	1,100	13.4	20.0	265	46
1995	na	1,104	14.6	20.5	297	50
1996	na	1,103	14.5	19.8	287	48
1997	na	1,033	13.6	17.0	267	18
1998	na	995	13.8	16.5	270	24
2000	na	984	14.8	16.2	278	13
2001	na	1,158	13.9	17.2	326	26

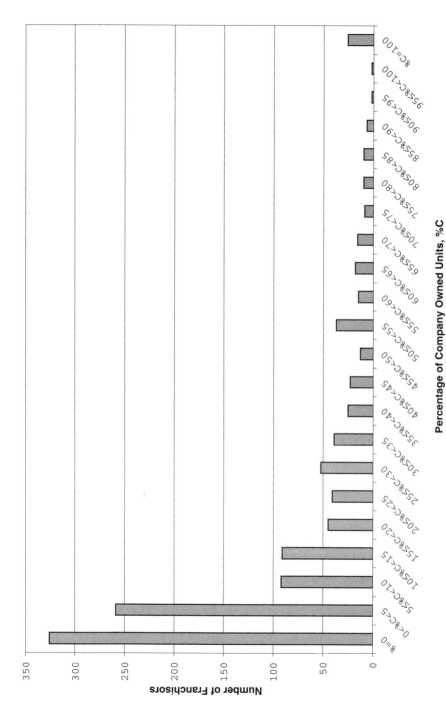

Figure 4-1: The distribution of the proportion of company-owned units in our data in 2001 (sample size = 1,158 franchisors).

proportion of their outlets, i.e., the distribution is quite skewed to the left. In fact, 28 percent of franchisors (326 out of 1,158) choose to own and operate no units. From Table 4-4, we see that the proportion of firms with no company units (column 6) has remained fairly stable, at 25 to 28 percent of the sample of franchisors, implying that a substantial number of franchisors make a conscious decision to operate no unit corporately. At the other extreme, Figure 4-1 also shows that a number of franchisors operate more than half of the units in their chain. In most cases, the chains that are at or close to 100-percent company-owned tend to be those that are just becoming involved in franchising and thus are still in their adjustment phase. We now explore this issue in more detail.

4.2.2 The Dynamics of Dual Distribution

Using a subset of our data on U.S. franchisors over the 1980 to 1997 period, Lafontaine and Shaw (2005) explored in some detail how the extent of company ownership varies not only between firms, but also over time within franchised chains. They have shown that in the first seven years in franchising, firms indeed reduce their proportion of company-owned units significantly. But they note that this effect of increased experience in franchising is simply an artifact: franchised chains almost all begin with one or two company-owned pilots, so they are 100-percent company-owned chains when they start franchising. As they open new franchised units, this proportion can only go down. It is this decrease in the early years in franchising for each chain that leads to the lower proportion of company outlets for mature or large franchised chains compared to new and small ones that we noted above. In other words, in a cross-section of franchisors of varying ages, there will be a tendency to find a systematic reduction in the proportion of company outlets as firms become established simply because newcomers to franchising are necessarily small chains of mostly corporate stores.

After the initial seven or so years of adjustment, however, the authors show that the proportion of company-owned units stabilizes at about 15 percent on average. Moreover, the proportion of company units becomes quite stable within individual franchised networks after this period: Lafontaine and Shaw show that franchisors open or close both company and franchised outlets in a way that maintains a stable mix. As the authors point out, a number of franchisors also publicly announce what they consider the optimal proportion of company-owned outlets in their chains to be, or answer inquiries about their targets in surveys.[89]

---

[89] See, for example, Ozanne and Hunt (1971) and Lafontaine and Kaufmann (1994).

Lafontaine and Shaw (2005) conclude that franchisors actively manage their portfolio of outlets with the goal of maintaining their target mix. For the majority of franchisors, the targets are neither zero nor 100 percent, confirming that dual distribution truly is an equilibrium strategy in franchising.[90] However, the targeted levels of company ownership vary tremendously across franchised chains. We illustrate this variation in Figure 4-2, where we show the proportion of company-owned outlets of each franchisor in our data that has been franchising for eight years or more. Each of the franchisors is counted only once in the figure: we take their proportion of company units in the last year they appear in the data, making sure that this last year is at least their eighth year in franchising. A total of 1,967 different franchisors are thereby included in Figure 4-2.

This figure confirms the large variation in the proportion of company units that franchisors target. The proportion of franchisors that have a strategy of operating no unit directly in the long term is about the same, at 28 percent, as in Figure 4-1. But only a few firms now are found in the fully company-owned category: most likely these are firms that never succeeded in becoming involved in franchising despite appearing in the surveys we use as our source of data. Finally, the distribution shown in Figure 4-2 is skewed to the left to a greater extent than is the distribution shown in Figure 4-1. Thus, franchisors tend to operate an even smaller proportion of their outlets directly in the long term. Specifically, more than 70 percent of the franchisors in Figure 4-2 operate less than 20 percent of their outlets directly, and less than 5 percent of them operate three quarters or more of their outlets directly.

Table 4-5 shows the sectoral variation in the stable proportion of company-owned outlets. Again this table is constructed using the proportion of company units of each franchisor in the last year in which they appear in our data if, and only if, this last year represents at least their eighth year in franchising.

Table 4-5 makes it clear that there is cross-sector variation in the extent of company ownership. Franchisors in the Hotels and Motels and in the Maintenance sectors, for example, are more likely to have no company units at all, while those in the sit-down Restaurant sector are more likely to have an above average proportion of company units. But the table mostly indicates that there is still much variation in the stable proportion of company units *within* sectors. This is consistent with Lafontaine and Shaw (2005) who found that sectoral differences explained some of the variation in the stable proportions of company units in established chains, but that variation in the value of the brand was an important factor affecting this

---

[90] See also Scott (1995) and Bradach (1998) on the value of dual distribution in franchising.

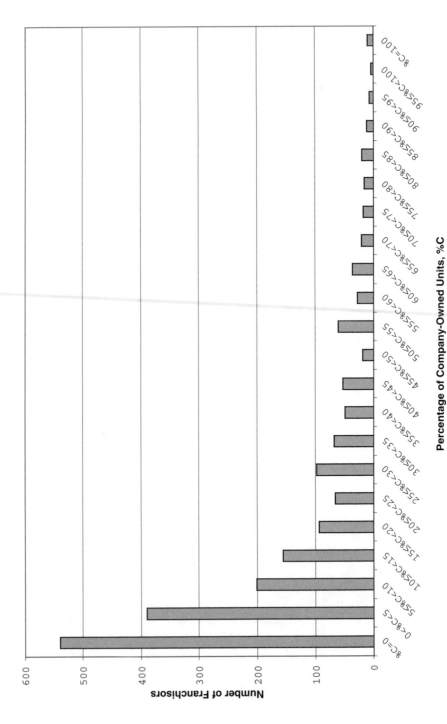

Percentage of Company-Owned Units, %C

Figure 4-2: The distribution of percent of company-owned franchisors with 8 or more years of franchising experience only (sample size = 1,967 franchisors).

Table 4-5: *The distribution of percent company-owned, per sector, for franchisors with 8 or more years of franchising experience*

Sector	$x=0$	$0 < x \leq 5$	$5 < x \leq 10$	$10 < x \leq 15$	$15 < x \leq 20$	$20 < x \leq 50$	$50 < x$	Total
Automotive	35	42	15	3	14	26	15	150
Business	83	37	24	10	14	37	27	232
Contractors	22	26	3	4	0	5	0	60
Cosmetic	10	7	7	6	1	13	4	48
Education	12	6	8	5	4	9	2	46
Fast Food	93	88	55	34	23	98	42	433
Health and Fitness	11	6	6	4	6	7	11	51
Home Furnishings	8	6	6	5	4	7	5	41
Hotels and Motels	21	6	3	0	1	9	9	49
Maintenance	40	33	12	8	3	14	7	117
Personal Services	32	32	10	4	4	22	10	114
Real Estate	28	6	0	1	1	3	2	41
Recreation	7	6	2	2	1	2	3	23
Rental	26	9	2	3	2	13	4	59
Restaurants	20	8	15	15	10	53	27	148
Retail Food	20	21	16	8	5	9	11	90
Retail Other	72	58	28	28	18	44	17	265
Total	540	397	212	140	111	371	196	1967

target both within and across sectors. They conclude that "franchisors with high trade-name value target high rates of company ownership [. . .] both in terms of controlling franchisee free-riding and in terms of franchisor incentives, one expects higher rates of company ownership in franchised systems with more valuable brands. The evidence we present supports this implication from the theories."

4.3 Contractual Equivalents

In this section, we consider various vertical restraints that may allow upstream firms (i.e., franchisors) to emulate the vertically integrated outcome (i.e., company ownership) without in fact resorting to vertical integration.[91] We begin by describing outcomes under the vertical integration benchmark and then move on to examine the effect of lump-sum franchise fees, royalties on sales, output royalties, tying, resale price controls, and, finally, output quotas on the decisions made by franchisees. In many instances we model the relationship for a single franchisor–franchisee pair, but the analysis applies similarly if the franchisor imposes these vertical controls to all the units in the franchised system.

4.3.1 Vertical Integration

If an upstream firm decided to distribute as well as produce its product, or own all its outlets, it would be fully vertically integrated. Its performance as a vertically integrated firm provides a useful benchmark against which various contractual arrangements can be measured as suitable alternatives. Accordingly, we first examine the profit potential under full vertical integration.

Because the vertically integrated firm both produces and distributes its product, we can write its profit function in a given downstream market as

$$\Pi = PQ - (MC_P + MC_R)Q,$$

where price and quantity sold in this market are P and Q, respectively, marginal (and average) cost of production is MC_P, and the marginal (and average) cost of retailing is MC_R.[92] The first-order condition for a maximum is familiar:

$$d\Pi/dQ = P + Q \, dP/dQ - MC_P - MC_R = 0,$$

---

[91] Much of this section is based on Blair and Kaserman (1983). More algebraic detail and formal proofs can be found there.

[92] Throughout, we use Π to refer to franchisor or franchised system profit, and π to refer to franchisee profit.

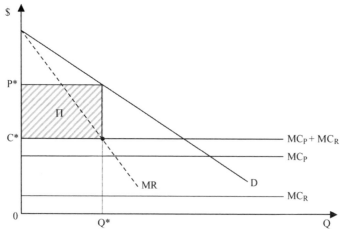

Figure 4-3: The vertically integrated outcome.

which implies that marginal revenue should equal the sum of the marginal cost of production and distribution. This solution is shown in Figure 4-3 for the simple case of linear demand and constant marginal cost.[93]

The optimal price and quantity are shown as P^* and Q^*, respectively. We can see that at Q^* marginal revenue (MR) equals the sum of the marginal costs of production and retailing. Under the assumed conditions, the vertically integrated firm is earning the maximum profits that can be squeezed out of this market:

$$\Pi^* = (P^* - C^*)Q^*,$$

where C^* represents the sum of the MC_P and MC_R. This solution provides a benchmark against which we can assess the efficacy of the various contractual equivalents considered below.

4.3.2 Lump-Sum Franchise Fees

In principle, an upstream firm could extract all the profit from a vertically separated retailer or franchisee through a franchise contract that required the payment of a lump-sum franchise fee equal to the profit inherent in

---

[93] We make the assumption that demand is linear and marginal cost is constant to simplify all the graphs in this section, but the results discussed generally hold for well-behaved demand and cost functions.

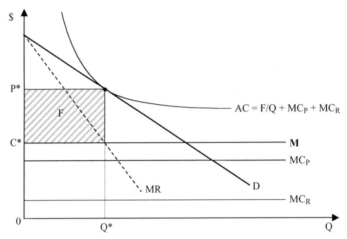

Figure 4-4: The effect of a lump-sum franchise fee.

the downstream market.[94] For the supplier-retailer case, or the traditional franchise context, this arrangement is depicted in Figure 4-4, which retains the same demand and marginal cost curves as those in Figure 4-3. The franchisor then sets the lump-sum franchise fee equal to $(P^* - C^*)Q^*$, i.e., equal to the profit that it could earn if it were vertically integrated, and sells its output to the franchisee at its marginal cost of production (MC_P). As a result, the franchisee's profit function is

$$\pi = PQ - (MC_P + MC_R)Q - F,$$

where F is the fixed franchise fee. As is clear from the first-order condition

$$d\pi/dQ = P + Q\,dP/dQ - MC_P - MC_R = 0,$$

the franchisee will sell Q^* units at a price of P^*, which is the same as the result with vertical integration. The retailer's positive cash flow from operations is then just sufficient to cover the lump-sum franchise fee of $(P^* - C^*)\,Q^*$. Since the output is the same, the quantity of inputs employed also will be the same. The franchised unit in this case will be identical to a company-owned unit in terms of both the choice of prices and quantities.

In a business-format franchise context, contrary to Figure 4-4, the franchisor need not sell any inputs to the franchisee. What is important, then, is that the franchisee must have access to all its inputs at competitive prices

[94] Lump-sum franchise fees are also discussed in Blair and Kaserman (1983) and Blair and Esquibel (1996).

regardless of who supplies them. The franchisor can then request the payment of a lump-sum fee equal to the franchisee's maximum profits, which, if all inputs are purchased at competitive prices, will again equal the vertically integrated level of profits.

From the upstream firm's perspective, a franchise contract involving a lump-sum fee thus is economically equivalent to vertical integration: price, quantity, and producer profit are all the same. The franchisee, however, earns only a normal return on its investment. The franchisor achieves this result by committing to sell its product to the franchisee at marginal cost (MC_P) in Figure 4-4. If the franchisor is not the supplier, as in a business-format franchise, the franchisor must ensure, as noted above, that the franchisee can buy all of its inputs at competitive prices.[95] Then, if there is a competitive supply of potential franchisees, competition among potential franchisees will bid up its "price," or franchise fee, to the present value of the future profit stream of the franchise. In other words, franchisees will pay in advance to obtain the franchise license and the profit stream that the franchise will generate over its lifetime. This fee will leave a competitive return for the franchisee's capital and effort, a return that is necessary over the life of the franchise contract for the franchisee to be willing to perform the distribution function. Graphically, in Figure 4-4, we can see that the lump-sum fee causes the winning franchisee's average total cost curve to be the rectangular hyperbola AC and, thus, economic profits to be zero.

In practice, however, the franchisor faces several problems in using the franchise fee as its sole means of compensation. First, most potential franchisees are wealth constrained and cannot pay the full present value of the future profit flow in advance.[96] As a result, the franchisor may not be able to extract all of the profit with this type of contract. For example, Kaufmann and Lafontaine (1994) have estimated, based on 1982 figures, that the present value of the profits of a McDonald's franchise over the duration of the contract was between $300,000 and $450,000, while the franchise fee was only $12,500 at the time. The authors argued that franchisee capital constraints explain at least part of this discrepancy. Klein (1995: 29) posits instead that "contract

---

[95] This can be difficult under some circumstances. Suppose, for example, that the franchisor has a recipe for its special sauce. If it can only license one or two firms to produce the sauce for its franchisees, it must make sure that the licensees do not overcharge the franchisees because such overcharges would reduce franchisee, and thus franchisor, profit.

[96] Of course, franchisees could borrow from third parties, and many do. This raises some selection and incentive issues as the franchisee may default on this loan. We examine incentive issues further below.

law and the good faith obligation of the *Uniform Commercial Code* imposes a duty on a franchisor in all states for good faith and fair dealing" and that this obligation makes it difficult to request large lump-sum fees such as those needed here.

Second, there is the potential for franchisor opportunism with a lump-sum franchise contract. Once the franchisor has extracted all of the future profits, it has no incentive to maintain product quality or to advertise on behalf of the franchise system. In a traditional franchise, the franchisor who has promised to supply the product at marginal cost will now have an incentive to misrepresent MC_P. In business-format franchising, franchisors that were not going to be involved in selling inputs to franchisees at all may now try to require franchisees to buy some inputs from them, inputs whose prices would be marked up above the competitive level. To the extent that the franchisor behaves opportunistically in these ways, the franchisee will not fully recover his costs. Anticipating those problems, franchisees will refuse to sign contracts involving large up-front fixed payments.[97]

Third, and finally, predictions tend to be less reliable the further into the future they go. Hence, the franchisor and franchisee may not be able to – or want to – rely on their estimates of demand and costs over the whole period of an average 15-year contract to set a single upfront franchise fee.[98] Therefore, although in theory the lump-sum franchise contract should leave the upstream firm indifferent between franchising and vertical integration, it is not likely to be employed by the franchisor. The fact of the matter is that franchisors generally do not extract the present value of all future profits in lump-sum franchise fees. As we saw in Chapter 3, upfront franchise fees are typically only a small proportion of the payments by franchisees to franchisors.

There is, however, a variant of the upfront fee that may be economically equivalent and viable. As we saw in Chapter 3, a small proportion of franchisors charge royalties that are fixed periodic amounts. For example, Fantastic Sam's charges its hair salon franchisees $225 per week in royalty and $104 per week as an advertising fee, while Chem-Dry Carpet and Upholstery Cleaning charges a fee of $198 per month.[99] Clearly, these periodic lump-sum royalty payments could be selected to extract all of the profit over the length of

---

[97] See, notably, Mathewson and Winter (1985) on this. Also, for a related form of franchisor opportunism that operates through the terms of the franchise contract, see McAfee and Schwartz (1994). We discuss franchisor opportunism on several occasions throughout this book as it relates to the subject of individual chapters.

[98] Data on contract duration are from the USDOC (1988).

[99] See Bond (2002) for these data.

the contract. That is, the present value of these weekly or monthly payments could be set equal to the optimal lump-sum franchise fee, which is equal to the present value of the profit stream. As we saw, however, this option is used infrequently in the U.S. – only 7 percent of the franchisors in our data in 2001 required franchisees to pay some such periodic lump-sum amount, and less than half of these relied solely on such payments, with no additional sales-based fee.[100] The reason for the relative infrequency of these periodic lump-sum fees is not entirely clear. After all, this option basically finesses the franchisee's wealth constraint by getting the franchisor to "finance" the lump-sum fee. However, this type of contract does not deal entirely with the franchisor moral hazard problem nor does it resolve the uncertainty issue. Thus, it is perhaps not really surprising that sales-based rather than lump-sum fees have become the norm in franchising.

4.3.3 Sales Revenue Royalties

As we saw in Chapter 3, extracting royalties as a percentage of the sales revenue of franchisees is extremely common in franchising. Under some market conditions, this also will be equivalent to vertical integration, but in others cases it will not be. First, consider the case where there is perfect competition among the franchisees. Under these conditions, price is set by market forces – it is exogenous to franchisees or, put differently, they are powerless to affect it. Taking this price as a given then, franchisees will maximize their profits by setting the output level such that their marginal cost equals the market price. The marginal cost, of course, includes the marginal cost of retailing and the wholesale price of the product or, in a business-format franchising context, the cost of all inputs and local production. By setting the wholesale price equal to the marginal cost of production, or allowing the franchisee to buy all inputs competitively, the franchisor can select a royalty rate that extracts all of the profit inherent in the franchisee's market. More specifically, the franchisor selects a royalty rate, r, such that

$$r P^* Q^* = (P^* - MC_P - MC_R) Q^*.$$

Dividing both sides by $P^* Q^*$ yields

$$r = (P^* - MC_P - MC_R)/P^*.$$

---

[100] According to Frazer (1998), some 17 percent of franchisors use lump-sum royalties in Australia. She advances some potential reasons why these are more popular in Australia than in the U.S.

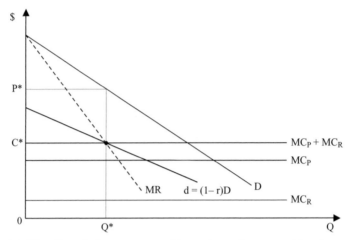

Figure 4-5: The effect of sales revenue royalties under perfect competition downstream.

Setting r at this level will allow the franchisor to extract exactly the profit that a vertically integrated firm could earn. This is illustrated in Figure 4-5. Here, the effect of the royalty rate is to rotate the net demand curve – or the demand that each franchisee sees – from D to d. This new demand curve (d) intersects the sum of the marginal costs at a quantity of Q^*. Consumers pay P^* for that output and, of course, total revenue in the market is P^* times Q^* (denoted P^*Q^*). The franchisee pays total royalties of

$$r P^* Q^* = [(P^* - MC_P - MC_R)/P^*](P^*Q^*),$$
$$= (P^* - MC_P - MC_R)Q^*$$

which is precisely equal to the profits available under vertical integration.

In contrast, if the franchisee has some measure of market power in his local market, then the franchisor will be unable to extract the fully integrated profit using only sales royalties. This can be seen by examining the resulting franchisee's profit function

$$\pi = (1 - r)PQ - (MC_P + MC_R)Q,$$

and the associated first-order condition

$$d\pi/dQ = (1 - r)(P + Q\, dP/dQ) - MC_P - MC_R = 0.$$

In other words, when the franchisee can exercise some market power, with $0 < (1 - r) < 1$, he will sell an output where marginal revenue exceeds the sum of the marginal costs, $MC_P + MC_R$. That output will be below Q^* and thus will generate less profits in the channel. Consequently, there will not exist an *ad valorem* royalty rate that could be applied to the reduced total revenue to generate the vertically integrated level of profit for the franchisor without imposing economic losses on the franchisee.

The conclusion that no percentage of sales royalty exists that can give rise to the vertically integrated level of profits for the franchisor when franchisees have some market power is somewhat troubling as we expect franchisees to have some market power in most retail and service industries if only because of location. Vertical integration and lump-sum franchise fees or ongoing fixed payments could achieve the optimal outcome for the franchisor under the same circumstances. This begs the obvious question: why do we find so many firms opting for franchising, and given that they do, why use sales-based royalties? The answer as to why they rely on franchising versus vertical integration, we argue below, has to do with franchisee incentives. As to why sales-based rather than fixed fees, this has to do at least in part with franchisor incentives and uncertainty, as mentioned above. To introduce these different incentive considerations, however, one needs to introduce demand and cost curves that depend on unobservable franchisee and franchisor effort. In the remainder of this section, we maintain our assumption of known demand and cost as this keeps our comparison of different types of vertical restraints relatively simple. We address incentive issues and how they affect the conclusions highlighted here in section 4.4.

4.3.4 Output Royalties

Another option for the franchisor is to levy a royalty on each unit of output sold by the franchisee. Specifically, the franchisor in a traditional franchise system would again commit to supplying its product at marginal cost but would charge a fixed sum each time the franchisee sells a unit. In a business-format franchise system, the franchisor would need to ensure that the franchisee is able to purchase all inputs competitively and then levy a per unit royalty on the franchisee's output.[101] As with sales revenue royalties, with perfect competition among franchisees, an output royalty will generate the maximum

---

[101] Most business-format franchisees sell a number of different products, such as the sandwiches, chips, soft-drinks, juices, and the like sold at Subway sandwich shops. This makes it difficult to define units and count units sold. One would have to set a per unit of output royalty for each product sold and keep track of the quantities sold separately for each. Alternatively, if the franchisor could set the price at which outputs are sold, then franchisee output could be measured in dollars of sales. In that case, an output royalty would be exactly the same as a sales royalty.

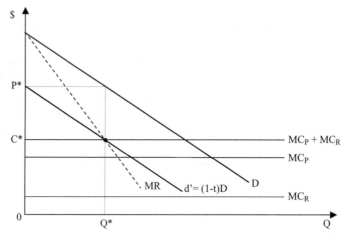

Figure 4-6: The effect of output royalties under perfect competition downstream.

profits for the franchisor. If the franchisees have some degree of local market power, however, the maximum profits cannot be extracted in this fashion.

When there is competition among the franchisees, the franchisor can set the per unit of output royalty, t, as follows:

$$t = P^* - MC_P - MC_R$$

where MC_P corresponds to the wholesale price in a traditional franchise, or the sum of all input prices for the business-format franchisee, and MC_R represents the constant retailing cost for a traditional franchisee or the cost of local production for the business-format franchisee. This output-based royalty gives rise to a net demand curve, d', that is parallel to the original demand, D, as shown in Figure 4-6. If the franchisor selects the correct t, the franchisees will produce Q^* and consumers will pay P^* per unit. The royalty revenue to the franchisor will be

$$tQ^* = (P^* - MC_P - MC_R)Q^*,$$

which is precisely equal to the profits that the franchisor could earn if it were vertically integrated.

If the franchisees have a measure of local market power, as we expect they would given differentiation (including spatial differentiation) in retail and service markets, the franchisor will not be able to extract the full vertically integrated level of profit with this franchise contract. As with the sales revenue royalties, the output royalty will lead the franchisee to restrict its output below Q^* and thereby reduce the royalty payments below the level that vertical integration would provide. This again follows immediately from the franchisee's profit function,

$$\pi = PQ - (MC_P + MC_R)Q - tQ,$$

and the franchisees' maximum profit condition,

$$d\pi/dQ = P + Q\,dP/dQ - MC_P - MC_R - t = 0.$$

Since $t > 0$, this condition shows that the franchisee will restrict its output below the quantity at which marginal revenue equals marginal cost of production and distribution (the sum of MC_P and MC_R). Thus, we reach the conclusion that no output royalty can generate the vertically integrated level of profits for the franchisor without imposing economic losses on the franchisees.

4.3.5 Input Purchase Requirements and Tying

Franchisors can also generate revenues by selling inputs to their franchisees. In fact, this is the standard way in which most manufacturers deal with their distributors, and as noted in Chapter 1, the way in which traditional franchisors – car manufacturers, oil companies, and soft-drink producers – all generate their stream of revenues. In business-format franchising, many franchisors do not have the option of selling a finished product to their franchisee as production usually takes place downstream. For example, meals are produced at the restaurant, not at the franchisor's head office. But business-format franchisors can sell various inputs, such as paper products, cooking equipment, pizza dough, hamburger patties, and so on. If such inputs are sold at a markup, the franchisor successfully extracts at least some downstream profit with this contractual requirement. Under certain circumstances, input purchase requirements are indeed economically equivalent to vertical integration. As with sales revenue and output royalties, they yield maximum profits for the franchisor if franchisees operate in a perfectly competitive environment, but not when the franchisees have local market power.

The effect of forcing franchisees in a perfectly competitive environment to purchase goods from the franchisor at a markup is illustrated in Figure 4-7, where the franchisor charges a wholesale price of

$$P_w = P^* - MC_R$$

for the good(s) it sells. Assuming for simplicity that no other physical inputs are needed downstream, franchisees in a perfectly competitive market then will sell Q^* since the competitive supply, $P_w + MC_R$, equals demand at Q^*.

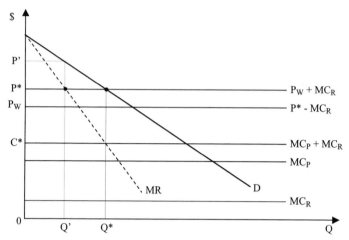

Figure 4-7: The effect of input purchase requirements under perfect competition downstream.

This, in turn, means that Q^* units of the input are sold at the wholesale price of $P^* - MC_R$ so that the franchisor's profit in this market is

$$\Pi = (P^* - MC_R)Q^* - MC_P Q^*,$$

which is precisely the profit that vertical integration yields.

This contract, however, will not generate the vertically integrated level of profits for the franchisor if franchisees have market power. In that case, the franchisee will see its marginal cost as $P_w + MC_R$. It will maximize its own profits by selling that output where $P_w + MC_R$ equals its marginal revenue. As inspection of Figure 4-7 reveals, this output Q' will be smaller than Q^* and, therefore, input purchase requirements, despite the markup, will fail to generate maximum profits for the franchisor.

Moreover, it is only if the franchisee needs a unit of the franchisor's input(s) for each unit of output that it sells, as in gasoline or car retailing, that requiring the franchisee to purchase inputs from the franchisor can be a sufficient condition to yield the vertically integrated level of profits for the franchisor under franchisee competition.[102] If instead franchisees must combine the inputs sold by the franchisor with some other inputs, and these other inputs

---

[102] See Vernon and Graham (1971) and Warren-Boulton (1974) for more on this. The equivalence between input purchase requirements and vertical integration in this case largely explains the lack of additional fees besides input markups in traditional franchising. Note that franchisee market power under these conditions will likely lead franchisors to impose some maximum price or minimum quantity requirement along

can be substituted for the ones provided by the franchisor, then input purchase requirements on the one input provided by the franchisor will not suffice even under perfect competition downstream.

Finally, input purchase requirements raise special legal concerns, especially for business-format franchisors. In legal terms, a tying arrangement is defined as a conditional sale in which product "A" is sold on the condition that the buyer also buys a second product "B" from the supplier of "A." In business-format franchising, the franchisor sells a license to do business as part of the franchise system. Thus, if the franchisor also sells products to a franchisee as a condition of obtaining the license, and these products are distinct from the license, then the franchisor is using a tying arrangement. If the goods sold are not really distinct from the license, as occurs, for example, for trademarked gasoline at a gasoline station or for particular brands of cars sold at authorized dealerships, there is no tying. In that sense, input purchase requirements do not raise the same degree of legal concerns in traditional franchising. We return to these issues in detail in Chapter 6, where we examine the conflicts between franchisors and franchisees that are created by input purchase requirements and tying.

4.3.6 Resale Price Controls

In circumstances where the franchisee has market power, the franchisor's concern is that the franchisee's prices may be set above the optimal level from the franchisor's perspective. We examine this problem in more detail in Chapter 7. Here, however, we show briefly how maximum resale price controls can generate the same outcome as vertical integration.[103]

Suppose that the franchisor sets its wholesale price as follows:

$$P_w = P^* - MC_R$$

Left to its own devices, the franchisee who has market power would equate its marginal cost to its marginal revenue:

$$MR = P_w + MC_R$$

with the exclusive purchasing requirement. On this, see, e.g., Shepard (1993) and our discussion of resale price maintenance in Chapter 7.

[103] Note that setting a minimum resale price, as opposed to setting a maximum price, is still *per se* illegal under U.S. antitrust laws. We focus on maximum resale price controls here as pricing disputes in franchising usually involve such controls. Maximum resale price controls are not illegal *per se*.

and produce an output Q' below Q^* (see Figure 4-7). From the franchisor's perspective, this is an unfortunate result because its profit falls below the maximum that vertical integration would yield. But all is not lost. Maximum resale price constraints can be employed to aid in this regard. In Figure 4-7, we can see that the franchisor could set its wholesale price as before equal to $P^* - MC_R$ and then also impose a maximum resale price of $P^* = P_w + MC_R$. This again will lead to an output of Q^* and profits of

$$\Pi = (P^* - MC_P - MC_R)Q^*$$

for the franchisor. At the same time, the franchisee earns a competitive return – zero *economic* profit – for performing the retail distribution function, as he would under perfect competition.

4.3.7 Output (or Sales) Quotas

The last option that we consider briefly here is the establishment, by the franchisor, of performance standards such as sales quotas.[104] Returning to Figure 4-7, one can see that the franchisor can obtain the desired result by establishing a sales quota of Q^* units. Given the demand function, the only way that the franchisee can satisfy the performance standard is by charging a resale price of P^*. The franchisor would still set the wholesale price at $P_w = P^* - MC_R$ and would earn precisely the same profit as under vertical integration. Again, the franchisee earns a competitive return on his or her investment.

Provided that the franchisor knows the demand in the franchisee's market, there is no problem in selecting the profit maximizing output quota. The practical difficulty is in enforcing that output quota. If the franchisee fails to meet the quota, the franchisor must impose a penalty of some sort. Termination is the sanction that comes to mind, but that may be too much of a penalty. Also, as we shall see in Chapter 10, there are legal constraints on a franchisor's freedom to terminate its franchisees. These legal constraints reduce the attractiveness of termination as a sanction and, by raising the costs associated with franchising, reduce the attractiveness of franchising as a distribution system from the perspective of franchisors.[105]

A variant of the performance standard is quantity forcing. This may take the form of "overfilling" orders from the franchisee. For example, an automobile manufacturer may decide how many of each car model will be supplied to

---

[104] See, e.g., Shepard (1993) for a discussion of the use of sales quotas in gasoline retailing.
[105] For an interesting analysis of the economic effect of imposing legal limits on termination, see Brickley, Dark, and Weisbach (1991b).

a dealer. Since the dealer must eventually pay for the automobiles that are supplied, these automobiles must be sold. Assuming that the manufacturer knows the local demand for its automobiles, it can select the quantity that it finds optimal. In Figure 4-7, the manufacturer would select quantity Q^* and ship it to the dealer. Again, there is only one way that the dealer can sell Q^* automobiles and that is to set price at P^*.

4.4 Incentive Issues and Agency Theory

In section 4.3, we have shown that various vertical restraints are economically equivalent to one another. In principle, by themselves or in combination, they are also economically equivalent to full vertical integration, that is, they generate the same profit for the franchisor. In practice, however, we showed in section 4.2 that most franchised chains are hybrids: partially vertically integrated and partially franchised. Moreover, initial franchise fees and sales-based royalties (and/or advertising rates) are by far the most frequently used contract terms in franchising, and sales-based fees represent the bulk of payments by franchisees to franchisors. We have hinted earlier at some reasons why some forms of vertical restraints – such as input purchase requirements and resale price maintenance – are not used as much as sales-based fees in franchise contracts. Throughout our discussion of vertical restraints, however, we have assumed that the level of demand and distribution costs are known by the franchisor and are independent of any effort by the franchisee or the franchisor. In this section, we relax this assumption in order to generate theoretical explanations for the levels of royalty rates and initial franchise fees chosen by franchisors.[106] We then return to dual distribution in franchising and explain how theories about optimal royalty rates can be used to understand some of the variation in the extent of company ownership across firms.

4.4.1 Royalty Rate and Franchise Fee Decisions

Agency theory has been the theoretical lens most frequently applied to the question of how firms select the terms of their franchise contract. The basic agency model views the primary purpose of contract design as a mechanism to provide appropriate insurance and incentives to risk-averse franchisees whose effort level is not directly observable by the franchisor. In this section, we first describe this basic model when the relationship between effort and sales is

---

[106] Much of this section is based on parts of Lafontaine and Slade (2001) and Lafontaine and Raynaud (2002).

deterministic. We then explain how non-observable effort by the franchisee changes the optimal affine contract. Finally, we add a role for franchisor effort in the basic model and consider how this affects the best sales-based royalty rate and franchise fee combination.

Suppose that a franchisee/manager must put in effort to generate outlet sales. Specifically, assume that downstream sales S are given by

$$S = PQ = \alpha e$$

where e is the manager's effort and α measures the importance of this effort in the sales generation process. For simplicity, we do not specify whether the franchisee's effort affects the price P at which the end product is sold to customers or Q, the number of units sold. Instead, we simply write that PQ, or sales, are affected by e, and assume specifically that sales are increasing in this effort level (i.e., $dS/de > 0$). Suppose also that the manager's effort is easily observed and verifiable by third parties such as the court system. The franchisor then can simply stipulate the desired level of effort to be exerted by the manager and write a contract contingent on whether or not this effort level is provided. On the cost side, assume simply that the cost of effort for the manager is $C(e) = e^2/2$, and that there are no other costs in running this business. Finally, suppose that the manager is risk-neutral. Under these circumstances, the risk-neutral franchisor would dictate the level of manager effort, or e, directly but would have to compensate the manager for the cost of exerting this effort. Hence, the franchisor would choose e to maximize:

$$\max_e[\alpha e - e^2/2]$$

The first-order condition for a maximum yields $e^* = \alpha$. In other words, the best thing for the franchisor to do is to request that the manager put forth a level of effort equal to α in the downstream production process. This solution generates the largest total surplus as well: it is the first-best outcome. Note that the franchisor here would not need to use a franchise contract – she could simply pay a wage to the manager to compensate him for the effort expended, that is, pay the manager $\alpha^2/2$. Alternatively, the franchisor could use any of the vertical restraints above that yield the vertically integrated outcome: demand and costs are observable under our current set of assumptions so the discussion of vertical restraints from the previous section applies here as well.

Now assume instead that the franchisee's effort is unobservable. Specifically, we write

$$S = \alpha e + \varepsilon,$$

where ε is a random variable with mean 0 and variance σ^2 that prevents the franchisor from inferring e from observed S. Then the optimal solution is to sell the outlet outright to the franchisee for a lump-sum franchise fee. This sale at a fixed price would make the manager a full residual claimant, thereby giving him incentives to put forth the optimal level of effort.[107] We can see this from the maximization problem of the manager/franchisee: using F to denote the lump-sum franchise fee that the franchisor charges, the risk-neutral manager/franchisee will want to maximize his expected profits, $E(\pi)$, given by

$$E(\pi) = \alpha e - e^2/2 - F.$$

The first-order condition for this maximization problem gives $e^* = \alpha$, which corresponds to the first-best level of effort and, thus, to the level of effort that the franchisor would have chosen if she had control over it. In that sense, selling the outlet at a fixed price to the franchisee completely resolves the franchisee's incentive issues. The franchisor can extract all the profits from the outlet operations by appropriately setting the price, F, equal to $\alpha^2/2$.[108] Note, however, that when franchisee effort is not observable, sales or output-based royalty schemes are not optimal: they prevent the realization of the first-best outcome. In particular, the risk-neutral franchisee who must pay a portion r of his revenues to the franchisor (where $0 < r < 1$ represents the sum of all revenue-based fees such as royalty rates and advertising fees) maximizes expected profits

$$E(\pi) = (1 - r)\alpha e - e^2/2 - F,$$

by setting effort $e' = (1 - r)\alpha$. In other words, the effort level e' chosen by the franchisee subject to royalty payments is strictly lower than the effort level e^* that the franchisee chooses under a pure lump-sum franchise fee contract. Hence, one would not expect revenue sharing to be used in this setting.

The standard agency model introduces one more complication to yield a contract that involves profit or revenue sharing. Specifically, assume now that the franchisee is risk-averse instead of risk-neutral. In other words, he values income levels that he knows he will obtain with certainty above the same income level obtained in expectation only. One simple way to represent

---

[107] See, for example, Rubin (1978) and Mathewson and Winter (1985) for more on this.

[108] To simplify the algebra, we ignore issues of contract duration and discounting. This in no way affects the generality of the result that a fixed price contract resolves all incentive issues when franchisees are risk-neutral. Note that F could be set at any level not exceeding $\alpha^2/2$. But any F below $\alpha^2/2$ means that the franchisor does not make as much as she could, and the franchisee earns above normal returns.

such preferences is to specify that the franchisee has a utility of income function given by $u(y) = -\exp(-\rho y)$, where y represents income and ρ is the franchisee's coefficient of absolute risk aversion. It is well-known that with this type of utility function, the agent behaves as if he were maximizing his certainty-equivalent income, CE, which is $E(y) - (\rho/2)\text{Var}(y)$, where E stands for the expectation operator, and Var refers to the variance.[109]

We saw in Chapter 3 that most franchisors use sales-based, linear compensation rules with franchisees.[110] Why franchisors use sales rather than profit-based fees is usually attributed to the fact that profits are too easy for franchisees to manipulate.[111] As for why franchisors rely on linear sharing rules, authors typically argue that the costs of implementing more complex contracts are too high. Beyond that, the models that address this question rapidly become quite technical and are beyond the scope of this book.[112]

Whatever the reasons for the reliance on simple franchise fee plus sales-based royalty contracts, the franchisee's profit under such a contract is $\pi = (1 - r)S - F - C(e)$, where F is the initial franchise fee and r is the royalty rate. The franchisee's certainty-equivalent, income, CE, then is

$$CE = E(y) - (\rho/2)\text{Var}(y)$$
$$= (1 - r)\alpha e - F - e^2/2 - (\rho/2)(1 - r)^2\sigma^2,$$

where $E(y)$ is his expected income, or outlet profit, and σ^2 is the variance of ε. Taking the first derivative of CE with respect to e and setting that equal to zero, the solution to the franchisee's maximization problem is to choose an effort level $e^\dagger = (1 - r)\alpha$. This level of effort is clearly lower than the first-best level, α, but given franchisee risk aversion and unobservable effort this is the best the franchisor can achieve.[113]

The franchisor's problem then is to choose r to maximize total surplus taking for granted that the franchisee will provide an effort level $e^\dagger = (1 - r)\alpha$,

[109] See Milgrom and Roberts (1992) at 217 for this proposition.

[110] In reality, the compensation rules are affine, that is the franchise fee is not zero. The literature, however, tends to refer to these as linear by opposition to non-linear. We follow that convention from here on.

[111] See, for example, Maness (1996). Rubin (1978) proposes instead that franchisors are paid a portion of outlet sales because these are what their effort affect. We return to Rubin's point below.

[112] See Holmstrom and Milgrom (1987), who show that such contracts are optimal in intertemporal settings, and Romano (1994) and Bhattacharyya and Lafontaine (1995), who show that such contracts are optimal under double-sided moral hazard with risk neutral parties.

[113] Specifically, under these assumptions, there is no contract that will allow the franchisor to achieve the first-best, even if we do not restrict ourselves to affine contracts.

and then set F to extract that surplus. Substituting $e^\dagger$ in the equation for expected total surplus (given by $\alpha e - e^2/2 - (\rho/2)(1 - r)^2\sigma^2$), we have

$$\max_r[(1 - r)\alpha^2 - (1 - r)^2\alpha^2/2 - (\rho/2)(1 - r)^2\sigma^2].$$

The first-order condition for the franchisor's problem implies that $r^\dagger = [\rho\sigma^2/(\alpha^2 + \rho\sigma^2)] > 0$. In other words, the best linear contract from the franchisor's perspective now involves some revenue sharing. This sharing arises as a way to balance the need to motivate franchisee effort (which makes the optimal r lean toward 0) while providing insurance to the franchisees given that they are risk-averse (which makes the optimal r lean toward 1).[114]

Finally, the standard agency model above has been amended to allow franchisor effort to also play a role in franchise contracting. Thus, instead of assuming that sharing occurs as a way to provide insurance along with incentives to risk-averse franchisees, a number of authors have focused on sales royalties as a franchisor incentive device under double-sided moral hazard.[115] Specifically, in addition to considering franchisee effort, models based on two-sided moral hazard formally recognize that the effort that the franchisor puts into maintaining the value of its trademark, updating the product offerings, selecting franchisees, and so on, also affects outlet sales. When both parties must provide effort in these ways, and neither effort level is observable, then, even if both parties are risk-neutral, the optimal contract will involve revenue sharing. To see this, assume now that outlet sales are given by

$$S = \alpha e_e + \beta e_r + \varepsilon,$$

where e_e stands for franchisee effort, and e_r for franchisor effort. The presence of a random term, ε, in the sales function implies that neither party can infer the effort level of the other from observing sales, S, and their own effort. Suppose further that the franchisee's and franchisor's cost of effort are given

---

[114] We do not model the choice of F explicitly but instead leave it intentionally vague given that this fee affects neither the choice of effort nor total surplus.

[115] See notably Rubin (1978), Lal (1990), Romano (1994), and Bhattacharyya and Lafontaine (1995). Carmichael (1983) has shown that with two agents or more, and moral hazard on the principal's side as well as the agents' side, the first-best can be achieved with a contract based on relative output. See also Gupta and Romano (1998) for more on relative performance contracts. In spite of their theoretical benefits, we do not observe explicit relative performance contracts in franchising. One could speculate that this is because the markets are too distinct to make performance comparisons meaningful, or perhaps that such contracts would lead to excessive intrabrand competition. Bradach (1998), Chapter 5, examines the less formalized, but still important, use of relative performance evaluation in practice.

by $C(e_e) = e_e^2/2$ and $C(e_r) = e_r^2/2$, respectively. The franchisee maximizing his expected profits given r will choose $e_r^* = (1 - r)\alpha$. The franchisor who gets a fraction r of outlet sales will set $e_r^* = r\beta$. Substituting these two effort levels into the franchisor's maximization problem yields

$$\max_r[(1 - r)\alpha^2 + r\beta^2 - (1 - r)^2\alpha^2/2 - r^2\beta^2/2].$$

The first-order condition for this maximization problem gives $r^* = \alpha^2/(\alpha^2 + \beta^2) > 0$, which once again implies revenue sharing even though we have assumed away franchisee risk aversion (i.e. $\rho = 0$). If we assumed instead that $\rho > 0$, the result would imply that both franchisee risk aversion and franchisor effort lead r away from 1.

The standard incentive-cum-insurance agency model and the double-sided moral hazard model just described generate clear predictions concerning factors that should influence the financial terms of the franchise contract or, more specifically, the share parameter (royalty rate). In the basic model, these are the level of risk, the degree of franchisee risk aversion, and the importance of the franchisee's effort. Double-sided moral hazard models add the importance of franchisor effort to this list. The empirical literature has found support generally for the notion that the need to provide incentives to franchisees and to franchisors play a role in the setting of the actual rates.[116] The evidence relative to the level of risk, however, does not conform to the predictions from these models.[117]

The basic agency model has been challenged also by the surprisingly high degree of franchise contract term uniformity and stability that has been observed empirically. While the framework predicts a different optimal

---

[116] See Lafontaine and Slade (1997, 2001) for reviews of the empirical literature. Though these authors mention the few studies that have examined the determinant of sales-based fees, they review the bulk of the literature that focuses instead on the mix of company-owned and franchised outlets. We discuss the relationship between the contract mix and contract terms in the next section.

[117] See Lafontaine and Bhattacharyya (1995) for a review of the empirical evidence establishing a positive rather than negative relationship between risk and franchising. This positive relationship runs counter to the idea that franchisees need to be better insured by franchisors when they face greater risk. The authors explain this result in a double-sided moral hazard setting where the variance of outcomes, i.e., measured risk, is endogenously greater for franchisees because they make better use of their own private information about the market. See also Prendergast (2002) for more on this. Ackerberg and Botticini (2002) provide an alternative explanation for this same empirical fact using the notion of endogenous matching. They argue that less risk-averse individuals will choose riskier contracts, making it difficult for the econometrician to correctly assess the relationship between risk and franchising. Finally, see Mazzeo (2004) on a related empirical analysis of motel owners' decisions to join chains or operate independently.

contract for each franchisor-franchisee pair due to different preferences of franchisees and to differences in the characteristics of individual outlets and their markets, in reality franchisors tend to offer a single franchise contract to all franchisees applying for a franchise at a given point in time (e.g., Lafontaine 1992a, 1992b). Furthermore, the frequency of changes in the financial terms of this single franchise contract is quite low (Lafontaine and Shaw 1999).

Authors seeking to explain the observed incidence of franchise contract uniformity have proposed a number of extensions to the basic agency framework. One set of arguments focuses on the *costs* of contract customization, including the direct costs associated with tailoring and enforcing a large number of contracts (e.g., Holmström and Milgrom 1987; Lafontaine 1992b) or with regulatory and disclosure constraints on contracting practices (Lafontaine 1992b). Cost-based explanations for the lack of contract customization also include arguments about the indirect costs of customization, such as the potential for franchisor opportunism once contracts are signed. From this perspective, a commitment to contract uniformity may reassure franchisees that the financial terms of the contract in a given chain will not be modified for new franchisees in a way that would be detrimental to existing franchisees (McAfee and Schwartz, 1994).[118] A second set of extensions to the basic agency framework focuses on a different rationale for contract uniformity, namely that the *benefits* of contract customization are quite low under double-sided moral hazard (Bhattacharyya and Lafontaine 1995).[119]

This tendency for contract uniformity and stability also has led researchers to examine whether adjustments to the ownership structure of the franchise chain may substitute for contract customization. We now turn briefly to an examination of how the agency-theoretic arguments above, or extensions of these, can help shed light on franchisors' decisions concerning contract mixing given the reality that franchise contracts terms tend to be uniform within any given franchise network and quite stable over time.

4.4.2 Dual Distribution Decisions

Starting from the assumption that contract terms are uniform within franchised chains, under certain conditions those factors that would ordinarily influence the terms of the contract instead affect the likelihood that particular

---

[118] This is an application of the Coase conjecture for durable goods; see Coase (1972).

[119] More specifically, Bhattacharyya and Lafontaine (1995) show that when the production function is Cobb-Douglas and the cost-of-effort function is exponential, the optimal-share parameter is independent of the scale of operation and, as a result, of the level of demand and the degree of competition in the market. The share parameter is also independent of both parties' cost-of-effort parameters.

outlets will be franchised or company operated. In particular, we are interested in whether the same factors that would lead to granting higher-powered
incentives to franchisees if contracts were allowed to vary within a chain instead lead to a higher fraction of franchised outlets in the uniform-contract
case. We now describe a setting in which this is the case.[120]

Suppose that each outlet or unit is associated with some outlet characteristic x that affects its profitability, and let the expected profitability of that
unit depend on the power of the agent's incentives (inversely related to the
royalty rate) as well as on this characteristic. One can express this relationship as $E[\pi(r, x)]$ and assume that as x increases, the marginal profitability
of higher-powered incentives (lower r) also increases. For example, x might
be the distance between the outlet and the closest monitoring headquarters
or a parameter indicating the need for local customization of the business. If
contracts were outlet specific, the franchisor's problem would be to choose a
series of royalty rates r_i^*, where $i = 1 \ldots n$ (and n is the number of outlets in
the chain), to maximize expected profit in each outlet, $E[\pi_i(r_i, x_i)]$, subject
to the constraint that the franchisee in each outlet will choose its effort level
to maximize its own profit given r_i. The assumption that the marginal profitability of higher-powered incentives increases as x increases guarantees that
the solution to this problem, r_i^*, is decreasing in x_i.

Now suppose that fine tuning the contracts is sufficiently expensive for the
franchisor to choose to offer only two contracts: a franchise contract with
$0 < r < 1$, where r is the same for all franchisees, and a vertical integration
contract that amounts to a contract with $r = 1$ and a negative F. If the franchisor has n units, one can order those units such that $x_1 \leq x_2 \leq x_3 \ldots \leq x_n$.
Then the franchisor's problem involves choosing r^* and an index i^* such that
all outlets with i's below i^* – in other words low x's – will be company-owned
and all others will be franchised. In this situation, an exogenous increase in
x at some units would lead the franchisor to adopt both higher-powered
franchisee incentives (lower r^*) for its set of franchised units and a greater
proportion of franchised units (lower i^*) in the chain.

In empirical tests, authors have found support for the idea that franchisors at least partly address issues of outlet or market heterogeneity through
their choice of contract *type*, that is, company-ownership versus franchising,
instead of tailoring the *terms* of their franchise contract. For example, the
evidence suggests that smaller, rural units that are farther away from headquarters are more likely than others to be franchised (see Lafontaine and

---

[120] This section borrows heavily from Section 3 of Lafontaine and Slade (2001).

Slade (1997, 2001) and the references therein). Thus, local market and unit characteristics clearly affect the ownership decision.

The evidence, however, also strongly suggests that the proportion of a company's units that are franchised versus company owned does not arise simply as a passive outcome resulting from a set of individual ownership decisions based on the characteristics of each of the outlets in a chain, as the agency models might imply. Using data on the proportion of company owned units in almost 5,000 franchised chains in the U.S. over the 1980 to 1997 period, Lafontaine and Shaw (2005) show that established firms – those with eight or more years of franchising experience – tend to hold their proportion of company units stable over time. Franchisors do this by adding both types of units when growing and closing both types when the chain decreases in size. The authors also cite a number of instances when franchisors have stipulated what they see as the optimal mix of franchised and company units in their chain.[121] Lafontaine and Shaw conclude that this mix is a decision variable that firms actively work toward, and that this decision variable then informs or constrains the individual outlet-level decisions on ownership.

Lafontaine and Shaw (2005) also show that the target mix varies substantially across franchised chains. They find that variation in brand-name value across chains is an important determinant of the targeted mix: franchisors with high brand-name value, as measured by advertising fees or major media expenditures per outlet, target high rates of company ownership. The authors argue that targeting high rates of company ownership is desirable in chains with more valuable brands because individual franchisees have incentives to free ride on brand-name value or to simply adopt policies that make them better off at the expense of the brand. Consequently, high-value franchisors need to exert more direct managerial control over outlets in their chain. In addition, according to double-sided moral hazard arguments, high company ownership rates give franchisors better incentives to maintain the value of their brand.[122]

---

[121] Lafontaine and Kaufmann (1994) further show that most franchisors will answer questions about their optimal mix, and the majority of them operate what they perceive to be the optimal mix.

[122] For further discussions of these arguments and others on the role of dual distribution in franchising, see notably Oxenfeldt and Kelly (1969), Caves and Murphy (1976), Brickley and Dark (1987), Dant, Kaufmann and Paswan (1992), Gallini and Lutz (1992), Lafontaine (1992a), Kaufmann and Lafontaine (1994), Scott (1995), and Bradach (1997, 1998).

4.5 Conclusion

In this chapter, we have reviewed the extent to which franchisors vertically integrate some outlets versus franchising others. We examined also a number of instruments that franchisors could use in their contracts to obtain, at least in theory, as much profit from their franchisees as with direct operations. In this discussion, we have abstracted from the underlying reason why franchisors choose to franchise rather than operate all their units directly: in particular, we assumed that outlet-level demand and costs were known by all and unaffected by the outlet manager's effort. When demand and costs are affected by local effort – and potentially by franchisor effort as well – we showed that revenue sharing arises as a way to motivate franchisees and franchisors. This is the central theme of the agency-theoretic arguments that we reviewed. These arguments suggest that franchisors will choose to give franchisees higher-powered incentives (i.e., lower royalty rates or rely on franchising more) the more important the franchisee's effort, an implication that has been supported in the empirical literature. We also discussed specifically how the same agency arguments can shed light on decisions about contract terms and decisions to both own and franchise outlets in a chain, but noted that the extent of contract mixing seems to reflect a stable policy decision in franchised chains. We described how franchisors with more valuable brands tend to own and control directly a larger proportion of their units, suggesting that such franchisors have a greater need for control given that brand-name value can be significantly eroded by franchisees' profit-maximizing behavior.

Finally, although our account of franchisor practices again focused on U.S. franchising, it is important to note that the few studies conducted elsewhere suggest that dual distribution also is the norm for non-U.S. franchisors. For example, Azevedo and Dos Santos Silva (2001), Pénard, Raynaud and Saussier (2003), and Windsperger (2002), who study the Brazilian, French, and Austrian franchise sectors respectively, all find that dual distribution is the norm in these countries as well. Moreover, Azevedo and Dos Santos Silva (2001), and Pénard, Raynaud and Saussier (2003) show that the contract mix is quite stable within established franchised chains in Brazil and in France, respectively, and that it also relates positively to measures of brand-name value in these countries.

5

Quality Control

5.1 Introduction

The strength of franchise systems typically does not lie in the *absolute* quality of the products offered. Instead, it resides largely in the capacity of the franchised chain to offer a *uniform* product at a reasonable price. Customers know what to expect when they patronize an outlet in a franchised chain, and it is important for the chains to successfully meet these expectations time after time. The importance of uniformity to mobile customers is clear. Speaking about airport restaurants, Nancy Kruse, of the restaurant consulting firm Technomic, notes: "Travelers love to see fast-food chains at airports. Even if they're 2000 miles from home, they can go into an airport McDonald's, order a Big Mac, and know exactly what they're getting and more or less what it's going to cost" (quoted in *Frequent Flyer*, March 1991). Similarly, the founder of Ember's America, a new franchise conversion concept for locally owned family restaurants, points out: "If Big Macs were different from McDonald's to McDonald's, people wouldn't stop at McDonald's very often."[123] In other words, it is the consistency of the system's operation, service, and product quality that attracts customers and induces loyalty: customers become loyal if the experiences they enjoy at diverse units of these chains routinely meet their expectations.[124]

Franchisors are, of course, well-aware of the importance of consistency to their customers. Bradach (1998) interviewed several managers and franchisees in five major fast-food franchised chains to gain insight into how these firms were organized and why. In characterizing the shared identity of outlets in these chains and the importance of product uniformity, Bradach quotes in

---

[123] Quoted in Johnson (1998).
[124] See, e.g., Kaufmann and Eroglu (1998) for more on this.

particular Gregg Reynolds, then vice-president of public affairs at KFC: "KFC chicken should taste the same and be served with the same friendly service regardless of whether it is purchased in Tiannamen Square in Beijing, China, or in Louisville, Kentucky" (Bradach 1998: 16–17). Franchisees also are well-aware of the importance of meeting customers' expectations at every visit. Franchisees will complain to the franchisor about under-performing outlets and request that the franchisor intervene because they know how a bad experience by a customer in one location can have an adverse impact throughout the entire franchise system and ultimately on them.[125] In other words, quality and service variation have external effects that damage other franchisees as well as the franchisor, and this creates a tension between the franchisor and individual franchisees. The problem is aptly described by Caves and Murphy (1976: 577):

> A franchisee who reduces the quality of the good or service he offers for a given price might increase his own profits, yet by disappointing buyers' expectations he could reduce by a greater amount the net returns to the common intangible goodwill asset – maintained by the franchisor and used jointly by his other franchisees.

Similarly, Klein (1980: 358) observes that

> there is an incentive for an individual opportunistic franchisee to cheat the franchisor by supplying a lower quality of product than contracted for. Because the franchisee uses a common trademark, this behavior depreciates the reputation and hence the future profit stream of the franchisor.

These statements highlight the fact that the individual franchisee's incentives are not aligned with those of its franchisor: the profit-maximizing behavior of an individual franchisee can have adverse external effects on the franchisor and other franchisees as well.[126] Thus, a donut shop owner might reduce costs, and so enhance profits, by selling rather than throwing away

---

[125] Tannenbaum and Mehta (1997) mention the case of Fernando Galaviz, an Hispanic who said he refused to book any travel with one national hotel chain because he and some colleagues "experienced specific racist attitudes" at one of the chain's hotels. Although Mr. Galaviz said he realized that he might be penalizing non–racist franchisees in the process, he felt that he was justified in doing this as "They're all part of the same family."

[126] For further analysis, see Dnes and Garoupa (2005). Note that the racist behavior mentioned in the previous footnote may be better explained by franchisee utility maximization rather than profit maximization, that is, the franchisee might be focused on what makes him happy rather than his profit. However, utility maximizing behavior is necessarily constrained in highly competitive markets where other firms focus on profits.

donuts that are no longer completely fresh. Such a strategy, in turn, is more likely to be profitable if most of his customers are transient: knowledgeable local customers would be unlikely to continue to patronize a place with low quality. At the same time, the more transient consumers are, the more this misbehavior will hurt the franchisor and other franchisees as it depreciates the value of the franchisor's trademark.

Franchisees can hurt the franchise system not only by using lower cost products or not observing performance requirements, but also by catering too much to the needs of their local market or by refusing to implement system-wide innovations. While local responsiveness can have positive effects on a unit's profits and be a source of innovative ideas for the system as a whole, local changes and adaptation affect the uniformity of the chain and can have a detrimental effect on the value of the brand. For example, if McDonald's franchisees offer "Cajun burgers" in New Orleans, "teriyaki burgers" in Honolulu, and "Tex-Mex burgers" in San Antonio, consumers will not know what to expect at a McDonald's in San Francisco or St. Louis. Given customer risk aversion, such uncertainty might result in lower system-wide sales.

Uniformity also brings with it several operational advantages.[127] First, uniform operations across outlets increase the opportunities for economies of scale in procurement and marketing. Second, uniform operations make it easier and less costly to develop and introduce new processes and products. If franchisees individualize their outlets, then procedures developed by the head office to increase productive efficiency or for the introduction of new products and production processes will not necessarily be adaptable in each franchised outlet. Finally, uniformity facilitates comparisons across outlets and thereby reduces learning and monitoring costs. More specifically, the more similar outlet operations are, the more useful will be the sales, cost, and best practices information that franchisors can collect from all of the outlets in their chains. Franchisors can then use this information to evaluate individual outlets and/or disseminate it throughout the system and thereby facilitate learning by franchisees and managers.[128]

For all these reasons, franchisors care about maintaining uniformity. To this end, they exercise control over many important aspects of the franchisee's business, including appearance, hours of operation, location, and product

---

[127] See Kaufmann and Eroglu (1998).
[128] See, e.g., Bradach (1998), p. 24. In Chapter 5 of his book and on several other occasions in it, the author also notes how comparisons between the company and franchised sides of these chains can be used to more effectively manage these chains.

quality.[129] A major function of the franchise agreement under these circum-stances is to specify contractual provisions that will remove or at least mitigate the fundamental incentive issue that arises because franchisees care about their own outlets' profits while the franchisor cares about system profits. Almost all franchise contracts contain specific provisions concerning expected fran-chisee performance. In fact, most franchise contracts incorporate by reference the whole set of directives contained in a very thick and detailed operations manual. Further, the contracts provide for the franchisor's right to moni-tor the performance of the franchisee through inspections, audits, mystery shopper programs, and so on. Most contracts also give franchisors the right to terminate the contract unconditionally or for good cause.[130] Finally, the terms of franchise contracts typically give rise to *ex-post* rent, namely amounts of money that the franchisee can earn within the relationship that are above what he could earn in his next best alternative. The amount of such rent in some chains is simply limited to the up-front franchise fee and potentially some other specific investments. In other words, the franchisee may only be able to earn quasi-rents on his operations that are just sufficient in total over the duration of the contract to compensate him fully for the franchise fee and the other sunk costs he incurred to join the chain. In order to recoup these investments, however, the franchisee will need to remain in the system – termination would mean he would lose the opportunity to earn the quasi-rent and thereby recoup his investments. But the rent *need not* be limited to the amount of such payments. All that matters from an incentive perspective is that the franchisee be better off remaining within the franchise relationship at any point in time in the contract period than moving on to the next best alternative use of his time and capital.[131] If the franchisee earns such rents,

---

[129] There are a few notable exceptions, such as conversion franchises like Best Western in the hotel industry and Embers America in the restaurant industry, and other franchise concepts such as the Great Harvest Bread Co. that cater to franchisees and customers who value local flavor (and hence these chains consistently offer such flavor). Embers America, for example, recruits owners of existing restaurants. To be attractive to such owners, they allow franchisees to "maintain their individuality and blend that with our marketing, purchasing, technology and other programs" (Walkup 2001). Still, such concepts have various criteria that franchisees must meet for consistency purposes. Thus, Embers restaurants must have the Embers signage, use the merchandising ma-terials of the system, and include Embers' signature menu items on their menus. The restaurants are allowed to maintain different looks, store sizes, additional menu items and other touches that have worked for them in their markets.

[130] We discuss termination in detail in Chapter 10.

[131] See Kaufmann and Lafontaine (1994) for the calculation of positive rents both *ex post* and *ex ante* at McDonald's and for more discussion of their incentive effects; see also Klein (1995) on the fact that it is the amount of rent that matters for incentives, not the amount of specific assets.

then he has something to lose from termination. This, in turn, will make him try to keep the likelihood of termination low, which requires that he abide by the rules imposed by the contract even if such rules prevent him from maximizing his short-term operating profits.

The rest of this chapter is organized as follows. In the next section, we present a simple model that illustrates the fundamental incentive misalignment problem generated by the use of the common brand name. We then examine how contractual performance requirements, product specification, tying, and vertical integration can be used to resolve this incentive problem. We describe how each of these mechanisms works and the costs of using them to solve this incentive problem. We then briefly look at the limited empirical evidence on the effect of franchising on quality and offer some concluding comments.

5.2 A Simple Model of Vertical Externalities[132]

In this section, we present a simple model that illustrates the externality problem that arises under common branding in franchising. Suppose that the franchisor has licensed exactly one franchisee in each of several distinct geographic markets. This, of course, means that each franchisee has a local monopoly on the distribution of the franchised good, which is differentiated from other substitute products by the goodwill associated with the trademark. In many instances, such as in gasoline retailing, the differences between the brands may not be great. But in other cases, as in car dealerships for Ford and Toyota, for example, the differentiation may be more pronounced. In the fast-food sector, Kalnins (2003) and Thomadsen (2005) examine the prices charged at a number of individual outlets at McDonald's and Burger King among others, and specifically analyze how the prices set at a given outlet relate to prices set at other outlets within and across chains. They both find evidence that cross-chain competition is relatively weak, implying that the amount of differentiation due to branding is quite large in this industry.

For present purposes, the degree of monopoly power enjoyed by a franchisee in his market is not important: we simply need the franchisees operating under the common brand to have some market power. Let

$$P = [P_1, P_2, \ldots, P_n]$$

represent the vector of output prices set by the individual franchisees for their product. In some instances, the franchisor may try to control these

---

[132] This section relies largely upon Blair and Kaserman (1994).

prices, but there are legal problems associated with franchisors controlling franchisee prices.[133] Thus, pricing decisions are usually in the hands of the franchisees. We assume also that franchisees control various other decisions in their outlet that affect the quality of the good or purchase experience that they offer customers. The quality of the products sold by the n franchisees can be represented by the following vector:

$$q = [q_1, q_2, \ldots, q_n].$$

If franchisees all chose the same quality level, then $q_i = q_j$ for all i, j. We posit that franchisee profits depend upon the prices and qualities in the entire system:

$$\pi_i = \pi_i(P, q) \qquad i = 1, 2, \ldots, n.$$

The externalities are captured by the partial derivatives of π_i:

$$\partial\pi_i/\partial P_j < 0 \text{ and } \partial\pi_i/\partial q_j > 0, i \neq j.$$

We are assuming for simplicity that the n franchisees are located in n separate geographic markets and, therefore, the external effects arise only from the use of a common trademark.[133] The assumptions that $\partial\pi_i/\partial P_j < 0$ and $\partial\pi_i/\partial q_j > 0$ capture the following influences: if a single franchisee raises its price or reduces its quality in its own market, the profits earned by all other franchisees in their own markets will fall. These external effects exist because a consumer's experience at one franchised outlet influences that consumer's decision of whether to patronize another outlet of the same franchised system in a different geographic location. If consumers are disappointed with their experience at one outlet because of an unexpectedly high price or unexpectedly poor quality, they will tend to shy away from other outlets of the same franchise system. Offering quality, however, is costly. Because quality is costly to the franchisee offering it, we assume that each franchisee's revenues increase at a decreasing rate with quality. Hence, there exists a quality level q_j^*, where $\partial\pi_j/\partial q_j = 0$, that maximizes each franchisee's profits.

Finally, we assume that the franchisor receives a proportion k of the profit earned by each of its franchisees, and that this proportion is the same for

[133] See Chapter 7 on the issue of maximum resale prices. Minimum resale prices are illegal *per se* under U.S. antitrust laws; see Blair and Kaserman (1985).

[133] What we really need is that the externality that arises from common branding be more important than any within-chain competitive effect. This should be the case if joining the chain is to be worthwhile for franchisees.

all franchisees.[134] As a result, the franchisor's total profit from the franchise system is

$$\Pi = \sum_{i=1}^{n} k[\pi_i(P, q)]. \tag{1}$$

We are now in a position to examine analytically the problem of incompatible incentives. The fundamental conflict of incentives that exists between the franchisor and its franchisees concerning product quality can be shown by proving the following proposition.

Proposition 1. *Under a franchise contract, the franchisee who owns a single unit will have a profit incentive to provide a lower level of quality than that which maximizes the franchisor's profit.*

Proof. Maximization of the franchisor's profits as per equation (1) requires that quality levels across the franchise system be set such that

$$\frac{\partial \Pi}{\partial q_j} = \sum_{i=1}^{n} k \frac{\partial \pi_i}{\partial q_j} = 0, \quad j = 1, \ldots, n. \tag{2}$$

We can write (2) as

$$k \frac{\partial \pi_j}{\partial q_j} = -k \sum_{\substack{i=1 \\ i \neq j}}^{n} \frac{\partial \pi_i}{\partial q_j} \tag{3}$$

or more simply

$$\frac{\partial \pi_j}{\partial q_j} = -\sum_{\substack{i=1 \\ i \neq j}}^{n} \frac{\partial \pi_i}{\partial q_j}. \tag{4}$$

Equation (4) implies that

$$\frac{\partial \pi_j}{\partial q_j} < 0 \tag{5}$$

since $\partial \pi_i / \partial q_j > 0$ for $i \neq j$. In other words, at the franchisor's profit maximizing level of quality, each franchisee has a profit incentive to reduce its

---

[134] From Chapter 3, we know that franchisors are much more likely to charge franchisees a fee that is a proportion of their sales rather than profits. Making the assumption that the fee is a proportion of profits, however, allows us to introduce less notation and simplify the exposition tremendously, and the conclusions we draw are qualitatively the same as if we assumed a sales-based fee.

quality towards q_j^*, where $\partial \pi_j / \partial q_j = 0$. This completes the proof of Proposition 1. Moreover, while the proposition is in terms of a single-unit franchise owner, it remains valid as long as the franchisee does not own all of the franchisor's units.[135]   □

Note that an analogous incentive conflict exists with regard to the price charged by the franchisees. This conflict is stated in the following proposition:

Proposition 2. *Under a franchise contract, the franchisee will have a profit incentive to charge a price above that which maximizes the franchisor's profit.*

In this case, at the set of prices that maximizes the franchisor's profits,

$$\frac{\partial \pi_j}{\partial P_j} > 0. \tag{6}$$

In other words, each franchisee has an incentive to raise its price at the expense of the rest of the franchise system. The proof of this Proposition proceeds in a completely analogous manner. We examine pricing conflict and controls in Chapter 7.

As for quality issues, Proposition 1 implies that a franchisee cannot be left free to select the product quality that maximizes its profit as this undermines the profitability of the franchise system as a whole.[136] This creates a need for some vertical controls that will more closely align the interest of each individual franchisee with those of the other franchisees and of the franchisor. The greater the effect of each franchisee's choice of quality level on other franchisees' profits, that is, the stronger the externality effects, the more important it will be for the franchisor to establish strong vertical controls. Conversely, the lower these effects, namely the more repeat customers franchised outlets face, the less important it will be for the franchisor to devise such controls. Brickley (1999) uses data from a large sample of franchised chains to examine the likelihood that firms use certain types of controls, specifically that they impose restrictions on passive ownership, mandate advertising expenditures, and rely on area development agreements. He finds that firms rely on these types of controls more often if they operate in industries that cater to mobile as opposed to mostly repeat customers. He also argues that franchised units

---

[135] The incentive incompatibility problem becomes less severe the larger the number of units that the franchisee owns, which is why multi-unit ownership can solve at least part of the incentive incompatibility problem.

[136] For a detailed account, including a comparison of control policies at McDonald's and Burger King, see Makar (1988).

are more likely to be affected by decisions made at other outlets if they are geographically close together as this increases the likelihood that the same patrons could frequent the different outlets. Consistent with his arguments, he finds that firms whose outlets are more geographically concentrated tend to use passive ownership restrictions and mandatory advertising requirements more often.

The use of various controls, however, can create tension and friction between the franchisor and its franchisees. These contractual controls chafe for two reasons. First, they limit the franchisee's ability to behave opportunistically. Second, and perhaps most importantly, these controls reduce the franchisee's independence and limit his capacity to personalize his business and cater more specifically to his local clientele.

Yet, franchisees clearly benefit from having these controls exerted on the other franchisees in the chain. In fact, franchisees request franchisor intervention when they are aware of other franchisees who are not "doing their job." Bradach (1998: 130–131) quotes a franchisee saying "if someone is running a poor operation it hurts the chain and it hurts my business... it is the job of the chain operator to get on the people running a shoddy operation." In all fairness, each franchisee must accept then that the same controls be applied to him as to all other franchisees. Milton Gurwitz, a Subway franchisee in Bellingham, Massachusetts, put it simply: "If you're a free-spirited person and want to do it your own way... you don't buy a franchise."[137]

5.3 Contractual Efforts to Resolve Incentive Problems

There are a number of contractual provisions that are designed to deal with quality control problems, such as specific performance clauses, product specifications, and input purchase requirements. Ultimately, the franchisor also can choose to resolve the quality issues by owning and operating outlets directly rather than franchising them. We discuss each of those options in this section. It should be clear at the outset, however, that none of these options represents a perfect solution to the control problem. For one thing, some of these vertical control mechanisms are legal while others are not. Moreover, none of them are free. Consequently, by using these controls, the franchisor will achieve profits that only approximate those that are possible in a perfect world of voluntary compliance among franchisees.

---

[137] Quoted in Flaherty (2001).

5.3.1 Specific Performance Clauses

Not surprisingly, incentive incompatibility regarding the franchisee's choice of product quality motivates each franchisor to include quality control mechanisms in their franchise contract directly. In other words, the franchisor will attack the incentive incompatibility problem by reducing the managerial discretion retained by each franchisee. Thus, franchisors often specify that they are allowed to dictate the exact set of products to be sold, the hours of operation, the type of information system to be used by the franchisee in running its business, and so on.

For example, McDonald's operates the most extensive fast-food restaurant chain in the world. By 2002, it had more than 30,000 restaurants worldwide, and around 70 percent of them were franchised while the others were corporate outlets. The golden arches are literally everywhere. At each McDonald's, however, one can expect basically the same overall experience. McDonald's franchise agreement itself points to the central importance of uniformity. It states that "[t]he foundation of the McDonald's System and the essence of this Franchise is the adherence by Franchisee to standards and policies of McDonald's providing for the *uniform* operation of all McDonald's restaurants within the McDonald's system . . ." (emphasis added). These standards and policies are spelled out in detail in its operations manual, which it updates regularly and includes by reference in its franchise contract: "Licensee agrees to promptly adopt and use exclusively the formulas, methods, and policies contained in the business manuals now and as they may be modified by McDonald's from time to time" (McDonald's "Franchise Agreement," as included in McDonald's *Uniform Franchise Offering Circular*, 2003).

From very early on, Ray Kroc, the founder of McDonald's System Inc., understood how vital uniformity was to the success of his enterprise. But despite his best efforts to convince and control his franchisees, he found that his California franchisees "were experimenting with new products, new procedures, and new (and higher) prices. Few maintained the high standards of quality and cleanliness that the (McDonald's) brothers had established . . ." (Love 1986: 68). Similarly, the Rolling Green franchisees – those small and medium business owners that Ray Kroc knew from his country club and to whom he turned when he needed investors – insisted on broadening the menu, increasing prices, and so on. Kroc reacted to these problems by refusing to renew licenses or refusing to grant new franchises to existing franchisees, or, in the case of egregious deviations from Quality, Service, Cleanliness (QSC) standards, suing franchisees for breach of contract. These types of reactions were unheard of in franchising at the time. Kroc faced these types of problems again later in the international arena, in particular with Raymond Dayan, who had bought an exclusive license for Paris:

> McDonald's in Paris was considered "a QSC wasteland" by everyone else in the system. The company's strict specifications on food products had been blatantly ignored. Hamburgers were prepared without all of the standard ingredients. Food was held so long and served so cold that McDonald's managers inspecting the stores found it difficult to eat . . . the stores were so unclean that McDonald's franchisees elsewhere around the world began hearing complaints about them from their own local customers who had seen Dayan's units while visiting Paris. . . . George Cohon, the president of McDonald's of Canada, wrote a letter . . . about Paris, insisting that "it is time to remove the cancer." (Love: 409–410)

Cohon attempted to negotiate a buyout of Dahan's license. When Dayan refused, McDonald's terminated his license, and Dayan sued in Illinois court. In the court's 1982 decision, Judge Curry found for McDonald's, rejecting Dayan's claim that McDonald's was trying to pocket the profits of the Paris operations:

> Far more realistic . . . is the conclusion that McDonald's herculean effort in this case is motivated by a zeal to rid itself of a cancer within its system before it grows and further infects the 6900 store organization . . . if Dayan, the grade 'F' operator in Paris, can thumb his nose at the system and its standards, then so too can operators everywhere. (Quoted in Love: 410)

This was McDonald's most significant QSC victory. Combined with a number of other decisions regarding termination, non-renewal, and its policy of controlling the real estate of its stores, McDonald's set numerous precedents and convinced the courts that for franchising to function properly, franchisors must be allowed to control their franchisee's behavior and impose sanctions on those that do not abide by the rules set forth in the contract.[138]

Similarly, Doctor's Associates, Inc., which is the franchisor of the Subway restaurant chain, imposes controls on its franchisees. In particular, the franchise agreement itself contains a number of controls on the managerial discretion of its franchisees. In addition, as for McDonald's, the franchisee must agree to operate the business "in accordance with our [Subway's] Operations Manual . . . which contains mandatory and suggested specifications, standards, and operating procedures, which may be updated from time to time as a result of experience, or changes in the law or marketplace." Moreover, "[t]he Operations Manual, as amended from time to time, is intended

---

[138] See Love (1986), especially Chapter 16 of that book, for a detailed account.

to further the purposes of this Agreement and is specifically incorporated into this Agreement" (Subway "Franchise Agreement," as incorporated in its *Uniform Franchise Offering Circular*, 2002).

McDonald's and Subway are not unusual in including their operations manual by reference in their franchise contract – many franchisors do just that. The contract also typically includes more general statements about best efforts. Dnes (1992a: 269) cites a Midas Franchise Agreement: "The franchisee shall diligently carry on the said business at the said premises and shall use its best endeavours to promote and extend the said business. . . ."

As McDonald's experience makes clear, however, specifying what the franchisee must do does not eliminate the franchisee's incentive to deviate from the prescribed behavior. Therefore, there must also be monitoring – audits, mystery shopper programs, and so on – and some sanctions for noncompliance. Dnes (1992a) and Bradach (1998) provide detailed accounts of the business practices of nineteen British and five U.S. franchised chains, respectively. Both show that noncompliance is dealt with generally under what Bradach refers to as "proportional response." In other words, noncompliance on minor issues is tolerated so that the chain can focus on those deviations that matter most to the value of the business. Bradach offers the following example:

> [D]uring an interview a Pizza Hut franchisee asked me if the vice-president of franchising (whom I had interviewed earlier that day) mentioned anything about the nonstandard window shades the franchisee had recently installed. He said that the franchise consultant "has been after me for awhile, and I wondered how big a deal they were going to make of this." Later, when I talked to the vice-president of franchising again, he said, "I might send him a letter, but it isn't a giant issue. As long as it doesn't affect the consumer on a day-to-day basis, we just keep up the pressure but we won't push it." (101)

Bradach also cites Dave Hoban, an area director of franchising at Hardee's: "You don't want to burn your goodwill bothering franchisees with little things. There are too many big issues that we have to deal with – like convincing them to install new ovens – to get caught up in the little ones" (102). Dnes (1992a) notes, "Mr. Rowntree of Mobiletuning . . . states that it is not worth his while to police minor infringements of the agreement" (283).

When faced with more important deviations from performance standards, franchisors will "quote the contract" and try to get franchisees to conform. If that does not yield the desired result, franchisors will at some point suggest that a franchisee leave the system, by selling to another franchisee or back to the franchisor, as McDonald's tried to do in the case of Raymond Dayan. Even if such a sale is constrained by the franchisor's insistence that it occur relatively quickly, the franchisee can sell the unit at a price that captures at least some of the future expected profits associated with the business. The ultimate threat or sanction, however, is termination. If his franchise is terminated, the franchisee loses the entire present value of the profits that he could have earned by operating the franchised outlet rather than using his time and capital in their next best alternative. If the present value of those profits exceeds the (expected) profits that can be earned by engaging in the kind of cheating on quality that could lead to termination, this type of cheating will be deterred; otherwise, cheating on quality will occur and franchise terminations will be necessary.[139]

Coupled with these penalties for noncompliance, the performance standards are designed to make it unprofitable for a franchisee to deviate from the product quality that is optimal from the perspective of the franchise system as a whole. The higher the penalties are, and in particular the more rent franchisees are apt to lose if they are terminated, the more likely franchisors will be successful in preventing major deviations from the business format by franchisees. Kaufmann and Lafontaine (1994) used data from McDonald's earnings claims in their disclosure documents to calculate the expected profits per outlet at McDonald's. They found that in 1982, franchisees at McDonald's could expect to earn economic profits of between $300,000 and $450,000 on average over the life of the contract for each new outlet they purchased.[140] In other words, franchisees at McDonald's had a lot to lose if they were denied expansion rights. *Ex post* economic profits were, of course, even higher, at about $600,000 on average after taxes, as *ex post* economic profits include the *ex ante* amounts plus all initial fees and specific investments. In other words, the average franchisee stood to lose $600,000 upon termination. With such amounts of money at stake, McDonald's is able to exert significant control over their franchisees' operations.

5.3.2 Product Specifications

In addition to specifying performance requirements such as hours of operation, cleanliness standards, management information systems, and so on, the

---

[139] Deviations will occur also if franchisees expect that franchisors will not terminate or will not be allowed by the courts to terminate noncompliant franchisees. This best explains why Dayan refused the buy-back offer.

[140] See also Michael and Moore (1995) for evidence of rent in other franchised systems, and Lafontaine and Raynaud (2002) for an argument that such rent, combined with the threat of termination, complement residual claims in providing incentives to franchisees.

franchisor can affect quality by using precise contractual language to limit the franchisee's discretion regarding the products and services it can use. This again does not remove the incentive to reduce quality for private gain, but it does limit the franchisee's discretion and provides grounds for termination if the franchisee behaves opportunistically.

For example, at Subway, the franchisee must agree to adhere to Subway's quality control standards regarding goods and services sold to the customer. Similarly, uniformity at McDonald's extends to "serving only designated food and beverage products" that meet McDonald's specifications. In this way, McDonald's can assure quality uniformity for the products sold at all of its restaurants. Again, early McDonald's franchisees did not all abide by these: for example, Kroc accused Richard Picchietti, one of the Rolling Green franchisees, of "purchasing inferior food supplies in order to get a cheaper price" (Love, 76). Even Kroc's first true owner-operator husband and wife franchisee team, the Agates – whose undeniable success in the business led a number of their peers to become franchisees themselves and helped Kroc identify good prospects at a critical juncture in the chain's development, became known as "price buyers" – franchisees who substituted cheaper products from non-approved suppliers. On particular, Sandy Agate signed a deal with Pepsi to sell their cola instead of Coke, the only approved cola at McDonald's. In both the Picchietti and Agate cases, Kroc reacted by denying them the opportunity to buy additional stores later on. In fact, Agate became known throughout the McDonald's system "as the one punished by Kroc for switching from Coke to Pepsi," although this was not the only reason he was denied the opportunity to expand (Love, 85). No other franchisee ever tried to make that switch after that.

Finally, Anheuser-Busch operates what amounts to a traditional franchise system in the form of an extensive network of wholesale beer distributors.[141] These distributors buy Anheuser-Busch beer from the nearest Anheuser-Busch brewery and resell the beer to retail accounts – convenience stores, grocery stores, bars, restaurants, and the like. Beer has three enemies: age, heat, and light. To deal with heat as a source of quality deterioration, Anheuser-Busch requires that its beer be kept in temperature-controlled warehouses under strict guidelines. To deal with age, all beer containers have a date code, and the distributors are required to remove from the market and destroy over-age (i.e., old) beer at their expense. No doubt, there are some distributors that

---

[141] The Anheuser-Busch wholesalers are not technically franchisees, but the wholesale contract and obligations of both parties amount to something very similar to a traditional franchise.

do not like having to incur the cost of meeting these contractual obligations, but they must do so or face penalties, including, ultimately, the possibility of termination and the associated loss of profits.

5.3.3 Input Purchase Requirements[142]

In some circumstances, a franchisor may assure quality by imposing a requirement that franchisees buy certain inputs from it directly, that is, by imposing a tying arrangement on its franchisees. In that event, the franchisee is obligated to buy a package of items from the franchisor that is designed to eliminate opportunities for the substitution of alternative (and, of course, cheaper) inputs. Unfortunately, despite these requirements, it may still be possible for the franchisee to supplement the tied inputs or replace them with unauthorized inputs and dilute product quality. Thus, franchisors need to monitor input use and punish transgressors even if the contract includes tying clauses. For example, Barnie's Coffee & Tea Co. sells specialty coffees along with the usual array of coffee mugs, coffee makers, and other supplies. Some of the specialty coffees are flavored according to the franchisor's own recipes. At times, some franchisees have tried to purchase similar coffees elsewhere (at lower prices) and substitute them for the more expensive coffees supplied by the franchisor. The franchisor, of course, insists that a franchisee distribute Barnie's coffee rather than someone else's coffee.[143] The offending franchisees were threatened with termination if they insisted on selling coffee supplied by unauthorized third parties.

The use of tying contracts to assure input quality and consistency and thereby protect the value of the franchisor's trademark has a long history in franchising. It is also subject to various legal restrictions under U.S. antitrust laws. In the early 1920s, Sinclair already required its licensed dealers to sell only Sinclair gasoline from pumps bearing its trademark.[144] And while this practice has been the subject of a number of court cases over time, all major oil refiners continue to require that lessee dealers operating under their brands sell exclusively their gasoline.[145] To the extent that the refiners can control

---

[142] The role of input purchase requirements in franchising is examined in detail in Chapter 6.

[143] A similar dispute was at the heart of *Krehl v. Baskin-Robbins Ice Cream Co.*, 664 F. 2d 1348 (9th Cir. 1982). The franchisee did not want to sell Baskin-Robbins ice cream, but wanted to use the Baskin-Robbins trademark. The court decided against the franchisee, a perfectly reasonable outcome for consumers.

[144] *Federal Trade Commission v. Sinclair Refining Co.*, 261 U.S. 463 (1923).

[145] *Redd v. Shell Oil Co.*, 524 F. 2d 1054 (10th Cir. 1975), and *Phillips v. Crown Central Petroleum Corp.*, 395 F. Supp. 453 (E.D. Mich. 1975).

the quality of what they produce, these requirements preserve that quality at the pump. Some oil companies even extended the requirements to tires, batteries, and accessories as a way, potentially, to assure the quality level of all the products offered for sale at the dealership. Such requirements, however, were found to be in violation of U.S. antitrust laws. The requirement that the dealers purchase the gasoline from the company under whose name they do business, on the other hand, has traditionally not been considered a tie by the courts as the trade name and the gasoline in those cases are not really separate products. For the same reason, Baskin-Robbins was able to impose a requirement in its franchise contract that its franchisees buy all their ice cream from Baskin-Robbins. But Chicken Delight's requirement that franchisees purchase paper products and other similar inputs from it was found to be an illegal tie. The court reasoned that the franchisor could ensure quality by providing its franchisees with a set of approved suppliers instead of selling the inputs itself, as the inputs and the trade name were two different products.

The practical result of this jurisprudence has been that most business-format franchise contracts rely on approved suppliers rather than tying arrangements. Recent court cases have thus been brought against franchisors not for tying, but rather for limiting the set of approved suppliers.[146] As an example, consider the dispute in *Subsolutions, Inc. v. Doctor's Associates, Inc.*[147] All Subway franchisees need a cash register or a computerized point-of-sale (POS) alternative. Most of the franchisees had signed franchise agreements that permitted them to make a choice from an array of specific alternatives. Subsequently, the franchisor decided that it wanted all of its franchisees to buy the same POS system, the one designated by Subway. A provider of an alternative POS system sued Subway on the grounds that it was illegally foreclosed from selling its product to Subway franchisees. The district court found that the *Kodak* ruling applied because the franchisor had changed the terms of its contract without prior disclosure. (See *Eastman Kodak Company v. Image Technical Service*, 1992.) The case subsequently settled. Note that one potential reason for the franchisor's insistence on uniformity in POS system is the resulting ease of measuring and monitoring franchisee performance.

5.3.4 Vertical Integration

The most extreme reaction to the incentive incompatibility problem regarding quality would be to replace the franchise system with company-operated

[146] See, e.g., *Queen City Pizza v. Domino's Pizza*, 124 F. 3d 430 (3d Cir. 1997).
[147] 62 F. Supp. 2d 616 (D. Conn. 1999).

outlets, i.e., to employ ownership, as opposed to contractual, integration. In this way, the franchisor might better ensure that quality is not sacrificed to increase the profit of a given franchisee.[148] In the context of the model developed above, it is still true under vertical integration that starting from the quality level that the franchisor finds optimal, a reduction in quality at any given location will increase profits at that location, i.e., $\partial \pi_j / \partial q_j < 0$ at the franchisor's choice of quality. But with vertical integration, there is no one to act on this fact because the manager of each outlet, contrary to the franchisee, typically is not rewarded heavily on the basis of his outlet's profits. Instead, to obtain desired results, managers of corporate units should be rewarded on the basis of their contributions to the system as a whole, bearing in mind the externalities. After all, it is the elimination of the residual claimant status of the franchisee in the vertical chain that is the distinguishing property of vertical integration and that reduces the free-riding types of incentive incompatibility problems encountered under franchising.

As noted in Chapter 4, Lafontaine and Shaw (2005) have found that franchisors with more valuable brands tend to own and operate more of their outlets directly. This is consistent with vertical integration being used in part to prevent franchisee free-riding on the more valuable brands. The move towards a more vertically integrated structure, however, comes at the cost of the store manager's reduced incentives to work hard – the original shirking or moral hazard problem that led to franchising in the first place. After all, with a franchisee, the franchisor benefits from the dedication and drive of an individual who is building a business for himself or herself. And this motivation and drive of the individual franchisee, as compared to the typical company manager, is a main reason why franchisors use franchising to begin with.

5.4 Costs of Control

As should be clear from our discussion, each of the quality control mechanisms described above has problems of its own. There are costs associated with ownership integration, which undermines the desirability of this strategy. For one thing, managers can still engage in opportunistic behavior. The precise form that it takes will depend upon the incentive and monitoring systems

---

[148] Katz (1989) points out that vertical integration does not eliminate or resolve moral hazard problems. In a vertically integrated firm, the principal–agent problems that gave rise to the need for franchising in the first place are likely to be quite severe. The free-riding problems, however, are alleviated because the manager is not a profit maximizer (assuming his pay is not based largely on his unit's profits).

that are in place for them. For example, if each location is treated as a profit center, the manager will continue to have an incentive to increase his location's profits at the expense of other locations. Moreover, company managers who are not residual claimants of their outlet's profits have lower incentives to work hard and make their outlet a success. The vertically integrated firm must balance these issues to arrive at an appropriate choice of compensation plans. Franchisors also complain about the lack of managerial stability with company managers, as the latter change jobs relatively frequently. For another thing, managerial diseconomies of scale may increase the cost of operating outlets directly in various ways. Finally, the cost of capital may be an increasing function of the quantity of capital demanded by the firm. In this event, the vertically integrated firm may face significantly higher capital costs.[149]

As noted earlier, tying arrangements pose other problems as they may violate the antitrust laws and thereby expose the franchisor to litigation costs and, potentially, both civil and criminal sanctions.[150] Under some circumstances, tying to assure quality control has been found legal, but there is still some risk of antitrust exposure. As if this were not enough, consider the problems when the franchisee employs a multi-input variable proportions production function. In that case, the franchisor would have a far more complicated task of specifying the optimal input proportions. These proportions will, of course, change whenever any input price changes. As a result, the provisions of a tying contract may be prohibitively complex to negotiate and enforce.

Finally, the monitoring and enforcing of contractual performance standards and product specifications are clearly not free. Periodic inspections have to be made to check franchisee behavior and verify what products are used and in what quantities. Moreover, one should anticipate that franchisees will resist penalties and/or termination, which means that litigation again may accompany enforcement efforts as it did for McDonald's and its Paris franchisee.[151]

---

[149] For a further examination of the difficulties associated with vertical integration, see Blair and Kaserman (1983), at pp. 23–25 and 77–78.

[150] As a *per se* violation of Section 1 of the Sherman Act, tying can be prosecuted by the Department of Justice and fines of up to $100 million may be levied on corporations. Further, private suits by franchisees can result in treble damage awards. See Chapter 6 of this book for a more detailed treatment.

[151] Franchisees often resist quality controls and litigation results in some circumstances. For example, see *Wilson v. Mobil Oil Corp.*, 940 F. Supp. 944 (E. D. La. 1996), and *Metrix Warehouse, Inc. v. Daimler-Benz A. G.*, 828 F. 2d 1033 (4th Cir. 1987). Terminating a franchisee can be especially difficult due to limits imposed by state termination laws or common law doctrines. See Eaton (1980: 1331–1350) and Chapter 10 of this book for more on this subject.

Efforts to control quality will only succeed if opportunistic behavior is deterred. As we mentioned above, the ongoing rents that the franchisee can expect to earn as part of the distribution system act as a "hostage" from an incentive perspective. As Williamson has explained, the use of hostages serves the interests of *both* parties and not just the franchisor's interests.[152] Although the loss of the hostage may appear to be a one-sided "unfair" contractual provision, in fact it simultaneously protects the interests of the franchisor in developing and promoting the goodwill associated with the franchise and the interests of the franchisees who have invested both their time and money based on the market value of that goodwill. Equivalently, according to Klein (1980, 1995), the potential loss of the stream of future profits makes the franchise contract self-enforcing.

Note that our discussion of the role of rent combined with termination in resolving the incentive issues inherent in the franchise relationship implies that franchisors should terminate only when franchisees are not performing according to the terms of their contract. But various state laws have been enacted to prevent termination without cause. Such laws presume that franchisors terminate contracts opportunistically, namely with the goal of appropriating the investments of the franchisee rather than to resolve a performance problem. We examine the issue of termination and non-renewal in detail in Chapter 10. For now, we note simply that the empirical evidence suggests that franchisors on average do not behave opportunistically but instead terminate poorly performing franchisees. Specifically, using data on 830 franchised outlets drawn from the Census Bureau's "Characteristics of Business Owners" database, Williams (1996) shows that greater outlet performance, measured by a higher return on investment, decreases the likelihood of contract termination by franchisors. Laws that make termination more difficult thus make it more costly for franchisors to rely on the threat of termination to discipline franchisees and enforce uniform quality standards in the chain.

5.5 Observed Quality Differentials between Company and Franchised Units

One issue that we have not addressed above is whether we observe franchisee free riding on quality, which would imply lower observed quality levels in franchised than in company-owned outlets. Empirically, this is a complicated issue for a number of reasons. First, the decision as to which outlet in a chain

---

[152] Williamson (1983).

should be franchised and which should be company-owned is not a random process. If, as argued by Brickley and Dark (1987), franchisors systematically choose to own those units where free riding would be especially problematic and franchise only those outlets where there is not much scope for free riding, then we would find no difference in quality between the two sets of units in a chain. Second, the various forms of vertical controls described above can be used by franchisors to generate a very similar outcome for franchised and company units. Finally, while franchisees' ownership of their outlets may lead them to free ride, it also gives them substantial incentives to succeed. If quality is partially a result of franchisee effort, then quality might actually be higher in franchised outlets than in corporate stores. In other words, economic theory can lead to different predictions depending on whether we focus on the basic incentive issue (too little effort) that is solved by having a franchisee own its outlet, as we did in the agency theory section in Chapter 4, or whether we focus on the fact that profit maximizing franchisees *who own their outlet* can then increase their individual profits through free riding. Our economic model in this chapter focused on the latter, but the existence of the former makes it less likely that we can identify free riding on quality.

Bradach (1998: 109) notes that most of the franchisees and company managers he interviewed (in five different fast-food chains) "agreed that the two arrangements exhibited similar levels of (standard adherence) uniformity." He adds that for the two firms in his sample that use third-party evaluators to assess quality, the average score was 94.6 (out of 100 points) for the franchised units and 93.9 for the company units in the first chain, and 89.7 and 90.6, respectively, in the other chain. Thus, one may reasonably conclude that there is no meaningful quality difference between the two types of units. Finally, Bradach refers a few times to instances where franchisees complained about under-performing company outlets, implying that company owned-outlets do not systematically outperform franchised outlets from a quality perspective.

Michael (2000a) examines the effect of franchising on the quality ratings published for restaurant and hotel chains in *Consumer Reports*. His sample includes fully corporate as well as franchised chains. He finds that within narrow industry segments – steakhouses, family restaurants, and dinner houses in the restaurant industry, and budget, moderate and high-end hotels in the hotel sector – and after controlling for price, chains that use more company ownership display higher quality on average than chains that rely more on franchising. Note that this result confuses somewhat the notion of quality level in an absolute sense with deviation from a quality standard no matter what the intended level is. Opportunism or free riding really refers to deviation from the intended standard, not to absolute levels.

Finally, Lafontaine and Shaw's (2005) finding mentioned earlier – that firms with a more valuable brand as measured by their advertising expenditures on average over time tend to use more company units – is consistent specifically with the idea that franchisors try to protect their brand by using more company units when their brand is more valuable. Note that the causality is reversed between the two studies in Michael (2000a), more company ownership leads to higher quality whereas in Lafontaine and Shaw (2003) it is the more valuable brand (actual or desired) that leads franchisors to choose a form of governance that affords them more direct control over the units. In either case, however, the causal effect is predicated on the notion that company managers have fewer incentives to free ride than franchisees do.

All in all, though very limited, the empirical evidence seems consistent with the concept that free riding, or individual profit maximization by opportunistic franchisees, is an issue in franchised chains. But Bradach's case studies, combined with the low levels of company ownership one finds in most franchised chains (see Chapter 4), support the idea that franchisors control franchise free riding and associated costs fairly well, and that the incentive and innovation benefits of having owner operators rather than hired managers outweigh the remainder of these costs in many different contexts.

5.6 Conclusion

Franchising is a pervasive contractual alternative to ownership integration in geographically dispersed retail and service industries, and it arises for a variety of reasons. These arrangements represent a market response to one or more problems of vertical control between successive stages of production where the use of an intangible asset is involved. Inherent in the franchise relationship, however, is incentive incompatibility regarding product quality. In this chapter, we have modeled the problem of incompatible incentives and examined several ways of reducing, if not resolving, the conflict between the individual franchisee and the franchise system. In the end, the limited evidence we have suggests that quality differentials between company and franchised units are fairly low in practice. In other words, it appears that most franchisors have sufficient ways to control franchisee behavior and thus obtain fairly consistent operations throughout their chain. This fact is not as surprising as might first appear. After all, if the outcomes were significantly different between company and franchised outlets along a dimension as central to these chains as outlet-level quality, one would expect that franchisors would always choose the organizational form yielding the better, or perhaps even more important, the most consistent level of quality. Instead, the coexistence of company and franchised outlets in most chains suggests that in some basic sense, these two modes of organization yield comparable outcomes from the franchisor's perspective.

6

Franchise Tying Contracts

6.1 Introduction*

A tying contract is a vertical restraint that involves a conditional sale. In its simplest form, the producer of product A agrees to sell that product, but only on the condition that the buyer also purchase product B. In this scenario, product A is the *tying good* while product B is the *tied good*. The situation can be more complicated, involving possibly a collection of tied goods rather than just one. Moreover, tying may involve services and other intangibles, or extend to leases as well as sales. Finally, the tying arrangement may involve third parties, that is, the buyer of A may have to buy the tied good B from a designated third party rather than from the seller of A. In all of these scenarios, however, the essence of tying is the condition that limits the buyer's freedom to purchase the tied good(s) wherever he deems optimal from his own perspective.

In the franchising context, the alleged tying good is usually the franchise license, which is normally subject to intellectual property protection. The tied goods may be other goods that are resold with little modification or they may be inputs into the production of a final good. An example of the former would be branded products such as Baskin-Robbins ice cream or Shell gasoline. The Baskin-Robbins franchisor licenses its franchisee on the condition that it buy Baskin-Robbins ice cream for resale. Business format franchisors, such as Domino's Pizza, provide an example of the latter as they may license their franchisees on the condition that they buy certain inputs from the franchisor or a designated supplier. Domino's, for example, may require that its franchisees buy pizza dough and perhaps other ingredients necessary for a *real* Domino's pizza from Domino's or from a designated third party.

* This chapter relies heavily on Blair and Herndon (1999) and Blair and Kaserman (1978).

Table 6-1 shows the frequency of mandatory purchase requirements in business format franchising in 1988 and 1989, the only years for which information on such requirements is available for some subset of firms in our data.[153] Not surprisingly, we find that franchisors involved in various types of retailing, including those in the Health and Fitness sector and the Food Retail sector, tend to impose such requirements rather frequently. Franchisors that provide mostly services, on the other hand, such as those in the Business, Hotel and Motel, Rental, and Real Estate services sectors, typically do not require that franchisees buy any inputs from them. On average, about 30 percent of franchisors impose some supply restrictions on their franchisees. Michael (2000b) has examined the disclosure documents of 100 restaurant and fast-food franchisors to provide more detailed evidence on tying in these sectors. Of the 100 chains whose documents he analyzed, he found that 30 imposed a requirement that the franchisee purchase some product from the franchisor. In other words, tying occurs with the same frequency in these sectors as it does on average in all franchises sectors. Franchisors that used tying were found disproportionately among the chicken, pizza, sandwiches, seafood, and sit-down restaurant chains while very few hamburger and hot dog chains and Mexican restaurants had such requirements. Among the 30 firms with purchase requirements, he found that on average the amount of purchases that were required represented about 8.4 percent of all the wholesale purchases of the franchisees. Most of the franchisors in the chicken, pizza, and seafood fast-food sectors, however, only imposed requirements for spices, batter, or sauces. Firms with the largest proportions of wholesale purchases subjected to a tie tended to be those that sold some proprietary products, such as batter for pancake houses, bread for sandwich shops (Subway), or ice cream for family restaurants (e.g., Brigham's and Howard Johnson).

In Chapter 4 we showed that through the judicious use of a tying contract, a franchisor can induce the same input usage and the same final output that would result under ownership integration if the downstream market is competitive.[154] At that stage, we assumed that there was only one downstream input, and that the production function was such that the franchisee had to use one unit of the franchisor's input for each unit of output, so he had no opportunity to substitute away from the franchisor's high-priced input.

---

[153] The data are obtained from *Bond's Franchise Guide* 1989 and 1990–91 editions, respectively, for 1988 and 1989. As only a subset of the firms described in the *Entrepreneur Franchise 500* – our main source of data for 1988 and 1989 – also appear in the corresponding Bond publication, our sample sizes for this variable are reduced to 643 and 630, respectively.

[154] See Blair and Kaserman (1978) for a detailed proof.

Table 6-1: *Mandatory purchase requirements*

Sector	1988			1989		
	Number of Franchisors	Number of Franchisors Requirement	Percent (%)	Number of Franchisors	Number of Franchisors Requirement	Percent (%)
Automotive	56	13	23.2	54	14	25.9
Business	96	19	19.8	93	14	15.1
Contractors	18	7	38.9	20	7	35.0
Cosmetic	14	3	21.4	17	4	23.5
Education	8	1	12.5	12	5	41.7
Fast Food	119	51	42.9	112	45	40.2
Health and Fitness	20	11	55.0	12	6	50.0
Home Furnishings	14	4	28.6	14	4	28.6
Hotels and Motels	9	1	11.1	5	1	20.0
Maintenance	45	12	26.7	47	16	34.0
Personal Services	52	14	26.9	56	14	25.0
Real Estate	15	1	6.7	17	5	29.4
Recreation	11	4	36.4	11	5	45.5
Rental	15	2	13.3	18	3	16.7
Restaurants	37	16	43.2	39	18	46.2
Retail Food	22	13	59.1	22	12	54.5
Retail Other	92	22	23.9	81	24	29.6
Total	643	194	30.2	630	197	31.3

This assumption reasonably describes gasoline or car retailing where each dealer sale must involve a unit of the franchisor's input. In the appendix to this chapter, we revisit the economic equivalence between vertical integration and input tying in the more general case of several downstream inputs that franchisees can use in variable proportions. We show that the economic equivalence between vertical integration and tying continues to hold under these conditions as well, provided that the downstream market remains competitive.[155]

Using an agency-theory perspective, we also showed in Chapter 4 that there are benefits associated with having highly motivated owners managing a chain's outlets and we argued that these benefits are what lead franchisors to choose franchising rather than corporate ownership. But corporate ownership remains a very feasible way to organize a chain of geographically dispersed outlets: Starbucks, for example, is not a franchise. It is important to realize that judicial hostility toward the kind of vertical controls used generally in franchise contracts, which of course include tying, may tilt more franchisors toward a greater degree of vertical integration. This outcome would be a perverse result of an antitrust effort to protect franchisees as it would reduce the set of franchised opportunities for potential and existing franchisees alike.

The rest of this chapter is organized as follows. In the next section, we examine what tying is and how it is treated under U.S. antitrust policy. We then review the major franchise tying cases and their outcomes. As *Kodak*[156] represented somewhat of a shift in the antitrust treatment of tying, specifically in the market power and market definition aspects of these cases, we discuss the *Kodak* case and its relationship to more recent franchise cases in the following sections. We next consider the argument made in many franchise tying cases that tying represents a form of post-contractual franchisor opportunism. Finally, we revisit the issue of franchisee evaluation of franchise opportunities in light of the possibility of explicit or implicit ties in franchise agreements and offer a few concluding remarks.

6.2 Antitrust Treatment of Tying Contracts in General

To the extent that tying benefits the franchisor at the franchisee's expense, there is apt to be conflict and, given the current status of tying under antitrust, such

---

[155] The incentive of firms to vertically integrate when they face variable proportions in downstream production was pointed out by Vernon and Graham (1971), which spawned a revival of interest in the theory of vertical integration.

[156] *Eastman Kodak Company v. Image Technical Service* (1992).

conflict can give rise to an antitrust suit.[157] After all, tying contracts restrain the freedom of the contracting parties just as all contracts do. If a tying contract *unreasonably* restrains trade, it violates Section 1 of the Sherman Act.[158] From its earliest decisions, the Supreme Court has displayed a hostile attitude toward tying contracts. In fact, the Court's rulings in *Northern Pacific Railway v. United States* (1958) and *Fortner Enterprises v. United States Steel Corporation* (1969) endorsed a harsh rule of *per se* illegality. Although subsequent decisions – *United States Steel Corporation v. Fortner Enterprises* (1977) and *Jefferson Parish Hospital District No. 2 v. Hyde* (1984) – appeared to soften this attitude and move the Court toward a rule of reason approach to tying, its most recent decision in *Eastman Kodak Company v. Image Technical Services* (1992) reconfirmed its earlier rulings that tying remains illegal *per se*.

As used in price-fixing cases, *per se* illegality means that the plaintiff need only prove the fact of price fixing for a finding of illegality. There is no need to assess the actual economic impact as it is presumed to be deleterious, which is an economically sensible view of price fixing. When it comes to tying contracts, however, the *per se* label is a bit misleading. In fact, extensive economic analysis is required to prove that a tying contract is illegal. There are five elements to a *per se* illegal tying contract:[159]

First, there must be two distinct products involved – a tying product and a tied product. In a franchise setting, the franchise license is usually the tying product while all sorts of supplies and equipment may serve as the tied product(s).

Second, there must be a conditional sale. That is, the franchisor must have agreed to accept a prospective franchisee but only on the condition that the franchisee agree to buy the tied product(s) from the franchisor or a designated third party.

Third, the franchisor must enjoy substantial economic – or market – power in the tying good market. Since proof of market power can be elusive,

---

[157] In most instances, the franchisee is the plaintiff in a franchise tying suit. But a tying arrangement arguably forecloses rival suppliers of the tied goods. These foreclosed rivals may also file suit, as in *Subsolutions, Inc. v. Doctor's Associates, Inc.* (1999), for example, a case that involved computerized cash registers that were prescribed for all Subway shops. A foreclosed cash register supplier was the plaintiff in that case.

[158] Section 1 holds that "[e]very contract, combination . . . , or conspiracy, in restraint of trade or commerce . . . is hereby declared to be illegal." 15 U.S.C. §1. In a tying case, the contract between the buyer and the seller may be deemed to be unreasonable if it restrains competition.

[159] For an extremely thorough treatment of antitrust tying, see Areeda (1991). For more compact treatments, see Blair and Kaserman (1978) and Hovenkamp (1999).

courts have been willing to infer the existence of market power from the franchisor's trademark, but this attitude may be changing since intellectual property does not confer *market* power.

Fourth, the tying contract must have anticompetitive effects or must injure the competitive process. In most Federal circuits, the franchisee would have to show *actual* foreclosure of rival suppliers of the tied product(s).

Fifth, the contract must involve a "not insubstantial" volume of commerce. Usually, this is a *de minimis* standard that can be met by showing that the dollar volume is not trivial; it does *not* require showing that a substantial market is involved.

A tying contract is unlawful *per se* when all five of these elements are present. The analysis involved is a far cry from the relatively simple matter of proving a *per se* illegal agreement to fix prices or allocate markets. In tying cases, there are thorny issues of defining markets, measuring market power, and assessing competitive impact. In private suits, there are also difficult problems in proving and calculating damages (if any).

6.3 Application to Franchise Tying Contracts

Franchisors often require their franchisees to purchase goods and services directly from them. In fact, traditional franchising is a distribution system whereby manufacturers engage dealers in selling their products to end customers under an exclusive dealing agreement. Of course, such systems involve the sale of products and services to the dealers. Business-format franchising arose from this tradition with the same goal of selling an end product to customers. But in this case, the end product, such as meals, haircuts, cleaning services, and so on, was largely produced locally rather than by the franchisor. Thus, franchisors evolved a system of royalty payments to compensate them for the use of the business format and the trade name when they had no product to sell to franchisees. Earlier on, however, some business-format franchisors tried a different formula: in addition to, or instead of, imposing sales-based royalty fees, they requested that the franchisee buy various inputs from them, inputs that franchisors sold to franchisees at a markup. In part, this strategy allowed franchisors to control the quality of the inputs used, but it was also a way for franchisors to extract fees from franchisees. Because business-format franchisors also sold the business format to their franchisees, and because the inputs that franchisors sold to their franchisees were separate from the business format itself, some of these input sales requirements were brought to the attention of the antitrust authorities. The result has been that franchising has been no stranger to antitrust suits involving tying contracts. These suits have played important roles in developing the standards regarding (1) the existence of two or more products, (2) proof of a conditional sale, and (3) proof of market power. In this section, we deal with the first two issues and introduce the third. Given its central role in a large body of recent cases, we then devote much more attention to the third issue in subsequent sections.

6.3.1 Proof of Separate Products

If the plaintiff franchisee cannot prove that there are at least two separate products, then his suit must fail because by definition tying cannot exist in that case. Ordinarily, the franchisee will argue that the franchise license is the tying product and something else that he or she might have to buy is the tied product. As we will see, whether this argument is valid depends upon the facts of the particular case.

Siegel v. Chicken Delight (1971). The *Chicken Delight* case involved a situation in which the franchisor charged neither a franchise fee nor a running royalty for the privilege of doing business as a Chicken Delight franchisee. In order to earn some profit from its franchise system, the franchisor did require that its franchisees buy a certain number of cookers and fryers as well as packaging supplies and mixes from Chicken Delight. The franchisees were precluded from buying these items at lower prices from Chicken Delight's rivals in the tied good markets. Siegel, who was one of the franchisees, complained that he was being overcharged on the tied goods and sued Chicken Delight. The court found that even though Chicken Delight had no separate charge for using its trademark, the trademark (or franchise license) served as the tying product while the cooking equipment and supplies were the tied products. In this situation, which involved business-format franchising, the trademark was deemed to be a separate product to which other distinct products could be tied.[160]

Principe v. McDonald's Corporation (1980). In a later case, however, the court looked more carefully at the business of franchising and found that the license was not always a distinct product. Frank Principe, a McDonald's franchisee, entered into two agreements with the McDonald's Corporation. Under the franchise license agreement, Principe was permitted

---

[160] Whether Siegel was actually injured is an interesting question. On the one hand, he was at least arguably overcharged for the cooking equipment and supplies. On the other hand, he paid no fees to Chicken Delight and, therefore, at least arguably, he was undercharged for the franchise license. On balance, was there injury?

to use McDonald's food preparation system and to sell food products under the McDonald's trademark. In return, Principe paid a $10,000 lump-sum license fee and a running royalty of 2.2 percent of his gross receipts. The second agreement was a store lease that permitted Principe to use the store to which the franchise pertained. In return, Principe agreed to pay 8 percent of his gross receipts as rent plus a non-negotiable, non-interest bearing security deposit of $15,000.[161] Since the two agreements were necessary to become a McDonald's franchisee, the store lease appeared to be tied to the franchise license, which is essentially what Principe argued.

The court observed that McDonald's is in the business of "developing and collecting royalties from limited menu fast food restaurants operated by independent business people." Development plans were carefully made and real estate specialists used economic and demographic data to find suitable locations for the new sites. The land was either bought or was secured under a long-term lease by McDonald's. Store design was dictated by the anticipated volume of business, lot size and shape, local zoning, and land elevation. Once it had built the store, McDonald's was ready to install the new franchisee.

The court noted that McDonald's does not simply license its franchisees to sell products under its "Golden Arches." Instead, it provides a complete method of doing business. The court explained that

> [McDonald's] takes people from all walks of life, sends them to its management school, and teaches them a variety of skills ranging from hamburger grilling to financial planning. It installs them in stores whose market has been researched and whose location has been selected by experts to maximize sales potential. It inspects every facet of every store several times a year and consults with each franchisee about his operation's strengths and weaknesses. Its regime pervades all facets of the business, from the design of the menu board to the amount of catsup on the hamburgers, nothing is left to chance. This pervasive franchisor supervision and control benefits the franchisee in turn. His business is identified with a network of stores whose very uniformity and predictability attracts customers. In short, the modern franchisee pays not only for the right to use a trademark but for the right to become a part of a system whose business

---

[161] The security deposit provided McDonald's with an interest-free loan for the life of the franchise agreement. In an economic sense, the cost to the franchisee is the difference between the value of the deposit when it was made and the value when it would be returned:

$$C = \$15{,}000 - \$15{,}000/(1 + r)^t$$

where r is the discount rate and t is the life of the agreement. This sum should be added to the lump-sum franchise fee to obtain the true initial cost.

methods virtually guarantee his success. It is often unrealistic to view a franchise agreement as little more than a trademark license.

Given the realities of modern franchising, we think the proper inquiry is not whether the allegedly tied products are associated in the public mind with the franchisor's trademark, but whether they are integral components of the business method being franchised. Where the challenged aggregation is an essential ingredient of the franchised system's formula for success, there is but a single product and no tie in exists as a matter of law.[162]

Applying this reasoning to the *Principe* facts, the court ruled that McDonald's lease was not separable from the McDonald's franchise system. The restaurant location and design was an integral part of McDonald's success. As a result, there was a single product and, therefore, tying could not exist.

Krehl v. Baskin-Robbins Ice Cream Company (1982). Both *Chicken Delight* and *Principe* dealt with pure business-format franchise systems. In contrast, *Krehl* involved a product distribution franchise system.[163] The franchisee alleged that Baskin-Robbins illegally tied its ice cream to the Baskin-Robbins trademark. The court pointed out that in a distribution franchise system, the trademark "serves merely as a representation of the end product marketed by the system." Thus, the trademark provides information to the consumer regarding the quality and source of the product that reduces search costs. Because the source of the product can be identified, the franchisor has an incentive to preserve quality.[164] Accordingly, "the franchised outlets serve merely as conduits through which the trademarked goods of the franchisor flow to the ultimate consumer." The court found that the Baskin-Robbins ice cream was not separable from the trademark and, therefore, there was no tying arrangement – illegal or otherwise. This, of course, is an economically sensible result. When consumers buy ice cream at a Baskin-Robbins ice cream store, they do not expect to get Breyer's ice cream. They quite reasonably expect to get Baskin-Robbins ice cream. If franchisees were free to sell other brands under the Baskin-Robbins trademark, consumers would be deceived.

---

[162] It is clear from the court's description that it is quite useful to think of franchising as vertical integration by contract. McDonald's control over the operation is apparent and not unlike the control exercised by a vertically integrated firm.

[163] Ice cream franchises are among those in the grey area between traditional and business-format franchising that we alluded to when we defined both types and noted that the distinction is more a matter of degree than anything else. Baskin-Robbins sells its ice cream to its franchisees – on which it may or may not charge a markup – but also provides a turn-key operation like business-format franchisors do, and charges a franchise fee and sales-based royalties to its franchisees.

[164] See, for example, Klein and Leffler (1981).

Moreover, as consumers became aware of the fact that the trademark no longer identified the source of the product being purchased, they would have to incur search costs to identify the source of various stores' ice cream and guarantee that they get the type that they want. Hence, the trademark would lose its informational value and its economic purpose.

In some of the recent franchise tying suits, the plaintiff franchisees do not dispute having to purchase proprietary ingredients, such as Little Caesar's pizza dough, or other supplies that would ordinarily be considered integral to the success of the franchise system. Instead, they complain that relatively generic supplies, such as "logoed" paper products and nonproprietary ingredients, such as pepperoni, are tied to the franchise license as per the *Chicken Delight* case. In these cases, the "system argument" offered in *Principe* is not likely to be persuasive and, therefore, the courts will reasonably conclude that the separate products condition has been satisfied. This is consistent with positions taken with respect to traditional franchising, where requirements that franchisees purchase products other than the main manufactured product of the franchisor have also been challenged and ultimately abandoned by franchisors. Specifically, the practice of requiring that gasoline dealers purchase tires, batteries, and accessories through their franchisor (the oil refiner to which they were affiliated), or from designated suppliers under sales commission plans that allowed refiners to profit from these sales, was challenged by the FTC in the 1960s. Ultimately, such sales commission plans were abandoned as a result of these challenges.[165] Thus, the legal constraints on tying apply to traditional franchisors if they try to control the sales of products other than the one that the franchise relates to directly.

6.3.2 Proof of Conditional Sales

In some instances, franchise agreements are *explicitly* conditioned on the franchisee's buying some specific good(s). In many others, the conditional sale is *implicit* in the sense that the actual implementation of the franchise contract results in de facto tying. Either situation can result in an antitrust suit by unhappy franchisees.

Explicit Conditioning. A recent example of explicit conditioning is provided by *Wilson v. Mobil Oil Corporation.* In *Wilson,* the plaintiffs were franchisees of the SpeeDee Oil Change Systems, which provided quick car-care services, such as oil changes. The franchise agreement explicitly required the franchisees to purchase automotive products, such as engine oil and

---

[165] See, e.g., Marvel (1995) for more details on this.

lubricants, as well as financial services from Mobil. One could not be in compliance with the franchise agreement if one did not purchase Mobil products. Thus, the conditioning in this franchise agreement was explicit and, therefore, quite easy to prove in court.[166]

Implicit Conditioning. In many franchise agreements, the franchisee is required to use inputs that meet certain specifications. In order to be sure that they do, the franchisor will supply these inputs – sometimes at inflated prices. Typically, the franchise agreement permits the franchisee to buy these inputs elsewhere provided that the inputs are approved by the franchisor as conforming to its standards and specifications.[167] If the franchisor provides alternative suppliers with incomplete specifications to hinder approval or simply refuses to approve an alternate supplier without good cause, the franchisee will have to purchase those inputs from the franchisor. In such instances, there will be an implicit conditioning in the franchise agreement. This, of course, will be much more difficult to prove in court than explicit conditioning. For example, a competent meat supplier may offer a perfectly good chicken breast for a chicken breast sandwich, but the franchisor may still contend that it does not conform to the franchisor's specifications. Whether it does or not is not subject to *a priori* reasoning.

6.3.3 Proving Market Power in the Tying Good[168]

If a seller conditions the sale of "A" on the purchase of "B," but lacks market power in "A," the tying arrangement will not be illegal. Absent market power in "A," buyers will only agree to the tie if it confers benefits to them, that is buyers cannot be coerced. Moreover, the seller's rivals (in the market for "A") can presumably offer the same set of options and, therefore, there can be no anticompetitive foreclosure. Proving market power in the tying good, therefore, is a crucial element of a tying suit. Clearly, to speak of market power presupposes a market definition. After defining the relevant markets for the tying and the tied goods, one can proceed to an evaluation of market power.

---

[166] The McDonald's franchise agreement at issue in *Principe* was also explicit as prospective franchisees had to enter into two agreements. Similarly, all product distribution agreements are explicit; see, e.g., *Krehl*.

[167] There are many recent examples; see, e.g., *Queen City Pizza, Inc. v. Domino's Pizza, Inc.* (1996), and *Little Caesar Enterprises, Inc. v. Smith* (1995).

[168] An excellent analysis of this issue is provided by Silberman (1996). Ordinarily, economists use "market power" and "monopoly power" to refer to the ability of a firm to raise price above the competitive level and thereby earn higher profits. See also Krattenmaker, Lande, and Salop (1987).

In the past, there was a tendency to infer the existence of market power from the existence of intellectual property: patents, copyrights, and trademarks. But there is an increasing recognition that the *legal* monopoly conferred by a patent, say, does not mean that there is an *economic* monopoly. For one thing, just because one can obtain a patent, copyright, or trademark is no guarantee that there will be a demand for the product or process. More importantly, in the franchise context, much of the intellectual property resides in trademarks and trade names. McDonald's, Burger King, Wendy's, and Hardee's may all have trademarks as well as somewhat differentiated product offerings, but they scarcely can be said to have monopoly power in fast-food franchise licenses. Yet, market power in that market is what would be required to support a tying claim.

In the case of firms that face competition from numerous rivals, one may modify the measure of monopoly power first proposed by Lerner (1934). As Landes and Posner (1981) have shown, a useful measure is

$$\lambda = \frac{s}{\eta + \varepsilon(1 - s)}$$

where λ measures the firm's power to deviate from the competitive solution, s is the firm's market share, η is the elasticity of demand, and ε is the supply elasticity of the rival firms. The actual measurement of λ is an empirical matter, but no franchise system has an overwhelming share of all franchise opportunities and, thus, the value of λ would tend to be low. Moreover, if one franchisor restricted the number of franchise licenses that it provided, other franchisors could readily expand the numbers that they offer. In other words, the supply elasticity would seem to be quite large, which would also tend to make λ small.

The more recent spate of franchise tying suits can be traced to a notion of market definition spawned by the Supreme Court decision in *Kodak*. To understand this new set of cases, it is useful to better understand the *Kodak* decision, to which we now turn.

6.4 The *Kodak* Decision and Its Progeny

The Eastman Kodak Company (Kodak) is involved in the sale and servicing of copiers and micrographic equipment to end users, a market where a number of other producers also operate. For years, Kodak sold its proprietary repair parts to independent service organizations (ISOs) so they could provide maintenance and repair services to the owners of Kodak copiers and micrographic equipment. When Kodak changed its policy and refused to sell its repair parts to the ISOs, Kodak became the only source of maintenance and repair services to its end customers. Image Technical Service and seventeen other ISOs sued Kodak alleging that it had illegally tied its service to its repair parts.[169] Thus, the *Kodak* case involved the tie of one aftermarket product to another. This raised an interesting question regarding the relevant market definition for antitrust purposes. Kodak argued that since it sold its equipment in competition with other manufacturers, it could not have appreciable economic power in the (tying good) aftermarket for repair parts. In essence, Kodak argued that the relevant product market for antitrust analysis is the primary market for photocopying and micrographic equipment, rather than the aftermarket for repair parts. Kodak argued that when a buyer is choosing among alternative copiers, he or she recognizes that buying a durable good involves a financial commitment to paying for future maintenance and repair in addition to the initial price of the copier. The Supreme Court, however, rejected Kodak's reasoning and ruled that the relevant market for determining market power is based on "the choices available to Kodak equipment owners." Accordingly, it held that the relevant market for determining market power was the market for replacement parts for Kodak equipment. Of course, the more narrowly the market is defined, the greater the market share a firm will have and the stronger the inference of market power. In this case, since the repair parts were proprietary, Kodak was found to have a market share of virtually 100 percent. Despite this large market share, however, Kodak maintained that it could not have any real economic power in the market for repair parts since it did not have market power in the primary equipment market. Specifically, Kodak argued that charging supra-competitive prices in the aftermarket would result in a loss of customers in the primary equipment market. But the Supreme Court was not persuaded and concluded that since repair parts for Kodak equipment are unique (i.e., neither IBM repair parts nor Xerox repair parts will fit a Kodak copier), the owners of Kodak copiers are "locked in" to Kodak if they want to keep their copiers operational. The only alternative is to switch to another brand of copier. But the Supreme Court reasoned that the high costs associated with switching prevented this option from being economically viable and provided Kodak with the power to exploit the locked-in owners.[170]

---

[169] *Eastman Kodak Company v. Image Technical Service* (1992a, 1992b).
[170] For an analysis of the reasons for vertical restraints by durable goods producers, see Blair and Herndon (1996). It should also be noted that switching to an IBM copier merely locks one in to a different repair parts supplier. As such, it does not solve the customer's problem.

6.5 Franchise Tying Cases After *Kodak*

The concept of being locked in to a particular manufacturer and thereby subject to aftermarket exploitation is the most significant of the Court's findings in *Kodak*. This is the foundation of its determination that the market power for Kodak repair parts – a single manufacturer's brand – was sufficiently great to restrain competition in the tied product market for service. Consequently, *Kodak* presented a new angle from which to allege an illegal tying arrangement. Plaintiffs may craft arguments that they are powerless, locked-in consumers, subject to all sorts of onerous demands by their supplier. When the relevant market is confined to a particular firm's product or service, that firm will appear to have market power in that "market." In the recent franchise tying cases, the franchisees all employed the lock-in argument to support their claims of illegal tying. Interestingly, these arguments have generally been unsuccessful.

The recent franchise tying cases have the following common characteristics:

1. All cases involve business-format franchises. As noted above, the *Krehl* decision has made it difficult for distribution franchisees to prevail on tying claims and *Kodak* did not change that. Consequently, it is not surprising that the post-*Kodak* suits have been filed by business format franchisees.
2. Plaintiffs define the relevant tying product market narrowly, typically asserting that it is restricted to the market for the defendant's franchise.[171]
3. Plaintiffs correspondingly offer a narrow definition of the tied product market, alleging that it is the market for supplies to a particular franchise system, rather than supplies in general. For example, in *Collins v. International Dairy Queen*, franchisees alleged that International Dairy Queen (IDQ) inhibited competition in the market for "food products and supplies that are sold to Dairy Queen franchises." Thus, the Dairy Queen franchisees would allege that the tied product market is hamburger patties sold to Dairy Queen franchisees, rather than hamburger patties supplied to fast-food restaurants or, more generally, the wholesale market for hamburger patties.

---

[171] *Collins v. International Dairy Queen* (1996) is an exception. The Dairy Queen franchisees apparently offered a market definition restricted to the Dairy Queen franchise system, but recognizing the narrowness of this market definition, also offered soft-serve ice cream as a relevant product market in which Dairy Queen had over a 90-percent market share. It is interesting to note that soft-serve ice cream specifically was proposed, rather than all ice cream (including both hard pack and soft-serve), or ice cream and frozen yogurt, or all franchise opportunities for that matter.

4. The cases focus on the franchisor's refusal to approve or allow alternate sources of supply. In *Wilson v. Mobil Oil Corporation*, this refusal was explicitly specified in the franchise agreement. In the other cases, the plaintiffs alleged that the franchisor had imposed a more restrictive policy of approving alternate suppliers than was contemplated in the franchise agreements.[172]
5. In each case, the franchisor has a financial interest in the sales of the tied products. Franchisors are more likely to escape antitrust condemnation when the franchisor does not have a financial interest in the sales of the tied product.[173]

Before proceeding to the economic analysis of franchise tying suits since *Kodak*, we summarize the central claims in recent cases to clarify how they appeal to the *Kodak* logic. This summary is divided into explicit and implicit tying arrangements.

6.5.1 Contractually Explicit Tying after *Kodak*

Wilson appears to be a classic case of tying. In *Wilson*, the plaintiffs were franchisees of SpeeDee Oil Change Systems, Inc. The franchisees, who provide quick car-care services such as oil changes and minor engine tune-ups, alleged that SpeeDee and Mobil Oil Corporation engaged in illegal tying by requiring that franchisees purchase automotive products and financial services from Mobil in order to acquire or retain a SpeeDee franchise license. SpeeDee received $650,000 from Mobil as part of a 15-year agreement that allowed Mobil to become the exclusive supplier of automotive products for the SpeeDee franchise system, and the franchisees were allegedly required to purchase these automotive products from Mobil at "undisclosed prices to be set by Mobil without negotiation." The plaintiffs identified the tying product market as the SpeeDee franchise and associated trade and service marks.[174] The plaintiffs then defined the tied product market as the market for Mobil lubricants and financial services. The franchisees asserted that the

---

[172] This raises the question as to why the appropriate complaint is not a breach of contract.
[173] See *Kentucky Fried Chicken Corporation v. Diversified Packaging Corporation* (1977).
[174] The court initially stated that "Plaintiffs define the relevant product market as the SpeeDee trademarks, trade names and copyrights, or alternatively, the market for providing quick automotive oil change, goods and services." The plaintiff's subsequent allegations, defendant's arguments, and the court's decision, however, are all based on a product market definition restricted to the SpeeDee franchise system and not the broader market for quick car-care services.

Mobil products that they were forced to purchase were more expensive and inferior to those that they would have preferred to purchase, thereby placing them at a competitive disadvantage. Notably, they did not explain how this would benefit the franchisor. The franchisees relied heavily upon *Kodak* to support their allegations, charging that (1) single-brand market power is applicable since the franchise agreement creates an "aftermarket" for the requisite automotive products and financial services; and (2) they are "locked into" the franchise system as a result of high "switching costs" due to a significant capital investment, penalty payments to Mobil and SpeeDee, and a non-compete covenant in their franchise agreement that prevents them from operating a similar business within a specified period of time and geographic region.[175] In its 1996 decision, the court refused to follow the *Queen City* approach and dismiss the case. However, in 1997, following discovery, the court granted defendants' motion for summary judgment and endorsed the views of the majority in *Queen City* (see below).

6.5.2 Implicit Tying Arrangements after *Kodak*

The rest of the post-*Kodak* franchise tying cases involve *de facto* tying that stems from the franchisor's alleged refusal to approve alternative sources of supply. To get a flavor of these complaints, we summarize the salient facts of some typical suits.

Queen City Pizza, Inc. v. Domino's Pizza, Inc. (1996, 1997). Domino's Pizza, Inc. (DPI) required that its franchisees buy the necessary ingredients and supplies from DPI or from a DPI-approved supplier. Consequently, Domino's franchisees purchased approximately 90 percent of their ingredients and supplies from DPI. Further, DPI typically did not produce these goods; rather, it purchased them from third parties and resold them to its franchisees.

Queen City Pizza and ten other franchisees along with the International Franchise Advisory Council filed suit against DPI, alleging various antitrust violations, including two tying claims. First, they alleged that DPI illegally tied ingredients and supplies to the purchase of fresh pizza dough. Second, they alleged that DPI illegally tied ingredients and supplies to the franchise license itself. Integral to these complaints were the allegations that (1) DPI unreasonably withheld its approval of alternative sources of supply and (2) DPI provided incomplete product specifications, thereby eliminating

---

[175] We discuss such covenants further in Chapter 10.

viable competitive sources of supplies to the Domino's franchise system. The net effect was that most of the necessary ingredients and supplies had to be purchased from DPI.

The *Queen City* litigation was notable in many respects. It is the only franchise tying case that has received substantive appellate court consideration in light of *Kodak*. Interestingly, the court concluded that *Kodak* is not applicable in the context of franchise tying suits, and the case ultimately was resolved in favor of the franchisor. In doing so, however, it raised additional questions and concerns about the appropriate analysis of franchise tying claims. We address these questions in the next section.

Collins v. International Dairy Queen (1996, 1997). International Dairy Queen (IDQ) purchased products that it approved and then resold to its franchisees directly or through independent distributors or warehouses that were designated as approved sources of supplies. Thus, many of the supplies purchased by Dairy Queen franchisees were, in effect, supplied by IDQ itself. But IDQ's franchise agreements allowed franchisees to purchase these supplies from alternate sources as long as they were approved by IDQ as being in conformity with certain standards and specifications. The franchisees alleged that IDQ violated the spirit of this agreement by providing incomplete specifications, altering specifications without good cause, and refusing to approve or unreasonably delaying approval of alternate sources of supply, thereby forcing the franchisees to purchase virtually all of their supplies from those distributors and warehouses designated by IDQ. The franchisees thus asserted that IDQ implicitly and illegally tied the purchase of supplies to the Dairy Queen franchise license. The franchisees restricted the relevant tying product market to the market for soft-serve ice cream franchises and the relevant tied product market to food products and supplies sold to Dairy Queen franchisees. The court in this case declined to follow district court's ruling in *Queen City*. The case subsequently settled.[176]

Little Caesar Enterprises v. Smith (1998). The franchisees of Little Caesar's Enterprises (LCE) alleged that LCE illegally tied non-proprietary supplies to

---

[176] In an order signed March 13, 2000, the U.S. District Court Senior Judge Wilbur D. Owens Jr. said the proposed settlement seemed reasonable. The agreement requires International Dairy Queen to pay $30 million in advertising, $250,000 to each of the suit's five original Central Georgia plaintiffs, and $11.3 million in legal fees. Defendants also must make concessions on supply and other franchise issues. Interestingly, in its 2000 decision on the matter of *Maris Distributing Company v. Anheuser-Busch, Inc.*, in the same federal circuit as *Dairy Queen*, the court went out of its way to state "we reject [*Dairy Queen*] in favor of what we consider to be the more persuasive rationale of *Queen City* and its progeny."

its franchise license.[177] It accomplished this by requiring that its franchisees buy all of their "logoed" paper products from a wholly owned subsidiary of LCE. Since there are economies of "one-stop shopping," that is dealing with a single outside supplier, the franchisees bought all of their non-proprietary supplies from LCE's subsidiary as well. LCE's market power was based on its intellectual property – copyrights, trademark, service name, and trade name. LCE allegedly rejected alternate sources of supply, which meant that the franchisees would buy the "non-logoed" supplies as well as the "logoed" supplies from the franchisor.

The franchisees alleged market power in two respects. First, they alleged that LCE had market power in LCE franchise licenses. They alleged that LCE also had market power over its logoed products and used it to foreclose rival suppliers of these paper products. Additionally, they claimed that this practice had the practical effect of tying non-logoed supplies as well. Since the LCE subsidiary was the only distributor from which the franchisees could obtain logoed products, including paper products and packaged condiments, the franchisees argued that this had the twofold effect of excluding other distributors from competing for sales of logoed products as well as making it economically unattractive to purchase non-logoed supplies from other distributors due to economies from "one-stop shopping." This argument appeals to an aftermarket type of tying claim. Based on its market power over its franchise licenses, LCE has market power over the "aftermarket" sales of logoed products to its franchisee and it effectively uses that power to (economically) compel franchisees to purchase other non-logoed supplies from it as well.

In the end, the court decided that franchisees could not use a *Kodak* type of lock-in argument because the risk of such a tie was known or predictable when they signed their franchise agreement. The court indicated that a *Kodak* type of analysis might have been appropriate on the exclusion of competing suppliers' argument but that there was no evidence that the franchisor had used its power over logoed supplies to exclude other distributors. The court thus granted summary judgment for the franchisor.

6.6 Identifying Market Power After *Kodak*

As noted above, courts are likely to find that the license to operate a business format franchise and the other inputs required to run the business are

---

[177] The plaintiffs did not dispute LCE's right to distribute its "Pan! Pan!" pizza dough mix or its secret spice mix.

separate products. The "system" argument, which was successful in *Principe*, will not be persuasive in cases concerning generic supplies that are not likely to be considered integral in and of themselves to the success of the franchise system. As a result, the fate of the franchisor lies primarily in the determination of market power in the tying product market. Indeed, this issue has been the major point of contention in all these cases. Assessing market power, in turn, hinges largely on the definition of the relevant product market. Naturally, the narrower the market definition, the greater the firm's market share will be and, therefore, the more likely is the inference of market power.[178] When evaluating market power for a pizza franchisor, for example, there are at least four possible market definitions: (1) all franchise opportunities, (2) the franchise segment, for example, fast-food, (3) all pizza franchises, and (4) a particular franchise system such as Domino's. Since there are thousands of franchise opportunities, no one has market power in the broadest market definition. At the other extreme, every franchisor controls all of its licenses. Applying *Kodak* to franchise tying cases, one would argue that the committed franchisee is locked in by high switching costs and is disadvantaged by information costs.

6.6.1 Locus of Competition: Pre-Contract v. Post-Contract

Following *Kodak*, franchisees typically adopt a post-contractual perspective, thereby asserting a very narrow market definition limited to the franchisor's own system. Franchisees appeal to *Kodak*'s focus on "the choices available to Kodak equipment owners." For example, in *Queen City*, the franchisees alleged that the relevant market for determining market power was Domino's Pizza franchises since "[o]nly Domino's-approved products may be used by Domino's franchisees without violating . . . Domino's standard franchise agreement." Naturally, DPI will have market power in a market so defined given that no one else can issue a Domino's franchise license.

Franchisors argue that a broader market definition is appropriate by correctly emphasizing that at the pre-contractual stage the potential franchisees have a substantial number of franchise opportunities from which to choose. The district and appellate courts in *Queen City* apparently understood the pre-contract versus post-contract distinction and thus observed that DPI had no market power in selling franchise licenses (the tying good): "The

---

[178] Although it has been pointed out that market share is not the sole determinant of market power, the judiciary continues to be persuaded by such evidence. See, e.g., Landes and Posner (1981).

franchise transaction between Domino's Pizza, Inc. and plaintiffs was subjected to competition at the pre-contract stage." Indeed, prior to signing a franchise contract, a franchisee has literally thousands of options. Information on opportunities is readily available. For example, the 2001 *Bond's Franchise Guide* provides detailed information on more than 1,000 franchise systems and lists yet another 1,000 or so. These franchisors must compete with one another for franchisees. While it is true that a DPI franchisee selling pizza does not compete for customers with a SpeeDee franchisee selling oil changes, the DPI and SpeeDee franchisors compete with one another in the sale of franchise licenses. Consequently, a single franchisor has no appreciable market power in the market for franchise licenses to exploit through a tying arrangement.

One might make a case, however, that franchisors only compete with other franchisors in the same business sector for franchisees. The few studies that have examined the decision process of prospective franchisees have found that the majority of franchisees – 63 percent in Bradach and Kaufmann (1988) and 75 percent in Kaufmann and Stanworth (1995) – expected they would choose a business sector first and then decide whether they should buy a franchise or start an independent business. Hence, for the majority of franchisees, it seems that only those franchises within the same sector are potential substitutes for one another. But even then, the franchisees have numerous choices within any segment. For example, in Bond (2002) there are fifteen detailed listings in the tune-up and oil change segment of the automotive products and services sector that SpeeDee belongs to, and thirty in the pizza segment. If one considers the firms listed but not profiled in *Bond*, or includes chains involved in other types of automotive services or of fast-food services, respectively, the number of options grows much higher. Finally, the figures above also imply that between 25 to 37 percent of franchisees are willing to consider different franchise opportunities from different business sectors altogether.[179]

When deciding on which franchise system to join from among these sets of options, the prospective franchisees will be aware of their obligations under the contracts offered after reviewing the franchising agreements. Presumably, those obligations will play a role in determining their investment decisions. From a pre-contract perspective, the relevant product market in *Queen City* cannot reasonably be defined more narrowly than pizza franchises. But it

---

[179] In fact, proprietary research by a large U.S. franchisor cited in Kaufmann and Stanworth (1995) revealed that 75 percent of that chain's franchisees had considered another category of franchise in the process of deciding which chain to join.

would not be unreasonable to argue for the broader market definition of all fast-food franchises, if not all franchise opportunities.[180]

6.6.2 Cost Comparisons

In each period, the franchisee's net operating revenue (π) can be expressed as

$$\pi = (1-r)PQ - \sum_{j=1}^{n} w_i x_i$$

where P is the franchisee's output price, Q is the quantity of output (which for simplicity we assume is just one product), r is the sales-based royalty, x_i represents the quantity of input i, and w_i denotes the price of input i. These inputs, of course, include ingredients, paper products with logos, and the like. Assuming that the w_i's are competitive prices, π then represents the maximum profit that the franchise location will generate per period. The franchisor wants all or at least a big part of this profit – whether and how the profit is obtained is not an issue that would normally fall within the scope of antitrust.

In comparing franchise opportunities, potential franchisees will compare the net present values (NPV) of investments in the various franchise systems:

$$NPV = \left(\sum_{t=1}^{T} \pi_t /(1+\delta)^t \right) - F$$

where F stands for the initial franchise fee and/or specific investments, π_t represents the net operating revenue in each period, T is the length of the franchise contract, and δ is the discount rate. Naturally, π_t is influenced by the costs incurred by the franchisee, including all periodic royalty payments to the franchisor. To the extent that the franchisee must also buy equipment, supplies, and ingredients from the franchisor at supracompetitive prices, initial investments or operating costs will be higher than they would be otherwise. This will reduce the net revenues and make that franchise opportunity less attractive, which will be reflected in a lower franchise fee. That is, *ceteris*

---

[180] A telephone survey of 500 franchisees and 200 potential franchisees conducted by a private survey firm for the FTC in 1984 indicates that 58 percent of franchisees considered other opportunities seriously enough to meet in person with other franchisors before they chose to invest in their franchise. Franchisees who comparison shopped considered four other opportunities on average. See Beales and Muris (1995) for more details.

paribus, those franchise systems that employ tying arrangements as part of the franchise agreement will have lower initial franchise fees since prospective franchisees will factor the potential for post-contractual exploitation on the part of the franchisor into their cost comparisons. This process of cost analysis is referred to as "life-cycle costing."[181]

There is no doubt that various business uncertainties make precise cost calculations problematic. For example, a potential franchisee cannot accurately forecast future prices of all necessary inputs, it cannot accurately forecast demand for its output, it cannot know the results of menu changes, and it cannot know in advance about competition from new entrants. But these sorts of uncertainties plague all business decisions. At least in a subjective sense, probabilities of various outcomes can be assigned and expectations formed. If one franchise contract subjects a franchisee to a higher risk of exploitation in aftermarkets than another contract, this should be factored into the franchisee's evaluation of profit potential for the two systems and thus into the final decision as to which franchise contract best suits him.

6.6.3 The Lock-In Argument

Kodak argued that it could not charge supracompetitive prices in the aftermarket because such pricing behavior would lead to lost sales in the competitive primary equipment market. But the Supreme Court rejected this rationale as it was persuaded by the plaintiffs that Kodak copier owners were effectively "locked-in" to Kodak repair parts and services and, therefore, subject to aftermarket exploitation. Franchisees have tried to adopt the same notion of lock in.

Queen City Pizza, Inc., for example, relied upon the *Kodak* court's reasoning in suing DPI, asserting that it was locked in to the franchisor's system. That is, it did not allege that DPI had *pre-contractual* power in the market for fast-food franchise licenses. Instead, it argued that DPI employed *post-contractual* power to coerce its franchisees into purchasing ingredients and supplies from DPI. In essence, the argument is that franchisees sign a franchise agreement in reliance on contractual promises that they can buy ingredients and supplies from approved sources. DPI's refusal to approve competitive sources of supply changes the rules of the game. The substantial time and money that each franchisee has invested in the franchise means that each will suffer a considerable loss if the franchise agreement is terminated. Thus, DPI has

---

[181] See Williams (1996) and Brickley (2001) for more details on this in the context of franchise contracts.

post-contractual power to coerce its franchisees to purchase ingredients and supplies from it. This power, however, derives from the franchise agreement itself and is not the sort of market power that raises antitrust concerns. Thus, while the dispute between DPI and its franchisees may well have involved legitimate claims of contract breach, it should not be confused with an antitrust concern. The franchisor's "power" flows from the terms of the contract. It is not a manifestation of *market* power, which is the proper concern of the antitrust laws.

The *Queen City* district court recognized this issue explicitly: "[t]he economic power DPI possesses results not from the unique nature of the product or from its market share in the fast food franchise business, but from the franchise agreement." The Third Circuit affirmed the lower court's reasoning and further noted: "If Domino's Pizza, Inc. acted unreasonably when, under the franchise agreement, it restricted plaintiffs' ability to purchase supplies from other sources, plaintiffs' remedy, if any, is in contract, not under the antitrust laws." In our view, this is precisely correct.

Recognizing that DPI's actions did not reflect true economic power, yet procedurally unable to ignore the *Kodak* decision, the district and appellate courts in *Queen City* distinguished *Kodak* by arguing that the service market for Kodak equipment arose out of the unique nature of the Kodak equipment whereas the sale of ingredients and supplies to the DPI franchisees arose from "a valid and binding franchise agreement." This reasoning, however, is not persuasive. Just as a Kodak equipment owner needs repair parts and service on a continuing basis over the life of the Kodak copier, a DPI franchisee needs ingredients and supplies on a continuing basis over the life of the franchise agreement.

The Supreme Court's finding that Kodak customers were locked in to Kodak repair parts and services hinged largely on its analysis of switching and information costs incurred by Kodak equipment owners. These elements have similarly played a major role in recent franchise tying suits.

Switching Costs. In *Kodak*, the equipment owners were "locked-in" as captive customers by the high costs of switching to a different brand of copier. The plaintiffs in *Wilson* asserted that franchisees face even greater switching costs than Kodak equipment owners due to the significant capital investments that are necessary to obtain a franchise license. At first glance, the higher initial investment associated with a franchise license would seem to indicate that a franchisee is every bit as locked in to the franchise as a Kodak copier owner is to Kodak repair parts. If so, there is no economically meaningful distinction between the two situations. But there is a meaningful difference between copiers and franchises.

Although it is true that the franchisees have a larger investment than copier owners, it is also true that franchisees have a revenue-generating asset that has significant resale value. Kodak equipment owners, however, had invested in a depreciating durable good with rapidly declining resale value.[182] Thus, while switching costs may have effectively locked-in the owners of Kodak copiers, switching costs may not present a similar problem for franchisees: franchisees can sell their franchise if they find that it does not live up to their expectations. Further, in contrast to a Kodak copier that depreciates rapidly, a franchise may, in fact, appreciate considerably. Franchisees may well be unhappy that their profits are lower than they would be if they were permitted to buy ingredients wherever they choose, and/or that they cannot sell their franchise at as high a price as they could obtain were it not for these restrictions on sources of supply, but that does not mean that they are earning no profits.[183] Importantly, that franchisee profits are not as high as they could be in the absence of a tying contract does not by itself implicate anticompetitive injury.

Information Costs. The Supreme Court was persuaded by the plaintiffs' argument in *Kodak* that information costs prevent buyers from effectively performing life-cycle cost calculations.[184] Similarly, plaintiffs in recent franchise tying cases claim to fall victim to information asymmetries. It is difficult to be swayed by such arguments, however, in an industry that has extensive disclosure requirements that should reduce asymmetric information. Specifically, since 1979, Federal Trade Commission Rule 436 has required the disclosure of information to prospective franchisees, including requisite supplies that must be purchased and whether they must be purchased from particular suppliers. Furthermore, many states have added their own disclosure requirements with the prospective franchisees' interests in mind. Consequently, most franchise systems now have some type of UFOC that provides information regarding expected costs for requisite supplies. In addition, existing franchisees serve as valuable and accessible sources of information to prospective franchisees. Indeed, prospective franchisees are encouraged by trade publications,

---

[182] Akerlof (1970) explains why market prices of used durables tend to be low. When durables are resold, some of them are better than average and some are worse. Sellers know the difference, but buyers do not. As a result, buyers rely on the average quality. This leads sellers to withhold those durable goods that are better than average, which causes the average quality of those on the market to fall further and thus leads to an even lower market price. Asymmetric information about product quality between buyers and sellers is the root of this problem.

[183] See Kaufmann and Lafontaine (1994) for an analysis of the profitability of a McDonald's franchise.

[184] See Blair and Herndon (1996) for a technical analysis of life-cycle pricing and a critique of *Kodak*.

attorneys, consultants, and franchisors themselves to contact existing franchisees of various systems before investing in any particular franchise opportunity.

Despite the prevalence of such information, Grimes (1996) argues that franchisors may have information advantages that allow them to engage in "pre-contract opportunism." That is, the franchisors are able to dupe would-be franchisees into making poor investment decisions. But he concedes that this is more likely to occur in newer, high-risk systems rather than for well-established franchise systems, such as McDonald's. This is because a large amount of information is readily available on such systems and they have valuable reputations at stake that make it expensive for them to engage in such deceptive practices. Interestingly, however, recent franchise tying cases concern well-established and relatively low-risk systems. This suggests that it may be the franchisees, not the franchisors, who are behaving opportunistically in these cases.

In explicit tying cases, such as *Wilson*, the potential franchisees know that post-contractual exploitation is possible because the obligation to buy the supplies is explicit even though the prices are not guaranteed. Indeed, asserting that *Kodak* was inapplicable, the defendants in *Wilson* noted that the franchisees were aware of the obligation to buy from Mobil prior to signing their franchise agreements. The court, however, stated that the facts of the case were not clear in indicating to what extent franchisees did indeed know about the arrangement and, moreover, that "it is not self-evident . . . that before-the-fact disclosure of the tie-in means in all cases that information costs are not so high as to preclude accurate life-cycle pricing. . . . It may well be that disclosure that a tie-in exists does not allow accurate life-cycle pricing of the long-term franchise agreement and the purchase of ten-years' worth of tied products, equipment, and financial services."

To the extent that an explicit tie creates uncertainty for the franchisee, it makes the franchise opportunity less attractive. This greater uncertainty will be reflected in a lower initial franchise fee as a risk-averse franchisee's willingness to pay will be reduced. It is clear that eliminating the tied sales of equipment and supplies would raise the periodic net operating revenues. Competition among potential franchisees for the opportunity to own this business, however, and/or the desire of the franchisor to capture the outlet profits to the same extent as before, would then lead to an increase in the initial franchise fee or in the periodic fees so that the net present value of joining the chain would be unaltered in the end. Note that those franchisees already "locked in," however, who agreed to pay the earlier set of fees under the presumption that they would pay relatively high prices for the inputs provided by the franchisor, stand to benefit if they can get these purchase requirements eliminated from their set of contractual obligations.

In the case of an implicit tie, the franchisor allegedly misleads the franchisee by promising to approve alternative sources of supply, but never doing so. In essence, the franchisee is led to believe that competition for sales of equipment and supplies will protect him from post-contractual exploitation, but that competition never materializes because the franchisor reneges on his promise.

There are two points to make here. First, while this is a breach of contract, it is not monopolization in the antitrust sense. A promise was made, but not kept. If there are damages, they are contract damages rather than antitrust damages. Second, this strategy of reneging on contractual obligations makes little sense. As potential franchisees become aware of the fact that the contractual guarantees are not guarantees at all, they must assume that they will be obligated to purchase all equipment and supplies from the franchisor. Thus, the implicit tie becomes an explicit tie.

6.7 Post-Contractual Opportunism

Whether the tie is explicit or implicit in nature, all of the recent franchise tying allegations essentially involve concerns of post-contractual opportunism by the franchisor. Basically, recent franchisee allegations boil down to the complaint that they are being overcharged for requisite ingredients and supplies. This overcharge must be the underlying source of the franchisees' complaint, for otherwise they would suffer no injury. It is important to emphasize that the alleged monopoly power that the franchisor has is *ex post* since the franchisee is presumably locked in to purchasing requisite supplies for the franchise operation. *Ex ante*, of course, the franchisor has no market power since it is competing with hundreds of other franchisors for the sales of franchise licenses.

Since the franchisor ultimately operates in a fairly competitive industry for franchise licenses, it will earn a competitive return no matter how it structures the cost to the franchisee. If the franchisee is effectively "locked in" to the franchisor's particular system once a commitment is made, the franchisor may indeed recognize that it has the opportunity to earn quasi-rents in the "aftermarket" for supplies. That is, the franchisor may be tempted to exercise post-contractual opportunism. But the economic reality is that the competition that exists for the sales of franchise licenses will cause the initial franchise fee to fall until a new competitive equilibrium is attained. In other words, vigorous competition for franchise licenses drives the franchisor's economic profit to zero. No matter how the franchisor structures its revenue stream, market forces will compel it to earn a competitive return. Interestingly, the Eleventh Circuit implicitly recognized this fact in *Kypta v. McDonald's Corporation* (1982) in its discussion of damages: "A determination of the value of the tied product alone would not indicate whether the plaintiff indeed suffered any net economic harm, since a lower price might conceivably have been exacted by the franchisor for the tying product. Unless the fair market value of both the tied and tying products are determined and an overcharge in the *complete price* found, no injury can be claimed; suit, then, would be foreclosed."

The franchisor has at least two rational and reasonable incentives to lower the initial franchise fee and earn quasi-rents on supplies. When one considers that there is typically a high initial lump-sum cost in obtaining a franchise license, this may be a particularly appealing strategy for both the franchisor and the franchisee since it allows the franchisee to pay a lower initial fee and spread more of the cost over time. A lower franchise fee may enable the franchisor to attract a greater number of potential franchisees.[185] The obvious question then is why not simply raise the royalty payments rather than employ a tying arrangement. One argument that has been offered is that by restricting the sources of supplies, franchisors are better able to monitor quality and prevent free riding by franchisees, that is, prevent post-contractual opportunism by the franchisee. Klein and Saft (1985) have noted that such a tying arrangement serves as an efficient means for "policing" the behavior of the franchisee. Michael's (2000b) data, which we mentioned in the introduction, support this argument as they show that franchisors that impose such requirements mostly do so for inputs that are central to the identity of the product and the chain. Of course, the same analysis performed in the late 1960s or early 1970s before the *Chicken Delight* decision may have revealed otherwise. But at this point, tied inputs in business-format franchising seem to be limited in scope to those types of inputs that the franchisor needs to ensure consistent product quality. The tie-in arrangement thus serves the twofold purpose of allowing the franchisor to compete in the sales of franchise licenses by offering a lower initial fee and to monitor quality and prevent free riding.[186] Ironically, it is the very

---

[185] The existence of numerous listings and articles advertising "low-cost" franchises based on low initial investments and fees suggests that indeed initial cost matters in a franchisee's decision or ability to join a franchise. Kaufmann and Lafontaine (1994) also argue that McDonald's leaves rents with franchisees above and beyond the initial fees and investments in specific assets because it could not successfully attract the type of owner operators it desires if it charged the level of fees upfront that would be required to recover all the *ex post* profits.

[186] See Chapter 5.

incentives that the franchisor has to implement tying arrangements that have been employed against it in antitrust litigation. The high initial franchise fee that is characteristic of many franchise systems, and that the franchisor may be lowering in its attempts to sell franchise licenses by making them more affordable, has served as the basis for the lock-in argument. The franchisor's incentive to deter post-contractual opportunism by franchisees has resulted in franchisees accusing the franchisor of post-contractual opportunism.

Indeed, the lure of treble damages under the Sherman Act may be inducing franchisees to engage in post-contractual opportunism by alleging illegal tying. For example, in *Wilson*, the franchisees were obviously aware of the tie since it was spelled out in the franchise agreement. The fact that they agreed to the franchise contract indicates that the value of owning a SpeeDee franchise was at least as great as the net present value of the associated costs and that despite the tie-in. As noted above, any uncertainty regarding future costs would only serve to decrease the franchisee's willingness to sign the franchise agreement. That they made this commitment in a competitive franchise environment indicates that they expected to receive at least a competitive return from joining the SpeeDee franchise system – even in the presence of uncertain future costs. The franchisees' tying allegations in that context thus indicate that franchisees also are apt to try and capture additional surplus by engaging in some post-contractual opportunism of their own.

6.8 Evaluating Franchise Opportunities

For a potential franchisee to select among the enormous range of franchise opportunities that exist, he or she must compare the anticipated profit flows that each affords. In order to do this, the prospective franchisee must have some ability to forecast future revenues and future costs at least in some rough fashion. He or she must also take into account any timing differences and estimate the present values of the profit flows, which must then be compared to the initial franchise fees demanded by the various franchisors. Clearly, this assumes that the prospective franchisee is well informed and somewhat sophisticated economically. In fact, prospective franchisees may be economically unsophisticated and not particularly well-informed. They may not be able to perform life-cycle cost calculations, net present value calculations, or revenue forecasts. Moreover, franchisees may not receive adequate information from the franchise disclosure documents to perform life-cycle cost calculations even if they did know how to perform them. Due to the complications related to documenting earnings claims, the vast majority of franchisors choose to not provide revenue and profit projections to prospective franchisees. According to the IFA Educational Foundation and Frandata (2000), only 25 percent of the 1226 franchisors in their data offered an earnings claim as part of their disclosure document.[187] The lack of relevant data on income and costs is compounded by the fact that most prospective franchisees are unable to project potential revenues given the economic and demographic characteristics of the trade area surrounding the proposed location. All these data limitations combine with the technical difficulty of the required calculations to undermine the prospect's ability to make a well-informed decision. They also put the prospect at the mercy of unscrupulous franchisors who may choose to inflate the potential franchisee's expectations of profitable investments in their systems, thereby adding to the confusion. In this event, the prospective franchisee will be hard-pressed to make intelligent choices among the extant franchise opportunities.

All of these considerations mean that prospective franchisees must use all of the resources that are available to them to evaluate available franchise opportunities. Irrespective of the fact that the franchisor may be friendly, he is not a friend, but rather a potential business associate. The same is true of franchisees. While they may be very cooperative during the courting stage, they are not friends. Both franchisors and franchisees must adopt a strictly business attitude toward one another. No unverified or unverifiable claims should be believed.[188] Prospective franchisees should consult existing franchisees to discover which franchisor claims are fact and which are fancy. Attorneys and accountants who are experienced with franchising should be, and in fact are, relied upon. They can offer valuable advice and protect franchisees from avoidable errors.[189]

Our point, however, in relation to tying contracts is that prohibiting their use does not improve the franchisee's access to information or ability to evaluate different franchise options. Tie-ins in franchising are simply one

---

[187] Franchised systems that do not divulge an earnings claim are then required by law to make no claim at all as to the likely financial results of the business they are trying to entice the franchisee to invest in. Not surprisingly, there are numerous claims in the trade press that franchise sales people try to get around this rule by "unofficially" disclosing financial information to potential franchisees even though this is not permitted.

[188] Some prospective franchisees refuse to take care of themselves; see, e.g., Gibson (1998), which reports on several prospective franchisees who ignored information on poor growth in sales. Some prospects do not even talk to other franchisees before making their own commitment.

[189] A telephone survey of 500 franchisees and 200 potential franchisees conducted by a private survey firm for the FTC in 1984 revealed that 69 percent of franchisees obtained outside assistance before signing franchise contracts, with 49 percent of franchisees consulting an attorney specifically. See Beales and Muris (1995) for more details.

of the mechanisms by which franchisors earn returns from their franchised outlets, and they should be recognized and treated as such by all concerned, including the antitrust authorities and the courts.

6.9 Conclusion

In traditional franchising as in most distribution channels, franchisors obtain revenues from their franchisees by selling goods to them at a markup. Whereas such practices are legal in traditional franchising, the antitrust definition and treatment of tying arrangements has meant that business-format franchisors are subject to litigation if they rely on input markups as a source of revenues because their franchisees already are purchasing "a business format" from them. Hence, most business-format franchisors limit input purchase requirements to just the few items that are indistinguishable from the trade name itself, and use approved supplier programs for the rest.

In this chapter, we have detailed the antitrust treatment of tying contracts generally, and specifically as it applies to franchising. We have also discussed how the treatment of tying cases has evolved over time, and especially how the *Kodak* decision affected the regulatory regime for franchisors, and reviewed some of the more important decisions since.

In the end, it is important to reiterate that tie-ins in franchising serve the double purpose of facilitating quality control and allowing franchisors to obtain revenues from their franchised outlets. Explicit contractual restraints should be treated as an integral part of the agreement – attempts by franchisees to have such components of the agreements they signed rendered void by the court system may best be seen as a form of franchisee post-contractual opportunism. And while after-the-fact changes in the extent of input purchase requirements by franchisors may constitute franchisor opportunism, these can give rise to claims of contractual breach, but are not a source of antitrust injury. Finally, as other forms of vertical control and, especially, vertical integration, are treated less harshly by the courts, the strict regulatory regime that prevents tying in franchised chains might lead franchisors to rely on franchising less, thereby reducing the set of future opportunities for potential and existing franchisees alike. This would be a perverse result indeed for a policy whose goal presumably is to protect franchisees.

6.10 Appendix: Vertical Integration and Tying Contracts

In Chapter 4, we showed that for a monopoly selling an input to a downstream firm, tying is economically equivalent to vertical integration if the downstream market is competitive and the franchisee uses only this input or, equivalently, when he must use one unit of the franchisor's input for every unit of output it produces. This type of downstream production process exhibits what are called fixed proportions. In our discussion of this result, we hinted that the situation is more complex when the franchisee uses several different inputs that he can combine in different proportions to generate his output, that is, when his production function exhibits what are called variable proportions. In this appendix, we show that the economic equivalence of tying and vertical integration holds under downstream competition if the franchisee's production function is characterized by variable proportions.[190] To achieve the vertically integrated outcome in this case, however, the franchisor must require that the franchisee purchase all inputs from him or her.

In what follows,[191] we let $P(Q)$ represent the inverse demand function for the franchisee's output, $Q(x_1, x_2)$ stand for a linearly homogenous production function so that we have constant returns to scale downstream, and c_i denotes the constant marginal cost of input x_i, $i = 1, 2$. We limit ourselves to two inputs, for simplicity. The result is the same with more inputs, but as will be clear, the tie then must involve all of them. We assume that the production of x_1 is monopolized while the markets for input x_2 and for the final good Q are competitive. If $Q(x_1, x_2)$ admits variable proportions, the full monopoly rents cannot be obtained solely from the sale of x_1 because the derived demand for the monopolized input will reflect both consumer and franchisee substitution in response to the supracompetitive price of x_1. Franchisee substitution leads to economically inefficient use of inputs in production that the franchisor can circumvent through forward integration.

Suppose that x_1 is only used in the production of Q, and that the producer of x_1 can successfully vertically integrate all producers of Q. This strategy would then yield the following profit function for the integrated monopolist (who would not be a franchisor),

$$\Pi_V = P \cdot Q(x_1, x_2) - c_1 x_1 - c_2 x_2, \qquad (A1)$$

since x_1 would be priced at marginal cost internally to achieve maximum profits.

---

[190] Vernon and Graham (1971) showed that with variable proportions downstream, a monopolist that would tie only his input would not achieve the vertically integrated level of outcome. This gave rise to a new reason to vertically integrate and fueled a revival in interest for theories of vertical integration.

[191] This section relies on Blair and Kaserman (1978).

Alternatively, the producer of x_1 could remain separate from the downstream firms and sign a franchise agreement with each of them. The producer could then purchase x_2 at the competitive price c_2 and tie the purchase of x_2 by its franchisees to the purchase of the monopolized input x_1. Following this strategy, the franchisor would have the following profit function,

$$\Pi_T = p_1(x_1, x_2) \cdot x_1 + p_2(x_1, x_2) \cdot x_2 - c_1 x_1 - c_2 x_2, \qquad (A2)$$

where p_i is the price charged by the franchisor to all its franchisees for the ith input. Note that both prices need to be set optimally as a function of the amount of both types of inputs purchased to induce the franchisees to use them in the right proportions; therefore they are both functions of x_1 and x_2. To simplify notation, however, we refer to them simply as p_1 and p_2 in what follows.

Under these conditions, vertical integration and tying are economically equivalent. That is, these strategies yield identical results with regard to both profitability and productive efficiency. This assertion can be shown by proving the following two propositions:

Proposition I. *Given a monopoly in x_1, vertical integration that results in the monopolization of the market for Q and tying the purchase of x_2 to the purchase of x_1 yields identical profits to the producer of x_1.*

Proof. We want to show that $\Pi_V = \Pi_T$. Canceling input costs from (A1) and (A2), this requires that

$$P \cdot Q(x_1, x_2) = p_1 \cdot x_1 + p_2 \cdot x_2. \qquad (A3)$$

Under the tying arrangement, the franchisees accept p_1, p_2, and P as given: p_1 and p_2 are chosen by the franchisor as a function of x_1 and x_2 so as to induce the optimal input mix, and P is exogenous to the franchisee due to competition. Profit maximization on the part of the franchisee requires that he set the value of the marginal product of each input equal to its price, i.e., that

$$P \cdot \frac{\partial Q}{\partial x_i} = p_i, \quad i = 1, 2 \qquad (A4)$$

Substituting (A4) into (A3) and factoring P, we obtain

$$P \cdot Q(x_1, x_2) = P \left(\frac{\partial Q}{\partial x_1} \cdot x_1 + \frac{\partial Q}{\partial x_2} \cdot x_2 \right), \qquad (A5)$$

which yields the desired result, namely,

$$P \cdot Q(x_1, x_2) = P \cdot Q(x_1, x_2), \qquad (A6)$$

as $\frac{\partial Q}{\partial x_1} \cdot x_1 + \frac{\partial Q}{\partial x_2} \cdot x_2 = Q$ by Euler's Theorem. This establishes the profitability equivalence of the alternative strategies. Now, we turn to the productive efficiency of input usage under tying:

Proposition II. *Inputs x_1 and x_2 will be employed in efficient proportions whether the franchisor obtains control of the final-good industry through vertical integration or engages in a tying arrangement.*

Proof. Efficient production requires that input proportions be adjusted such that

$$\frac{\partial Q/\partial x_1}{\partial Q/\partial x_2} = \frac{c_1}{c_2}, \tag{A7}$$

that is, the downstream firm uses the inputs in proportion to their relative marginal costs. The first-order conditions for profit maximization by the monopolist if she vertically integrates the downstream industry are

$$\left(P + Q \cdot \frac{\partial P}{\partial Q} \right) \cdot \frac{\partial Q}{\partial x_1} = c_1, \tag{A8}$$

and

$$\left(P + Q \cdot \frac{\partial P}{\partial Q} \right) \cdot \frac{\partial Q}{\partial x_2} = c_2. \tag{A9}$$

Dividing (A8) by (A9) yields expression (A7), which establishes efficient input utilization under vertical integration. To establish the equivalent result under a tying arrangement, note that (A4) describes how the franchisees will choose the amounts of inputs to use. The franchisor's goal therefore will be to maximize Π_T given (A4). Thus, we substitute (A4) into (A2) and differentiate with respect to x_1 and x_2. This yields the first-order conditions:

$$\left[P + \frac{\partial P}{\partial Q} \cdot \frac{\partial Q}{\partial x_1} \cdot x_1 + \frac{\partial P}{\partial Q} \cdot \frac{\partial Q}{\partial x_2} \cdot x_2 \right] \cdot \frac{\partial Q}{\partial x_1}$$
$$+ P \left[x_1 \cdot \frac{\partial^2 Q}{\partial x_1^2} + x_2 \cdot \frac{\partial^2 Q}{\partial x_2 \partial x_1} \right] = c_1, \tag{A10}$$

and

$$\left[P + \frac{\partial P}{\partial Q} \cdot \frac{\partial Q}{\partial x_1} \cdot x_1 + \frac{\partial P}{\partial Q} \cdot \frac{\partial Q}{\partial x_2} \cdot x_2 \right] \cdot \frac{\partial Q}{\partial x_2}$$
$$+ P \left[x_2 \cdot \frac{\partial^2 Q}{\partial x_2^2} + x_1 \cdot \frac{\partial^2 Q}{\partial x_2 \partial x_1} \right] = c_2. \tag{A11}$$

Linear homogeneity of the production function implies that the second bracketed term on the left-hand side of (A10) and (A11) is zero. Dropping these terms, we factor $\frac{\partial P}{\partial Q}$ from the last two terms of the first bracketed expression, apply Euler's Theorem, and write conditions (A10) and (A11) as

$$\left(P + Q \cdot \frac{\partial P}{\partial Q}\right) \cdot \frac{\partial Q}{\partial x_1} = c_1, \tag{A12}$$

and

$$\left(P + Q \cdot \frac{\partial P}{\partial Q}\right) \cdot \frac{\partial Q}{\partial x_2} = c_2. \tag{A13}$$

Dividing (A12) by (A13) again results in expression (A7), thereby confirming efficient input utilization under a tying arrangement.

Propositions I and II establish an equivalence between both the private and the social effects of vertical integration and tying under input monopoly and variable proportions with downstream competition. Given such symmetry, the firm holding monopoly power over an input for which (imperfect) substitutes exist must select between alternative strategies on the basis of factors that lie outside our simplified model. Important considerations that will influence this choice include the number of substitutable inputs that must be tied to the monopolized input in order to ensure efficient downstream production; the frequency of changes in the costs, c_i, and the cost of changing the prices to franchisees in response to those changes in costs; potential cost savings that may be available through vertical integration because of transactional efficiencies or technological inseparability of the various stages of production; the feasibility of vertical integration with the whole downstream sector; and the comparative treatment afforded the alternative strategies by the antitrust authorities. The latter is determined by the policy thrust of the antitrust enforcement agencies as well as legal precedents.

Of course, if the franchisor cannot impose requirements on all inputs, then vertical integration will dominate franchising unless there are incentive issues under vertical integration (e.g., paid managers have weaker incentives to provide effort than owner operators do). Moreover, while in many industries manufacturers cannot reasonably vertically integrate all downstream resellers – their product is just one of a large mix of products sold at supermarkets or in large department or discount stores – in the franchising context, however, vertical integration is a readily available option. As we saw in Chapter 4, most franchisors operate some of their outlets directly as it is. Increasing their reliance on vertical integration is always an option they can turn to if they find that their capacity to contract with franchisees is too constrained by the regulatory regime.

7

Vertical Price Controls in Franchising

"Why do your prices vary from one restaurant to another and why do some restaurants charge for extra condiments?[*]
Approximately 85 percent of McDonald's restaurants are locally owned and operated. As independent businesspeople, each individual determines his or her own prices taking their operating costs and the company's recommendations into consideration. Therefore, prices do vary from one McDonald's restaurant to another. Also, for this same reason, charges for condiments may vary from one McDonald's restaurant to another. (McDonald's Corporation Web site, June 2003)

7.1 Introduction*

Prices vary somewhat from outlet to outlet in most franchised chains. This has been confirmed in several empirical studies, including Lafontaine (1995b), Graddy (1997), Thomadsen (2002), and Kalnins (2003), all of which examined price data they had gathered from the individual outlets of large fast-food chains within relatively small geographical markets. Moreover, Lafontaine (1999) has examined the relationship between the extent of franchising and the degree of price dispersion in local markets, namely the Pittsburgh and the Detroit metropolitan areas. She finds that several fast-food chains allow some price dispersion even within their set of corporate stores. The amount of price dispersion, however, is larger for fully franchised than for fully corporate chains. She finds the greatest total amount of price dispersion among those chains with a mix of corporate and franchised stores.

Although the quote above from the McDonald's Web site suggests that price differences across outlets are a normal and accepted part of franchising,

---

* This chapter relies heavily on Blair and Lafontaine (1999).

it is not uncommon for franchisors and franchisees to disagree about the prices that the franchisees charge their customers. In fact, earlier in the history of McDonald's, Ray Kroc became furious at one of his first franchisees, Bob Dondanville, for raising his price from 15 to 18 cents. "The 15-cents hamburger was central to McDonald's image.... As soon as he learned of Dondanville's price increase, Kroc fired off a telegram ... 'Take down your arches,' it demanded" (Love 1986: 75). More recently, Gibson (1996) reported that McDonald's franchisees were complaining about their franchisor's use of "value meals" as they found the prices of these meals too low. In an early survey of franchisees, Ozanne and Hunt (1971) found that franchisees' "...complaints about the poor quality of pricing assistance center around franchisors trying to keep prices low" (158).

In the United States, franchisors have been on shaky legal ground historically when they have tried to impose resale price controls on their franchisees. In 1968, the Supreme Court decided *Albrecht v. Herald Company* and thereby made vertically imposed *maximum* resale prices illegal *per se*.[192] The resulting *Albrecht* rule meant that upstream firms could not impose a ceiling on the prices charged by their resellers. This rule applied not only to arm's length seller–reseller relationships, but also to franchisors, in their relationships with their franchisees, as the latter are independent businesses under the law. After some 30 years of sustained academic criticism, of firms finding and implementing alternatives to maximum price controls, and of lower courts evading the dictates of *Albrecht*, the Supreme Court recently overruled *Albrecht*. In *State Oil Company v. Khan*, the Court returned the antitrust treatment of maximum resale price fixing to the rule of reason. For all intents and purposes, this ruling will permit maximum resale price restraints in the U.S.

In our view, this change in the Court's treatment of maximum resale price maintenance is a good thing in general and for franchising in particular.[193]

---

[192] Minimum resale price maintenance is also *per se* illegal in the U.S., but the economic rationale for minimum resale price maintenance, and the set of precedents governing the *per se* rule against it, are different from those that govern maximum resale price maintenance. Given that the complaints from franchisees, and the legal cases against franchisors, have been about franchisors imposing price ceilings or pushing franchisees' prices down, we focus exclusively on maximum resale price maintenance. For treatments of minimum resale price maintenance under U.S. antitrust, see Blair and Kaserman (1985).

[193] In addition to Blair and Lafontaine (1999), see Blair and Lopatka (1998a, 1998b) for extended analyses.

Because such restraints preclude franchisees from raising prices, they obviously benefit consumers. As we shall show below, they also increase the profits of franchisors and thereby make them better off – in fact, therein lies their desire to impose such restraints. Not so obviously, however, actual and prospective franchisees as a group may also be better off because a franchisor's ability to restrict the pricing freedom of its franchisees makes franchising more attractive and thereby expands available franchise opportunities.

Interestingly, a similar change in the treatment of maximum prices has occurred in Europe: the stance adopted by the European Commission in its new block exemption for vertical restraints, which took effect on June 1, 2000, is in line with *Khan*. The block exemption specifically distinguishes maximum price restraints from other vertical price controls – minimum resale prices or set prices – treating the latter as "hardcore restrictions" that take an agreement outside the block exemption. Maximum prices, on the other hand, like suggested prices, are treated much less harshly: They are completely legal for suppliers whose market share is below 30 percent, and are subject to review, but not presumed illegal still, when a supplier has more than a 30 percent market share.[194] Under the old block exemption for franchises, all forms of price controls – maximum, minimum, or direct – were "blacklisted," meaning that their presence in an agreement took the agreement outside the scope of the exemption.

In this chapter, we provide a thorough examination of the U.S. antitrust law and the economics of maximum resale price restraints. Because the antitrust prohibitions have been so severe, we begin by examining briefly the forerunners of *Albrecht*, the landmark *Albrecht* decision, and the *Khan* decision. We then turn our attention to an economic analysis of the three main reasons why franchisors may want to impose a ceiling on the prices charged by their franchisees. The first flows from the standard successive monopoly argument, common to all retailing, where upstream and downstream firms both have some degree of market power. The second stems from the use of a common tradename in franchising, a tradename that gives rise to positive demand externalities. The third is based on the argument that franchisors may behave opportunistically toward their franchisees. This last explanation is the one that franchisees explicitly or implicitly rely on when complaining about their franchisor's attempt to control their prices. Finally, we combine the law and the economics when we examine the public policy implications of *Khan*.

---

[194] See European Commission (2002) and Flohr (2000).

7.2 The Legal History of Maximum Resale Price Fixing in the United States

7.2.1 Forerunners of *Albrecht*

In the case of *United States v. Socony-Vacuum*, against the backdrop of a horizontal agreement among competitors to *raise* prices, the Supreme Court sweepingly stated that "[a]ny combination which tampers with price structures is engaged in an unlawful activity" (*Socony-Vacuum* at 221). To underscore the point, the Court went on to say that "[u]nder the Sherman Act a combination formed for the purpose and with the effect of raising, *depressing*, fixing, pegging, or stabilizing the *price of a commodity* in interstate or foreign commerce is illegal *per se*" (*Socony-Vacuum* at 212–213; emphasis added). Through this expansive ruling, the Supreme Court set the stage for specifically condemning maximum resale price fixing, a practice that tends to depress prices and thus benefit consumers.

The pronouncement of the *per se* illegality of "depressing" prices was not tested until the Supreme Court's 1951 ruling in *Kiefer-Stewart v. Joseph E. Seagram & Sons*. In response to a horizontal conspiracy among Kiefer-Stewart and other wholesale liquor dealers to *raise* their resale prices to retailers, two liquor suppliers, Calvert and Seagram, agreed to refuse to sell their products to these wholesalers unless the wholesalers agreed not to charge more than a specified maximum price (*Kiefer-Stewart* at 212–213). When Kiefer-Stewart refused to respect these maximum resale prices, its supplies were cut off. Kiefer-Stewart subsequently sued for the lost profits on the lost sales of Calvert and Seagram products. Despite the obvious benefit to consumers of lower prices, the Court ruled in favor of Kiefer-Stewart. Embracing the *Socony-Vacuum* pronouncement, the Court ruled that agreements to fix maximum resale prices "cripple the freedom of traders and thereby restrict their ability to sell in accordance with their own judgment" (*Kiefer-Stewart* at 213).[195] As a result, such agreements were declared illegal and the first step was taken in depriving franchisors of their ability to control the resale prices of their franchisees.

In *Socony-Vacuum* and *Kiefer-Stewart*, the facts suggested the existence of horizontal agreements among competitors. As horizontal agreements regarding price are among the most pernicious evils that the antitrust laws are designed to thwart, the Court in these cases had some cause for alarm.

---

[195] This, of course, ignores the impact on their customers as well as on their suppliers who want to restrict their pricing freedom.

Therefore, the question remained as to whether – absent any hint of horizontal collusion among competitors – the Supreme Court would still stand so solidly behind its *Socony-Vacuum* pronouncement. In other words, it was not yet clear how the *Socony-Vacuum* test would be applied in a case where there was a purely vertical attempt (e.g., by a franchisor) to impose maximum resale prices (e.g., on a franchisee). In *Albrecht*, the Court was confronted with these simplified facts and gave a clear answer favoring resellers.

7.2.2 The *Albrecht* Rule

The Herald Company, which published the *Globe-Democrat* newspaper, awarded exclusive territories to its carriers, thereby giving each carrier a local monopoly. The carriers purchased the newspapers at wholesale prices from the *Globe-Democrat*. The carriers then performed the retail distribution function by delivering the newspapers to subscribers' homes. The Herald Company advertised a home delivered price and required, under threat of termination, that its carriers honor that price. Despite this threat, one of the carriers, Albrecht, decided to charge his customers more than the advertised price. When the Herald Company terminated Albrecht, a lawsuit ensued. The lower courts found that the *Globe-Democrat*'s policy did not constitute a restraint of trade, but the Supreme Court reversed and ruled for Albrecht.

In its ruling, the Supreme Court, reaffirming *Kiefer-Stewart* and echoing *Socony-Vacuum*, once again condemned maximum resale price fixing: ". . . schemes to fix maximum prices, by substituting the perhaps erroneous judgment of a seller for the forces of the competitive market, may severely intrude upon the ability of buyers to compete and survive in that market" (*Albrecht* at 152). Without specifying what "forces of the competitive market" it thought were operative in Albrecht's exclusive territory, the Court went on to explain:

> Maximum prices may be fixed too low for the dealer to furnish services essential to the value which goods have for the consumer or to furnish services and conveniences which consumers desire and for which they are willing to pay. Maximum price fixing may channel distribution through a few large or specifically advantaged dealers who otherwise would be subject to significant nonprice competition. Moreover, if the actual price charged under a maximum price scheme is nearly always the fixed maximum price . . . the scheme tends to acquire all the attributes of an arrangement fixing minimum prices. (*Albrecht* at 152–153)

Thus, erroneously equating the economic effects of maximum resale price fixing with those of minimum resale price fixing, the Court found that fixing maximum resale prices is illegal *per se* under Section 1 of the Sherman Act. Unilateral restraints on a reseller's freedom to raise price became illegal *per se*, irrespective of their potential benefits to consumers. *Albrecht*, in that sense, gave resellers a considerable weapon to wield against upstream firms who might seek to limit their pricing decisions. The *Albrecht* decision gave resellers a treble damage claim against upstream firms that imposed maximum resale prices.[196] It also provided an appealing rationale for failing to give customers lower prices. This rationale was, in essence, that the imposition of lower prices by upstream firms would ultimately harm consumers by squeezing profits out of the resellers, which would in turn lead to a reduction in the availability of desired products and services. Although such a rationale has superficial appeal, it ignores the fact that it would be contrary to the upstream firm's interest to prevent resellers from offering goods and services that consumers value as this would ultimately damage the market for the upstream firm's product.

In fact, because maximum resale price maintenance implies lower consumer prices, it is difficult to comprehend why the practice should be illegal *per se* under our antitrust laws. Not surprisingly then, the decision generated substantial academic criticism.[197] Despite this criticism and a judicial opportunity to respond to it, the Supreme Court let the rule stand. In *Atlantic Richfield Co. v. USA Petroleum Co* (or *ARCO*), for example, Atlantic Richfield had imposed maximum resale prices on its gasoline dealers.[198] As a result of Atlantic Richfield's low, but not predatory, prices, one of its gasoline dealers' competitors, USA Petroleum, alleged that it lost sales and profits. It sued on the grounds that its injuries were the result of Atlantic Richfield's illegal policy of imposing maximum resale prices on its dealers.

On these facts, the Supreme Court might have seized the opportunity to overturn the *Albrecht* rule or at least severely curtail it. But it did not expressly do so. Instead of confronting *Albrecht*, the Court observed that USA Petroleum was merely frustrated by its inability to raise prices.[199] Therefore, the Court

---

[196] Section 4 of the Clayton Act provides in relevant part that "anyone who shall be injured in his business or property by reason of anything forbidden in the antitrust laws may sue therefor . . . and shall recover threefold the damages by him sustained, and the cost of suit, including a reasonable attorney's fee. . . . " 15 USC § 15.

[197] For the earliest, severe criticisms, see the dissenting opinions of Justices Harlan (*Albrecht* at 156) and Stewart (*Albrecht* at 168). In addition, see Blair and Kaserman (1981), Easterbrook (1981), Blair and Fesmire (1986), and Areeda and Hovenkamp (1993 Supp.).

[198] For an analysis of this case, see Blair and Lang (1991).

[199] On remand from the Supreme Court, the Ninth Circuit affirmed the district court's original grant of summary judgment (*USA Petroleum Co. v. Atlantic Richfield Co.*).

ruled USA Petroleum had not suffered antitrust injury (*ARCO* at 337–338).[200] But the Court did not address in its decision the potential benefit to consumers from maximum resale price maintenance, perhaps because the case was filed by competitors of the dealers that were subject to the alleged maximum vertical pricing arrangement. Although it had sidestepped the *Albrecht* rule, there was, nonetheless, a skeptical tone in the Court's opinion about *Albrecht*'s continuing vitality. Moreover, the finding of no antitrust injury (a requirement to maintain all private antitrust actions) suggested that the practice did not warrant the *per se* label. Despite this, *Albrecht* still remained as precedent for the *Khan* case.

7.2.3 State Oil Company v. Khan

Khan was a lessee-dealer of Union 76 brand gasoline. He leased his station and bought gasoline from State Oil Company. The price agreement in the franchise contract was a thinly veiled attempt to evade the *Albrecht* rule. Under this agreement, State Oil suggested a retail price for Khan to charge. The wholesale price[201] was set 3.25 cents below this suggested retail price. If Khan decided that he wanted to raise price above the price suggested by State Oil, he was free to do so, but he could not profit from that change because he had to rebate the premium to State Oil. In other words, Khan was obligated to pay State Oil the wholesale price plus a sum equal to the difference between his actual price and State Oil's suggested price, all the times the quantity sold at the higher price. Thus, at the higher price, Khan would still receive the same gross profit of 3.25 cents per gallon. But he would sell fewer gallons and, therefore, his net profit would be lower due to unexploited economies of scale and to fewer related sales (motor oil, cigarettes, beer, and so on). In effect, Khan would have no incentive to raise price above the level suggested

---

In response to the Supreme Court's ruling that a competitor did not have standing to challenge vertical maximum resale pricing if the prices are not predatory, USA Petroleum wanted additional discovery to gather evidence of below cost (predatory) pricing (*USA Petroleum Co.* at 1277–1278). But the panel majority found that USA Petroleum had waived its right to present evidence of below cost pricing (*USA Petroleum Co.* at 1279). Thus, it refused to permit additional discovery.

[200] For an examination of *antitrust injury*, which is injury that flows from the anticompetitive consequences of a practice that violates the antitrust laws, see Blair and Harrison (1989).

[201] This price included all taxes and transportation charges; it was the laid-in cost of the gasoline to Khan.

by State Oil. Thus, the contract was equivalent to a maximum resale price restraint.[202]

Albrecht was decided in 1968 and the Supreme Court had not had a case until *Khan* that squarely posed the same question, namely, whether vertically imposed maximum resale price restraints were so pernicious (and predictable) in their competitive effects that they deserved to be illegal *per se*. In other words, *Khan* offered an opportunity to revisit the competitive concerns expressed in *Albrecht*. After some 30 years of critical commentary and an improved understanding of vertical relationships, the Court decided that it was "difficult to maintain that vertically-imposed maximum prices could harm consumers or competition to the extent necessary to justify their *per se* invalidation" (*Khan*, 282). The Court recognized that the competitive concerns in *Albrecht* were purely theoretical. Moreover, it found that "Albrecht's dire predictions have not been borne out, even though manufacturers and suppliers appear to have fashioned schemes to get around the *per se* rule against vertical maximum price fixing" (*Khan*, 283).[203] Finding that the conceptual foundations of *Albrecht* were "gravely weakened," the Court overruled Albrecht's *per se* prohibition of maximum resale price restraints.

We believe that this was a wise decision in general, and in particular for franchising. In the next section, we provide an economic analysis of three main reasons why franchisors may want to impose maximum resale prices on their franchisees. We show that consumer welfare is enhanced by maximum resale price maintenance under at least two of these, namely the successive monopoly and the positive demand externalities arguments. In addition, we argue that the third, which has to do with franchisor opportunism, is a popular but much less likely explanation for this practice. Most importantly for our purposes, it does not generate antitrust injury. Thus, we conclude that *Khan* is a positive policy change.

---

[202] Based on local market conditions, if Khan believed that the suggested retail price was too high, it could request a reduction. If State Oil agreed, it would adjust the wholesale price to maintain the 3.25 cents margin. If it did not agree, and Khan wanted to reduce the retail price anyway, then Khan would have to absorb the reduction and earn a reduced margin. Given the realities of gasoline retailing, such price reductions were extremely unlikely because a gross margin of 3.25 cents per gallon was already probably too small to make Khan's gasoline sales operations profitable. Hence, State Oil effectively controlled price reductions as well as price increases.

[203] See Blair and Esquibel (1996) for an extensive look at economic equivalents to maximum resale prices.

7.3 An Economic Analysis of Maximum Resale Price Restraints

In order to better understand the economic irrationality of the *Albrecht* rule, it is useful to examine the potential motivations for setting maximum resale prices. As we now demonstrate, consumers normally benefit from the reduced prices that maximum price restraints yield. Thus, assuming that consumer welfare is the primary concern of the antitrust laws, one is driven to the conclusion that the demise of *Albrecht* was long overdue.

We begin with an examination of the standard successive monopoly argument, which applies to all supplier-reseller relationships, including traditional franchising. We then move on to show that even though business-format franchising may not involve any product sale from the franchisor to the franchisee, the double-marginalization problem still arises there due to franchisors' reliance on sales-based royalties.[204] Finally, we discuss two other reasons why franchisors, traditional or business format, may want to impose maximum resale price restraints, namely positive demand externalities and franchisor opportunism.

7.3.1 The Successive Monopoly Argument for the Supplier-Reseller (or Traditional Franchising) Case

Suppose, for the sake of simplicity, that a single producer holds the patent for the production and sale of the proverbial widget; in other words, there is a perfectly legal monopoly in the market for widgets. This manufacturer decides to franchise the distribution of his widgets. In each local market, the franchisor appoints a single franchisee with an exclusive territory. Because the franchisee faces no local competition, *it* also enjoys some monopoly power. In this event, the market structure is one of *successive monopoly*.[205] Empirically, maximum price restraints arise mostly in these kinds of markets where there is some element of successive monopoly, that is, where there is market power at the production stage and independent market power at the distribution

---

[204] Our point is that even if there are no sales of products by the franchisor to the franchisees, the argument still goes through. Obviously, if there are such sales in some business-format franchised chains, the successive monopoly argument applies to these as well.

[205] A full understanding of successive monopoly dates at least to Spengler (1950). See also Machlup and Taber (1960). The argument follows through in the same way if the markets are oligopolistic. See, in particular, Greenhut and Ohta (1979).

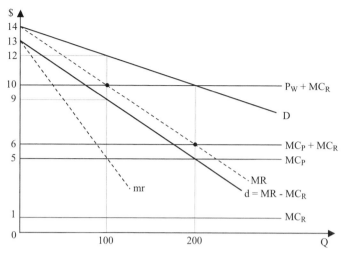

Figure 7-1: Double marginalization.

stage, as is typically the case in traditional franchising.[206] As the subsequent analysis makes clear, from the perspective of consumer welfare, this market structure is worse than having a single, integrated monopoly involved in both production and distribution.

Under conditions of successive monopoly, the franchisor must set its price and quantity taking into account the profit-maximizing behavior of the franchisee. Now, each franchisee will maximize its profit in the usual way by selling that quantity where its marginal revenue equals its marginal cost. In this endeavor, the franchisee must have widgets to sell. It demands widgets for resale – not for its own use. As a result, the franchisee's demand is derived from the consumer demand for widgets. It is this derived demand that the franchisor then faces. To begin the analysis, then, we must find the derived demand for widgets.

In Figure 7-1, we assume that the consumers' inverse demand for widgets in a representative territory is given by $D(Q) = P$, and the associated marginal revenue is MR.[207] This, of course, is the demand that the franchisee faces. The derived demand for the franchisor's product that arises from each

---

[206] The upstream market power found in the reported court cases stems from the (nearly) pure monopoly of local newspapers or the branded products such as automobiles, soft drinks, gasoline, packaged meats, and prefabricated farm buildings. The downstream (successive) market power stems primarily from exclusive territories.

[207] In the example shown in the figure, the consumers' inverse demand is $D(Q)$, where

$$D(Q) = P = 14 - 0.02Q,$$

market can then be ascertained from the franchisees' profit maximizing calculus. Without loss of generality, we focus on a single franchisee market in
what follows. As mentioned above, the franchisee will maximize its profits by
equating its marginal revenue (MR) to its marginal cost. Now, the franchisee's
marginal cost equals the marginal cost of goods sold, which is the wholesale
price (P_W) charged by the franchisor, plus the marginal cost of performing
the retailing function. The latter is shown in Figure 7-1 as MC_R. Thus, the
franchisee will sell that quantity where

$$MR = P_W + MC_R.$$

Rearranging this condition yields the following derived demand:

$$P_W = MR - MC_R.$$

In other words, given the profit-maximizing behavior of the franchisee, the
maximum price that the franchisor can charge for any specific quantity of
widgets is the difference between the franchisee's marginal revenue at that
quantity and the marginal cost of performing the distribution function. In
Figure 7-1, we show this derived demand as $d(Q) = MR - MC_R$, and the
associated marginal revenue, which we denote by mr.[208]

The franchisor maximizes its profits by producing the quantity where its
marginal revenue (mr) equals its marginal cost, where the latter is the marginal
cost of production (MC_P). Hence, the franchisor produces the quantity where:

$$mr = MC_P.$$

As shown in Figure 7-1, the profit maximizing quantity is 100 widgets.[209] The
profit maximizing wholesale price that corresponds to an output of 100 is

so that the associated marginal revenue is

$$MR = 14 - 0.04Q.$$

This specific numerical example is traced through the analysis to make the general
analysis more concrete. Note that while our example and figures assume a linear demand
curve for the sake of simplicity, the results hold for general well-behaved demand curves.

[208] The derived demand facing the manufacturer is $P_W = MR - MC_R$. Assuming that
$MC_R = \$1$, we can use the equation for MR – see last footnote – to write $P_W = 14 -
0.04\ Q - 1$ or $P_W = 13 - 0.04Q = d$. In this case, the derived marginal revenue is
$mr = 13 - 0.08Q$.

[209] In Figure 7-1, we have assumed that the marginal cost of production is $5. Equating
marginal revenue – see last footnote – to the marginal cost of production gives $13 -
0.08Q = 5$. Solving for Q yields the optimal output of 100.

found by substituting 100 for Q in the derived demand, d. In our numerical example, the optimal wholesale price is \$9.[210]

Once the franchisor selects a wholesale price, the marginal cost of the franchisee is set since the franchisee's marginal cost is P_W plus MC_R. The franchisee then will maximize its profits by selling that quantity where its marginal revenue (MR) equals its marginal cost:

$$MR = P_W + MC_R.$$

In our numerical example, the franchisee's marginal cost is \$10, so its optimal output is also 100 (as it must be), and the price charged to consumers is \$12.[211]

The profits of the franchisor and the franchisee are easy to calculate. For the franchisor, profits (Π) are the difference between wholesale price and production cost times the quantity sold:

$$\Pi = (P_W - MC_P)Q.$$

In our numerical example, this amounts to \$400.[212] For the franchisee, profits (π) are calculated in a similar fashion:

$$\pi = (P - P_W - MC_R)Q.$$

In our example, the franchisee's profits are \$200.[213] Thus, total channel profits when there is a successive monopoly are $\Pi + \pi = \$600$.

This market structure is inefficient because it is possible to generate more profit. We can see this by considering what would happen if the franchisor were vertically integrated. By this, we mean that the franchisor would produce the widgets and also perform the retailing function itself, through company-owned retail outlets. In that case, the manufacturer would produce *and* distribute that quantity of widgets where the marginal revenue equals the marginal cost of production plus the marginal cost of retailing:

$$MR = MC_P + MC_R.$$

In Figure 7-1, we have added the marginal cost of production and retailing ($MC_P + MC_R$). In our numerical example, this marginal cost is \$6 and

[210] The derived demand is $P_W = 13 - 0.04Q$ so that when $Q = 100$, $P_W = 9$.
[211] Since the wholesale price is \$9 and the marginal cost of performing the distribution function is \$1, the franchisee's marginal cost is \$10. The franchisee sells the quantity where $MR = P_W + MC_R$ or $14 - 0.04Q = 10$, which yields an optimal quantity of 100. Substituting $Q = 100$ into the demand function yields $P = 14 - 0.02(100) = 12$.
[212] Substituting \$9 for P_W, \$5 for MC_P, and 100 for Q gives $\Pi = (9 - 5)100 = 400$.
[213] Substituting \$12 for P, \$9 for P_W, \$1 for MC_R, and 100 for Q gives $\pi = (12 - 9 - 1)100 = 200$.

the profit maximizing output is $Q_V = 200$. At this output, the corresponding profit maximizing price is $10.[214] The integrated firm's profit is then given by

$$\Pi_V = (P - MC_P - MC_R)Q_V,$$

which is $800. This level of profit exceeds the combined profit of the franchisor and the franchisee found above.

Our example has shown that in a successive monopoly context, vertical integration leads to an *expansion* of output, a *reduction* in price to consumers, and an *increase* in total channel profits. In spite of the fact that price is lower, the profit of the vertically integrated monopolist is larger than the sum of the profits earned by a production monopolist and a separate distribution monopolist. This reflects the inefficiency associated with the double marginalization problem inherent in a successive monopoly. Consequently, one would expect vertical integration to occur under these structural conditions, which would mean the end of franchising.

There is, however, "more than one way to skin a cat." Vertical integration is not necessary to achieve the same economic results because there are contractual alternatives.[215] One of these contractual alternatives is maximum resale price maintenance. In our setup, the franchisor knows the demand curve faced by the franchisee and thus also knows what retail price will maximize channel profit. In our example, that price is $10. The franchisor can then agree to sell its widgets to its franchisee on the condition that the franchisee not charge more than $10 to its customers. In that event, the franchisee will sell 200 widgets (given the demand it faces for widget). The franchisor will sell those 200 widgets to its franchisee at a wholesale price of $9. This wholesale price will permit the franchisee to sell 200 widgets at a retail price of $10 because the marginal cost to the franchisee is the wholesale price ($9) plus the marginal cost of distributing the widgets ($1). Thus, maximum resale pricing yields results that are the same as those of vertical integration: $Q = 200$ and $P = \$10$. The franchisor's profit is

$$\Pi = (P_W - MC_P)Q = (9 - 5)200 = \$800.$$

Even though the franchisee has a monopoly on retailing in its territory, it is forced to behave as a competitive firm would, namely, to sell that output

---

[214] Given the marginal revenue of $MR = 14 - 0.04\,Q$, and marginal cost for an integrated firm of $MC = 5 + 1 = 6$, the optimal output for the integrated case is found by solving $14 - 0.04Q = 6$ for Q, which yields a profit maximizing quantity of 200. Substituting $Q = 200$ in the demand equation yields $P = 14 - .02(200) = 10$.

[215] For extensive examinations, see Blair and Kaserman (1983) and Warren-Boulton (1978). See also Katz (1989) for a survey of the related literature.

where price equals marginal cost. As a result, the franchisee's profit is zero:

$$\pi = (P - (P_W + MC_R))Q = 0,$$

because $P = P_W + MC_R$. This is not to say that the franchisee just barely breaks even or makes no accounting profits. But it does mean that he makes no economic profits, that is, the franchisee is limited to a competitive return on his investment and time, a competitive return that is already reflected in its economic costs.

It should be clear that the franchisor employs maximum resale price restraints not because this is good for consumers, but rather because it improves her profits. Indeed, in our numerical example, her profits double from $400 to $800. But the franchisor's interests and those of consumers happen to coincide in the context of successive monopolies. To show this more clearly, note that we have already established that quantity doubles from 100 to 200 widgets, and that price to the consumer falls from $12 to $10, when the franchisor imposes the maximum price restraints. One would suspect that consumer welfare rises as a consequence and, indeed, it does. We can measure consumer welfare using the net consumer surplus (CS), which is the area below the demand curve and above the price. In our numerical example, this area will be

$$CS = 0.5(14 - 12)100 = 100$$

in the presence of successive monopoly. But when maximum resale price maintenance is imposed (or when the producer is vertically integrated), consumer surplus rises substantially to

$$CS = 0.5(14 - 10)200 = 400.$$

Thus, the use of maximum resale price restraints leads to increased output, reduced prices, and increased consumer welfare.

All else being equal then, a ban on maximum resale price restraints is inconsistent with the promotion of consumer welfare. Of course, existing franchisees who operate under no pricing constraints are worse off when maximum resale price maintenance is imposed on them. In our example, the franchisee's profits go from $200 to zero, or from supracompetitive to competitive levels. In that sense, franchisees are hurt by the imposition of maximum prices in a successive monopoly context. But total welfare (the sum of consumer surplus and channel profits) increases when we allow maximum resale price maintenance, and, therefore, it is socially desirable to do so. Furthermore, franchising is much more likely to be used by manufacturers if they can control prices. In our example, the franchisor would most likely integrate rather than forgo the extra $400 in profits that are available under an integrated channel. Thus, franchise opportunities are much more likely to arise in successive monopoly contexts if franchisors are allowed to control resale prices. In that sense, franchisees as a group (including potential and existing franchisees) may well benefit from these price controls as this will make it possible for them to become or remain franchisees in the future.

7.3.2 The Successive Monopoly Argument for Business-Format Franchises

Our previous analysis was conducted in the context of traditional franchising, where the franchisor generally sells a product under exclusive marks to its franchisees. We now want to show how the same "successive monopoly" problems arise in the context of business-format franchising. In other words, we show that the use of royalties on sales in business-format franchise contracts gives rise to increased prices in the same way and for the same reason that successive markups in the more traditional analysis lead to non-optimal downstream prices. As a result of these royalties (or percentage advertising fees), franchisees face a net demand curve that is lower than it would be at the same unit if it were operated corporately or without such payments. This, in turn, leads franchisees to sell less, and to demand a higher price – once adjusted to include the royalty payment – than would occur under vertical integration (or corporate ownership).[216]

The "successive monopoly" effect of a royalty or advertising fee on sales on optimal downstream prices can be shown algebraically using a simple example. Assume a linear demand curve at the outlet level,

$$P = a - bQ,$$

a constant marginal (and average) cost of retailing, $MC_R = c$, and a royalty rate, and/or advertising fee, (r), which is a percentage of total sales revenue,

$$0 < r < 1.$$

Given any value for the royalty rate (r), the franchisee's profits are given by

$$\pi = (1 - r)PQ - cQ$$

---

[216] See Schmidt (1994) for an algebraic example of the "successive monopoly" problem under a royalty payment. Note that in a linear demand example, the marginal cost of performing the retail functions must be greater than zero for the optimal quantity to be reduced under a royalty on sales. This condition does not appear overly restrictive since marginal cost is necessarily positive in a world of scarce resources.

or

$$\pi = (1 - r)(a - bQ)Q - cQ.$$

Now, the franchisee will maximize its profit by operating where

$$d\pi/dQ = (1 - r)(a - 2bQ) - c = 0,$$

which yields the optimal output

$$Q_D^* = [a(1 - r) - c]/[2b(1 - r)]$$

where the subscript D refers to downstream. By substituting this quantity into the demand curve, we find that the franchisee's optimal retail price, once adjusted to include the royalty payment or advertising fee, is

$$P^* = a - bQ_D^* = [a(1 - r) + c]/[2(1 - r)].$$

This price is higher than it would be if there were no royalties or advertising fees based on sales. This is easily seen if we set r equal to zero. In that case, the optimal price becomes

$$P' = (a + c)/2,$$

which is lower than P^* for any $r \in (0,1)$.[217] Thus, the franchisee's price is higher when the franchisee pays some royalties on sales than when these are set equal to zero. Note also that if the franchisor had been operating the unit directly, it would have chosen to set the price at P' rather than at the higher P^* as total channel profits are higher with a price of P'. In that sense, the franchisor will find the price that the franchisee selects to be too high just as he does in the traditional "successive monopoly" analysis. So again, both franchisors and consumers will benefit from maximum resale price restraints. Finally, as P^* is increasing in r, it should be clear that franchisee prices will be higher the higher the proportion of sales revenue paid by the franchisee to the franchisor.

7.3.3 Demand Externalities

Aside from the "successive monopoly" problem, franchisors may impose maximum prices on their franchisees for two main reasons: first as a way to force franchisees to internalize positive demand externalities; second, because they

---

[217] $P^* - P' = cr/(2(1-r))$, which is positive whenever $0 < r < 1$.

are behaving opportunistically. Here, we consider the demand externality argument.[218] We discuss franchisor opportunism in the next subsection.

We live in a mobile society. As a result, in a chain of units operating under a common tradename, it is likely that what one franchisee does can affect other franchisees. For example, a franchisee who does not maintain his premises well will hurt the brand image generally, and likely have a negative impact on all units in the chain. Similarly, a franchisee that provides a particularly positive experience to his customers will probably have a positive influence on demand at all units as satisfied customers from his units will choose to patronize other units when the occasion arises. Both of these situations imply that demand is positively correlated across units sharing the same brand name, which in turn means that there exist positive demand externalities in branded chains. In other words, low prices at one unit (which is one way to generate a positive customer experience) will increase demand at all units in the chain. But no franchisee has an incentive to modify its behavior for the benefit of the other franchisees: the positive effect of one's prices on demand at other units is ignored by franchisees in their pricing decisions because it does not affect their individual profits. Corporate chains, on the other hand, would internalize this effect in their pricing decisions as they obtain the profits from all outlets. As we show below, this means that the franchisor would want prices to be lower in any given unit than the price that the franchisee chooses.

We can examine this conflict analytically.[219] Assume that a franchisor has n franchisees located in n separate geographic markets. Let $\boldsymbol{P} = [P_1, P_2, \ldots, P_n]$ be a vector of prices set by the franchisees. Positive demand externalities exist when the profit of each franchisee depends upon the vector of prices:

$$\pi_i = \pi_i(\boldsymbol{P}),$$

where $\partial \pi_i / \partial P_j < 0$, for all i, j. Thus, if one franchisee raises its price in its own market, the profits of other franchisees suffer. This, of course, arises because a customer's experience at one franchised location influences his or her decision to frequent another unit in the same system.

The reason why the franchisor cares about this is because its profits depend on how well all franchisees do. To highlight the fact that this conflict is not due to franchisors levying royalties on sales rather than profits, we show how this conflict would arise even if the franchisor shared in outlet profits. However,

---

[218] See also Barron and Umbeck (1984), Blair and Kaserman (1994), Lafontaine (1995b) and Lafontaine and Slade (2001) for more on this argument.

[219] This analysis is based on Blair and Kaserman (1994) and follows the same logic we used in Chapter 5.

we should say at the outset that royalties on sales rather than profits would make this problem even worse, that is, the optimal price from the franchisor's perspective will be even lower and the franchisee's optimal price higher if the franchisor levies sales royalties. For completeness, we cover this case in the appendix to this chapter.

If we assume that a franchisor collects a proportion of each franchisee's profits, we can write the franchisor's profit as

$$\Pi = \sum_{i=1}^{n} k \cdot \pi_i(\boldsymbol{P}), \tag{1}$$

where k is the profit-based royalty rate, or the uniform share of franchisee profits that the franchisor collects, with $0 < k < 1$. In order to maximize these profits it is necessary that

$$\frac{\partial \Pi}{\partial P_j} = \sum_{i=1}^{n} k \frac{\partial \pi_i}{\partial P_j} = 0, \ j = 1, \ldots, n$$

or

$$k \frac{\partial \pi_j}{\partial P_j} = -\sum_{\substack{i=1 \\ i \neq j}}^{n} k \cdot \frac{\partial \pi_i}{\partial P_j}, \tag{2}$$

which amounts to

$$\frac{\partial \pi_j}{\partial P_j} = -\sum_{\substack{i=1 \\ i \neq j}}^{n} \frac{\partial \pi_i}{\partial P_j}. \tag{3}$$

At the level of prices that maximizes the franchisor's profit, equation (3) implies that

$$\frac{\partial \pi_j}{\partial P_j} > 0,$$

since $\partial \pi_i / \partial P_j < 0$ for $i \neq j$. In other words, beginning at the franchisor's profit maximizing vector of prices, each franchisee has an independent incentive to raise its price to the detriment of the franchisor and the other franchisees.

We can get a somewhat better understanding of this phenomenon by examining a simple algebraic illustration. Assume that a franchised chain is composed of only two outlets, that demand is linear and identical for both outlets, and that marginal (and average) cost, c, is also the same for both outlets. Further, assume that the cost is unaffected by whether the outlet is corporately owned or franchised.[220] Finally, to operationalize the positive externality, assume that the quantity demanded at one outlet depends not only on the price set at this outlet, but also on the price at the other outlet. Thus, we have

$$Q_i = a - b P_i - d P_j, \text{ for } i, j = 1, 2,$$

where $b > 0$ and $d > 0$. Note that the assumption that $d > 0$ implies that these two units are not competing for customers. Presumably, the outlets are in different geographic markets, but customers' goodwill toward the brand depends on the prices they see at both units.

If these outlets are franchised to different individuals, the two franchisees will choose their prices to maximize their own outlet's profits. We discuss in the appendix the case where royalties are based on sales. Here, both for simplicity and to make clear that the conflict is not due to the difference between sales and profit maximization for franchisors and franchisees respectively, we assume that royalties are collected in proportion to outlet profits. Thus, we write franchisee profits as

$$\pi_i = (1 - k)[(P_i - c)(a - b P_i - d P_j)], \quad i = 1, 2.$$

Each franchisee selects its optimal price by solving

$$\partial \pi_i / \partial P_i = (1 - k)(a - 2b P_i - d P_j + bc) = 0 = a - 2b P_i - d P_j + bc$$

for P_i. Thus, the optimal prices for the franchisees are independent of the share of profits that franchisees earn. Specifically, they are:

$$P_1 = (a - d P_2 + bc)/2b$$

and

$$P_2 = (a - d P_1 + bc)/2b.$$

Since we assumed that demands and costs in each market are the same, it is not surprising to find that solving these leads to identical optimal prices:

$$P_1^* = P_2^* = (a + bc)/(2b + d).$$

While these prices are the ones that the two franchisees would select independently, that is, when ignoring the positive demand externality, they are not optimal from the franchisor's perspective. This is because the franchisor

[220] In other words, we are assuming away any agency costs, which are a major explanation for the existence and use of franchising.

wants to maximize the sum of the profits earned at the two outlets, that is,

$$\Pi = k(\pi_1 + \pi_2) = k[(P_1 - c)(a - bP_1 - dP_2)$$
$$+ (P_2 - c)(a - bP_2 - dP_1)].$$

As a result, the franchisor is compelled to take the demand externalities into account.[221]

The franchisor's optimal prices are given by the solutions to

$$\partial \Pi / \partial P_1 = k[a - 2bP_1 - 2dP_2 + bc + dc] = 0$$

and

$$\partial \Pi / \partial P_2 = k[a - 2bP_2 - 2dP_1 + bc + dc] = 0.$$

Solving these first-order conditions for the optimal prices yields

$$P_1' = P_2' = [a + bc + dc]/(2b + 2d).$$

Comparing these prices to the franchisees' optimal prices, prices in franchisee-owned units will be higher than franchisor prices if $a > c(b + d)$, which is the condition that is necessary for the franchisor (and hence franchisees) to want to produce positive quantities in the first place. In other words, if this market exists, franchisee prices will be above those that the franchisor would like them to choose. Hence, the franchisor will have a profit incentive to impose maximum prices at

$$P_1 = P_2 = [a + bc + dc]/(2b + 2d).$$

By the fact that the imposed prices are lower than those that the franchisees would choose, consumers will benefit from the franchisor's use of price ceilings in this context as in the successive monopoly case. But as these are not the prices that maximize the franchisees' profits, existing franchisees will be hurt if such restraints are imposed on them. Still, as in the successive monopoly case, the divergence between the franchisor's and the franchisee's optimal prices may well lead franchisors to vertically integrate and thereby reduce franchise opportunities if they cannot control prices. Thus, once again, maximum resale price maintenance may be beneficial to franchisees in the sense that it makes franchising more attractive to franchisors, thereby increasing

---

[221] Note that if the two units were franchised to the same individual, this individual would internalize the externality just like the franchisor does. But the point is that as long as different individuals own different units in a chain, they will not fully internalize these externalities whereas these are fully internalized in a corporate entity.

the likelihood that they will continue to operate with their existing franchised networks and even allow new franchisees to join.

7.3.4 Franchisor Opportunism

As noted by Ozanne and Hunt (1971), Hadfield (1990), and Stassen and Mittelstaedt (1991), franchisors may also push franchisee prices down because they are opportunistic.[222] In other words, because franchisors extract their revenues as a percentage of the sales revenue rather than the profits of their franchisees, a franchisor might want its franchisees to maximize unit sales revenue rather than profits. Franchisees, on the other hand, are interested in maximizing their unit's profits, which requires a higher price than that which maximizes sales. Hence, franchisors might exert pressure on franchisees to reduce their prices and increase their sales volume. The result, of course, is conflict between the franchisor and its franchisees.

While this is a popular explanation for the pressure imposed by franchisors on franchisee prices, it fails to recognize some of the effects of this behavior. First, if franchisors systematically force franchisee prices down to levels that maximize sales, they may not earn a sufficient return in the short run and so would close down. This, of course, cannot ultimately be beneficial to the chain as it reduces the availability of its product and the visibility of the trademark. If the prices are pushed down a bit less so that the franchisee can cover its variable costs in the short run, the franchisee can remain open for a time. But in the longer run, again, the unit will close and the franchisor will be hurt by this. Furthermore, assuming that potential franchisees can see that this is happening, it will become very difficult for this franchisor to find new franchisees, which will limit the growth and size of the chain.

It is sometimes argued that the franchisor will push prices down enough so that the franchisee will nearly fail. The franchisor then exploits the struggling franchisee by buying back the unit at a very low price and reselling it at a profit to a new franchisee. But for this to work, it is necessary that new franchisees remain unaware of such behavior. Otherwise, they would refuse to buy and expose themselves to the same opportunistic treatment. Other franchisees in the chain also must be unaware of this behavior or they would start to take protective actions. They might even stop investing in their franchise. These

---

[222] The trade press often refers to this to explain why franchisors exert pressure on franchisees to lower their prices.

actions again will ultimately hurt the chain and, therefore, cannot be in the franchisor's interest.

The point of this discussion is not to say that franchisors never behave opportunistically. Rather, our point is that reputation concerns, combined with the inefficiency the franchisor presumably faces if he has to operate corporately because he can no longer find franchisees willing to work with him, will by themselves curb the franchisors' tendency to behave opportunistically toward their franchisees.[223]

In addition, the empirical evidence to date reveals that prices are higher in franchised than in company-owned stores of the same chains.[224] This is consistent with the general idea that franchisors find franchisee prices too high and try to push them down. But it is not consistent with franchisor opportunism as an explanation for this behavior. This is because company-owned outlets are profit centers for the franchisors. Thus, franchisors would not want to maximize *sales revenues* in those outlets. Instead, they would want to maximize *profits*. As a result, the franchisor would choose the higher price, the one that maximizes profits, in its company-owned units rather than the lower price that maximizes sales revenue. In other words, post-contractual opportunism by franchisors implies that prices at company-owned outlets would be *above* the prices they would be trying to get the franchised units to charge, which is contrary to the existing evidence. Under successive monopoly and the positive demand externality arguments, on the other hand, prices in franchised units would be above those in company units, as the evidence shows they are.

We conclude that franchisor opportunism, while still a possible explanation in some cases for franchisors imposing maximum resale prices, is not the most likely explanation for this practice. Rather, we believe that the issues of successive monopolies and demand externalities play a much larger role in a franchisor's desire to adopt these restraints. In addition, franchisor opportunism is not an antitrust issue. Thus, we conclude that the decision

---

[223] Klein (1980, 1995) explores these issues in more detail.

[224] See Lafontaine and Slade (1997) for a review of this evidence. This literature includes studies of gasoline retailing (Shepard 1993), soft-drink bottling (Muris, Scheffman, and Spiller 1992), pubs (Slade 1998a), and fast food (Graddy 1997 and Lafontaine 1995b). In all cases where a significant difference in prices was found, the franchisee's prices were *higher* than those in the franchisor-owned outlets. More recent studies of the prices at the outlets of major fast-food chains in specific markets performed by Thomadsen (2002) and Kalnins (2003) also confirm this pattern of higher prices in franchised than in company units.

to overturn the *Albrecht* rule in *Khan* can only be viewed as a positive policy change.

7.4 The Public Policy Implications of *Khan*

We have seen that there are procompetitive reasons for franchisors to employ maximum resale price restraints. We have also seen that post-contractual opportunism provides an alternative explanation and this is not procompetitive. The public policy implications of these conflicting incentives are examined in turn in what follows.

7.4.1 Antitrust Policy

First, and foremost, *Khan* was an antitrust case that dealt with vertically imposed maximum resale prices. For some 30 years, we had a *per se* prohibition of this business practice. When a practice is deemed illegal *per se* that means that the Supreme Court has determined that the practice inevitably has anticompetitive consequences. While this is generally true of *horizontal* agreements on price, it is usually not true of *vertical* price agreements. Under conditions of successive monopoly or in the presence of positive demand externalities, the *per se* ban on maximum resale price restraints is perverse. Instead of promoting consumer welfare, the *Albrecht* rule protected downstream monopoly and thereby reduced consumer welfare. We have shown this quite clearly in the preceding section. Thus, as an antitrust matter, the *Khan* decision was correct and should lead to consumer welfare gains. Similarly, the new attitude toward maximum resale prices embodied in the recent block exemption for vertical restraints in the EU should benefit consumers.

7.4.2 Opportunism

As an economic matter, we do not want to encourage opportunistic behavior. It is not socially productive. In fact, opportunism is unproductive because resources are wasted by those engaging in such behavior and by those who try to defend against it. In the case of maximum resale pricing, franchisees will waste resources in devising ways to protect themselves. They may debase product or service quality in an effort to evade the effects of maximum resale prices. This is especially likely if their economic survival is at stake. Alternatively, they may refrain from making certain investments if they are concerned about having them confiscated by the franchisor.

Post-contractual opportunism by franchisors is also not good for the franchise community at large. To the extent that it makes franchising less attractive to prospective franchisees, this hurts all franchisors. Opportunistic behavior, however, is not a *competitive* evil. That is, it is not an antitrust problem. Rather, it is a contractual problem. If a franchisor restricts the franchisee's pricing freedom to the point that total revenues cover variable costs, but do not provide a competitive return on the franchisee's sunk investment, then the franchisee faces economic duress. The choices are unpleasant: if he refuses to adhere to the restriction, he faces termination; if he acquiesces, he will slowly slide into bankruptcy. Neither option is appealing. There may, however, be some contractual relief.

Plaintiff-franchisees and their attorneys surely prefer antitrust relief because the antitrust laws provide for treble damages plus a reasonable attorney's fee. Clearly, this is more lucrative than contract damages, which are confined to the actual lost profit and do not provide for an attorney's fee. But if there is no real anticompetitive significance to maximum resale price restraints, there can be no antitrust violation and, therefore, no antitrust damages.

7.5 Conclusion

The Supreme Court overruled *Albrecht* in its recent *Khan* decision. This should bring to a close some 30 years of criticism of a misguided prohibition of maximum resale price restraints. Under conditions of successive monopoly or positive demand externalities, franchisors will have an incentive to limit the maximum prices that franchisees can charge. We have argued that this will benefit consumers along with the franchisors. It is therefore appropriate that franchisors should be free of antitrust prosecution to pursue this business strategy.

We have been mindful of the possibility that franchisors could use maximum resale price restraints in an opportunistic fashion to abuse their franchisees. Our concern is that the franchisor could reduce resale prices to the point where the franchisees are not earning a competitive return on their sunk investments. One cannot prove that this behavior makes no economic sense. But we have discounted the likelihood of post-contractual opportunistic behavior because of its adverse reputation and operational effects. Franchisors have a continuing interest in licensing new franchisees and in keeping their existing franchised networks in good working order. If a franchisor develops a reputation for engaging in opportunistic behavior, its system will not be attractive to prospective franchisees and it will find it difficult to expand. It will also face uncooperative franchisees. In other words, market forces will blunt the incentives for opportunistic behavior on the part of franchisors. Furthermore, we have noted that existing empirical evidence contradicts the franchisor opportunism argument. Perhaps most importantly for public policy purposes, franchisor opportunism is not anticompetitive, and thus not an antitrust issue. In fact, allowing franchisees to sue franchisors for treble damages in the U.S. when they face pressure to reduce their prices may well amount to endorsing opportunistic behavior on the part of some franchisees. Thus, in our view, the new attitude toward maximum resale prices embodied in the *Khan* decision in the U.S. and in the new block exemption on vertical restraints in the EU represent a change for the better in general, and for franchising in particular.

7.6 Appendix: Sales-Based Royalties and Demand Externalities

In this appendix, we show that the demand externality problem is exacerbated when franchisors levy royalties based on sales rather than profits. In this case, we can write the franchisor's profits as

$$\Pi = \sum_{i=1}^{n} r[TR_i(\boldsymbol{P})],$$

where TR_i represents the total revenue or sales of franchisee i, r is the uniform sales-based royalty rate, with $0 < r < 1$, and $\boldsymbol{P}$ is the vector of all prices chosen by franchisees. To maximize Π by choice of price we must have

$$\frac{\partial \Pi}{\partial P_j} = \sum_{i=1}^{n} r \frac{\partial TR_i}{\partial P_j} = 0, \ j = 1, \dots, n,$$

or

$$r \frac{\partial TR_j}{\partial P_j} = - \sum_{\substack{i=1 \\ i \neq j}}^{n} r \cdot \frac{\partial TR_i}{\partial P_j},$$

which amounts to

$$\frac{\partial TR_j}{\partial P_j} = \sum_{\substack{i=1 \\ i \neq j}}^{n} \cdot \frac{\partial TR_i}{\partial P_j}.$$

In other words, at the level of prices that maximizes the franchisor's sales royalties, $\frac{\partial TR_j}{\partial P_j} > 0$ since $\partial TR_i / \partial P_j < 0$ for $i \neq j$. Hence, beginning at the franchisor's profit maximizing vector of prices, each franchisee would have an incentive to raise its price further if it wanted to maximize its own total revenues. But in reality, franchisees whose royalties are based on sales want to maximize the difference between the portion of sales that they retain and their cost. Since they bear the full cost of selling an extra unit, but only receive part of the extra revenues, their incentives will be to choose a price that is even higher than the sales revenue-maximizing price at the outlet level. To see this, assume that the cost of selling a unit of the good for an outlet j is constant and equal to c. The franchisee's profits then can be written as

$$\pi_j = (1 - r)TR_j - c_j Q_j.$$

Maximizing these by choice of P_j entails setting the first derivative equal to zero, that is

$$\frac{\partial \pi_j}{\partial P_j} = (1 - r)\frac{\partial TR_j}{\partial P_j} - c_j\frac{\partial Q_j}{\partial P_j} = 0.$$

As $(1 - r)$ is positive by assumption, and $\partial Q_j/\partial P_j < 0$, this condition implies that $\partial TR_j/\partial P_j < 0$ at the price that maximizes the franchisee's profits. This in turn requires that the price be set at a level that is even higher than the price that would maximize outlet revenues, which in turn is higher than the price that maximizes the sum of outlet revenues and thus franchisor profits. Of course, such a result makes sense if we consider that the franchisee only gets a portion of the sales revenue associated with selling more but bears the full cost of extra sales himself, making extra sales less attractive and, correspondingly, the optimal price higher. Moreover, we have assumed that the franchisor only cares about outlet sales, so his incentive is to have franchisees sell even larger amounts at lower prices than would occur under profit sharing.

Here again, we can get a better understanding of the problem by examining our simple algebraic illustration – with two outlets – linear and identical demand for both outlets, and constant marginal (and average) cost, c, for both that is unaffected by whether the outlet is corporately owned or franchised. As before, the quantity demanded at one outlet depends not only on the price set at this outlet, but also on the price at the other outlet. Thus,

$$Q_i = a - bP_i - dP_j, \text{ for } i, j = 1, 2,$$

where $b > 0$ and $d > 0$. If these outlets are franchised to different individuals, the two franchisees will choose their prices to maximize their own outlet's profits. Assuming a sales-based royalty rate of r, the franchisee's profits are

$$\pi_i = (1 - r)[P_i(a - bP_i - dP_j)] - c(a - bP_i - dP_j).$$

Each franchisee selects its optimal price by solving

$$\partial \pi_i / \partial P_i = (1 - r)(a - 2bP_i - dP_j) + bc = 0$$

for P_i. Thus the optimal prices for the franchisees now depend on the sales royalties. Specifically, they are:

$$P_1 = \frac{\left(a - dP_2 + \frac{bc}{1-r}\right)}{2b}$$

and

$$P_2 = \frac{\left(a - dP_1 + \frac{bc}{1-r}\right)}{2b}.$$

Solving these gives:

$$P_1^* = P_2^* = \frac{\left(a + \frac{bc}{1-r}\right)}{2b + d}.$$

When $r = 0$, there are no royalties on sales and we get the same solution as when the franchisor shares in the franchisees' profits directly. We would also get this solution if the franchisor extracted only a fixed fee with neither sales nor profit royalties – the solution with $r = 0$ is the one that maximizes each franchisee's profits directly. With $0 < (1 - r) < 1$, P_1^* and P_2^* are higher than those we found under profit sharing, and they are higher the higher r is. In other words, the franchisee's optimal prices are higher under sales royalties than under profit sharing. Again this is not surprising: sales royalties mean that the franchisee gets a smaller part of revenue per unit but bears all costs. This makes him want to stop selling when the contribution of a unit to his revenues equals the contribution to his cost which, with a tax on revenue, occurs for a smaller quantity and higher price than the one that would arise if he did not face this tax on revenue.

As for the franchisor, they would now want to maximize:

$$\Pi = r(TR_1 + TR_2) = r[P_1(a - bP_1 - dP_2) + P_2(a - bP_2 - dP_1)].$$

From this perspective optimal prices would be given by the solutions to

$$\partial \Pi / \partial P_1 = r[a - 2bP_1 - 2dP_2] = 0$$

and

$$\partial \Pi / \partial P_2 = r[a - 2bP_2 - 2dP_1] = 0.$$

Solving these first-order conditions for the optimal prices yields

$$P_1' = P_2' = a/(2b + 2d).$$

Comparing these prices to the franchisor's solution under profit sharing, we see that these are even lower. In other words, we have shown that under sales royalties, the franchisee wants even higher prices than under profit sharing, while the franchisor's optimal prices go down further. Hence, the pricing conflict is even more acute with sales instead of profit royalties. Part of this conflict now relates to the different objectives of the franchisor and franchisee: the franchisee wants to maximize outlet profits, which are the difference between what he retains of revenues and all costs, while the franchisor now wants the franchisees to maximize sales instead of profits. In the body of the chapter, we have focused on profit maximization to highlight the part of the conflict that arises from the presence of demand externalities only. In other words, we showed that even when we eliminate the component of the conflict that comes from the different objectives, franchisees still would want higher prices than those that maximize the franchisor's profit if there are demand externalities in the franchise system, something that common brands are meant to generate.

8

Encroachment

8.1 Introduction

Many of the business sectors where franchising occurs are mature, and franchising itself has become a fairly mature mode of organization in these industries. As a result of this maturity, competition has intensified and the issue of "impact" or "encroachment" has come to the forefront. In fact, as some industry analysts would have it, traditional encroachment – "the franchisor's placement of a new company-owned or franchised unit too close to an existing one – has emerged to be one of the most vexing, emotional and yet least understood [franchising] problems of today." (Barkoff and Garner 1994a)

While encroachment is defined most often in terms of geographic competition, it can take many different forms. All alternative channels through which a franchisor can distribute its products or services to customers will potentially "encroach" on its franchisees' businesses and impact their profitability. For example, when Carvel sells its frozen desserts at the supermarket, customers who purchase them there might reduce the frequency of their visits to individual Carvel restaurants. Franchisees thus can claim that they are hurt by such sales. On the other hand, customer awareness of the Carvel brand may be increased by the availability of the product at non-franchised locations, thereby increasing traffic at the chain's franchised outlets. A similar set of potentially negative and positive impacts on franchisees can occur with internet sales, non-traditional franchised or company outlets, and any other alternative route used to reach the ultimate customer. In the end, whether distribution through such alternative channels has a negative impact on any individual franchisee is an empirical matter that depends on how customers react to this new option as well as how the franchisor chooses to organize the distribution through this alternative channel. In particular, it will be a function of whether this activity is centralized at the franchisor's headquarters or involves the local franchisee directly, either in the sales process or in the servicing of the same, whether the franchisor shares the revenues or profits from such sales with local franchisees, and so on. In other words, we cannot draw general conclusions on the effect of "encroachment" decisions based on *a priori* reasoning – the net effect on franchisees always depends on the specific circumstances and methods involved. Whatever strategy is used, however, conflict between franchisees and their franchisor will emerge if either party feels constrained by the other, or finds that it is being unfairly treated by the other.[225]

The same basic trade-off that we just described between building brand presence and visibility while minimizing the negative impact on existing units occurs, of course, under the traditional, or geographic, notion of encroachment as well. Increasing the geographical density of stores can have a harmful effect on nearby units' sales, yet it can also increase demand for the products or services sold under the common, and now more visible, brand and thus benefit the same nearby stores. In fact, disputes about chains developing "too few" units in particular geographic markets also arise regularly in franchising. As Bassuk (2000) puts it, "encroachment is the disease of the rich and successful" while "lack of clusters and adequate market penetration is the disease of the masses." Indeed, for the majority of franchised systems, encroachment is not really an issue – as we discussed in Chapter 2, most franchised chains simply do not operate enough outlets for geographical encroachment to arise. But as we established also in Chapter 2, the majority of *franchisees* are part of large chains, and, as such, encroachment by new nearby outlets is indeed an issue for many of them.[226] Since growth within franchised chains mostly occurs through the development of new outlets rather than outlet level sales growth, the issue of geographic encroachment in franchising, in some sense, is here to stay. Finally, encroachment through alternative channels or concepts can occur even in relatively small franchised systems.

In general, whether the negative "impact" on sales or the positive business generation effect dominates in any particular instance of "encroachment" ultimately must be addressed on a case-by-case basis by franchisors and their franchisees. Calls for regulatory intervention must be tempered by the

---

[225] Problems with alternative channels are not limited to franchising. See, e.g., Gertner and Stillman (2001) on how apparel manufacturer internet policies were shaped, at least in part by channel conflict issues.

[226] See Chapter 2 for data on the size distribution of franchised chains, most of which are much too small for traditional encroachment to be an issue. However, those data also establish that most franchisees are associated with a relatively few, very large, franchised systems.

recognition that encroachment is not as simple an issue as some proponents of legislative remedies suggest.

This chapter begins with a discussion of geographical encroachment, the types of industries most affected by it, and the potential motivations behind it. We then describe, in section 3, various ways in which industry members have reacted to this issue, along with current legislative solutions, actual and proposed. In section 4, we discuss encroachment through alternative channels and alternative concepts, from both a theoretical and a practical perspective. Here as well, we present information on various solutions implemented by industry members and on current legislative proposals. We conclude in section 5.

8.2 Market Coverage and "Traditional" Encroachment

Franchisors and their franchisees all want their franchise systems to thrive. They also all understand that more outlets in a chain means greater visibility and customer brand awareness. Moreover, an increase in the number of outlets leads to larger marketing and advertising budgets not only globally, but also regionally and locally. In addition, it leads to increased bargaining power vis-à-vis suppliers. In other words, a larger number of outlets in a chain theoretically benefits everyone as it simultaneously increases demand and reduces costs.

Geographic encroachment comes into play at the local rather than regional or national level. While franchisees agree in principle that more outlets in their chain is a good thing, they do not necessarily feel the same way about their local markets. In other words, franchisees expect to do better if they do not face "too much" competition from their own brand nearby.

8.2.1 Defining Geographic or Traditional Encroachment

The word encroachment has a very negative connotation. Its origins are found in real estate law, where it was defined as an illegal invasion or intrusion by a landowner's building or other structure on someone else's property. As used in franchising, it has come to refer to any interference by the franchisor with a franchisee's perceived market rights. Contrary to the real estate situation, then, the franchisor's behavior need not be unlawful at all to be deemed a form of encroachment.

In 1992, the Iowa legislature enacted what has remained, through its various revisions, the most comprehensive franchise relationship law in the United

States. This law addresses directly the issue of encroachment. In its most recent version, this statute defines encroachment as follows:

> If a franchisor develops, or grants to a franchisee the right to develop, a new outlet or location which sells essentially the same goods or services under the same trademark, service mark, trade name, logotype or other commercial symbol as an existing franchisee and the new outlet or location is in unreasonable proximity to the existing franchisee's outlet or location and has an adverse effect on the gross sales of the existing franchisee's outlet or location, the existing adversely affected franchisee has a cause of action for monetary damages. . . . (*Iowa Code* 2001 Supplement, Section 537A.10)

Though "unreasonable proximity" is not explicitly defined, the statute further refines its encroachment definition by eliminating recourse where the effect on the existing outlet's gross sales, relative to the twelve months immediately preceding the opening of the new outlet, is below 6 percent. Further, for franchisees to have recourse when there is more than a 6 percent effect, it must be established that the sales reduction is not due to other factors, such as changes in the business environment or changing consumer tastes. Other factors that eliminate the possibility of franchisee action include (1) the franchisee was offered the right to develop the new unit under then current contract terms, (2) the franchisee is not in compliance with the franchisor's "then current reasonable criteria" for eligibility for a new franchise, or (3) the existing franchisee has been granted "reasonable" territorial rights and the new outlet does not violate those rights.

Note that the definition above replaced an earlier one that used a 5 percent "impact" threshold (*Iowa Code* 523H, 1995), which in turn had replaced an even earlier version that based the definition of encroachment strictly on physical proximity and population density (3 miles/30,000 population base around the outlet) (*Iowa Code* 523H, 1992).

The Small Business Franchise Act of 1999, proposed in November 1999 by Congressman Coble (HR 3308) at the federal level, used a similar definition of encroachment:

> A franchisor may not place, or license another to place, one or more new outlets for a franchised business in an unreasonable proximity to an established outlet of a similar kind of franchised business, if. . . the intent or probable effect of establishing the new outlets is to cause a diminution of gross sales by the established outlet of more than 5 percent in the 12 months immediately following establishment of the new outlet.

Under this proposal, franchisors can prevent franchisees from bringing an action only by paying the owner of each established outlet whose sales are

affected by more than 5 percent an amount equal to 50 percent of the new
outlet's gross sales for the first 24 months of operation of the new outlet. This
would seem to be a high price indeed.[227]

The idea behind these definitions, of course, should be to capture what is
perceived to be the central problem with encroachment, namely franchisor
market development and expansion policies that are not based on legitimate
commercial interests but instead are intended directly to hurt franchisees.[228]
After all, franchisees themselves want their franchisor to develop the chain
aggressively and compete well with other product offerings in the market. In
what follows, we use a very stylized example to examine diverse circumstances
where the "impact" threshold is likely to be operative, and yet the expansion
not only serves the franchisor's commercial interests, but is desirable also
from the perspective of consumer welfare and the commercial interests of
potential franchisees. One of our goals in this process is to show that the
type of territorial protection requested by individual incumbent franchisees
is often not in the chain's or society's best interest.[229]

8.2.2 Territorial Conflict – Pinpointing the Source(s)

In what follows, we use a stylized example to illustrate the basic source of conflict between franchisors and franchisees in geographic markets. The specifics
of this example have been chosen purposely to allow us to highlight the most
common sources of conflict within a single framework. As our goal is simply
to illustrate the issues at hand, we abstract from many real-world considerations. However, even though our example is very stylized, we use realistic

---

[227] This would also provide an enormous windfall for the franchisee. Suppose that the
franchisee's yearly sales were $1,000,000. Thus, a 5-percent reduction would be $50,000.
If the profit margin on those lost sales were 40 percent, profits would fall by $20,000 per
year. At a discount rate of 10 percent, the present value of the perpetual stream of lost
profits would be $200,000. If the new franchisee's annual gross sales were expected to
be $1,000,000, the incumbent would receive a $1,000,000 payment (50% of $1,000,000
for two years) to offset its loss of $200,000, which amounts to an $800,000 windfall.

[228] See *Far Horizons Pty Ltd v. McDonald's Australia Ltd.*, VSC 310 (August 18, 2000) for
a case where an existing franchisee specifically argued that the franchisor's decisions
to open two new outlets and not offer them to him were meant to apply pressure on
him to sell his stores and leave the McDonald's system, and to make an example of
him so as to intimidate other franchisees as well. For a discussion of this case, see Terry
(2001).

[229] See also Smith (1982) and Eckard (1985) for evidence that the territorial protection
afforded to car dealers has been costly for consumers in that the result has been both
higher prices for cars and fewer hours of operation for dealers.

figures to calibrate it and the main points it illustrates are, in fact, quite general.[230]

Assume a circular market – say an island – where consumers are uniformly distributed along the circumference of the island. To make things concrete, we assume this circumference to be 120 miles long.[231] Each consumer is willing to consume some amount of the good offered by a firm – say a fast-food restaurant chain. But consumers do not frequent these restaurants as often if they are located far away from their home. More specifically, we assume that consumers incur travel costs and that these reduce the frequency of their visits or, equivalently, induce a smaller proportion of the population in the region to frequent the restaurant regularly. In particular, we assume that consumers who live within a mile from a restaurant will visit it on average six times per time period. We abstract from issues of pricing by measuring units of the goods in dollars, assuming that each visit costs the consumer $5. Thus, customers living within a mile of a restaurant will spend $30 per time period there. We assume also that customers who live between one and two miles visit their closest restaurant four times and thus spend $20 per time period there, whereas those who live between two and four miles visit twice, and those who live between four and six miles visit the restaurant only once per time period. Finally, we assume that people will not travel more than six miles to go to these restaurants, so those who live further than six miles away from any of the outlets do not purchase any meals there.[232] To finalize our characterization of the demand side, we need to specify the number of consumers per mile and what a time period is. To get relatively realistic but "round" numbers, we assume that population density is 1,000 people per mile, and the number of periods per year is 10 (so our time periods are slightly longer than a month each), for a total of 10,000 potential customers per year per mile.

On the cost side, we assume, again for concreteness, that the yearly fixed cost of operating one of these stores is $320,000 and the variable costs (cost of goods sold plus crew labor) represent 60 cents out of every dollar in sales.

---

[230] See Schmidt (1994) for a more complete model demonstrating some of the points below.

[231] We choose this number not because it represents any particular reality, but because it has a large number of divisors such that the solutions to our many scenarios tend to be round numbers.

[232] Our stylized assumptions about the trade areas around a restaurant are consistent, for example, with McDonald's location policy as described in Salvaneschi (1996: 76): "McDonald's used to follow a distance rule of 3, 5, and 7 minutes of travel time. A restaurant's core part of its RTZ (retail trade zone) was under three minutes of travel time, the secondary part of its RTZ was within 3 to 5 minutes, and the outer area was within 5 to 7 minutes."

While these figures are chosen somewhat arbitrarily, they approximate the costs of operating certain types of fast-food restaurants. Using S to denote yearly sales, we can write the yearly total costs as

$$TC = \$320,000 + .6S,$$

with yearly profits at the store level then equal to

$$\pi_i = S - TC = .4S - \$320,000.$$

As is standard in economics, we consider that the costs described here include all opportunity costs such as a normal return on investment and compensation for the owner's time spent managing the store. When economic profit, π_i, is greater than zero, the owner is making economic or "above-normal" profits. When economic profits are zero, accounting profits are positive and amount to normal compensation for the owner's capital and time. Put differently, with zero economic profits the owner is as well off using his capital and time in this business as he would be in his next best alternative. Hence, zero economic profit is the minimum required profit for the owner to be "just satisfied" with the outlet's performance. Finally, for simplicity, we assume that the stores described by the cost function above are always large enough to serve all customers who come under our various scenarios.

Given this setup, we now turn to an assessment of the optimal number of stores in this market from different perspectives and under different scenarios. As a benchmark, we first consider the competitive solution, which is what independent business owners, who would establish independent fast-food outlets all around the island, would choose to do. For simplicity, we assume that the lack of a common brand does not affect local demand levels nor outlet costs. This assumption, of course, rules out some of the main reasons why a franchisee would opt for franchising rather than independent business ownership or why a franchisor would prefer franchising to company ownership. While restrictive in that sense, it is worth making as it simplifies our analyses significantly and the results obtained under this assumption in fact give a good sense of the general issues at hand.

8.2.2.1 The Competitive Benchmark

Under this scenario of independent businesses all around the island competing with one another locally, we ask how many stores one would expect to see ultimately, what would be individual store sales and profits, and how well off consumers would be.

Fundamentally, under competition, entry into this market will continue as long as business owners can earn more profit doing this than in their next best alternative. This means that entry stops only when each owner earns normal returns, or zero economic profits, which amounts to $\pi_i = S - TC = .4S - \$320{,}000 = 0$. Solving for S gives a sales level of \$800,000 per store. This level of sales per store, in turn, occurs if stores locate every 3 miles so that they each attract all those customers living within 1.5 miles from them in both directions.[233] Each store then gets the \$30 per period per customer for all those living within a mile of it in either direction, for a total of two times 10,000 times \$30, or \$600,000 in sales, plus the demand from all those who live in the next closest half mile in either direction. Their demand is \$20 per customer per period for 5,000 customers on each side, for \$200,000 in sales. Thus, if we have unaffiliated business owners competing with one another to serve this market, we expect to get a total of 40 stores with revenues of \$800,000 each and zero economic profits. Consumers are very well off under this scenario as they get to purchase 6.4 million "units" of the good each year, at \$5 each. Put differently, consumers are well off because everyone has a store nearby, within 1.5 miles of their home.

8.2.2.2 The Optimal Store Configuration under Monopoly

Assume now that a single chain provides fast food on the island, and no other firm is considering entering this market. Thus, we have a monopoly protected from entry. Supposing that all the stores are corporately owned and operated, what is the optimal number of stores for this monopolist to set up along the circumference of the island? Presumably, the chain will want to maximize the profits it derives from all the stores. With individual store profits of $\pi_i = S - TC = .4S - \$320{,}000$, the firm wants to choose n to

$$\max \Pi = \sum_{i=1}^{n} \pi_i = n(S - TC) = .4n \cdot S(n) - \$320{,}000 \cdot n,$$

where $S(n)$ represents the fact that sales at an individual outlet depend on the number of outlets in the market. Since demand was assumed to be a step function, we cannot use calculus to solve this problem. Taking as given

---

[233] Customers who live more than 1.5 miles away will have access to another restaurant that is closer to them than this one. In equilibrium, as prices are the same at all restaurants, consumers frequent only the restaurant that is closest to them. Hotelling (1929) first proposed and solved this type of location model in economics. See also Carlton and Perloff (2000) for a textbook treatment.

the fact that the number of stores must be an integer, however, by trial and error one finds that the firm maximizes Π by establishing 15 stores, each eight miles apart. With average expenditures of $30 by all customers within a mile of the store, on either side, followed by $20 for those between miles one and two, and $10 for all those living two to four miles away on each side – the point where the customers instead choose to visit the adjacent store – we get total store revenues per year under this configuration of 10,000 · (30 + 30 + 20 + 20 + 10 + 10 + 10 + 10) = $1.4 million. Store profits are .4 · $1,400,000 − $320,000 = $240,000 per year. With 15 stores generating such profits, the chain as a whole earns $3.6 million.

As one would expect, consumers are worse off under monopoly than under competition: they get to consume only 4.2 million units per year compared to the 6.4 million they purchased under competition. Put differently, some consumers are not served as well under monopoly because the closest store to their homes is up to four miles away rather than just 1.5 miles away. As we will see below, however, consumers are better off under monopoly than under the configuration that maximizes the profits of individual stores. Hence, if consumers value having access to a branded product, where a firm necessarily holds some market power associated with its brand, they are better off under the solution that the brand owner prefers than under the solution that those who might purchase the rights to distribute the branded product would prefer.

8.2.2.3 Franchisees' Optimal Configuration

Instead of operating all the units corporately, the same chain might franchise all the restaurants. Suppose for now that the chain allows each franchisee to own only one restaurant. For simplicity, assume also that the franchise contract requires that the franchisee pay a fixed fee each year to the franchisor rather than sales-based royalties.

Franchisees of course would prefer not to face any competition from other restaurants operating under the same brand. Since any given restaurant can draw customers from up to six miles away, the franchisee will maximize its profits if it has an exclusive territory extending six miles from its store in both directions around the island. With a total market length of 120 miles, single-unit franchisees then would find it optimal if the chain established a total of ten restaurants distributed uniformly every twelve miles around the island. In other words, they would not mind if the franchisor set up another restaurant twelve miles away from theirs in either direction as such restaurants would not "infringe" at all on their sales given that consumers will not travel more than six miles to buy this product.

With a total of ten restaurants around the island, each of them would generate yearly sales of $10,000 \cdot (30 + 30 + 20 + 20 + 10 + 10 + 10 + 10 + 5 + 5 + 5 + 5) = \$1.6$ million. Each franchisee would earn $.4 \cdot \$1,600,000 - \$320,000 = \$320,000$ per year, minus whatever yearly fee they have agreed to pay to the franchisor. Total sales in the market would be equal to $10 \cdot \$1.6$ million $= \$16$ million. In other words, consumers are worse off under the single-unit franchisee scenario than under the monopoly solution: they now consume only 3.2 million units per year versus 4.4 million. Equivalently, some consumers now live quite far, up to six miles away, from their closest restaurant.

Note that franchising will be less appealing than company ownership to this firm if it is bound to establish only the number of stores that franchisees prefer. Under the 10-store configuration favored by franchisees, total profits in the market are $3.2 million as opposed to the $3.6 million generated under the monopolist's 15-store configuration. Thus, even if the franchisor were to extract all the franchisees' profit through the annual fixed fee, namely setting that fee at $320,000 per year so that in the end the franchisee only earns "normal returns," the franchisor would still not fare as well under this scenario as under company ownership. This illustrates the most fundamental source of conflict between franchisors and franchisees as it relates to store location: the franchisees' preferred number of stores is below the number of stores that maximizes chain profits. The franchisor will always want to locate other stores "too close" to the existing franchisees' stores except in the one particular case where a single franchisee owns all the stores in the market. In that case, the franchisee will choose to maximize the sum of store profits in the market just as the franchisor would and will reach the same conclusion as the franchisor regarding the optimal configuration to achieve this goal. What this last point illustrates is that as long as the franchisee does not own **all** of the outlets in a market, he or she will want other outlets to be fewer in number and farther away than what the franchisor finds best.

From a public policy perspective, it is important to note that franchisors that choose to locate outlets "too close" to one another for their franchisees are in fact serving their customers and society better than they would if they followed the wishes of their franchisees. Of course, vertical restraints such as exclusive territories can have procompetitive effects due to increased interbrand competition, as the Supreme Court recognized in *Sylvania*.[234] In that particular case, Sylvania imposed location restrictions on its distributors. This strategy resulted in an increase in market share from 1–2 percent to about 5 percent. But when such procompetitive effects are present, franchisors have every

---

[234] *Continental T.V., Inc. v. GTE Sylvania, Inc.*

incentive to rely on these vertical restraints. When they instead choose to not provide exclusive territories or to locate outlets "too close" to one another from the franchisees' perspective, this is presumably because they do not believe that the restraints will benefit them. In those cases, the restraints also will not benefit consumers. And indeed, studies of the effect of state laws that have conferred territorial protection on car dealers have confirmed this. Smith (1982) and Eckard (1985) have studied the prices charged at car dealerships before and after such territorial protection, and both found that consumers pay more for their cars due to state statutes that restrict the car manufacturers' ability to establish new car dealerships. They also find evidence that customers obtain less service after the imposition of these restrictions, as evidenced by a reduction in hours of operation. While our stylized example abstracts from potential pricing effects, higher prices would ensue in our model, as well, if we allowed price competition among our more or less densely located stores. In that sense, it is troubling that courts and public policy decisions, under the notion of protecting small businesses, have sometimes favored the franchisees' position in encroachment disputes at the expense of consumers. We will return to the legal treatment of encroachment claims later.

8.2.2.4 Franchisees' Optimal Configuration – Revisited

The discussion above suggests that single-unit franchisees will always want fewer units than franchisors in any given market. This is true, however, only for those single-unit franchisees who own one of the original ten outlets. As they are the ones who bring up the issue of encroachment, they are the correct group of franchisees on which to focus to understand the source of the basic conflict. There is another set of franchisees, however, the ones who will not get one of the ten outlets, who would rather that the franchisor establish more than ten outlets in the same market. In fact, fundamentally, when a franchisor sells a new franchised outlet that is "too close" to existing outlets, it must be that some franchisee is willing to purchase an outlet in that location. Alternatively, if the chain sets up a new company-owned unit, it must be willing to operate one in that new location as well. This suggests that such an outlet is expected to be profitable. But how could it be profitable if it is so close to other outlets as to render them unprofitable? Of course, for franchisees the issue is not really one of profitability versus no profitability – it is a question of the **level of** profitability.[235] And franchisees do better if they do

---

[235] Franchisees sometimes argue that because it is clean and new, the new outlet "unfairly" draws their customers away, and that is what makes the new outlet profitable (see, for

not compete with other restaurants operating under the same brand, as seen above. But the owner of the new outlet can still expect to make some amount of positive profit. He may not expect as much as the existing franchisee had been making, but it is still enough to entice him to invest and entice a bank or other lender to lend. In fact, were it not for the franchisor restricting entry or the number of outlets in the market, individuals would be willing to continue to purchase restaurants in a market until they drive economic profits to zero, as we saw above in our analysis of the competitive benchmark. In that sense, relative to the case of free entry – the situation they would face were it not for their belonging to a chain – the franchisor already reduces substantially the number of restaurants they must compete with in the market and thereby increases the amount of profits each of them can earn. Of course, as the owner of the brand, the franchisor extracts at least some, if not all, of those profits through its franchise fees.[236]

As for existing franchisees, if they were offered a choice at the outset between investing in a restaurant belonging to a chain that would establish 15 outlets in our stylized market or going on their own, they would opt for investing in the chain as long as the franchise fees were below $240,000 per year. This is because the positive economic profits they would earn imply that they still earn a higher return on their time and capital within the chain, even with 15 outlets, than they could earn in their next best alternative.

This points to one important component of a solution to the encroachment problem: franchisors need to be as explicit as possible about target sales levels per outlet in markets where they sell franchises, and let franchisees know beforehand that sales levels much above those – whether they occur because demand is high in the market to begin with or because the market has grown over time – will induce them to locate other units in that same market just as such sales levels would induce the franchisee to do so if he or she owned the chain or were granted the rights to fully develop the chain in this market. In

example, Zarco's points in Zarco and Dienelt 1994). If this were the main reason for new outlet profitability and thus attractiveness to investors, it should be countered by renovations and good service and aggressive pricing by the owner of the old outlet. Such actions would prevent customers from leaving the established outlets, which in turn would mean that the new outlet would not be profitable, and thus no one would want to establish such an outlet.

[236] See Lafontaine and Kaufmann (1994) for evidence that McDonald's leaves at least some of the profits to the franchisees. The authors explain this as part of McDonald's self-enforcement policy with franchisees, which functions in part, at least, via promises of additional outlets. Michael and Moore (1995) show evidence that other chains also leave some rent with their franchisees.

other words, if expectations are set correctly, then conflict over encroachment will be minimized.[237]

8.2.2.5 Franchisor Opportunism and Sales Maximization

Using our stylized example, we have shown that franchisors and franchisees will typically disagree on the optimal number of franchises that should be established in a given market. This conclusion is based on simple profit maximization by both parties, where neither party was intentionally taking advantage of the other. Yet many accounts of encroachment situations – specifically many franchisee complaints about franchisor encroachment – suggest that encroachment is a form of franchisor opportunism, namely that franchisors intentionally harm their franchisees. In some cases, it is assumed that the franchisor gains from the resulting churning in outlet ownership as the franchisor collects new franchise fees each time a store is sold. In other cases, the source of the misbehavior is traced to the fact that franchisors may be interested more in sales revenue maximization than in profit maximization at the outlet level given that the typical franchise contract entails sales-based royalty payments.

Let us first consider the sales maximization argument. In our example, a franchisor who would want to maximize sales revenue rather than profits would locate a large number of stores in the market. Specifically, since consumers consume more if they live within a mile of a store than if they do not, a sales maximizing franchisor would want to establish enough outlets so that every customer can frequent a store within a mile from his or her house. In our hypothetical example, this means a store every two miles, for a total of 60 stores. Individual stores then achieve yearly sales levels of $(30 + 30) \cdot 10{,}000 = \$600{,}000$ as they only sell to those customers living within a mile from their store in both directions, and profits per store are $.4 \cdot \$600{,}000 - \$320{,}000 = -\$80{,}000$. Of course, with the break-even level of sales revenue calculated above at $800{,}000, it is clear that this store density, optimal from a sales revenue maximization perspective, would give rise to losses for all stores in our example. This, of course, cannot persist in the long run.

---

[237] One might worry that franchisees would react to such information by keeping effort low so as to not achieve sufficient sales for the franchisor to want to add an outlet. If franchisee effort mostly affects costs, this will of course not be an issue. But if franchisee effort affects sales revenues, this is something the franchisor will need to be on the lookout for. Franchisors can, for example, compare outcomes across similar markets and/or operate company units to get better information on the demand side and thus be able to identify these types of behaviors.

The question then becomes whether this is really profitable for the franchisor. Obviously, if the franchisor announced from the outset that this was its goal, no franchisee would purchase any of the 60 stores. This cannot be profitable. So this sales revenue maximization goal must set in later, after at least some franchisees have signed on. Suppose then that the franchisor sells the first ten franchises and locates them sequentially and symmetrically around the whole market. This is exactly the configuration that franchisees find optimal so that, during this initial market development period, each franchisee earns the largest possible profits and is very happy with the franchise. The franchisor who is ultimately interested in maximizing sales revenue would then want to establish more outlets. Let us assume that he now locates one more outlet halfway between each existing pair of outlets, for a new total of 20 outlets in the market, one every six miles. Franchisees who owned the first ten units now earn less revenues and profit so they would complain of encroachment. But new franchisees would be willing to purchase these units as the expected profit per outlet is still positive (assuming of course that they do not predict that the franchisor is headed toward 60 units, and assuming also that the yearly fees are set below the yearly expected profits of $160,000). The last phase of development to achieve sales revenue maximization would be to establish two new units within each of the six miles separating the current 20 units. Assuming the franchisor succeeded in attracting investors to these – a dubious assumption given the "writing on the wall" – all the units would earn negative profits and fail. Again, this could not be profitable for the franchisor. So franchisors are very unlikely to ever reach the revenue maximizing number of stores.

In essence, opportunism refers to the fact that the incentives of the franchisor may become different once the contracts have been signed and the franchise fees paid. And indeed there is some basis for this concern: once an initial set of contracts is signed and the franchisees have made their investments and paid their fixed fees, the franchisor can exploit any quasi-rent[238] the franchisees may be earning *ex post* by selling additional franchises close by at different terms. The terms of the new contracts would have to be different because new franchisees would not agree to sign under the old contract since they face a higher level of competition.[239] Note that franchisees who bought franchises in the first stage will regret this decision. Had they known that the

---

[238] A quasi-rent is a payment above the opportunity cost, in this case, any positive profit.

[239] This can be seen in our example from the fact that the franchisor could charge franchise fees up to $320,000 for the first 10 units – assuming franchisees expected that there would be no more than 10 units in the market. For the second set of 10 units, the new

franchisor would sell more later, they would not have agreed to the original terms.

This type of intertemporal "inconsistency" or regret about one's purchasing decision due to an incorrect assessment of the future behavior of the seller was analyzed by Coase (1972). In general, a monopolist can charge a price above the competitive level by restricting the quantity of its product below the competitive level. Coase argued that for durable goods (i.e., those that are consumed over many periods), the monopolist will have to develop some sort of contractual assurance that it will not sell additional units at necessarily lower prices in the future, otherwise the original set of customers will not agree to pay the monopoly price. The same reasoning applies here. Franchisors would need to look for ways to commit to "monopoly" contract terms, or would find they cannot sell their contracts at prices above the "competitive" price unless franchisees are myopic.[240] In other words, for franchisor opportunism to be a major issue, franchisees must not see how their welfare can be affected by their franchisors' future decisions. In that context, there are good reasons to be somewhat skeptical about how widespread this problem is likely to be. The reasons for this skepticism relate to why opportunism through outlet churning is unlikely to be profitable as well. We turn, therefore, to an examination of the latter.

To analyze the possibility of franchisor opportunism related to churning, it is important to consider what franchisors stand to gain and lose if they mistreat their franchisees. As noted by Klein (1980, 1995), franchisors presumably have opted for franchising rather than corporate ownership as an organizational form because the cost of operating the chain in this way is lower than under full corporate ownership. Shelton (1967) and Krueger (1991) provide very convincing empirical evidence that costs are indeed lower under franchisee management. Of course, if franchisee effort affects customers' experiences, it is easy to imagine that outlet revenues also may be higher under franchisee ownership than under company management. Evidence on the effect of franchisee ownership on revenues is more anecdotal, but still

---

franchisees see that they will not get as much of the market as if they had been among the initial 10, and so they will not pay above $160,000 each.

[240] One way to achieve this will be to offer franchisees an exclusive territory. McAfee and Schwartz (1994) show that when sellers can charge a two-part tariff (i.e., both an initial franchise fee and running royalties) and buyers compete with one another, promises to offer any future discounts also to initial buyers do not resolve the franchisor commitment problem. The authors thus discuss the potential role of exclusive territories as an alternative source of commitment. They also examine franchisor policies of using uniform and stable "take-it-or-leave-it" contracts in this light.

compelling. For example, in a private conversation with one of the authors of this book, a franchisor mentioned how, if he had hired one of his franchisees, he could never have brought himself to pay him a salary commensurate with the level of profit that this franchisee was earning. But the franchisor also admitted that he never considered buying back this franchisee's outlets because he could not make as much money under corporate ownership as he was getting in royalties given this franchisee's management skills and effort. Of course, implicit in this analysis was the expectation that this franchisee, if hired as a company manager, would not have put forth an equivalent level of effort. Another franchisor put it simply: "You can't pay a manager enough to make them get up in the morning and do what the franchisee will do!"[241] The reason, he argued, is that the franchisee has his own money on the line.[242]

The bottom line is that, though our simple analysis so far has not addressed the issue of why firms franchise, in the end we expect franchising to be chosen by franchisors if it is more profitable for them than company ownership.[243] This, in turn, has consequences relative to their incentives to mistreat their franchisees, consequences to which we now turn.

Let us consider what happens if a franchisor, after establishing a number of franchised units, behaves opportunistically toward its franchisees by, say, requiring new fees, establishing competing outlets nearby, and so on. If these

[241] David McKinnon, Chairman and CEO, Service Brands International, during a panel discussion organized as part of Entrepalooza 2002, held on September 13, 2002, at the University of Michigan Business School.

[242] See Lutz (1995) for a model showing that asset ownership is a major aspect of the differential incentives of franchisees compared to managers as it gives them residual claims on future profits. Thus, even if the incomes of hired managers are made contingent on outlet profits, their incentives to put forth effort to increase sales or reduce costs will not be as strong as a franchisee's because they do not share in the outlet's future profits to the same extent that franchisees do. Note that the franchisee's longer-term incentives due to asset ownership work through the continuation of the franchise relationship or the option that franchisees can exercise to sell their outlet at any given point in time.

[243] An alternative, and potentially complementary, reason for franchisors to adopt franchising is that it gives them access to capital. This explanation was first proposed by Oxenfeldt and Kelly (1969). But, empirical analyses contradict this argument in that they find that chains do not become fully corporate when they become established and thus have greater access to financing; see Lafontaine and Kaufmann (1994) and Lafontaine and Shaw (2005) and the references therein for more on this. Established franchisors mention, generally, the stronger motivation of franchisees as the main reason they continue to rely on franchising. They do, however, associate these stronger incentives with the capital investment that franchisees make in their business, as per Lutz (1995).

behaviors become public knowledge, the franchisor will no longer be able to convince new franchisees to join the chain. Thus, not only will she no longer collect franchise fees from such sales, but the growth of the chain will be limited to growth in the number of corporate units. Moreover, many existing franchisees ultimately will abandon the chain, leaving the franchisor to operate as a corporate entity. To the extent that the profits are lower under corporate operations, the chain will earn lower returns after this transformation. It may even fail if its competitors can continue to operate more efficiently as franchised chains. Thus, to the extent that it becomes public, the cost of mistreating franchisees is high for any established franchisor.[244]

Perhaps the more important point, however, is to note how low the benefit of opportunistic behavior really is for franchisors. The franchisor may be able to appropriate a few outlets and resell them to new franchisees. But these new individuals must be unaware of the opportunistic behavior as they would not buy the outlets otherwise. The profit that the franchisor can earn from such churning is basically limited to the franchise fee, a very small proportion of total payments by franchisees to franchisors.[245] This is because both the old and the new franchisee typically pay the same royalties on sales, so churning does not affect the level of these revenues. And the extra franchise fees themselves will rapidly go to zero as the reputation of the franchisor is eroded and new owners can no longer be attracted to the chain. The alternative, rather than sell the outlet to a franchisee, will be to operate it corporately. If, as argued above, this is a less profitable way to organize the business, the benefit is again very small compared to the cost imposed on the franchisor's reputation and operations. After all, the old unit that the chain will now operate directly is unlikely to be very profitable with the new unit(s) now established close by (which is what led to the initial encroachment claim).

---

[244] It is less clear that this disciplines new franchisors to the same extent. Of course, if a new franchisor wants to grow and become an established franchisor, it needs to offer an attractive business to potential franchisees, and its desire to sell units in the future will curb any tendency to behave opportunistically. There can be, and in fact have been, some less scrupulous individuals who have sold just a few franchises and collected the associated fees, but made no effort to really develop viable franchised chains. When there is no desire to sell future outlets, there is nothing to prevent this opportunism. For this reason, among many others, it is always riskier for a franchisee to invest in a new franchise opportunity. Our discussion above, of course, presumes that the franchisor is "real" in that this is a firm that at least plans to develop a franchise system if it has not yet done so.

[245] Lafontaine and Shaw (1999) note that on average, franchise fees represent only about 8 percent of all payments from franchisees to franchisors.

8.2.2.6 Extensions

To provide clear intuition about the main issues, our stylized example has abstracted from many relevant complications. In particular, ours is a static market, where demand and costs are stable, yet market expansion is one of the main reasons why franchisors would want to establish new outlets. Furthermore, we have ignored the effect of competitive pressures on the franchisor by assuming that there was a single provider of fast food on our island and that there was no threat of entry by a competing chain. Yet franchisors often argue that they need to establish new outlets to prevent other chains from gaining market share. Finally, we have ignored one of the central arguments made by franchisees in relation to encroachment, which is their role in developing both the local market and the value of the brand. We briefly discuss each of these issues and their effects on our conclusions in this section, beginning with market stability.

Instead of assuming stable market conditions, suppose now that each year the population around the island grows by 5 percent or, equivalently, the income of island residents increases and that leads them to increase the amount they spend on fast food by 5 percent each year. As these increases do not affect the distance – which remains at a maximum of six miles in both directions from the store – over which stores can draw customers, the franchisee's optimal configuration is unaffected by this growth. But the franchisor whose goal is to maximize chain profits will want to adjust the number of stores upward over time. Thus, the potential for market growth only reinforces our earlier conclusion about the basic conflict that exists between franchisors and franchisees on store density. This holds *a fortiori* if the profits earned in each location become much larger than the initial contract envisioned and yet the fees cannot be adjusted within the contract period.[246]

Second, we have ignored the possibility that other firms might enter the market. In defending their choices of location, franchisors often point out that if demand warrants it, a competitor will open a new outlet if they do not, and the franchisee will be no better off. Franchisees counter that increased intra-brand competition is more damaging to them than increased inter-brand competition.[247] Consistent with franchisees' claims, Kalnins (2003) finds that prices of goods at a chain's outlets are negatively correlated to prices set at nearby outlets of the same chain, but not with the prices of nearby units from

---

[246] In that context, one can think of franchisors' right of termination and non-renewal as a mechanism through which they can exercise a call option. See Chapter 10, as well as Williams (1996a, b) and Brickley (2001) for more on this.

[247] See, for example, Zarco and Dienelt (1994).

competing chains.[248] In other words, franchisees respond more aggressively to prices at same-chain stores in the vicinity than they do to those of stores from different brands, which, given the lack of differentiation among same-chain stores, is what one would expect. Thus, the fact that a competitor might have taken the particular location may not be a compelling reason to locate two stores near one another under the same banner. Still, the possibility that other chains might enter the market will affect a franchisor's decisions as to the optimal location and density of its stores. Specifically, assuming that there are some sunk costs related to establishing a store in a particular location, it has been shown that one way to prevent entry by a competing chain or by independent competitors would be to proliferate the number of outlets in the market or enter earlier than these competitors.[249] Though franchisees also would want their franchisor to be aggressive in preventing entry or expansion by other firms, they are unlikely to agree with their franchisor as to the extent of intra-brand development that this entails. [250]

Finally, we turn to the argument that franchisees who take the risk of being the first few in a market, and who work hard developing brand recognition in their market, should reap the fruits of their labor. There is no denying that franchisees need to be compensated for the risks they take and the effort that they put in their business. But it is also true that franchisees that establish themselves in markets that their franchisors have not developed yet choose these markets because they know the markets in question and believe the chain would be successful there. This is a gamble, but one that each such franchisee is embracing based on the information he possesses about the market and the chain. Most likely, if he is right, he will earn high returns during at least some period of time before the franchisor decides that this

---

[248] See also Thomadsen (2002) for an analysis emphasizing the effect of geography on prices and Mazzeo (2002) for evidence that price competition is more intense when outlets offer more similar goods.

[249] See Schmalensee (1982) and Eaton and Lipsey (1979). See also Hadfield (1991) on the possibility that franchising makes proliferation credible. Note that *sunk costs* are expenditures on highly specialized inputs that cannot be recovered if one withdraws from the market.

[250] The notion that firms should proliferate their number of competing divisions or of franchisees arises also in the strategic divisionalization literature. Here, franchisors that face competitors should establish more outlets – each of which should be owned by different individuals for maximum competitive effect – to capture a bigger share of the market. See especially Baye, Crocker, and Ju (1996) on this. But see Rysman (2001) for a model where firms can also use the terms of their contracts strategically. In this case, there is no more strategic advantage associated with divisionalization. Instead, firms should place only one outlet in each market but sign a contract with a low wholesale price to generate high output levels from that one franchisee.

market is ripe for additional outlets. These higher returns are in some basic sense the compensation he gets for developing this market. If the franchisee needs more than those early returns to make the gamble worthwhile, he must negotiate lower fees, or the right to develop further outlets himself, or the right to some other form of exclusivity, **before** he agrees to purchase his first franchise. In other words, he cannot wait until after he experiences success to request guarantees on the level of returns he desires.

Note that if franchisors want franchisees to invest in the value of the brand, they need to compensate franchisees specifically for that. One way to achieve this is to offer franchise contracts involving lower fees or some form of long-term guarantee, such as those implied by the right to develop a specific number of additional outlets, or the right to develop auxiliary businesses, or exclusive rights within a particular territory over the long run. For franchisees to have incentives to develop the brand, however, these rights must be granted *ex ante* and explicitly. The converse then is also true: if the franchise contract gives franchisees no long-term guarantees, but on the contrary is explicit about the franchisor's full ownership of the brand and states that the franchisees' rights are limited to the right to operate an outlet at a given address for a certain period of time, then the franchisee must recognize his contract for what it is. It is not an opportunity to develop a business and invest in developing a brand in partnership with the franchisor, but rather a shorter-term license from which the franchisee must derive short-term benefits. Rental contracts are a standard solution to the type of durable goods monopoly problem that the encroachment issue is akin to. In that context, it makes sense to think of a franchise contract as a rental contract over an intangible asset, namely the brand with the terms of the franchise contract clearly defining the relationship. After-the-fact complaints that it should be otherwise ought to "fall on deaf ears."

From a franchisee's perspective, then, perhaps the biggest problem with franchising lies not so much in what it is, but rather in what it is not, and yet sometimes appears to be. The franchise contract confers certain rights on the franchisee for a period of time. It does not grant him generally any form of ownership of the chain or the brand and therefore should not in any sense be construed as a mandate to develop the brand beyond what will serve the *franchisee's* best interest locally and for the expected duration of the relationship. Any franchisor that wants more than a local finite-term focus from its franchisees *must* embed extra franchisee rights and expectations within the contract: verbal promises to the franchisee about future prospects should never suffice from the franchisee's perspective (they are not worth the paper they are written on!), especially in light of the frequent use of integration clauses in franchise contracts.[251] In other words, we conclude again that if expectations are set correctly and both parties fully understand what each is getting from the contract, conflict over encroachment – and over many other aspects of the contract – will be minimized. But when expectations are set unrealistically, conflict almost invariably ensues.

In the following section, we examine some mechanisms through which franchisors have offered guarantees to franchisees, and other related practices that address franchisee concerns over territorial encroachment.

8.3 Industry Responses

8.3.1 The Role and Extent of Territorial Guarantees

One simple solution to the issue of geographical encroachment is for franchisors to offer exclusive territories to franchisees, that is, to guarantee that they will not open another unit within a certain area around the franchisee's business.[252] Until the U.S. Supreme Court's decision in *Sylvania*, such territorial guarantees would have been *per se* illegal under U.S. antitrust laws. Since then, however, non-price vertical restraints, such as exclusive territories, have been analyzed under the rule of reason. Without this change in the Court's attitude toward non-price vertical restraints, encroachment claims could not be levied against franchisors as franchisees could not have claimed any explicit right to a territory without breaking the antitrust laws.[253]

Table 8-1 shows the frequency with which franchisors in different industries offer an exclusive territory to their franchisees according to the International Franchise Association (IFA) and Frandata (1998) survey of disclosure documents. Any form of exclusive territory, described by geography, population, miles, or number of vehicles, is counted as a "yes" in this table.

---

[251] See Cohn (1998) on the use of integration clauses in franchise contracts.

[252] This is common, for example, in the beer industry. Wholesale beer distributors usually are granted exclusive territories that contractually protect them from dual distribution (or non-traditional encroachment) as well as from distributors in adjacent territories. These arrangements have been analyzed by Sass and Saurman (1993, 1996) and found to be efficient in the sense of promoting greater sales.

[253] Special industry state laws in automotive and liquor distribution provide territorial protection to dealers. As noted earlier, Smith (1982) and Eckard (1985) have shown that the resulting territorial exclusivity for car dealers has led to higher car prices and lower service, namely fewer hours of operation, for customers.

Table 8-1: *Exclusive territories*

Sector	Number of Franchisors	Number with Exclusive Territories	% with Exclusive Territories
Automotive	89	62	70
Baked Goods	39	28	72
Building & Construction	70	61	87
Business Services	57	42	74
Children Products and Services	27	24	89
Education Products and Services	21	20	95
Fast Food	197	136	69
Lodging	39	13	33
Maintenance Services	77	49	64
Personnel Services	35	33	94
Printing	21	14	67
Real Estate	39	26	67
Restaurants	99	79	80
Retail Food	60	27	45
Retail Non-food	130	101	78
Service Businesses	105	90	86
Sports and Recreation	37	31	85
Travel	14	8	57
Total	1,156	844	73

Source: IFA Educational Foundation, 1998. Exclusive territories are defined as per item 12 of UFOC. Any territory, described by geography, population, miles, or number of vehicles, counts as a "yes". "No" means the territory is limited to the store itself.

Table 8-1 shows that the majority of franchisors offer some form of territorial protection to their franchisees. Since the industry (or sector) definitions are rather broad, the average frequency of territorial protection probably masks a good deal of within-sector variance. Despite this, Table 8-1 also shows substantial variation in the use of exclusive territories across industry sectors. In particular, in franchising sectors such as personnel services, franchisees specifically purchase the right to be the sole provider of personnel for businesses that operate in a specified territory. The same is true in education-related and services businesses more generally. Thus, most franchisors in those industries include territorial protections in their contracts. But even in mobile businesses, exclusivity is not a given: Murphy (2000), for example, cites the case of a franchisee in the mobile windshield repair industry who was surprised to find that his Novus franchise did not guarantee him any exclusive business territory. At the other extreme, in sectors such as lodging, food retail, travel and fast food, so there is no explicit territory embedded in the definition of the business concept and a larger proportion of franchisors choose not to offer any exclusive territory.

The grant of an exclusive territory, moreover, does not eliminate the possibility of encroachment. For example, if a territory is a geographical area, say one mile around an outlet, establishing a new outlet one mile away does not constitute an incursion in the exclusive territory of the original franchisee, yet it may still give rise to decreased sales at his outlet. Using the definition of encroachment in current and proposed legislation, namely a decrease in sales for the original outlet of 5 or 6 percent, this new outlet may well encroach. In that context, what an exclusive territory does is make it clear what the franchisor may not do, which in our hypothetical example would be to open a unit within the one-mile region. The grant of an exclusive territory then offers some level of security to franchisees, or at least communicates to them more clearly how the franchisor's future plans may affect them.

It is undeniable that exclusive territories provide at least some form of security against encroachment. In this light, Azoulay and Shane (2001) find that a contractual guarantee of an exclusive territory significantly increases the likelihood that new franchised chains survive beyond their first few years in business. They interpret their finding to mean that territorial protection is so important to franchisees that those franchisors that fail to offer such protection from encroachment are unable to attract franchisees, which then leads to their failure.

In a 1993 study of territorial restrictions as described in chains' disclosure documents, the Frandata Corporation found that only 26 of the largest 50 restaurant franchisors offered some territorial exclusivity. This is much lower than the 80 percent reported for the sit-down restaurant industry in Table 8-1, or the 69 percent reported for the fast-food industry. In contrast, for their set of 170 new franchisors from a variety of business sectors, Azoulay and Shane (2001) found 83.5 percent offering exclusive territories as compared to an overall rate of 73 percent in Table 8-1. Together, these data suggest that larger franchisors, for which encroachment is more likely to be an issue, have a lower tendency than average to offer territorial protection. New franchisors, in contrast, offer it more often than average, potentially to counteract the likely negative effect of their newness and small size on franchisee recruiting. Anecdotal evidence from Love (1986) further supports this conclusion: he mentions that while Ray Kroc offered territories to early McDonald's franchisees, he reduced the size of the territories over time and then eliminated them entirely by 1969.

The desire to maintain flexibility in developing their franchised system is the main reason franchisors give for not granting exclusive territories to franchisees.[254] This is consistent with the results of our stylized example: if franchisors cannot modify the terms of their contract in a growing market, they will want to increase store density. Thus, they may choose not to grant exclusive territories because they want to maintain the required flexibility to add outlets. But the need for flexibility as the market grows is not the only source of encroachment friction. Azoulay and Shane (2001) report that the main concern of franchisors that did not offer exclusive territories was that "exclusivity would allow franchisees to hold them up through underdevelopment." They cite the rationale of one franchisor: "If they (franchisees) can't afford new stores and they don't operate well, they will slow down our growth if we can't put someone else in the area." In other words, even if franchisors expect franchisees who are granted the whole local market ultimately to choose the same level of market development as the franchisor, this development may be postponed due to liquidity constraints or, even worse, because a particular franchisee is not talented enough or ambitious enough to operate more stores. Such concerns clearly make it harder for franchisors to provide guarantees at the start of the franchise relationship.

The problem, however, is not insurmountable. Basically, it requires that guarantees of exclusive territories be made contingent upon some objective measures of franchisee performance. Some of this is typically done in master franchise agreements: These contracts not only provide territorial guarantees to the franchisee, they also stipulate a development schedule within the territory in question. Thus, the franchisor evaluates the franchisee's performance using the number of outlets opened as the performance measure, and the territorial guarantee is predicated on this number reaching specific target values over time. The drawback, of course, is that these targets may be unrealistic and the master franchise agreement then fails.[255] A more flexible approach would involve more regular assessment of the market and its potential. In any case, franchisors should state explicitly what they consider to be reasonable sales and profit levels per outlet, and franchisees should know that new outlets will be added when outlet sales in the region go above these

---

[254] See, for example, Mathewson and Winter (1994) for a model emphasizing the role of exclusive territories in determining the starting point of future renegotiation processes in franchise relationships.

[255] See Kalnins (2004) on the frequency of failure of master franchise agreements in international markets, a large failure rate he argues is due to development schedules that are too aggressive.

levels.[256] These types of safeguards for franchisors and franchisees go much beyond the simple grant of a territory, and more closely align with other types of practices that franchisors currently use to minimize tension over geographic expansion. We now describe some of these alternatives.

8.3.2 Other Franchisor Practices

Franchisors can do a number of other things to mitigate the negative reactions that establishing new outlets in a franchisee's perceived market area might generate. First and foremost, they need to ensure that potential franchisees have the correct expectations when they purchase a unit. If franchisees are sold franchises under vague promises of exclusivity and options to grow within the chain, then they will expect that these opportunities will be offered to them. If, on the other hand, franchisees know what to expect in terms of sales and profits per unit, and it is made clear that the franchisor intends to continue to establish outlets and develop the market further when these unit sales levels are achieved in current outlets, then there will be no surprises for the franchisee whose sales are much above average when new outlets are opened nearby.[257] Moreover, the franchisor must draft a clear language contract, one that sets out whether or not the franchisee has an exclusive territory and, if so, just how it is defined.

In addition to candid disclosure of future plans and contract terms, some chains have found that instead of *ex ante* territorial protection, they can establish a policy of offering new outlets to the existing franchisees whose stores are most affected by each new outlet, assuming that the franchisee has performed satisfactorily. As seen in the legal definition of encroachment in Iowa (Iowa Code 2001), offering the outlet to the owner of the impacted unit is one way to prevent encroachment claims under that law. Empirically, whether or not franchisors have an explicit policy to this effect, Kalnins and Lafontaine (2004) show that franchisees in large fast-food chains are much more likely to become the owners of a new unit if they already own units nearby. This effect is even stronger if they own units that share a market boundary with the new unit. Of course, problems arise with these solutions when more than one existing owner has units that are impacted by the new outlet or when the existing franchisee is not performing well. Thus, one might still find some level of conflict arising with those franchisees that are not awarded the new

---

[256] Of course, franchisors again will need to be wary of franchisees providing low effort to keep their outlet sales below the level that will lead the franchisor to want more outlets.

[257] Of course, this does not mean that the incumbent franchisee will be happy about the newcomer, but at least he or she will not be surprised.

unit. Nevertheless, such policies can go a long way toward resolving territorial issues surrounding the growth in new units.

Many other tools are available to franchisors that want to lessen the costs associated with encroachment issues in their chain. First, franchisors can try to develop markets in a more focused way, with each individual market developed all at once, thereby eliminating the apparent encroachment associated with sequential development.[258] In our earlier numerical example, this would involve establishing all 15 of the desired outlets on the island at once. If this is not feasible for any reason, the franchisor can make it clear at the outset to the first few franchisees that this is the development plan and that the goal will be to establish the 15 locations quite rapidly. This strategy of rapid development has the advantage of providing for the type of cluster marketing economies mentioned earlier, thereby facilitating the establishment of the brand in the market.[259]

Franchisors also can minimize encroachment conflict arising from the establishment of new outlets over time as markets grow by involving existing franchisees in the decision process, or providing market analyses and other information supporting their actions. This strategy has the additional advantage of allowing franchisees, who may be in a unique position to provide very useful local market intelligence, to propose amendments to the company expansion plans that may address their concerns while still allowing the chain to achieve its goals. McDonald's and Dunkin' Donuts, for example, both have instituted impact policies whereby they provide notice of new outlets to franchisees whose current units may be affected and conduct studies to establish how large the impact is likely to be. Both firms have established criteria under which they may reconsider their plans to open new outlets based on the outcome of such studies.

Franchisors can also address the franchisees' legitimate impact concerns by offering some form of compensation to their franchisees. Compensation can take the form of modifying (perhaps for a limited period) the terms of the agreement under which the owner of the impacted unit operates. For example, the royalty rate could be reduced. Alternatively, the franchisor could provide direct compensation as the current federal proposal requires.[260] Both

---

[258] On planning ahead for multiple outlets, see Achabal et al. (1982). For an extension of the total market entry approach that recognizes the reality of opening delays, see Kaufmann, Donthu, and Brooks (2000).

[259] In other words, the franchisor can pool more advertising dollars and benefit from marketing and advertising economies of scale in each well-developed market.

[260] This compensation need not exceed the actual adverse effect on profit, i.e., there need not be a windfall for the franchisee as the proposed federal statute provides.

the McDonald's and Dunkin' Donuts impact policies mentioned above include provisions involving potential fee reductions or direct franchisee compensation. Contrary to the proposed federal law, however, this should *not* be done each time a franchisee's sales are negatively affected by a new outlet's entry. Indeed, most cases of "measurable" impact will arise from normal chain development processes over time.[261] The high profits that franchisees can earn in their first few years in business when they own the first units in a market should probably be viewed as compensation for bearing the higher risk of being first, not as a permanent franchisee entitlement. Franchisees, of course, are apt to see this differently as they build these returns into their household budgets.

Finally, when the risk of encroachment conflict is too high, franchisors may turn to large investors who develop whole regional markets or toward more company ownership of units in their system. As we saw in our illustrative example, a franchisee who would be given the right to the whole island would choose to establish exactly the same number of outlets as the franchisor finds optimal. Thus, the likelihood of encroachment conflict is much reduced when franchisors use area development agreements with large franchisee investors instead of allocating individual units to small owner operators. There is some evidence that a number of franchisors, including Quizno Subs and Applebee's, are choosing this option; whether they do so to minimize encroachment or for other reasons is not clear.[262] Similarly, current evidence suggests that units in urban areas are more likely to be owned and operated by franchisors directly (see Lafontaine and Slade, 1997 2001). This evidence is consistent with the idea that decisions about which units should be owned or franchised may be made partially on the basis of where encroachment claims are most likely. Note, however, that if franchisors choose to operate outlets to prevent encroachment claims and the associated penalties – actual or potential – this hardly benefits potential franchisees as the latter now face a reduced set of opportunities. The same conclusion applies for small franchisees when franchisors turn to large investors to whom they delegate the development of complete markets as a solution to potential encroachment claims.

8.3.3 Legal and Legislative Treatment

There is currently no general franchise law at the federal level in the U.S. that addresses the issue of encroachment. Over the last 20 years, however, there

---

[261] However, see Kalnins (2004b) for evidence that "impact" due to new hotels is greater within franchised than company-owned chains.

[262] See Vogel (1996) and Prewitt (2003).

have been regular federal proposals to regulate the franchise relationship, including encroachment. As of this writing, the proposed 1999 Small Business Franchise Act mentioned above was still under consideration, but had not left the Commercial and Administrative Law Subcommittee of the House Judiciary Committee. In July 2001, the FTC, the body that enforces the federal franchising disclosure rules, and the General Accounting Office (GAO) released a report of the 4,512 complaints received by the FTC from 1993 to 2000. The report indicated that only 6 percent of those complaints were about franchising, as opposed to business opportunities, and the franchising complaints were about earning claims and failures to disclose. The lack of data on franchise relationship problems prevented the FTC and GAO from assessing the extent of these problems, but the FTC noted that it did not believe that the situation warranted developing a new rule to address post-contractual problems in franchising.

There are both federal- and state-level special industry laws that govern franchise relationships in gasoline, automotive, liquor, and farm machinery distribution. These laws may require that franchisees be given territorial exclusivity. Furthermore, a few states have franchise relationship laws, some aspects of which apply to territorial encroachment.[263] As noted earlier, the most stringent anti-encroachment provision is found in the Iowa franchise relationship law.

---

[263] Besides Iowa, the states of Hawaii, Indiana, Minnesota, and Washington have franchise relationship laws with anti-encroachment provisions. These provisions, however, are much less extensive than those in the Iowa statute. For example, the Hawaii, Minnesota, and Washington state laws simply reaffirm the territorial exclusivity contracted for in the franchise agreement. Specifically, the Hawaiian law states:

[I]t shall be an unfair or deceptive act or practice or an unfair method of competition for a franchisor or subfranchisor to:

Establish a similar business or to grant a franchise for the establishment of a similar business at a location within a geographical area specifically designated as the exclusive territory in a franchise previously granted to another franchisee in a currently effective agreement, except under the circumstances or conditions prescribed in such agreement. The fact that other franchisees or the franchisor may solicit business or sell goods or services to people residing in such geographical territory shall not constitute the establishment of a similar business within the exclusive territory." (Haw. Rev. Stat. § 482E-6[2])

The Indiana law (Ind. Code §§ 23–2–2.7–1(2) & 23–2–2.7–2[4]) prevents a franchisor from establishing a permanent company unit within "unreasonable proximity" of a franchisee-owned unit, but does not prevent the establishment of additional franchised units. Finally, Wisconsin's Fair Dealership Law does not contain a specific anti-encroachment provision, but it prohibits a grantor of a dealership from changing the competitive circumstances of a dealer without good cause.

Outside of the specific industries or state laws noted above, two opposing forces are at play in encroachment cases, namely the specific language found in the franchise contract versus the implied covenant of good faith and fair dealing that protects the reasonable expectations of parties involved in a contractual relationship.[264] In general, courts have refused to apply the covenant of good faith in derogation to a contract's express terms. Thus, if the franchise agreement expressly states that the franchisor has the right to establish other locations outside of the existing unit's defined territory, franchisees have not been able to rely on the implied covenant of good faith to argue a case against their franchisor's development decisions outside their territory even if such decisions have a measurable impact on their sales.[265] Further, almost all franchise agreements contain an integration clause stating that the written agreement encompasses the full agreement between the parties. As a result, prior oral representations or even franchisor policies concerning territorial guarantees and exclusivity are inapplicable if not contained in the written agreement. [266]

When the franchise contract expressly reserves to the franchisor the right to open outlets in close proximity to franchisees' units, the courts have been unsympathetic to franchisees' encroachment claims.[267] Further, when the contract expressly denies territorial protection to the franchisee by stating that the franchise is limited to the outlet's address, but does not expressly reserve for the franchisor the right to open additional outlets nearby, courts again have been generally unsympathetic to claims of encroachment.[268] There have been exceptions, however, most notably the *Scheck v. Burger King* cases (*Scheck I* and *Scheck II*), where the court found that the denial of territorial protection in a franchise agreement did not imply that the franchisor had the right to establish outlets just anywhere. Though the logic behind this argument was criticized directly in *Burger King v. Weaver*, it may still be relied upon.[269] Finally, when the contract fails to establish the parties' rights in unequivocal language, the facts of the case and the franchisor's representations and policies become more central. [270]

---

[264] Restatement of Contracts § 205 (1977).

[265] See, e.g., *Vicorp Restaurants, Inc. v. Village Inn Pancake House of Albuquerque, Inc.* and *Cook v. Little Caesar Enterprises.*

[266] See, e.g., *Schubot v. McDonald's, Payne v. McDonald's Corp.,* and *Cohn v. Taco Bell Corp.*

[267] See, e.g., *Cohn v. Taco Bell Corp.*

[268] See *Barnes v. Burger King Corp, Burger King Corp. v. Weaver,* and *Payne v. McDonald's Corp.*

[269] See, e.g., *Vylene Enterprises, Inc. v. Naugles, Inc.* and *Foodmaker, Inc. v. Quershi.*

[270] See *Photovest Corp. v. Fotomat Corp.* and *Vylene Enterprises, Inc. v. Naugles, Inc.*

8.4 Non-Traditional Encroachment

In its study of the largest 50 fast-food franchisors in the U.S., Frandata Corp. found that 26 offered exclusive territories. These 26, however, all reserved some rights to themselves even within the franchisee's territory. Most common were franchisor rights to develop franchises under different trade names (18 of the 26 franchisors) and the right to develop institutional locations, such as in stadiums, hospitals, airports, and so on (9 of 26 franchisors). Further, among the full set of 50 franchisors, 31 explicitly reserved the right to sell their products through alternative channels.

These different rights that franchisors embed in their contracts make it clear that they feel a need to reserve for themselves the right to respond to new market opportunities or challenges, as they see fit. And indeed, a franchised chain's long-term survival and growth is intrinsically tied to the franchisor's market strategy and its capacity to adapt to changing circumstances. But franchisees may not benefit at all from the resulting changes and, if they do, they may not benefit equally. For example, when Popeye's acquired Church's Fried Chicken, some Popeye's franchisees sued their franchisor, America's Favorite Chicken Co. (AFC), because the new strategy of the firm was to specialize the two chains, Popeye's for quality and Church's for value. The plaintiff Popeye's franchisees were in markets where they believed a value strategy like that of Church's would be more profitable. The court found for the franchisor, however, as the terms of the contract were quite clear that the franchisor could run outlets under different marks in the franchisee's territory. Moreover, the court noted that the franchisor believed its strategy was best for the two chains, and the fact that "AFC's marketing strategy for the Popeye's system had made [the franchisee] less competitive" in his market did not constitute bad faith.

More generally, claims of non-traditional encroachment will likely arise whenever franchisors react to new market opportunities in ways that either do not benefit, or even directly impinge, on their franchisees' businesses. Examples have included franchisors using alternative channels such as supermarkets or the Internet, or serving national accounts or business customers directly without resorting to franchisees, or establishing outlets in non-traditional settings, or, finally, operating competing brands obtained through acquisition or internal development. In all cases, franchisees worry about losing business to these alternatives while franchisors argue that the increased visibility of the brand brings additional customers and prevents entry by others in the same markets. When franchisors operate competing brands in the same market, they rely primarily on arguments of efficiency and/or argue that the offerings of the different concepts target different market segments and thus complement one another. But whether this turns out to be good or bad for an individual outlet, or even the chain, will again depend on the specific market situation and the way in which the franchisor organizes these activities.

The precedents established in legal disputes over geographic encroachment also apply, generally, to non-traditional encroachment. In particular, the courts have ruled that where a franchisor has expressly reserved the right to distribute its product through alternative channels in the contract, the provision is enforceable. For example, in the landmark Häagen-Dazs cases, franchisees sued after Pillsbury decided to start mass distribution of its ice cream via supermarkets.[271] But the franchise agreement provided that "the Häagen-Dazs trademark owner (i.e., Pillsbury) has the right and may distribute products identified by the Häagen-Dazs trademarks through not only Häagen-Dazs shops but through any other distribution method which may from time to time be established." As a result, the court found in favor of Pillsbury. Similarly, in the case of AFC, described above, the court ruled for the franchisor given that the franchise agreement explicitly reserved the right of the franchisor to compete with its franchisees under different marks.[272] However, in October 2002, the U.S. District Court for the District of Connecticut ruled in favor of franchisees in a series of cases involving the Carvel Corporation's supermarket distribution program, awarding franchisees more than one million dollars in compensatory and punitive damages. The Carvel Corporation has appealed these decisions. It also has modified its franchise agreements to make it very clear that franchisees are not granted any "proprietary or territorial rights or protections of any type" (see the appendix to this chapter for the text of the original and modified contract, per Kanouse 2000).

The advent of the Internet has raised a number of new opportunities for both franchisors and franchisees. The effect of this new way of reaching customers in at least some segments of the retail and service industries, such as travel services and accounting services, is yet to be fully understood. Two recent arbitration decisions suggest that here again the language of the contract is paramount in determining the respective rights and duties of franchisors and franchisees. In the *Emporium Drug Mart Inc. v. Drug Emporium Inc. of*

---

[271] See *Carlock v. Pillsbury Co.* (1989) and *Rosenberg v. Pillsbury Co.* (1989).

[272] *Clark v. America's Favorite Chicken Co.* For more on the issues raised by mergers or acquisitions in the context of franchising, see Vines (1996).

Denton case, an arbitration panel decided that an online drugstore was in fact a drugstore, and that its operations encroached on the exclusive territories granted to franchisees in the franchise agreement. Similarly, an arbitration panel found that H&R Block franchisees were harmed by the company's new Internet tax preparation activities and, given their contractual right to an exclusive territory, franchisees may have claims for damages against H&R Block.[273]

As in the case of traditional encroachment, many franchisors also have instituted programs by which internet sales are made through local franchisee-owned shops or other mechanisms whereby franchisees share in the revenues or profits thus generated. In fact, in the *Drug Emporium* case, the arbitration panel ordered the franchisor to direct customers to local stores instead of shipping directly to customers living in franchisees' exclusive territories.[274]

Above all, whether for internet sales or for other channels, the decisions above again point to the importance of explicit language covering all alternative channels in franchise agreements so that both parties are clear as to what is permitted and what is not.

8.5 Conclusion

The franchise contract confers certain rights on the franchisee for a period of time. In the best of cases, these rights, and the limits upon them, are clearly spelled out in the contract. When they are not, ambiguities and disputes are the logical consequence.

Encroachment is one of these complex, emotional issues for franchisees. In terms of economic effect, encroachment amounts to increased *intrabrand* (as opposed to *interbrand*) competition. Such enhanced competition within a brand threatens the financial well being of the incumbent franchisees and they complain. Some of these complaints resonate with legislators. In Iowa and several other states in the U.S., these complaints have resulted in legislation that is intended to protect incumbent franchisees from such intrabrand competition. Currently, there is also federal legislation under consideration that is intended to accomplish the same goal.

In this chapter, we have used a simple, stylized illustration to analyze the alleged problem of geographic encroachment. But our focus has not been

---

[273] See the Goldstein Law Group (2003).
[274] Before the order was even implemented, Drug Emporium sold its Web site to Health-Central.com. Shortly thereafter, it underwent a bankruptcy restructuring and was acquired by another drugstore chain.

limited to the incumbent franchisees. We have also examined the effect on franchisors, would-be franchisees, and consumers. As one might suppose, the protectionist legislation confers benefits on the incumbent franchisees, but makes everyone else worse off: franchisors make less profit and would-be franchisees must look elsewhere to presumably less attractive business alternatives. In our simple model, consumers are also worse off in that they have less access to the franchisor's product and thus consume less of it. Empirical evidence indicates that consumers in reality pay higher prices and enjoy less convenience as a result of legislation that has been enacted to protect car dealers.

The sad thing about legislation of territorial protection is that it is largely unnecessary. The legislation corresponds to governmental intervention in what is fundamentally a contractual relationship. The rights and the responsibilities of the franchisor and the franchisee are contract matters. When disputes arise, they can be resolved as any contract dispute is resolved. We are mindful of the fact that resorting to litigation is very costly and some franchisees may discover that justice is out of their financial reach. But the protectionist legislation is not self-enforcing and, therefore, franchisees who feel victimized still have to resort to the judicial system and bear the associated costs.

We also have examined various ways in which franchisors and their franchisees can avoid conflicts and misunderstandings. Importantly, many of these strategies focus on enhancing the flow of accurate information, which results in more realistic expectations on all sides. When everyone knows what to expect upon entering a franchise relationship, and then at every stage during the contract, surprises and disappointments are less likely and conflict is thus minimized.

8.6 Appendix: Carvel Corporation's Contract: Before and After

Having been sued by franchisees for encroachment when it developed its supermarket strategy, the Carvel Corporation has substantially modified its franchise agreement to prevent further suits (Kanouse 2000). The agreement involved in the lawsuit read:

> So long as Licensee complies with all of the terms of this Agreement, Carvel agrees not to establish or license another person to establish a Carvel Store on [name of street] for the sale of Carvel products, within one-quarter of a mile on said street in either direction from Carvel Store.

A rider to the latest Carvel Franchise Agreement now states:

Route Dealer [Carvel franchisee] expressly acknowledges and agrees that absolutely no proprietary or territorial rights or protections of any type, nature or degree are afforded by this Rider to Route Dealer with regard to any House Account or Approved Dealer Account [includes supermarkets]. To the contrary, Route Dealer expressly understands and agrees, under the terms of the Rider, that *Carvel (with or without participation of Route Dealer) may, in its sole and exclusive discretion, establish House Accounts or Approved Dealer Accounts anywhere and everywhere, now or in the future, and without regard to the impact such activity may have on the volume of business then being transacted between Route Dealer and any of his Supermarket Route Franchise Program accounts.* Such newly established House Accounts or Approved Dealer Accounts may be situated proximate to then-existing House Accounts or Approved Dealer Accounts. *Route Dealer expressly waives any claim he may have that Carvel violated* any law, rule or regulation; any decisional law; this Rider; *the implied covenant of good faith and fair dealing;* any principles of tort law; the International Franchise Association's Code of Principles; and, any other standards that might otherwise apply, *by virtue of Carvel's future approval of House Accounts or Approved Dealer Accounts in direct proximity to then-existing House Accounts or Approved Dealer Accounts being serviced by Route Dealer.* Further, *Route Dealer expressly understands and Agrees that Carvel,* its parent, and the affiliates, Subsidiaries and designees of either entity, *have the right, in their sole discretion, to themselves own and operate (outright, through contract, joint venture or otherwise) Supermarket Route businesses servicing accounts anywhere and everywhere; except as otherwise precluded by contracts, to own, and/or grant franchises and/or licenses for the operation of, Carvel Stores anywhere and everywhere (and regardless of the impact that the establishment of any such Carvel Store may have on House Accounts or Approved Dealer Accounts then being serviced by Route Dealer); to offer and sell Carvel products anywhere and everywhere; and,* in connection with the foregoing, *to exploit the Carvel name and Trademarks, reputation and know-how.* [Emphasis added by Kanouse 2000]

9

Advertising and Promotion

9.1 Introduction

The benefits of joining an established franchised chain for a franchisee, and thus the reasons why franchisees are willing to pay fees to be part of a franchised chain, can be grouped into two broad categories: cost-reducing and demand-enhancing benefits. The cost-reducing benefits include established supply relations and economies of large-scale purchasing, comprehensive and ongoing programs to develop efficient production processes, management training and consulting, and so on. Demand-enhancing benefits arise mostly from the brand and the products associated with it. In other words, when franchisees join a chain, they do so under the expectation that the brand that they get to operate under will bring in customers who might otherwise not have visited their store. A rare case of a McDonald's franchisee who "lost his arches" illustrates how important the brand can be to franchisees: the restaurant in question was operated very similarly by the same individuals in the same place after terminating its relationship with the McDonald's system. Despite all that, its sales fell by 60 percent immediately. Sales continued to go down after the initial shock, and never again exceeded 35 percent of the level they had achieved as part of the McDonald's system. The restaurant closed for good some 12 to 18 months later.[275]

It should come as no surprise then that advertising, a main determinant of brand value, plays a central role in franchise relationships. In Chapter 3, we documented how most franchisors today require franchisees to contribute some specified proportion of their sales towards advertising. Advertising fees most often range between 1 and 3 percent of total sales. Further contributions

---

[275] See Atkins, D., (1990), Affidavit In the Matter of *Canterbury et al. v. Commissioner of Internal Revenue.*

to local advertising are sometimes added to the franchisees' obligations in this regard.

In this chapter, we first review briefly the role that advertising plays in generating demand, focusing on consumers' need for information about products, prices, and availability. We then describe how differing economies of scale in advertising versus local production make it efficient for retail and service firms to be organized as chains of physically separate outlets. Next, we describe the public-good nature of advertising in franchised chains, and discuss the setting of optimal advertising budgets in this context. We then move on to a more detailed discussion of advertising requirements in franchised chains, followed by an examination of franchisor–franchisee conflict over advertising. We offer a few concluding remarks in the last section of this chapter.

9.2 A Simple Model of Advertising as Information[276]

Advertising has many functions, but one of its principal functions is to provide information to consumers about product price and quality, store location, hours of operation, and so on.[277] In this section, we present a simple model of advertising as a source of information. This view of the information role of brands, and of the advertising expenditures that support these brands, accords particularly well with the oft-heard idea that mobile customers, in particular, value chains because they *know* what to expect when they frequent them.[278]

9.2.1 Advertising as Information: Some Fundamentals

There are two reasons why it is necessary to advertise continuously to make consumers aware of the firm's existence, the quality of its products, and so on. First, the identity of buyers and sellers changes over time. Of particular interest to any one firm is the changing identity of its customer base. New customers

---

[276] Much of the material in this section is drawn from Stigler (1961). This treatment relies on Blair and Kenny (1982).

[277] Non-informative advertising is often viewed as an attempt by firms to alter consumers' preferences – see, notably, Dixit and Norman (1978). But see also Becker and Murphy (1993) for an analysis that treats non-informative advertising as a complement to advertised products in stable meta-utility functions.

[278] Brands also allow customers to punish firms that do not deliver what they claim to deliver. Because of this opportunity to punish brand holders by refusing to consume their product in the future, advertising investments become likely indicators of actual performance. This role of brands also depends on their information content. For more on this, see Klein and Leffler (1981).

continuously enter a market: some buyers move from different geographic markets (mobile customers), while others become of age financially and begin to purchase goods. Both sets of new customers require information about the firm's identity, the type and quality of the products it offers, and so on. Advertising performs this function. Second, customers sometimes forget some of what they learned or other firms provide conflicting information. For this reason, a firm needs to regularly refresh the knowledge of infrequent customers.

The amount and quality of advertising that takes place each period is a major determinant, therefore, of the fraction of potential customers who are aware of a particular firm's location and product offerings in any given period. In what follows, we present a simple model that illustrates these effects. For simplicity, we abstract from issues of advertising quality in this model – we come back to these briefly later. We also abstract from all the different forms that advertising can take and consider advertising in homogeneous units (e.g., the number of minutes of prime time television commercials per week or the number of quarter-page ads in the local newspaper).

Suppose that during each period a firm purchases α units of advertising and that as a result of this advertising, some fraction γ of potential customers become informed about the firm's existence and the products it offers. In other words, the fraction γ is a function of α, or $\gamma = g(\alpha)$. Moreover, if the advertising is effective – and we will assume that it is or it would be worth nothing – then increasing the level of advertising (α) in any given period increases the fraction of potential customers who are informed that period (γ), that is, $d\gamma/d\alpha > 0$. We assume also that there is a constant number N of potential customers in the market who, at the time the firm enters the market, are all uninformed. Thus, one period after entry, given a level of advertising α, γN customers are informed about the firm's existence, products, hours of operation, and so on.

Another determinant of the fraction of potential customers who are aware of a firm and its products at a given time is the amount of information that is lost each period. Let us suppose that at the beginning of each period, some fraction b of the informed customers either lose their knowledge or leave the market and are replaced by new ones. We should expect that b is high in communities characterized by high rates of turnover of permanent residents, a large fraction of tourists, or sizable mortality and birth rates. Of the γN customers who were informed in the first period, $(1-b)\gamma N$ remain informed at the beginning of the second period.

In the second period, there is another round of advertising. For those $(1-b)\gamma N$ customers who remain informed, advertising is unnecessary. But the advertising will reach some of those who were not reached in the first period, $(1- \gamma)N$, and those who had been informed but somehow became uninformed, $b\gamma N$. Once again, advertising at a level α will reach a fraction γ of these two groups. Thus, by the end of the second period, a fraction (λ) of N will be aware of the firm's offerings:

$$\lambda N = (1 - b)\gamma N + \gamma [b\gamma N + (1 - \gamma)N]. \qquad (9.1)$$

Equation (9.1) may be simplified to yield

$$\lambda N = \gamma N[1 + (1 - b)(1 - \gamma)].$$

Continuing this process over k periods, it can be shown that at the end of k periods,

$$\lambda_k N = \gamma N[1 + (1 - b)(1 - \gamma) + (1 - b)^2(1 - \gamma)^2 + \ldots \\ +(1 - b)^{k-1}(1 - \gamma)^{k-1}]$$

potential customers are informed. This is a series with the property that as k approaches infinity,

$$\lambda_\infty N = \frac{\gamma N}{1 - (1 - \gamma)(1 - b)}. \qquad (9.2)$$

In other words, the number of informed buyers equals γN in the first period and increases in each successive period, approaching $\gamma N/[1 - (1 - \gamma)(1 - b)]$ in the limit.

An examination of equation (9.2) shows the relationship between the number of informed buyers and both the effectiveness of the advertising in reaching customers, γ, and the retention rate, $(1 - b)$. As one would expect, an increase in the retention rate of advertising knowledge $(1 - b)$ results in an increase in the number of informed buyers in each period. We can see that as $(1 - b)$ rises, the denominator in (9.2) falls, which increases the fraction of total customers who are informed.[279] Similarly, for a given level of advertising α each period, more consumers know about a firm's existence at the end of every period if the advertising reaches more people each time (i.e., when it is more effective). Thus, we see that an increase in γ leads to a rise in $\lambda_\infty N$.[280] That is why firms are interested in influencing the retention rate $(1 - b)$ and the contact rate (γ) of their advertising messages.

In the remainder of this section, we pursue our model of advertising as information by discussing how a monopolist, and then a firm in a more competitive environment, would set its advertising budget.

---

[279] Analytically, the sign of $\partial(\lambda\infty N)/\partial(1 - b)$ is positive.
[280] Analytically, the sign of $\partial(\lambda_\infty N)/\partial\gamma$ is positive.

9.2.2 Optimal Advertising: The Monopoly Solution

If advertising informs customers as per the discussion above, a monopolist will set its price (P) and its quantity of advertising (α) to maximize profit. Since profit equals total revenue less total costs, including total production costs, $C(Q)$, and expenditures on advertising, we may express the monopolist's profit as

$$\pi = PQ - C(Q) - C_a\alpha, \tag{9.3}$$

where Q denotes the total quantity sold and C_a represents the cost of a unit of advertising (e.g., the cost of a minute of prime-time television, where we maintain the assumption that advertising is homogeneous). We assume, again for simplicity, that every potential customer who is aware of this monopolist's existence buys some quantity q from him.[281] Thus, the total quantity sold is equal to the product of the number of customers who buy from the firm (λN) and the quantity purchased by each customer (q):

$$Q = \lambda Nq. \tag{9.4}$$

By substituting equation (9.4) into equation (9.3), we get

$$\pi = P\lambda Nq - C(\lambda Nq) - C_a\alpha, \tag{9.5}$$

an expression that shows the firm's profit as a function of the number of informed buyers (λN), the quantity purchased by each customer (q), the product price (P), the costs of production $C(\bullet)$, and the expenditure on advertising ($C_a\alpha$).

In order to maximize profit, the firm will adjust its output and the amount of advertising until the profit can no longer be increased by changes in these variables, that is, until the first partial derivatives of π with respect to Q and to α are equal to zero:

$$\frac{\partial \pi}{\partial Q} = \left(P + Q\frac{dP}{dQ}\right) - \frac{dC(Q)}{dQ} = 0 \tag{9.6}$$

$$\text{or } MR - MC_p = 0,$$

and

$$\frac{\partial \pi}{\partial \alpha} = PqN\frac{d\lambda}{d\alpha} - qN\frac{dC(Q)}{dQ}\frac{d\lambda}{d\alpha} - C_a = 0 \tag{9.7}$$

$$\text{or } P - MC_p = \frac{C_a}{qN(d\lambda/d\alpha)}.$$

---

[281] Alternatively, we could assume that some constant proportion of them buy – all results would go through in the same way except we would need to keep track of an extra parameter describing this proportion.

For simplicity, we are considering a one-period model. Those who are informed by advertising buy the monopolist's product. Thus, λ measures the advertising penetration for this period alone.

Condition (9.6) is the usual profit maximization condition that output should be expanded until marginal revenue equals the marginal cost of production. Condition (9.7) states that the monopolist should increase informative advertising until the markup over production cost, $P - MC_p$, equals the per unit cost of advertising, C_a, divided by the marginal impact on quantity sold due to increasing the amount of advertising.

9.2.3 Optimal Advertising Under Imperfect Competition

A slightly more complicated, but more interesting situation arises when many firms are selling close substitutes. For example, most retail markets contain many different gasoline stations selling different brands of gasoline as well as many different hamburgers sold under the McDonald's, Burger King, Wendy's, and other trademarks. Changes in demand and supply conditions continually alter the equilibrium price. At any point in time, there will be a distribution of prices offered by the different sellers in a market. Consumers will have to go from one firm to the other searching for the best deal: their search is costly. One of the primary functions of advertising in that context is to induce consumers to visit a particular firm in their search for the best deal.

To make this point more precise, let us assume that each consumer goes to several stores before deciding where to buy. Suppose also that, given what all the other firms are doing, each firm i is able to increase the number of potential customers who canvass its store in any given period (δ_i) by increasing its advertising (α_i), and that the manager of firm i can increase the fraction of those canvassers who ultimately buy from his store (M_i) by lowering his price. In other words, as consumers shop around but incur costs in doing so, they will stop searching and buy when they find a price that they believe is relatively low. Hence, a lower price induces a high proportion of canvassers to stop searching and actually buy.[282]

The total revenue received by firm i equals

$$TR_i = P_i q(P_i)\delta_i M_i,$$

where P_i is the price per unit, $q(P_i)$ denotes the quantity bought by each buyer, which we assume depends on the firm's price but not its advertising, δ_i represents the number of customers who canvass the store, and M_i is the

---

[282] See Lewis (2003) for a model where consumers set their "reference" price based on prices observed during previous purchase occasions.

fraction of those canvassing the store who buy from it. The firm's profit is

$$\pi_i = P_i q(P_i) \delta_i M_i - C(Q) - C_a \alpha_i.$$

Where $Q = q(p_i)\delta_i M_i$. Holding fixed what all other firms are doing, maximizing profit is accomplished by setting the appropriate price and level of advertising.

As in the monopoly case, advertising has its benefits and costs. The optimal level of advertising occurs where the marginal benefit of selling one more unit through advertising equals the marginal cost of selling that unit. As before, the marginal benefit of selling one more unit through advertising equals the difference between the price at which it is sold and the marginal cost of generating the demand for, and of producing, this extra unit. Let us now examine the cost of generating the demand for this extra unit. By definition, the number of consumers who canvass a store rises by $d(\delta_i)/d\alpha_i$ when the level of advertising is increased. Because only a fraction M_i of canvassers buy from a store and each buyer purchases $q(P_i)$ units, a unit increase in advertising brings about an increase in sales of $M_i q(P_i)(d\delta_i/d\alpha_i)$. But it costs C_a to bring this about. Accordingly, the cost of selling an additional unit through advertising equals $C_a/[M_i q(d\delta_i/d\alpha_i)]$. In other words, profit is maximized when

$$P_i - MC_p = \frac{C_a}{q M_i(d\delta_i/d\alpha_i)}, \tag{9.8}$$

where for simplicity we write $q(P_i)$ simply as q.

We can illustrate the intuition behind condition (9.8) as follows. Suppose that a Goodyear tire distributor sells a particular model for $100 per tire. The purchasing, inventory, and installation costs are $70 per tire. Based on experience and marketing surveys, the distributor estimates that one minute of local TV advertising, which costs $200, brings 10 new potential customers into his store. His experience is that at $100 per tire, one-third of those potential customers on average will actually buy tires, and each of them will buy four tires. Given these facts, we have $P_i = \$100$, $MC_p = \$70$, $C_a = \$200$, $M_i = 1/3$, $q = 4$, and $d\delta_i/d\alpha_i = 10$. Thus, the distributor earns a $30 profit on each tire sold: $P - MC_p = \$100 - \$70 = \$30$. The cost of selling an additional tire through increased advertising is

$$\frac{C_a}{q M_i(d\delta_i/d\alpha_i)} = \frac{\$200}{4(1/3)10} = \$15.$$

The distributor in this example should expand his advertising effort as there is additional net profit to be earned: the benefit of selling one more unit, $30, is greater than the cost of the same ($= \$15$).

In our discussion above, we have not addressed competitors' reactions to the firm's choice of advertising level. If competitors also all know that they can get more customers to canvass their stores if they advertise, all of them will do so. In equilibrium, the effect that a single store's advertising has on the number of new customers will be smaller than it would be if other stores did not advertise, but the optimal amount of advertising by each store will be larger than under monopoly as each firm now has to counter the "business stealing" effect of its competitor's advertising. Any rents that might accrue to the firms as a result of advertising are dissipated by competition.[283]

Similarly, we have not addressed yet the issue of pricing. To maximize profit, the manager must not only pick the correct level of advertising but he must also choose the correct price. And the pricing decision, just like the advertising decision, is more complicated when there are other firms selling essentially the same product than when the firm is the only one selling a particular product.

We have seen that the manager of a monopoly maximizes the firm's profit by equating the increase in total revenue from selling one more unit to each customer to the marginal cost of production. We will now derive a similar condition for a seller competing with other sellers in a market characterized by imperfect information.

At any given level of advertising, a firm is able to sell more of its product when it lowers its price. This is true for two reasons. As the price falls, each customer may purchase more – that is, as we saw before, q is a function of P_i. A price decrease also causes a greater fraction of canvassers to purchase from this particular firm. Both of these effects are incorporated in the negative slope of the demand curve facing the firm and so both will influence the profit-maximizing price.

Holding advertising levels and prices of all other firms in the industry constant, the firm facing competition from sellers with slightly different products will determine its optimal price from its profit function:

$$\pi_i = P_i q(P_i) \delta_i(\alpha_i, \alpha_{-i}) M_i(P_i) - C(Q) - C_a \alpha_i$$

where the notation $\delta_i(\alpha_i, \alpha_{-i})$ simply denotes the fact that the number of customers canvassing the store is a function of this firm's and all other firms' advertising levels. Holding these fixed, optimization requires that the firm choose the price that causes the first partial derivative of profit with respect

---

[283] Stigler (1968) explains that while non-price competition does not lead to price reductions, it instead leads to the dissipation of non-competitive profits.

to its price to be equal to zero:

$$\frac{\partial \pi_i}{\partial P_i} = \delta_i \left[\frac{M_i d(P_i q)}{d P_i} + \frac{(P_i q) d M_i}{d P_i} \right] - MC_p \delta_i \left[\frac{M_i dq}{d P_i} + \frac{q d M_i}{d P_i} \right] = 0.$$

We can rearrange this condition as

$$MC_p = \frac{M_i(d(P_i q)/d P_i) + P_i q(d M_i/d P_i)}{M_i(dq/d P_i) + q(d M_i/d P_i)}.$$

This expression can be further simplified. If we define the price elasticity of individual demand as

$$\varepsilon_{q,P} = \frac{dq}{d P_i} \cdot \frac{P_i}{q},$$

and the elasticity of M_i with respect to price as

$$\varepsilon_{M,P} = -\frac{d M_i}{d P_i} \cdot \frac{P_i}{M_i},$$

we can write the profit maximization condition as

$$MC_p = P_i \left[1 - \frac{1}{\varepsilon_{q,P} + \varepsilon_{M,P}} \right]. \tag{9.9}$$

In this context, price deviates from marginal cost because information is costly; that is, customers incur costs of searching for the best value. If information were free, all customers would buy from the firm offering the lowest price. In other words, the sum of the elasticities would be infinite and condition (9.9) would require setting price equal to the marginal cost of production, the standard competitive result.

9.3 The Effect of Scale Economies

In our discussion above, we have described how advertising can be used by firms to provide information to customers: once they are aware of the firm and its products, customers will choose whether or not to canvass a store and whether or not to purchase some amount q of the good. Advertising can, of course, serve other roles, but the bottom line for firms is that it increases the demand for their products. This, in turn, means that it is worth investing in advertising. In this section, we take it as given that advertising increases demand and focus on the cost of advertising as a factor that can influence how firms are organized. Specifically, we explore how differences in the scale economies associated with production or distribution versus advertising can influence the organizational form of the firm.

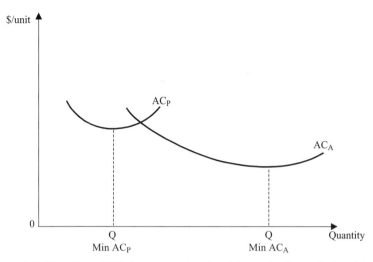

Figure 9-1: The effect of differing economies of scale in production and advertising.

When the economies of scale in advertising are much larger than the economies of scale in production and distribution, meaning that the firm size required to exhaust economies of scale for advertising is much larger than that needed to minimize production costs, multi-establishment or chain organization may be the solution. The chain organization can exploit relatively large-scale economies in advertising by combining the purchasing power of the different units in the chain, and promoting the chain at a national or regional level. At the same time, the individual establishments that are part of the chain can exhaust the scale economies in production and distribution at the local level.

Consider the illustration in Figure 9-1, which depicts the average cost of advertising per unit of output sold as AC_A and the average cost of production as AC_P. In this example, we can see that the minimum-cost output level for advertising is much larger than the minimum-cost output in production. Specifically, as drawn, the efficient size for advertising is about three times larger than the efficient size for production. As a result, a chain with at least three units would perform well: the chain can specialize the head office, or the franchisor if it is franchised, in advertising and brand-building activities while the local units, or franchisees, focus on the production and distribution activities. In doing so, the chain efficiently exhausts all economies of scale in both sets of activities.

The economic motivation for chain organization thus depends upon the relative scale economies in advertising and production. Products for which the minimum cost levels of production are low yet brand recognition can be highly valuable, for example, retail and service activities, are good candidates. It is not surprising then that the fast-food industry, and other types of businesses that must operate close to their geographically dispersed customers in order to attract their patronage, such as home cleaning, car repairs, real estate services, and the like, are organized as chains. In these cases, a good deal of the advertising is designed to make us aware of the chain's existence and to remove uncertainty in the customer's mind regarding product quality. This, in turn, explains the focus on consistency in most franchised chains (see Chapter 5). If products and implementation differed considerably across outlets, there would be little information to provide to customers through advertising! With generally consistent implementation throughout the chain, customers have a good idea of what to expect when they walk into a McDonald's restaurant, a Holiday Inn motel, or an Ace Hardware store anywhere in the country or even the world. Moreover, it would be much too costly for an individual restaurant, hotel, or hardware store to organize a similar level of promotional effort on its own. Thus, it makes sense for the central entity, or franchisor if the chain is franchised, to take on this burden. The local restaurant, hotel and hardware store, on the other hand, can easily exhaust the scale economies in producing and selling meals and hotel services, and in retailing hardware products locally.

In fact, exhausting economies of scale in branding and in purchasing have been main drivers behind the tendency to organize much of the retailing and services sectors with large chains of individual units. Access to lower-cost inputs, including advertising, historically has been, and remains to this day, an important part of the package that franchisors sell to potential conversion franchisees. In other words, when franchisors like Best Western, or ReMax, or Embers try to convince owners of existing businesses to join their chain, they strongly emphasize the economies and demand-enhancing benefits associated with operating under a common, well-known brand.[284]

9.4 Advertising as a Public Good in Franchised Chains

System-wide advertising is common for chains of outlets. It is also common specifically in franchised systems: we have all seen national television ads for automobiles, gasoline, fast-food restaurants, beer, accounting services, and hotels, to mention just a few. When a chain is organized as a single corporate

---

[284] See, e.g., http://www.bestwestern.com/aboutus/memdev/main.asp, http://www.remax .com/join/advantages.shtml, and http://www.embersamerica.com/franchise.htm.

entity operating all of its outlets directly, shareholders as a group both bear
the cost of, and receive the benefits from, advertising decisions. When a chain
is franchised, however, many separate individual franchisees benefit from the
same advertising. In other words, advertising is a *public good* for the members
of the franchise system. It is both *non-rival* and *nonexclusive*, which are the two
central characteristics of a public good.[285] Being non-rival simply means that
all owners of all the units can benefit at no extra cost.[286] When McDonald's
places a national ad during the Olympics television coverage, the benefits to
a franchisee or to a franchised unit in Florida are not reduced by the benefits
enjoyed by a franchisee or franchised unit in Michigan. Similarly, whatever
positive effect a Ford ad during the Super Bowl may have in New Jersey
does not diminish the benefits for Ford dealers in Texas. Being nonexclusive
means that no franchisee or franchised unit can be excluded specifically from
the benefits of the advertising campaign. Since the campaign pertains to the
franchise system as a whole, all units and franchisees will benefit to one extent
or another.

While advertising is a public good in a franchised chain, each franchisee
individually has a demand for advertising that flows from its own efforts to
maximize the profits of its outlets. The individual franchisee's optimal level
of advertising is the one that makes the cost to it of an extra unit of advertising
equal to the benefit:

$$C_a = P_i \partial Q_i / \partial \alpha_i,$$

where Q_i is the quantity sold in a franchisee's outlet, and α_i is the amount of
advertising benefiting the outlet.[287] These individual demands for advertising,
of course, will vary across outlets and franchisees due to the unique economic
and demographic characteristics of each market. Because the benefits to the
franchisees are not subject to rivalry, that is, the benefit to one franchisee
does not reduce the benefits to any other franchisee, the marginal benefit
schedules (i.e., the individual franchisee demands for advertising) should
be added *vertically* to obtain the system-wide demand. That is, the system-
wide marginal benefit of an ad is the vertical sum of the individual marginal
benefits, where the summation is taken over all outlets. This effect, that the
benefit to the system is the sum of individual benefits, is separate from the
issue of economies of scale discussed above, and is what makes big-ticket

---

[285] See, e.g., Pindyck and Rubinfeld (2001) at pp. 644–649.
[286] This is not true of a *private* good; we cannot both wear the same T-shirt.
[287] Though franchisees often own more than one outlet, we equate franchisee and outlet
in what follows to simplify the discussion.

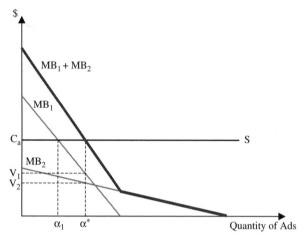

Figure 9-2: The optimal number of ads in a chain of two outlets.

advertising economically feasible for large chains. Certainly, no McDonald's franchisee, Anheuser-Busch wholesale distributor, or Ford dealer would find it sensible to pay for an ad during the Super Bowl coverage because 15-second time slots cost $2 million. But the system as a whole may well find it both affordable and beneficial.

We illustrate these ideas with a stylized example in Figure 9-2 for two franchisees. The cost of an ad is assumed constant and equal to C_a, reflecting a horizontal supply of advertising (that is, we are assuming away economies of scale to emphasize the effect of additive marginal benefits). Franchisee 1's marginal benefit schedule is shown as MB_1 while franchisee 2's marginal benefit schedule is MB_2. The aggregate benefit is shown as the vertical sum $MB_1 + MB_2$. For this two-outlet system, the optimal number of ads is found where

$$MB_1 + MB_2 = C_a.$$

In this simple example, the joint profit maximizing number of ads is α^*. On their own, neither franchisee would buy α^* ads because that is not individually optimal: As Figure 9-2 reveals, franchisee 1 would have bought only α_1 ads and franchisee 2 would have bought none. For the chain as a whole, however, even α_1 is too small because $MB_1 + MB_2 > C_a$ at α_1. This means that further advertising is desirable at that point.

As can also be seen in Figure 9-2, $MB_1 > MB_2$ at α^*, or put differently, $V_1 > V_2$. If franchisee 1 paid the value to him of this advertising, namely V_1 per ad (for a total of $V_1 \cdot \alpha^*$) and franchisee 2 paid V_2 (for a total of $V_2 \cdot \alpha^*$), these contributions would add up exactly to $C_a\alpha^*$ since by definition $V_1 + V_2 = C_a$. Moreover, at a "price" per ad of V_1, franchisee 1 would demand exactly α^* ads. Similarly, if franchisee 2 paid a "price" per ad of V_2, it would demand α^* ads. But, because $V_1 > V_2$, it seems "unfair" or discriminatory for franchisee 1's share of total expenditures to be greater than franchisee 2's. This easily could cause some complaints.

An alternative is for each of the two franchisees to pay $C_a/2$. In this case, however, $V_1 > C_a/2$ at α^* and franchisee 1 would want to expand the number of ads. At the same time, $V_2 < C_a/2$ at α^* and franchisee 2 would want fewer ads along with a reduced proportion of its budget going toward advertising. Thus, a seemingly fair and nondiscriminatory payment scheme, that is splitting the cost equally between the two franchisees, will leave both franchisees dissatisfied with the level of advertising even though it is the profit maximizing quantity for the chain as a whole.[288]

Finally, another problem will be getting franchisees to reveal their demands so that $MB_1 + MB_2$ can be calculated and thus the correct amount of advertising potentially can be purchased. If franchisees are charged in proportion to their stated demand, each franchisee has an incentive to free ride and say that it does not value advertising, or, at the very least, say that it values it less than it actually does. The franchisor can solve this problem somewhat imperfectly by requiring that franchisees contribute a certain fraction of their total revenue, no matter what their stated demands or preferences might be, into an advertising fund that the franchisor (e.g., Burger King) administers. Alternatively, the franchisor (e.g., McDonald's) may require that each franchisee spend a minimum fraction of its total revenue on advertising. It will then make sense for franchisees to spend these advertising dollars in an optimal way as they will get more benefit that way for the same expenditure level. If we assume that franchisees with higher sales on average value advertising more than owners of smaller or lower sales outlets, an advertising requirement based on outlet sales at least partially resolves the equity problem described above. In other words, in this case, those franchisees that value advertising the most pay a higher share of total advertising expenditures, yet the fees do not look so "unfair" since the same proportion of sales is required from all franchisees.[289]

---

[288] It is only in the unlikely event that the franchisees have identical marginal benefit schedules that fair and nondiscriminatory contributions do not lead to dissatisfaction with the quantity of advertising. Then, $V_1 + V_2 = C_a$ and $V_1 = V_2$.

[289] One might argue, however, that it is franchisees with low sales who might benefit most from advertising, in which case an advertising contribution based on sales levels would tax more heavily those who value the ads the least, contrary to what would be optimal. See Dant and Berger (1996) who argue that the more established franchisees

9.5 Advertising in Franchised Chains in Practice

In Chapter 3, we noted that most franchisors today require that franchisees contribute some proportion of their sales toward advertising. In Volume III of the *Profile of Franchising*, 634 (or 52 percent) of the 1,221 franchisors that provided advertising fee data required that franchisees pay a percentage of their sales toward advertising. The remaining franchisors either had no requirement (340, or 28 percent), or demanded contributions only to local or regional advertising funds (149, or 12 percent), or a flat fee (66, or 5 percent of them), or a per transaction fee (13, or 1 percent of the sample). Our data show a similar tendency to use sales-based advertising fees at the end of our sample period.

Interestingly, the reliance on separate advertising fees was not so popular earlier on. In 1980, the majority of franchisors charged neither sales-based nor fixed advertising fees (see Table 3-9 in Chapter 3). In part, this change seems to reflect a form of contract evolution: whereas franchisors used to specify royalties only and use some of the funds thereby collected for advertising purposes, the majority of them now explicitly separate the royalty and advertising requirements. Brickley (1999) surmises that the increased reliance on separate fees may be a response to a franchisor moral hazard problem in that franchisors may have an incentive to use funds for other purposes if they are not slated specifically for advertising.[290] And indeed, as he points out, some franchise contracts specify that moneys collected via the advertising fee cannot be commingled with other funds. But authors such as Sen (1995), Stassen and Mittelstaedt (2002), and Lafontaine and Shaw (2005) have examined the relationship between advertising fees and actual advertising expenditures per *Ad $ Summary*.[291] They found only a weak, or no, correlation between the two. Of course, advertising outlays need not be contemporaneous to the collection of fees. These authors tried to account for this however, by looking at advertising expenditures over long periods, between five and ten years. Other reasons for the lack of correlation include the fact that some of the funds may

who already enjoy considerable local market reputation and patronage are most likely to think that their franchisor advertises too much.

[290] Brickley, however, mostly views these fees as a constraint on franchisee behavior. He argues and finds empirically that the presence of separate advertising fees is related to the extent of sales externalities among outlets; that is, chains with more externality problems (more non-repeat business) must impose such requirement more often.

[291] *Ad $ Summary*, published by LNA/Media Watch (now TNS Media Intelligence/CMR) reports the estimated expenditures on advertising in ten separate media by brand. The estimates are generated by measuring the amount of advertising per brand in the various media and using going rates to transform these measures into dollars spent.

be spent on regional or local advertising or promotional efforts not captured by the publishers of *Ad $ Summary*. Moreover, for many franchisors, especially those with low or no fees, advertising outlays need not be limited by the amount of fees collected specifically for this purpose. Thus, it may not be surprising that there is little correlation between estimated outlays and percentage fees. In other words, as we noted in Chapter 3, many franchisors today still may not draw a really clear distinction between royalty and other revenue and advertising-related funds.

We also saw in Chapter 3 that there is much variance in how franchisors specify their advertising requirement; how they divide it among national, regional, and local expenditures; and what the franchisor commits to exactly. Some franchisors establish an advertising fund while others do not. In its franchise contract, Bruegger's Bagels, for example, requires that each

> Franchisee shall contribute weekly to the advertising Fund established by Franchisor for the System two percent (2%) of the Gross Sales of the Franchised Bakery.
>
> . . .
>
> In addition to its contribution to the Fund, Franchisee shall spend monthly for local advertising and promotion two percent (2%) of the Gross Sales of the Franchised Bakery.
>
> . . .
>
> Franchisee acknowledges that the Fund and any earnings thereon will be used to maximize general public recognition, acceptance, and patronage of BRUEGGER'S Bakeries, and that Franchisor is not obligated, in administering the Fund, to make expenditures for Franchisee which are equivalent or proportional to Franchisee's contribution, or to ensure that any particular franchisee benefits directly or PRO RATA from expenditures by the Fund. Franchisee acknowledges that its failure to derive any such benefit will not serve as a basis for a reduction or elimination of its obligation to contribute to the Fund. (Bruegger's Bagels New Bakery Franchise Agreement, per its 2000 UFOC)

The language of this agreement makes it clear that the franchisee must pay 2 percent of gross sales for national advertising and that it is up to the franchisor to decide how best to expend these funds. By acknowledging the uncertain benefits to be derived from this advertising, each franchisee agrees that he may be paying more than the advertising is worth to him. Based on the plain language of the contract, the franchisee surrenders any right to complain about the quality or geographic allocation of the franchisor's promotional efforts.

McDonald's, of course, also recognizes the value of advertising and demands that its franchisees spend a significant sum on this activity. In 1990, the McDonald's franchise system spent approximately $80–90 million to produce television and radio commercials and \$245 million to purchase national media time, mostly on network television.[292] Advertising on the national as well as the local level is organized by co-operatives. Each franchisee member of the national cooperative must pledge the same contribution rate, 1.65 percent of sales in 2003 as per McDonald's disclosure document. Local cooperatives are formed by restaurant owners who join together in various geographical locations and decide on local promotions and advertising campaigns. In 1990, these cooperatives spent approximately \$190 million on advertising, most of which was spent on local television time. The franchise contract simply stipulates that franchisees must spend at least 4 percent of their sales revenue in total on advertising:

> McDonald's employs both public relations and advertising specialists who formulate and carry out national and local advertising programs for the McDonald's System. Franchisee shall use only advertising and promotional materials and programs provided by McDonald's or approved in advance, in writing, by McDonald's [...] Franchisee shall expend during each calendar year for advertising and promotion of the Restaurant to the general public an amount which is not less than four percent (4%) of Gross Sales [...] for such year. Expenditures by Franchisee to national and regional cooperative advertising and promotion of the McDonald's System, or to a group of McDonald's restaurants which includes the Restaurant, shall be a credit against the required minimum expenditures for advertising and promotion to the general public. (McDonald's Franchise Agreement, per McDonald's UFOC, 2003)

McDonald's thus controls the quality of the advertising and the minimum amount that each franchisee must spend. However, none of the advertising moneys are paid to McDonald's corporation. Instead the funds are administered directly by the advertising cooperatives and independently audited. The franchisee has the freedom to participate in these cooperative advertising efforts with other franchisees, but cannot choose to expend less than the 4 percent stated in his franchise agreement on advertising and promotion. In practice, however, franchisees who want to be considered for additional units or even contract renewal are expected to participate consistently in the national and local cooperatives. Note that company-owned restaurants may also elect to be members of these cooperatives.

Stassen and Mittlestaedt (2002) report the advertising requirements imposed in a few different restaurant franchise chains, as described in their 1999 10-K reports. They note that Wendy's franchisees are required to contribute

---

[292] See the June 5, 1993 testimony of David B. Green, McDonald's Senior Vice President for Marketing, http://www.mcspotlight.org/people/witnesses/advertising/green.html.

2 percent of their sales to the "Wendy's National Advertising Program Inc." and another 2 percent for local and regional advertising (including, in many cases, cooperative advertising). Thus, like Bruegger's Bagels, Wendy's stipulates clearly how a franchisee's total advertising expenditure is dedicated to national versus regional or local advertising.

A number of franchisors also establish programs that allow them to share with franchisees some of the cost they incur for local or regional advertising. Specifically, according to Dant and Berger (1996), almost 75 percent of franchisors in the auto products and services industry, and 86 percent of the franchisors in the fast-food industry, engage in some form of cooperative advertising program with their franchisees.

Finally, franchisors leave themselves much leeway to make changes over time in their contracts when it comes to advertising contributions. For example, Stassen and Mittlestaedt (2002) report that in its 10-K report, Wendy's states "the Company may increase the total advertising and promotions contribution to 5% . . . if such increase is approved by an affirmative vote representing 75% or more of all domestic Wendy's restaurants." At Applebee's, though the contribution to the national advertising fund had been 1.5 percent through 1999, the 10-K report for that year stated that "the required contribution to the national advertising fund will increase to 2.1% of gross sales in 2000, and may increase from 2.1% to a maximum of 2.5% in 2001. Beginning in 2002, the required contribution will be 2.5% of gross sales." Further, "The Company can increase the combined amount of the advertising fee and the amount required to be spent on local advertising and promotional activities to a maximum of 5% of gross sales." Finally, in 1997, Mail Boxes Etc. implemented a new *ad hoc* cooperative effort in which the franchisees matched the franchisor's contribution. The focus of the effort was on local marketing, which was being ignored by some franchisees.[293] Of course, raising the amount that franchisees must devote to advertising at any point in time is apt to cause some conflict in a franchise system. In what follows, we examine this and other sources of conflict relating to advertising in franchised chains.

9.6 Franchisor–Franchisee Conflict

When the franchisor selects the advertising message and determines its placement, as most franchisors do, the franchisee's concern is with the marginal benefit to his store. In that context, conflicts over advertising-related issues between a franchisee and its franchisor can arise for several reasons.

---

[293] See Tannenbaum (1997).

First, the franchisee may believe that the amount that the franchisor spends or, more to the point, the amount that the franchisee is required to spend on advertising, is excessive. This belief is understandable, albeit perhaps unfounded, because the individual franchisee may not appreciate the benefit that he derives from a Super Bowl ad on national television or ads in *Time* magazine. Moreover, there is always the desire to be a free rider. To the extent that everyone else advertises, a single franchisee could free ride on the efforts and expenditures of others – that is, not spend any effort or dollars on advertising himself – and not suffer any appreciable loss in sales volume.

Second, the distribution of advertising nationally, regionally, and locally may cause dissatisfaction in some quarters. That is, some franchisees may feel that they have been shortchanged, that the advertising dollars of the system are being disproportionately spent elsewhere so that insufficient amounts reach their own particular market.

Third, the franchisee may feel that the franchisor has simply not done a good job with the advertising that it has done. The complaint in this case is not so much with the cost as it is with the effectiveness of the advertising. The franchisee thinks that he is not getting a sufficient "bang for the buck." Franchisees of Benetton in Germany, for example, sued their franchisor in 1996 alleging that its advertising campaign hurt their businesses.

Finally, some franchisees may object to the way in which the franchisor administers the advertising fund. For example, they may believe or find that advertising moneys are spent on ads to recruit new franchisees instead of being spent on growing the brand.

The recent *Meineke* case brought some of these issues into play.[294] Meineke's Franchise and Trademark Agreement (FTA) required its franchisees to contribute 10 percent of their weekly receipts to fund national and local advertising. The money was paid into the Weekly Advertising Contribution (WAC) account that Meineke maintained and administered. The terms of the FTA required Meineke to purchase and place advertising that promoted the goods and services sold by the franchisees. Meineke reserved the right to make strategic and creative choices in administering the WAC fund:

> [A]ll decisions regarding whether to utilize national, regional, or local advertising, or some combination thereof, and regarding selection of the particular media and advertising content, shall be within the sole discretion of Meineke and such agencies or others as it may appoint.

---

[294] The following discussion relies on the appellate court decision, *Broussard v. Meineke Discount Muffler Shops, Inc.*, 155 F. 3d 331 (4th Cir. 1998), and Killion and Schnell (1998).

Some of the franchisees objected to Meineke's performance. According to the Court of Appeals, Broussard testified that "some franchisees were growing increasingly dissatisfied with the cost, amount and quality of Meineke's advertising." Thus, the primary concern of the franchisees appeared to be Meineke's allegedly poor advertising strategy. But the franchise agreement gave Meineke sole discretion over decisions on advertising strategy, which foreclosed the franchisees from pursuing any legal action along these lines. The franchisees thus chose to sue their franchisor over something else, namely the way in which Meineke administered the fund.

There was language in some of the franchise agreements that indicated that Meineke would administer the WAC fund without any charge beyond the franchisee's initial license fee. At the same time, however, another provision of the agreement suggested that some of the WAC funds could be spent on related expenses:

> Meineke agrees that it will expend for media costs, commissions and fees, production costs, creative and other costs of such advertising, with respect to Meineke franchisees, an amount equal to the total of all sums collected from all franchisees [in the WAC account].[295]

This language suggests that commissions and fees paid to those entities that place the advertising and other related costs are covered among the set of permissible expenses. Meineke disbursed some $32.2 million over the years in three categories of costs that caused the dispute. First, it spent some $1.1 million of WAC money to defend and settle a suit filed by its former advertising agency. Second, Meineke established an in-house advertising agency, New Horizons, which paid about $14 million in commissions to outside advertising agencies for placing advertising. It used WAC account funds to cover these commissions. Finally, New Horizons collected $17.1 million in commissions on the advertising that it placed on behalf of the franchisees. These sums also came out of the WAC money.

The plaintiffs claimed that Meineke had no right to pay commissions to New Horizons or to the outside agencies with WAC funds. Instead, the plaintiffs argued that Meineke was supposed to absorb those costs out of the royalty payments that franchisees paid. The franchisees contended that all WAC dollars were to be spent on the advertising itself. Meineke, of course, disagreed. As the circuit court of appeals observed: "This case is a study in the tension that can beset the franchisor-franchisee relationship."

---

[295] *Id.* at 335. The court is quoting Meineke's Franchise and Trademark Agreement.

Whether the franchisees or Meineke was right, this case highlights the conflict that can result when the franchisor requires that it controls fully and administers the advertising funds contributed by the franchisees. A good deal of the ambiguity can be cleared away by carefully worded contracts. The rancor over poor advertising effectiveness, however, cannot be alleviated in this fashion; only a better performance will rectify that problem.

In addition to conflict relating to the amount or usage of advertising moneys, advertising can give rise to conflict if it is used by the franchisor to entice the franchisee to participate in certain promotions or set its price at a certain level. For instance, suppose that a franchisor would like to see its franchisee charge a price of $2.25 while the franchisee would prefer a more profitable price of $2.75. Without actually getting into specific price controls, the franchisor may be able to publicize prices to consumers in ways that make it very difficult for franchisees to charge more than the announced price. One example would be to simply include price information in an ad with fine print that contains a disclaimer such as "only at participating dealers." This leaves the franchisee with the option of not participating but at the risk of losing goodwill with his local customers. As a result, franchisees may be "forced," albeit legally, into participating in a particular price promotion.

In the Seventh Circuit at least, it is permissible to go even further according to the decision in *Jack Walters*.[296] Morton was a manufacturer of prefabricated buildings that it sold as kits to its franchised dealers. Jack Walters and other franchisees bought the kits from Morton and resold them as assembled buildings to consumers. On occasion, Morton advertised special prices for its buildings. In addition to including the discounted retail price in its ad, Morton listed the names of participating franchisees. In *Jack Walters*, Judge Posner explained that such price advertising by a franchisor was perfectly legal:

> Walters concedes as it must that it is perfectly lawful for a manufacturer to advertise his product to the ultimate consumer, and to mention in that advertising the retail price of the product – the only price the consumer is interested in.[297]

Judge Posner explained further that the legality of advertising retail prices extends to the minimum steps necessary to make the advertising useful to the franchisor. This includes reasonable measures to ensure that franchisees do not charge more than the advertised price.[298] Judge Posner found Morton's threats of termination, offers of direct sales to retail customers, and

---

[296] *Jack Walters & Sons Corporation v. Morton Building, Inc.* (1984).
[297] *Id.* at 707.
[298] *Id.* at 708.

other policing efforts to be reasonably necessary to make its price advertising credible.

Instead of using its ad directly to entice franchisees to charge a given price, a franchisor may also obtain the desired pricing behavior by conditioning the reimbursements stipulated in its cooperative advertising plan, that is, in its offer to share the cost of local advertising, on a franchisee's advertising the product at the price that the franchisor wants.[299] As long as the franchisee can set the price on actual transactions at whatever level seems appropriate to the franchisee, there is little danger of antitrust liability.[300]

9.7 Conclusion

In this chapter, we have examined the role of advertising in franchised chains. Given the importance of the brand's value to both franchisors and franchisees, it is not surprising that advertising plays a central role in the franchise relationship. It is also not surprising then that it is the source of much dispute and conflict. We began by reviewing the information role of advertising and brands as this view aligns well with the mobile society argument for the value of chains in today's society. We then described how economies of scale in advertising increase the likelihood that firms will want to develop common branding and jointly advertise. The presence of economies of scale and the public good nature of advertising in the context of a common brand both explain why franchisors and franchisees often disagree not only about the type of advertising, which is partially a matter of taste, but also about the amounts spent, the placement, the division of expenditures between franchisors and franchisees, and so on. But while there is much potential for disputes, the judicial treatment has been rather straightforward. If the contract provides for full franchisor discretion as to how and when to spend the advertising dollars collected from its franchisees, then franchisees have little legal recourse. If the franchisor has an obligation to maintain a separate fund and to report its usage to franchisees, then franchisees who believe that their franchisor has used advertising funds in inappropriate ways will be able to air their grievances in court. Thus, litigation will resolve these types of disputes.

---

[299] For a model of cooperative advertising for optimal system-wide returns, see Dant and Berger (1996).

[300] In *In re Nissan Antitrust Litigation* (1979), the key was that the Nissan dealers were not compelled to make sales at the advertised prices. Moreover, participation in the advertising program was not mandatory.

10

Termination and Non-Renewal

10.1 Introduction

The vast majority of franchise contracts are of finite duration, but contract duration varies considerably across franchise chains: some contracts are as short as 5 years while others are as long as 20 or 30 years. The contracts also usually stipulate an option to renew and the duration of the potential renewal period(s). In their 1998 survey of franchise contracting practices, Frandata and the IFA found that 91 percent of franchise contracts included an option to renew. Moreover, most of the time, franchise agreements are indeed renewed. In a small number of cases, however, even franchisors who offer such an option choose not to renew a specific contract. Further, franchisors sometimes terminate a franchisee's existing contract within the contract period.

In this chapter, we first describe in more detail what we know about contract duration. We show in particular that franchise contracts are typically quite long-term. We also provide some information on termination and renewal rates. We then examine the role of contract duration, termination, and non-renewal in franchising, specifically the effect these have on franchisees' willingness to invest both capital and effort in their franchised unit.[301] We also discuss the issue of franchisee and franchisor opportunism and how these relate to termination and non-renewal. Next, we examine how the common law treats the termination and non-renewal of franchise contracts in the United States, and then describe how several states within the United States further regulate termination and non-renewal in their franchise relationship laws. Finally, we review the economics behind various ways to calculate damages in

---

[301] See Lutz (1995) for a model illustrating how outlet ownership provides incentives to franchisees that go beyond pure current residual claims. This result follows because ownership allows franchisees to capture the returns on the part of their effort that increases the **future** value of the outlet.

cases involving wrongful termination. Note that while we use this particular setting to discuss issues related to the calculation of damages, many of the points we make about calculated damages in this context apply generally to the calculation of damages in cases involving other forms of contract breach.

10.2 Franchise Contract Duration, Termination, and Renewal:
A Look at the Data

10.2.1 Contract Duration

In their 1998 survey of franchisors, Frandata and the IFA Educational Foundation found an average duration for franchise contracts of 10.3 years. They also found that 91 percent of franchisors offer a renewal period, which lasted for 8.2 years on average. Table 10-1 shows the mean duration of the initial contract and its standard deviation across sectors in the first and last year for which we have duration information in our data, namely 1993 and 2001. This table shows that there is some important variation in the duration of these contracts across sectors. For example, the average contract length in the sit-down restaurant industry is 14 plus years, which is twice as long as the average contract duration in the real estate sector. Moreover, duration varies more within some sectors than others, as indicated by the differences in the standard deviation of contract duration across sectors. Thus, firms offer contracts of very variable length in the recreation sector: the standard deviation of contract duration in this industry is almost as large as the mean contract duration. For franchisors in the contractor and rental sectors, on the other hand, the standard deviation is only 3 or 4 years around a mean duration of roughly 9 years. The data also suggest that there has not been any trend toward shorter or longer contracts on average in franchising, nor within the various sectors, between 1993 and 2001. The only exception may be the Hotel and Motel sector. Finally, Table 10-1 includes information on the number of firms in our data in each of the two years covered in the table, and documents the low frequency with which franchisors choose to rely on an infinite or an indefinite contract duration.

It is important to realize that these average durations hide some interesting discrete patterns in the data. Specifically, contract duration varies mostly in 5-year increments (see also Brickley et al. 2003 on this). In 2001, 20 percent of the franchisors in our data offer 5-year contracts, while 53 percent use 10-year contracts, 7 percent offer 15-year contracts, and 14 percent use a 20-year contract. Thus, 94 percent of all franchise contracts offered in 2001 were of one of these four possible durations. The corresponding total in 1993 is almost

Table 10-1: *Initial franchise contract duration, per sector*

	1993				2001			
	Number of Obs.	Mean Contract Duration in Years	Standard Deviation	Number infinite or indefinite	Number of Obs.	Mean Contract Duration in Years	Standard Deviation	Number infinite or indefinite
Automotive	70	12.2	4.9	1	76	12.6	5.2	3
Business	132	11.0	6.7	6	118	11.0	6.4	4
Contractors	39	8.3	3.6	1	52	8.8	2.9	0
Cosmetic	27	9.9	3.8	1	22	9.5	3.2	1
Education	27	8.0	3.7	0	39	8.3	3.4	0
Fast Food	212	12.1	4.6	3	229	12.3	4.9	2
Health and Fitness	31	8.8	3.7	1	27	9.0	3.9	1
Home Furnishings	24	10.0	6.4	0	25	9.1	3.9	0
Hotels and Motels	22	12.9	6.2	0	19	16.7	5.2	0
Maintenance	76	9.4	5.2	0	98	9.7	4.7	3
Personal Services	88	9.3	4.1	2	86	9.1	4.1	3
Real Estate	22	7.9	4.0	1	35	7.1	2.7	0
Recreation	18	10.3	9.1	1	18	10.4	8.2	2
Rental	26	9.6	3.4	0	26	8.6	3.6	2
Restaurants	70	14.0	4.7	0	70	14.7	4.7	0
Retail Food	40	8.9	2.4	3	42	9.6	3.9	1
Retail Other	128	9.5	4.5	2	129	9.5	3.6	1
Total	1,052	10.6		22	1,111	10.7		23

the same, at 93 percent, and the individual proportions are very similar as well. When we look at this from the perspective of franchised outlets, by weighing the contract duration of each franchisor by the number of franchised units they have, the discrete patterns remain. The 1,158 franchisors in our data in 2001 operated 329,803 franchised units in total.[302] Of these, 91 percent were under a 5-, 10-, 15-, or 20-year contract. The proportion of contracts of each duration, however, were quite different. Specifically, the proportion of 20-year contracts is much higher, at 37 percent, while the others are all smaller: the proportions of 5-, 10-, and 15-year contracts are 13, 37, and 4 percent, respectively. In other words, the data imply that larger franchisors tend to offer 20-year contracts much more frequently than average, while franchisors with fewer franchised outlets rely more on shorter-term contracts. Again, the same patterns arise in the 1993 data.

Brickley et al. (2003) analyze the factors that affect the duration of initial franchise contracts. Consistent with our comparison of duration at the franchised unit level versus franchisor level, they find that larger chains and franchisors with more years of experience tend to use longer-term contracts. Moreover, although firms rarely change the duration of their contracts, the authors find a tendency toward longer-term contracts over time within firms. Finally, they show that contract duration is positively related to the amount of physical and human investment (weeks of training) that franchisees must make in the business. We discuss the importance of franchisee investment in more detail in the next section.

Table 10-2 shows the duration of franchise contract renewals, that is, the number of years by which the initial contract period will be extended upon first renewal, on average per sector and, again, for 1993 and 2001. This table shows that first renewals tend to be somewhat shorter, by a year or two on average, than initial contracts. But this is not true in all sectors, especially sectors where initial contracts are relatively short, such as contractors, cosmetics, and real estate franchisors.

In part, the lower average duration of renewals is due to the 7 percent of firms in our data that offer no renewals, as shown in Columns 4 and 8.[303] But

---

[302] This total represents the number of franchised units of these chains that year, not their total number of units. According to the USDOC (1988), in 1986, business-format franchised chains operated a total of 246,664 franchised units (see Chapter 4 of this book). Thus, while our data does not include all franchisors in 2001, it undoubtedly includes the vast majority of franchised outlets.

[303] Note that we include in this set those few respondents that left the field blank when asked "What is the term of the renewal period," as well as those that answered NA or N/A as we presume that respondents that do not offer a renewal are the ones who

Table 10-2: *Renewal period, per sector*

	1993				2001			
	Number of Obs.	Mean Renewal Duration in Years	Standard Deviation	Number at zero*	Number of Obs.	Mean Renewal Duration in Years	Standard Deviation	Number at zero*
Automotive	66	9.4	4.9	6	71	10.2	5.6	5
Business	129	9.7	6.3	4	115	9.3	5.9	4
Contractors	38	8.3	3.7	3	50	8.5	3.0	2
Cosmetic	24	9.6	3.3	3	21	8.5	3.7	2
Education	25	8.8	4.5	1	37	8.2	2.8	2
Fast Food	186	9.5	4.1	21	206	9.4	4.2	23
Health and Fitness	30	7.6	2.6	2	26	6.8	2.5	3
Home Furnishings	24	9.0	6.4	0	25	8.0	3.3	1
Hotels and Motels	18	8.8	5.7	4	10	9.5	1.6	9
Maintenance	72	8.2	6.4	4	98	8.5	4.7	0
Personal Services	85	8.2	3.8	3	80	8.1	4.0	5
Real Estate	21	7.6	4.1	1	35	6.4	3.2	0
Recreation	17	6.3	2.8	1	17	8.5	3.0	1
Rental	23	8.0	3.3	3	26	7.2	2.9	0
Restaurants	62	10.2	4.9	7	60	9.7	5.0	6
Retail Food	36	8.0	2.8	4	37	8.4	3.5	6
Retail Other	120	7.9	4.2	7	123	8.4	4.2	7
Total	976	8.8		74	1,037	8.8		76

* These include a few actual zeros and "none" as well as cases where the data field was left blank or contained NR (no response), NA or N/A.

it also reflects a real duration difference between initial contracts and renewals in most of the sectors. A full 36 percent of the franchisors in our 2001 data offer only a 5-year renewal, as compared to 20 percent of initial contracts being this short. Another 41 percent of franchisors offer a 10-year renewal, while only 5 and 6 percent, respectively, offer 15- and 20-year renewals. Thus, the whole distribution of duration for renewals is shifted downward relative to what we find for initial contracts. The same is true if we examine the renewal durations from the perspective of franchised units as opposed to franchised firms. Among the 329,083 franchised units of the 1,158 franchisors in our data in 2001, we find no renewal clauses in 17 percent rather than only 7 percent of the cases, while 25, 26, 2 and 19 percent have contracts with 5-, 10-, 15- and 20-year renewals, respectively.

10.2.2 Renewal and Termination Rates

While most franchisors offer franchisees an opportunity to renew their contracts, what matters to franchisees is the likelihood that their contract indeed will be renewed. This probability not only affects the profits they themselves can expect to earn from their franchise, it also affects the resale value of their franchise. Although the USDOC (1988) does not report renewal and termination rates in traditional franchising, it shows that renewal is the norm in business-format franchising: of the 12,999 agreements up for renewal in 1986, 12,073, or 93 percent, were renewed. Of the 926 that were not, 359 were cases where the franchisee did not want a new contract, 374 were cases of mutual agreement not to renew, and 193 were cases where franchisors refused to renew. As for contract terminations, these are more common according to the same data source. Specifically, 3,075 agreements were terminated by franchisors in 1986, while 3,914 were terminated by franchisees and another 372 franchises were terminated by mutual agreement. These 7,361 terminations correspond to a 3 percent termination rate that year given that there were 246,664 franchised outlets in operation in 1986 according to the same source. The USDOC (1988) further documents that more than half of the terminations instigated by franchisors were due to franchisee non-payment of fees or financial default. Finally, the same source indicates that franchisors approved all but 94 of the 4,202 requests for ownership transfers – bequests

would give such answers. This leads to an estimate of 93 percent of all franchisors in our data offering a renewal period, which is very close to the corresponding proportion in the *Profile of Franchising* (1998).

or sales of the franchise to new owners – that they received from franchisees in 1986.

Williams (1996) used the Characteristics of Business Owners (CBO) database compiled by the U.S. Census Bureau to study termination rates. He found 1,001 franchise contracts with full-time owner involvement and at least one employee in 1987 in these data. In this sample, he observed a termination rate of 15.7 percent over a 4-year period, including terminations instigated by franchisees and franchisors. Consistent with the figures from the USDOC on terminations and ownership transfers, Williams further found that slightly more than 50 percent of the franchise contract terminations in his data were motivated by a desire, by the franchisor or franchisee, to transfer ownership to another franchisee. One-third of all contract terminations resulted in the outlet being closed. Finally, Williams showed that the types of outlets that were most subject to termination were those that were underperforming, suggesting that franchisors use termination to enforce performance standards or eliminate poor locations. We return to this issue below.

In sum, franchise contracts usually are quite long-term, with a very high tendency for the relationship to continue beyond the original term. In what follows, we explain the long duration of franchise relationships based on the franchisor's need for its franchisees to invest both capital and effort in their outlet. We then examine the effect of contract renewal and possible termination on franchisees' incentives to invest, followed by a discussion of the role of franchisee and franchisor opportunism in determining termination and non-renewal rates.

10.3 The Role of Duration, Termination, and Non-Renewal in Theory

10.3.1 Determinants of Contract Duration

Franchisors need franchisees to make significant investments of both time and money (capital) in their businesses. But, of course, such investments are only worth making if the franchisee can expect to earn some reasonable return on these investments over a sufficiently long period of time. If it takes five years, for example, to fully recoup one's investment in a franchise, then no franchisee should invest unless the relationship is expected to last for at least five years.

In general, the value of any asset on the market is given by the net present value (NPV) of the returns one can expect to earn from it during its "workable" life. In other words,

$$V = \sum_{t=1}^{T} \frac{R_t}{(1+\delta)^t}, \qquad (10.1)$$

where V stands for the value of the asset, R_t is the return from this asset at time t, δ is the interest (or discount) rate, and T is the workable life of the asset, that is, the amount of time until the asset is no longer worth anything. The uncertainty of the returns and the attitude of the potential investor toward risk are captured via the discount rate, δ: More uncertain returns are discounted more highly over time, and the more risk-averse the investor, the more he will discount the future. Thus, both risk and risk aversion are captured in the NPV formula through higher discount rates.

Applying the formula above to the valuation of a franchise contract, we have:

$$F = \sum_{t=1}^{T} \frac{\pi_t}{(1+\delta)^t} + S, \qquad (10.2)$$

where F is the present value of the contract or, put differently, the maximum amount of resources, including effort, capital and upfront fees, all of which are evaluated in present value terms, that a franchisee should invest in total in this business. In this formula, π_t is the period t economic profit from the franchise net of all payments to the franchisor but before compensating the franchisee for his investment and effort, T is the duration of the contract, and S captures the salvage value of the physical and other assets that have not been fully utilized within the contract period. In other words, S reflects the fact that the franchisee may still have valuable assets to sell at the end of the franchise contract. The implication to be drawn from equation (10.2) then is that if the franchisee invests exactly F in total in his franchise, and sells the assets for S at the end of the contract term, he earns normal returns overall. Note that our formulation assumes that S does not depend on T. In reality, the salvage value of the assets will be a function of T if the investment in such assets is made upfront and allowed to depreciate over time. In many cases, however, the contracts require regular upgrades and reinvestments that maintain the value of the physical assets over time, making S independent of T.

Everything else the same, this formula shows that franchisees can afford to invest more, that is F is larger, the longer the contract (the larger T is). It is also true, however, that the incremental value of extending the contract, $\partial F / \partial T$, declines as T grows due to discounting over longer periods. For example, if $\pi_t =$ \$20,000, changing T from 10 to 11 increases F by $\$20,000/(1+\delta)^{11} = \$7,010$

at a discount rate of 10 percent. If T were increased instead from 20 to 21, F would increase only by $\$20{,}000/(1 + \delta)^{21} = \$2{,}703$ assuming the same discount rate.

10.3.2 The Effect of Termination and Renewal

The possibility of contract renewal and within-contract termination complicates the calculations above somewhat. Now, the franchisee must assess the probability of renewal and termination and embed these in his assessment of the value of the franchise. Specifically, using ρ to represent the per-period probability of a contract termination, which we assume for simplicity to be constant from period to period, and η to account for the probability of contract renewal,[304] we have

$$F = \sum_{t=1}^{T_0} \frac{\pi_t (1 - \rho)^t}{(1 + \delta)^t} + \eta \left(\sum_{t=T_0+1}^{T_0+T_1} \frac{\pi_t (1 - \rho)^t}{(1 + \delta)^t} \right) + S, \qquad (10.3)$$

where T_0 represents the duration of the original contract and T_1 represents the duration of the renewal. Although we do not make this explicit, note that S may be affected not only by the period t, but also by whether or not the franchise is being terminated since the franchisee may not be able to sell the assets at the same price, or at all, if he faces termination. Also, for simplicity, we assume that the contract can be renewed only once. Of course, as subsequent renewals occur further in the future, the *NPV* of profits associated with such renewals becomes quite small. Finally, we have assumed no renewal fee. If assessed at the beginning of the renewal period, at time T_0, such a fee, R, would reduce F by $R/(1 + \delta)^{T_0}$. Little is known about the use or level of such fees in the U.S. but, according to Frazer (1998), they are common in Australia. In the U.S., what is most important is that franchisors often require that franchisees reinvest significant amounts in their franchise at the time of renewal. The discounted value of these new investments should be subtracted from the present value of the profit stream in the formula above, or be included in the definition of F.

Equation (10.3) shows that everything else constant, franchisees will be willing to invest more in their franchise (1) the longer the original contract (i.e., the higher is T_0); (2) the longer the renewal period, T_1; (3) the higher

---

[304] For purposes of this analysis, we are assuming that these probabilities are exogenous, independent of both franchisee and franchisor behavior. In fact, they are endogenous to some extent. From the franchisee's perspective, however, it makes sense to treat them as exogenous since the future is uncertain and most franchisees are entering what, for them, are uncharted waters.

the probability of renewal, η; and (4) the lower the per-period probability of termination, ρ. Conversely, the more franchisors want franchisees to invest, the more they will need to offer long-term contracts with high renewal probability and a low likelihood of termination.[305]

Three other aspects of the franchising relationship related to duration will intervene and affect the value of a franchise. First, the more restrictions a franchisor imposes on a franchisee's right to transfer (sell or bequeath) his franchise, the lower the price at which the franchisee is likely to sell his franchise or the lower its inheritance value, that is, the lower S is. This, in turn, will reduce the franchisee's willingness to pay upfront and to invest generally in the franchise.[306] Second, non-compete clauses can restrict the franchisee's options geographically or the types of activities he or she can engage in after leaving the franchise or both. The presence of such clauses in the contract decreases the value of the human capital that a franchisee can expect to build through operating the franchise. This again will reduce the value of the franchise to the franchisee and his willingness to invest in it relative to the case where no such restrictions are imposed. Finally, buy back clauses may increase or decrease the value of the franchise. Those clauses that require franchisees to sell their business back to the franchisor upon request, like those used recently by Ruby Tuesday, will reduce the value of the franchise. In contrast, clauses that guarantee buy backs at a given price from the franchisor if the franchisee wants to sell – a type of clause also included in Ruby Tuesday's new franchise contract – will increase the value of the franchise and thus the franchisee's willingness to pay or invest in it.[307]

Finally, in discussing the effect of renewal and termination rates above, we have treated the probability of these events as though they are independent of the franchisee's and the franchisor's behavior. But franchisors decide to terminate or not renew contracts. As any possibility of termination or non-renewal reduces the franchisee's incentives to invest in his franchise, why would franchisors ever choose to not renew or even terminate a contract in our scenario? The answer lies in the fact that outlet and franchisee performance vary across outlets, and franchisors also may change their approach to particular markets.

---

[305] Gasoline lessee dealers do not invest or own facilities but rather are "hired" to manage a station whose assets belong to the oil company. Their contracts usually last only one or a few years, renewable at will, which is consistent with the rule that franchisors requiring large franchisee investments need to use long-term contracts.

[306] This includes the possibility that the franchisor may impose a transfer fee, that is, a fee that a franchisee must pay to the franchisor when selling his franchise to another franchisee, as Frazer (1998) indicates many franchisors in Australia do.

[307] See Prewitt (1998).

Perhaps most important, franchisees may not always behave in ways that are consistent with what the chain needs, at least from the franchisor's perspective, so franchisors may choose to not renew or terminate the contracts of such individuals to protect their brand and business format. Finally, some have proposed that termination and non-renewals occur because franchisors take advantage of franchisees, that is, they behave opportunistically. In what follows, we consider the relationship between franchisee, and then franchisor, opportunism and the termination or non-renewal of franchise contracts.

10.3.3 Franchisee Opportunism

As should be clear from the discussion in many other parts of this book, franchisees who have purchased ownership and residual claimancy rights in the profits generated by their own outlets may not always behave in ways that are optimal from the franchisor's perspective. What they own is different from what the franchisor owns and cares about, and thus their objectives also differ. The franchisee is focused on maximizing the profits of his outlet(s), as he should be, while the franchisor is focused on the profits of the overall chain, also as she should be. Those two objectives, while broadly consistent, are not the same, and they do not always imply the same desired behavior at the outlet level. The issue, in essence, is one of externality that arises because of the common brand under which all outlets operate. This common brand makes it possible for customers to punish the chain for the behavior of a single franchisee. A customer dissatisfied with the value of the goods or services purchased at one outlet can cease to purchase from all outlets under the same brand. This means that pricing, quality, menu choices, cleanliness, staff demeanor, and so on at each outlet affect not only the future purchases that a customer will make at a given outlet, but also their decision to frequent other units in the same chain. Yet, the franchisee does not bear the cost of the reduced sales at all other outlets, and hence does not consider the cost of its decisions on these other outlet sales and profits. The consequence is a tendency for the franchisee to under-invest in quality, charge higher prices than those that the chain finds optimal, offer products that local customers like even if this erodes the value of the brand, and so on. All of these franchisee profit maximization strategies correspond to "misbehaviors" from the chain's perspective given its "raison d'être," which is to offer consumers a predictable, homogeneous product across a large number of geographically dispersed establishments.

To curb these behaviors, Rubin (1978) and Klein (1980, 1995) have argued that franchisors rely on self-enforcing contracts, namely contracts that give incentives to parties to put forth effort by ensuring that they derive a benefit from the relationship, a benefit that is at risk if they do not behave as requested. Specifically, they suggest that franchise contracts leave some stream of ongoing rent that franchisees must forgo if they are caught "misbehaving."[308] In other words, the rent plays the role of a hostage as per Williamson's (1985) analysis. The incentives embedded in a franchise contract in this context stem from the combined effect of three elements: (1) the ongoing stream of rent, (2) the franchisor's monitoring of the franchisee to assess whether the franchisee is "misbehaving" and, (3) the franchisor's ability to terminate the franchise contract. Thus, termination rights, and non-renewal rights, are central to the concept of self-enforcement. While other punishments are surely available and used by franchisors, ultimately it is the threat of termination that prevents franchisees from engaging in behavior that the franchisor does not approve of.[309] If franchisors cannot punish franchisees who "misbehave" by terminating their relationship with the chain, then controlling the behavior of franchisees through self-enforcement becomes much less viable.

Klein (1980) notes that franchise contracts are one-sided, meaning that the terms impose many restrictions on franchisees and often subject them to termination at will by their franchisors. He argues that this one-sidedness arises because the contracts focus on giving incentives to franchisees only. The franchisor's behavior in this setting is controlled already by her desire to maintain her reputation, a reputation that is put at risk if the franchisor behaves opportunistically vis-à-vis her franchisees. The presumed higher cost of finding franchisees once the franchisor is known to have behaved opportunistically, and ultimately of operating the chain as a corporate entity – an option that the franchisor would have chosen from the outset if it were more efficient than franchising – both prevent the franchisor from misappropriating the assets of its franchisees. The result is that franchise contracts are one-sided as they explicitly constrain the behavior of franchisees but let

---

[308] Readers familiar with efficiency-wage theory in labor economics will recognize the similarity with the theory of contractual self-enforcement. See, for example, Becker and Stigler (1974) and Shapiro and Stiglitz (1984). Akerlof and Yellen (1986) provide a collection of important contributions in this area.

[309] Bradach (1998) at p. 35 notes that termination, or even the threat of termination, is rarely used to control franchisee behavior. He interprets this as evidence that the self-enforcement mechanism does not play a central role in the management of franchise relationships. But the theory is completely consistent with termination being a rather rare event. Termination is the ultimate threat that prevents franchisees from behaving in ways that are really detrimental to the chain. If the mechanism works, franchisee behavior remains within the bounds of what franchisors want and so no termination need occur.

reputation rather than contract terms govern the behavior of the franchisor. Klein (1995) further develops, clarifies, and refines these ideas.

Brickley, Dark and Weisbach (1991b) provide empirical support for the claim that termination provisions play an important role in franchise relationships. Specifically, they exploit variation in the existence and timing of state laws requiring good cause for termination of franchise contracts to show that franchisors use franchising to a lesser degree in states where they face laws that restrict their ability to terminate franchisees. This is true especially for franchisors operating in industries with mostly transient customers as the consumption decisions of such customers do not discipline franchisees that free-ride directly. They conclude that such franchisors rely on termination as a potential disciplining tool and, when this tool becomes more onerous to use, they modify the extent to which they rely on franchising itself. Brickley, Dark, and Weisbach also find evidence that the passage of a law requiring good cause for termination in California in 1980 was associated with relatively large losses for the shareholders of publicly traded franchisors with franchise operations in California. Based on these empirical results, the authors conclude that these laws have increased the cost of controlling outlet-level quality in the franchised part of these chains.

Kaufmann and Lafontaine (1994), on the other hand, examine in detail the profit and loss statements from typical McDonald's outlets, and the resale prices of a small set of such outlets. They conclude that McDonald's leaves rent with its franchisees, rent that the franchisees lose if they are found in violation of firm policy and are terminated.[310] Moreover, McDonald's does not require franchisees to pay upfront for the full amount of *ex post* rent. In other words, it allows franchisees to earn rent from an *ex ante* perspective. The authors explain this in part based on the type of franchisees that McDonald's desires, namely individuals who will devote themselves to their role as owner-operators of their restaurant(s). The authors also note that the company further reserves the right to decide which franchisees are granted expansion rights, that is, which franchisees are offered additional McDonald's restaurants, based on a franchisee's degree of compliance with firm policies. Thus, these *ex ante* rents also serve an incentive role for current franchisees at McDonald's, encouraging those who aspire to expand their set of restaurants to continue to function within the bounds set by their franchise contract.[311]

---

[310] See also Michael and Moore (1995) for a similar analysis showing evidence of rent at other chains.

[311] See also Klein (1995) for an explanation for *ex ante* rent based on a legal environment that makes it difficult for franchisors to terminate franchise relationships if they demand large bonds upfront that they do not reimburse upon termination.

10.3.4 Franchisor Opportunism

Historically, franchisees have voiced concerns that franchisors may use contract termination and non-renewals to appropriate the units that are most profitable within the chain. In other words, franchisees complained that they do not reap the benefit of their hard work because once they make a market profitable, the franchisor behaves opportunistically and simply terminates or does not renew their contract. The franchisor then presumably appropriates the profits of the outlet either by operating the outlet directly, or by selling it to a new franchisee under a contract involving higher fees.

As noted earlier, Williams (1996) used the Census Bureau Characteristics of Business Owners database to examine the reasons why franchisors terminate contracts with franchisees, ending the relationship within the term of the contract. He found that one-third of all contract terminations resulted in the outlet being closed, evidence that these were not the most profitable outlets. More generally, he found that the types of outlets that were most subject to termination were those that were underperforming, leading him to conclude that franchisors usually rely on termination to enforce performance standards or eliminate poor locations (see also Chapter 5). The USDOC (1988) data moreover shows that franchisees as well as franchisors sometimes want to terminate their franchise relationship. The most likely interpretation of franchisee terminations is that the franchisee either wants to change affiliation (most common in the hotel and motel industry), become independent, or close the business. As noted earlier, another 4,202 franchisees requested permission to sell their outlet (and franchisors granted those in 4,108 of these 4,202 cases). Some of these franchisees most likely were not doing very well, but many of the transfers and terminations by franchisees also are due to a change in the life circumstances of a franchisee (such as retirement, moving on to other business endeavors, or sickness). Company buy-backs and allowing transfers are the main ways in which franchisors can accommodate a franchisee's desire to move on to other things.[312] Finally, while company buy backs of outlets do occur, they remain rather infrequent. According to the USDOC (1988), franchisors bought back 827 units in 1986 out of 246,664 franchised outlets in operation that year. At the same time, they converted 1,726 units back to franchisee ownership.

Franchisors also buy back franchises simply because they are changing their strategy, moving toward a higher proportion of company units, or even

---

[312] See, e.g., Shelton (1967).

getting out of franchising altogether. The USDOC (1988) data is informative in this respect as well. It reports the number of franchisor failures and departures, where the latter are defined as franchisors that have decided to "discontinue franchising as a method of doing business." Out of an estimated total population of 2,177 franchisors in 1986:

> A total of 104 franchisors operating 5423 outlets failed during 1987 [. . .] The volume of 1986 sales represented by the failed firms amounted to $1.7 billion, of which the franchisee-owned portion was $1.5 billion. [. . .] In addition, 80 franchisors decided in 1987 to discontinue franchising as a method of doing business; these companies operated 2104 units in 1986 with $932 million in sales, of which 1519 outlets with $472 million in sales were franchisee-owned. (USDOC 1988: 12)

Franchisors who decide to discontinue franchising or move toward a greater degree of company ownership have the option of either buying back franchisee-owned outlets or closing them down. Of course, buy backs will be the preferred option for the franchisees. Thus, some companies are now entering into franchising with a contract that not only allows the franchisor to purchase its franchisees, but also guarantees to franchisees that the company will buy them back if they choose to sell.[313] As noted by Williams (1996) and Brickley (2001), liberal termination and non-renewal rights, like buy-back clauses, provide franchisors with valuable call options on units in their chain. A call option gives its owner the right, but not the obligation, to purchase an asset at a fixed exercise price prior to the expiration date of the option. This option is valuable if the market value of the asset covered by the option is higher than the exercise price at some time prior to the expiration of the option – assuming it can be exercised at any time. While stock options are the best-known types of options, options are available in many other contexts. Here, liberal non-renewal rights give franchisors the option to terminate the contract of an existing franchisee at the end of the contract period. Liberal termination rights provide an equivalent option within the term of the agreement. In either case, franchisors may exercise these rights simply because it is profitable for them to do so. This is the essence of a call option. Of course, franchisees are quite correct when they point out that such behavior by franchisors can reduce their ability to reap the rewards associated with their investment of time and money into the franchised business. Whether it does so fundamentally depends on the relationship between the exercise price, that is, how much the franchisor has to pay for the business, and what

---

[313] Prewitt (1998).

the franchisee could get otherwise if he continued to operate the business or sold it on the market. In turn, whether the franchisor has the option to terminate or not renew the contract depends on the terms of the franchise contract and applicable laws. To the extent that a franchisee worries that the franchisor can appropriate the fruits of his labor through her termination and non-renewal rights, the franchisee should not be willing to pay as much for the franchise. And indeed, using data on the fees charged by a large number of franchisors across a variety of industries, Brickley (2001) finds evidence that franchisees pay more over the life of the contract for franchises sold by franchisors whose termination and non-renewal rights are constrained by applicable state law than they do for franchises where franchisors are not subject to such restrictions.

Finally, while franchisor opportunism may be an issue in specific cases, it is unlikely to be the main explanation for franchisor termination and non-renewal decisions generally. First, if franchisors were systematically buying back all profitable outlets, established chains likely would show a tendency toward more company ownership over time. Yet we do not find that in the data.[314] Second, as discussed also in Chapter 8, to analyze the possibility of franchisor opportunism, it is important to consider what franchisors stand to gain and lose if they mistreat their franchisees and repossess outlets. As noted by Klein (1980, 1995), franchisors presumably have opted for franchising rather than corporate ownership as an organizational form because it is more profitable for them. This, in turn, has consequences relative to their incentives to mistreat their franchisees.

Specifically, in the context of non-renewal and contract termination, franchisor opportunism would amount to a franchisor who terminates highly profitable franchisee-owned business with the purpose of appropriating those profits. For this to be worth doing, it must be the case that the franchisor appropriates the outlet at a price that is much below the market value. If the franchisor pays market value for the outlet, then the franchisee does not lose. If a below-market price is achieved using what was an *ex ante* agreed upon buy-back price, we are back to the option scenario. If the franchisee agreed to this buy-back price at the outset, we would expect that he did so based on his assessment of the likely value of the business at the time and that this has all been priced into the contract. If the appropriation at below-market price is done by "unreasonably" withholding the right to transfer the franchise, presumably the franchisee can sue for contract breach. Moreover, as such behavior becomes public knowledge, it will tarnish the reputation of

---

[314] See Chapter 4 of this book and Lafontaine and Shaw (2005) for more on this.

the franchisor and thus increase the cost of recruiting new franchisees into the franchise system. Thus, the chain's future growth will be impacted. Also, to the extent that the chain may not be as efficient at running the outlets, which we presumed was the reason it initially chose to rely on franchising, profits for the units it buys back will be lower under corporate operation. If it buys back and then resells the outlet, it will only do better if the new franchise contract contains higher fees, especially higher royalty rates as these represent the bulk of payments from franchisees. But as franchisors offer the same contract terms to all franchisees at a point in time, this requires that the franchisor's current contract contains higher royalty rates. While this situation sometimes arises, the reality is that franchise contract terms and royalty rates in particular do not change much over time either.[315] Thus, waiting for contract renewal – where renewals normally occur at the "then going rates," which means under the terms offered to new franchisees – will often be the better option. We conclude that in terms of non-renewals and termination, as with other aspects of the contract, the benefits of "mistreating" franchisees is typically low, and the cost of doing so can be quite high.

Having said all this, it is important to recognize also that reputation effects do not discipline all franchisors to the same extent. Established franchisors that are no longer expanding may not need to offer an attractive business proposition, though they still need to consider the effect of their behavior on remaining franchisees if they do not intend to buy back all outlets. Such consideration will tend to prevent them from mistreating franchisees. But if they are leaving markets altogether, or transforming their business into a fully corporate entity, or rationalizing their networks after a merger, their incentives to minimize the cost this imposes on franchisees can be quite weak. This is therefore the type of situation where we expect to find established franchisors imposing damages on franchisees. As for new franchisors, those who want to grow via franchising need to offer an attractive business proposition to potential franchisees. Thus, their desire to sell units in the future will curb any tendency to behave opportunistically. But there have been instances where unscrupulous individuals simply sold a few franchises and collected the associated fees, but made no effort to really develop viable franchised chains. If there is no real desire to sell future outlets, there is nothing to prevent opportunistic behavior. Our discussion above, of course, presumes that the franchisor is "real" in that it at least plans to develop a franchise system if it has not yet started to do so. This requirement that the franchise be "real," in turn, makes it clear how important it is for potential franchisees to thoroughly investigate

---

[315] See Chapter 3 of this book and Lafontaine and Shaw (1999) for more on this.

different franchise opportunities and assess the franchisors' prospects and incentives before committing to any particular business proposition.

10.4 Termination and Non-Renewal: Legal Considerations

Garner (2000; § 10.01) points out that "the most important change in the franchise relationship is its termination by the franchisor or its . . . non-renewal" at the end of its term. As a result, termination and non-renewal are apt to be challenged by very unhappy franchisees. The rights and obligations of the respective parties in the U.S. are determined by the franchise contract, common law rules, and individual state statutes. One thing is clear: if a franchisor can convince a court that she had a good reason for terminating the franchise relationship, she will be free to do so.[316]

Generally, the courts recognize that the franchisee is a "middleman" between the franchisor and the ultimate customer. The franchisor must be allowed to determine how his goods and services are to be marketed. When a franchisee deviates significantly from the prescribed method of distribution, the franchisor must be able to replace the offending franchisee through termination or non-renewal.[317] Absent this ability, the franchisor would lose control of the franchise system (see also Chapter 5 for the role of termination in quality control). Garner points out that many courts further respect the franchisor's desire to make a change even if the resulting termination is wrongful. That is, the courts do not want to force the parties to continue doing business with one another. Accordingly, when the termination is deemed wrongful, the franchisee should not expect the court to order his or her reinstatement. Instead, the remedy will be an award of monetary damages.[318] In this section, we briefly review the treatment of termination and non-renewal

---

[316] See Love (1986), Chapter 16, for an account of the role that McDonald's played in legitimizing the use of termination and non-renewals to discipline franchisees. The case of McDonald's Paris franchisee was particularly important in this regard. Love notes: "Indeed, the McDonald's franchising cases established important legal precedents. Previously, court rulings on franchising described practices that were so unfair to franchisees that collectively they gave franchising a bad reputation. McDonald's cases had the very opposite effect. The courts essentially used them to define franchising practices that were equitable, and taken together they created a body of case law that gave franchising a degree of legitimacy it had never had before." The author further states "McDonald's also succeeded in convincing courts of the fairness of its renewal policy. . . . Even more important, McDonald's defended its right to terminate franchisees for failing to meet its QSC [quality, service, cleanliness] standards" (407–408).

[317] For a clear statement, see *Amerada Hess Corporation v. Quinn* (1976).

[318] See Garner (2000, § 10.05).

under common law and state franchise relationship laws. In the next section, we discuss how damages may be calculated in cases involving wrongful termination.

10.4.1 Termination Under Common Law

In states that do not have a franchise relationship statute, common law rules govern such business relationships and dictate a franchisor's right to terminate or not renew a franchise contract. The precise limits will vary from state to state and, therefore, categorical generalizations are hazardous at best. There are, however, a few central tendencies that we briefly summarize in what follows.

First, if a franchise contract contains no provision for termination and has no definite duration, the contract is *terminable at will* by the franchisor or the franchisee. No notice need be given and no cause for the termination is required. As a result, most – if not all – franchise agreements contain some provisions related to duration, termination, and non-renewal. These contractual terms then explicitly limit the freedom of the parties. In particular, when the contract specifies the grounds for termination, courts will usually honor the agreement and not substitute their judgment for that of the parties. Disputes can still arise over whether there has been behavior giving grounds for termination, but the courts will then focus on assessing whether the behavior has occurred, not whether termination on these grounds is reasonable.

In reality, however, even contracts that are silent on duration and termination are not completely *terminable at will.* The Uniform Commercial Code (UCC §2-309(2)) modifies the common law to some degree by imposing a *reasonable* term when the contract is silent: "Where the contract provides for successive performance but is indefinite in duration it is valid for a reasonable time but unless otherwise agreed may be terminated at any time by either party." Thus, an agreement that is silent on duration cannot be terminated until a reasonable time has elapsed. This, of course, is somewhat vague since what is a *reasonable* time will vary from case to case. As described earlier, it makes economic sense, however, that a franchisee who pays a lump-sum franchise fee and further invests in facilities, inventory, equipment, training, and the like surely does not expect to be terminated after a brief time. One way to define a reasonable duration is in terms of *recoupment.*

Garner (2000; §10.13) traces the recoupment rule to an 1894 case in Missouri.[319] He explains that the recoupment rule "provides that when a

---

[319] *Glover v. Henderson* (1894).

distributor, dealer or franchisee makes a substantial investment . . . , it is entitled to continue the relationship for a period of time sufficient to recoup the investment in the absence of cause for termination." For otherwise terminable-at-will franchise agreements this rule imposes some reasonableness. After all, as we noted in the previous section, a franchisee would invest neither a substantial sum nor substantial effort to develop a business if he did not expect to be a franchisee long enough to recoup this investment. The legal rule, however, focuses on the franchisee's financial investment only. Specifically, let I denote the franchisee's financial investment in the franchise. According to the recoupment rule, the minimum term of the contract, T, is given by the following equation:

$$\sum_{t=1}^{T} \frac{C_t}{(1+\delta)^t} - I = 0 \tag{10.4}$$

where C_t is the franchisee's cash flow in period t and δ again is the discount rate. The cash flow is the profit plus depreciation on the fixed assets (if any), and amortization of intangible assets (if any). Depreciation and amortization are accounting "costs" that do not require actual expenditures and, therefore, provide cash that may be taken out of the business. Solving equation (10.4) for T provides a minimum term under the recoupment rule. Since I and C_t vary across franchise opportunities, generalizations regarding the value of T across franchise companies or even across franchised units within a chain are problematic.

While this rule imposes some minimum reasonable duration to the relationship, the calculation above will yield a value of T that is questionable from an economic perspective for a number of reasons. First, the net present value (NPV) of the opportunity cost of the franchisee's effort over time must be added to the investment figure to yield an estimate of total investment. Alternatively, the opportunity cost of the franchisee's effort can be deducted from the estimation of cash flow each period. If a Subway franchisee, for example, could earn $35,000/year putting the same effort level in an alternative occupation, then that sum should be excluded from the measure of cash flows because it is not part of the return on the investment.[320] If the franchisee pays himself some salary, which appears on his income statement, this amount will need to be adjusted up or down so that the total cost of

---

[320] Of course, one could instead add the NPV of the opportunity cost of effort over the duration of the contract to the measure of franchisee total investment. This approach is somewhat more complicated, however, when one is estimating the reasonable duration. Thus, we describe the simpler method, which consists of removing the cost of the franchisee's effort in the calculation of cash flow each period.

the franchisee's time is exactly his opportunity cost, namely $35,000. Second, in the event of termination prior to T, any sums that the franchisee may recover by selling equipment, land, or facilities (namely S in equations 10.2 and 10.3) should be deducted from the award. Otherwise, the franchisee will be overcompensated. Third, there is the question of what should be included in I. For example, suppose a franchisee must move to a new location in order to become a franchisee. Should the expenses associated with relocation be included in I? Most likely, the answer to this question will be "yes," that is unless the franchisee used the occasion of buying the franchise to relocate to a new place that he was already planning to move to. Similarly, the time spent in training to obtain the franchise should be included in the investment figure except for the portion of this training that is useful outside of the franchise relationship.

Finally, under the common law, franchise termination may require good cause even when the agreement is silent on this issue.[321] There is variation across jurisdictions and, therefore, broad generalizations are hazardous. The judicial instinct to require cause for termination is captured by a Utah court: "*[I]t seems fair and reasonable to assume both parties entered into the arrangement in good faith, intending that if the service is performed in a satisfactory manner, it will not be cancelled arbitrarily.*"[322] This reasoning has intuitive appeal. Thus, many state courts will not permit termination of the franchise contract if the franchisee has not breached the contract by failing to perform its part of the bargain. There are, however, a wide array of suitable grounds for termination. Garner (2000; §10:16) lists several:

> ... the failure of the franchisee to perform a substantial obligation of the agreement, either generally or with respect to agreed sales goals or quotas; failure to pay for products when payment was due; fraud; indictment or conviction of a crime relevant to the business; carrying a competitor's products; failure to purchase and install required equipment; failure to pay taxes; underreporting income; drunkenness; falsification of financial information; and trademark infringement or product trademark disparagement.

10.4.2 Termination and Non-Renewal Under Dealer or Franchise Relation Statutes

Many individual states in the U.S. have statutes that regulate the relationship between franchisors and their franchisees. Further, at the federal level,

---

[321] Garner (2000; §10:15) points out that courts seldom infer a requirement of cause when agreements are oral because such agreements are inherently terminable at any time.

[322] See *Miller v. Western Men, Inc.* (1968), quoted by Garner (2000; §10:16).

non-renewal of gasoline franchises without good cause is proscribed by the Petroleum Marketing Practices Act,[323] and in most states, an automobile manufacturer cannot refuse to renew a dealership contract.[324] These statutes are usually designed to protect franchisees from opportunistic franchisors. Accordingly, most of them require *good cause* for termination and non-renewal. For the most part, a good cause for termination is the franchisee's failure to comply *substantially* with the *material* terms of the franchise contract.[325] This failure alone may not be sufficient, however, as most statutes demand that an offending franchisee be given an opportunity to cure its failure. Thus, a franchisee's failure to follow the franchisor's operating manual may be grounds for termination, but the franchisee must be put on notice and given a chance to adhere to the procedures and standards set out in the operations manual. Only after the opportunity to cure has been offered can a franchisor pursue termination in cases where the failure persists.

In spite of the protectionist nature of state dealer relation statutes, there are a host of failures that have been deemed good causes for termination or non-renewals. Garner (2000; §10:20) mentions the following:

> ... failure to conform to quality standards; failure to maintain prescribed hours of operation; noncompliance with warranty procedures; failure to provide adequate premises for operation of the business; refusal to comply with a system-wide requirement that the franchisee's shop have a computer; and failure to meet a customer's request for delivery of a product, or failure to comply with payment terms.

Franchisees are agents of their franchisors in distributing products or dispensing them in a business format developed by the franchisor. Recognizing the fact that the franchisor must depend on its franchisees for its livelihood, franchisors also are entitled to demand financial stability and honesty. Accordingly, franchisees also may be terminated for a variety of financial failures including the following: late payment of fees or rent, deliberately underreporting revenues to the franchisor, and failing to maintain a minimum net worth.[326]

Failure to meet performance standards can also be adequate grounds for termination. For example, a franchise contract may include a sales quota.

---

[323] 15 U.S.C. §2802.

[324] See, e.g., Ala. Code §8-20-5; Cal. Veh. Code §3060; Conn. Gen. Stat. §42-133v; Fla. State. §320.64(1)(a); Ill. Rev. Stat. ch. 121 1/2¶ 754(d)(6); Mass. Gen. L. ch. 93B, §4(3)(e), §9; Tex. Rev. Civ. Stat. Ann. art. 4413(36) §5.02(3). For an analysis, see Smith (1982).

[325] Garner (2000; §10:19)

[326] *Id.* Garner also points out that a franchisor can lose its right to terminate a franchisee for late payment if it has ignored a pattern of late payments in the past.

Failure to meet a reasonable sales quota may be good cause for termination. This is particularly important when the franchisee has an exclusive territory because if he does not make the sales, there is no one else (including the franchisor) who can make those sales. When the franchisor maintains a system of exclusive territories, a franchisee who trans-ships product, that is, sells outside its assigned territory, may be terminated.[327]

10.5 Assessing Damages for Wrongful Termination[328]

Once a franchisee has been terminated, the breach cannot be repaired. In most cases, a court will not order reinstatement of the franchisee as it is not fruitful to force the parties to work together. Thus, the only remedy for wrongful termination is an award of damages. There is some confusion regarding the proper measure of damages: "loss of goodwill," "lost profits," "going concern value," and "reasonable market value" have all been mentioned as potential candidates. Ideally, the damage award should make the wrongfully terminated franchisee whole. In other words, it should put the franchisee in the economic position that he would have occupied had the wrongful termination not occurred. From this perspective, the proper measure of damages is the present value of the expected future economic profits lost as a result of the wrongful termination. As we shall see, much of the confusion surrounding the proper measure of damages is simply a matter of semantics. In what follows, we use a simple hypothetical illustration to untangle the issues.

10.5.1 Measuring the Present Value of Lost Profits: An Illustration

Being something of an entrepreneur at heart, Fran considered several franchise opportunities before joining the fledgling Blair Burger franchise system. The most promising location available was in Gulf Harbour, Florida. Fran signed a 20-year franchise contract, uprooted her family from their comfortable midwestern home, moved to Gulf Harbour, and invested $500,000 in her franchise there. As the proud owner of a Blair Burger franchise, Fran worked hard and prospered along with the franchise system as a whole. By the end of five years, Fran's business was generating an annual accounting profit of $140,000 and the future looked rosy. Fran estimated that the work she performed as a franchisee was worth $60,000 per year. Given the level of risk in the business, and what she knew about returns she could earn in

---

[327] *Id.* This is necessary to protect other franchisees.
[328] Much of the following analysis relies on Blair (1988).

alternative investments, she thought she should earn a 12 per cent rate of return on the $500,000 she had invested in her franchise. So, she estimated that she was earning economic profits, or above normal returns, of $20,000 per year. Then disaster struck: her franchise contract was wrongfully terminated. Knowing that she could never get her franchise back, Fran sued her franchisor for damages.

Fran's Blair Burger franchise was an income-generating asset, which would have produced a stream of profits into the future. To put Fran back in the position that she enjoyed before the wrongful termination, the damage award should be sufficient to replace the flow of income (economic profit plus a competitive return on her investment) that she lost. Generally, a wrongfully terminated franchisee is entitled to a lump-sum award equal to the present value of the lost stream of future income. If Fran receives such an amount, she can invest it and use the principal and interest to replace the stream of above normal profits that she would have earned "but for" the termination. In its simplest form, the damage award (D) can be expressed as

$$D = \sum_{t=1}^{\tau} I_t/(1 + \delta)^t \tag{10.5}$$

where I_t denotes income at time t, δ is the discount rate, and the summation is taken over the expected remaining term of the relationship, τ. Though the logic of defining the damage award in this way is quite clear, each component of the estimation may be hotly contested.[329]

10.5.1.1 Estimating Future Profits

Valuing the lost stream of income requires estimating the future profits that would have been earned but for the wrongful termination. These estimates are bound to be challenged. There is an unavoidable element of uncertainty surrounding any forecasting exercise, and the estimation of future profits is no exception. But as long as the underlying methodology for estimating the lost profits is sound – economically and statistically – some degree of imprecision will be tolerated by the courts. In other words, although judges and juries may not award damages on the basis of speculation or pure guesswork, they may award damages on the basis of fair and reasonable inference based on relevant

---

[329] In addition to lost expected income, Fran could also ask for transition damages, namely forgone wages and returns during a reasonable transition period, as these losses are also due to the wrongful termination.

data. The fundamental reasoning behind this tolerance for imprecision is that the franchisor, by her wrongful termination, created the necessity for determining damages in the first place. As the Supreme Court has observed, "[t]he most elementary conceptions of justice and public policy require that the wrongdoer shall bear the risk of uncertainty which his own wrong has created."[330] This does not mean that just anything goes, but it does mean that objections about imprecision will "fall on deaf ears" provided that the estimates are based upon reasonable inferences drawn from the best evidence available.[331]

In a case such as Fran's, where the franchisee's business is mature, there exists an established financial track record. In that event, past profits are likely to be the best evidence of what one reasonably could anticipate in the future.[332] But past accounting profits do not provide an appropriate measure – they must be adjusted downward to account for the fact that part of the accounting returns are in fact compensation for the use of Fran's time, time that she can now use in another revenue-generating activity. As we discuss further below, the discounted value of the profits must also be adjusted downward to account for the value of the assets upon termination. Moreover, even once adjusted in these ways, past profits cannot be used without accounting for the possibility that future changes may undermine their reliability. For example, one should take into account the likely presence of new competitors, anticipated growth in the market, inflationary changes in cost, and anything else that will influence profits. It may be sensible to calculate future profits under various sets of assumptions regarding these variables (i.e., to do a sensitivity analysis). In this way, one will be able to see how robust any single estimate is and the jury will know how changes in those variables influence the magnitude of the damage calculation.

Unlike Fran, if the franchisee's business is not mature, that is, the wrongful termination occurs early in the life of the business, then estimation of future profits cannot rely upon the fledgling franchisee's past performance. Naturally, this makes the estimation of lost profits much more difficult. A court

---

[330] *Bigelow v. RKO Radio Pictures* (1946).

[331] In some cases, lost profits are admittedly too speculative to be the basis for a damage award, but are accepted anyway because the alternative would be to deny recovery to a wronged party. See Areeda and Turner (1978; ¶ 344C).

[332] Precisely how one uses the past profit performance depends upon the circumstances. It is preferable to use data from several years to establish a benchmark rather than just one year, which may not be typical. If the prior years indicate a pattern of growth, this fact may be useful for forecasting future performance. If one year is aberrational for identifiable reasons, this may provide an adequate justification for excluding it – whether it is particularly favorable or unfavorable is irrelevant.

could decide that the available evidence is inadequate to sustain a damage estimate. If so, that would leave the wrongfully terminated franchisee without any compensation. This is not a satisfactory state of affairs as an estimate of zero clearly understates actual damages unless the business was expected to never earn any profits, an unlikely scenario.[333]

The franchisee in this situation may discover a fruitful source of data in the franchisor's own business records. Specifically, the franchisor's files may contain data on the economic and demographic characteristics of each of its company-owned and/or franchisee-owned locations. Combining these data for each location, one may estimate how the average location fares in the marketplace. This relationship can be used to estimate how the terminated franchisee would have fared, given the characteristics of its market, but for the termination. In other words, the plaintiff would create something akin to a composite "yardstick" for estimation purposes.[334] This would be accomplished by using multiple regression analysis that employs actual data to estimate a relationship among several variables.[335] In particular, if the franchisor has reasonably complete data on each of its locations, the franchisee can explain variation in profit across locations by building a multiple regression model and fitting it with the data characterizing the actual franchise locations.

For example, one may specify outlet profit as a function of several explanatory variables: age of the outlet, number of competitors within the same geographic market (e.g., a three-mile radius around the outlet), population within the same geographic market, median household income, median age of the population, the size of the outlet (if there is any variation in size), and whether the outlet is company-owned or franchised. This information would be collected for each of the franchisor's outlets and used in a multiple regression analysis to determine the influence of each explanatory variable on the dependent variable (profit). The regression technique, in fact, provides estimates of the influence that each explanatory variable has on profits. In that sense, one obtains an estimated relationship that permits reasonable inferences regarding an average performance on the part of the terminated franchisee.[336]

---

[333] The franchisee still may sue for reasonable reliance expenditures, but these may be a far cry from the lost profits that it cannot prove with sufficient credibility.

[334] On "yardstick" methods in antitrust damage calculations, see Blair and Kaserman, (1985: 78–82).

[335] Excellent introductions to multiple regression techniques are provided by a number of introductory econometrics texts, including Kmenta (2d ed. 1986) and Kennedy (2003).

[336] Of course, the franchisor will want to present testimony to show that the terminated franchisee would not have done as well as an "average" franchisee. The plaintiff will

The regression results also can be used to test the reasonableness of other estimates of lost profit. For example, if one were to use the past performance of the terminated franchisee to project future profits, these projections can be compared to those flowing from the regression model. If the two projections are not terribly dissimilar, then some useful information is provided. On the other hand, if the results are quite different, some reconciliation will be necessary. In either event, what magnitude of differences should raise concerns is a matter of judgment and, perhaps, some dispute as well.

Another measure of lost profits that courts have accepted at various times is one that relies explicitly on the so-called *yardstick* methodology. To implement this approach, the wrongfully terminated franchisee must find a similarly situated franchisee who has not been terminated. The profit of this franchisee serves as a yardstick to measure the wrongfully terminated franchisee's loss. Although the use of yardsticks to gauge the profit potential of a wrongfully terminated franchisee is completely logical in principle, it is fraught with problems in practice. It is one thing to say that a suitable yardstick should be a "similarly situated franchisee," but it is quite another thing to actually find one. What one is searching for is a second franchised outlet that is as similar to the terminated franchise outlet as possible. Ideally, the yardstick ought to be an identical twin or a clone. Their ages should be the same as should the markets in which they compete. The latter includes the identities of competitors in each location, the economic and demographic characteristics of consumers within the relevant geographic market (e.g., per capita income, unemployment rate, educational attainment, female labor force participation, racial composition, and the like), the skills and abilities of the two franchisees, and any other factor that influences a franchisee's success, such as consumer tastes. To the extent that any of these factors vary between the terminated franchisee and the proposed yardstick, some questions arise as to the reliability of the yardstick's performance as a basis for measuring damages. Resolution of this uncertainty requires the sort of regression analysis described above.

10.5.1.2 Discount (or Interest) Rate

In order to calculate correctly the present value of Fran's lost profits, one must select the correct discount rate from a wide array of alternatives. Interest rates on loans, for example, vary according to the riskiness of the loan among other things. At one end of the spectrum are short-term government obligations

---

offer evidence to the contrary. Thus, multiple regression estimates are not immune from criticism and are also likely to be disputed.

that carry very low interest rates because the loan commitment is of short duration and because there is no meaningful default risk. At the other end of the spectrum are extremely risky ventures with significant prospects for default such as those that venture capitalists fund. There is, of course, a host of options in between these extremes. Specific rates reflect the time value of money and inflation risk as well as all of the risks inherent in business generally.

We should not lose sight of the purpose behind the discounting. A lump-sum damage award is made to Fran so that she (in principle) can invest the award and thereby generate a flow of payments to replace the estimated stream of profits. Accordingly, a long-term flow of profits should not be discounted at a short-term interest rate. On the contrary, one should attempt to match the terms in order that the interest rate selected will incorporate the appropriate expectations regarding inflation risk as well as the time value of money. Depending upon how the profit stream was estimated, no further adjustment for risk may be necessary.

There are also tax consequences that come into play. Awards of lost profits are taxed fully in the year they are received. Thus, the pre-tax flow of future profits should be discounted to provide a lump-sum payment that Fran can then invest in order to replace the lost profits. If post-tax profits were used in this calculation, the after-tax lump-sum amount would be too small to compensate Fran fully.[337]

10.5.1.3 Duration

As a general proposition, economists view businesses as having indefinite lives. In the case of a franchised business, however, this may not be appropriate due to specific contractual provisions. For example, Fran's franchise agreement had a 20-year life. When the contract has a specified term, the expiration date of the contract may be used to define τ in the valuation formula. In particular, τ would equal the difference between 20 and the age of the contract upon termination, that is, the number of years left in the contract. In Fran's case, τ equals 15.

A wrongfully terminated franchisee may, however, look at the franchisor's previous behavior and applicable law relating to renewal as well. For franchise contracts that specify a fixed term, it is of some interest to know whether

---

[337] Of course, if the tax rate on the award is different from what the tax rate on Fran's profits would have been, or the tax rates do not apply to the full amounts in one case or another, then other corrections will be needed.

the franchisor usually renews the contracts. If so, Fran may argue that the franchisor's usual practice should apply. Similarly, if the contract contains indefinite termination provisions, the franchisor may be bound by his past practices in this regard. In states with statutes that provide that a franchisor may not refuse to renew the franchise agreement without cause,[338] or in industries to which such legislation applies,[339] the duration of the lost future profits may extend well beyond the original term specified in the contract.

One aspect of duration that tends to be ignored in these estimations is the possibility of business mortality.[340] Although there is some positive probability that the business would have failed in the future, many analysts disregard this. In adopting this attitude, they implicitly assume that the probability of failure is zero. If the discount period is short enough, this may be an appropriate assumption. In contrast, however, if the discount period is very long, this assumption may be wholly inappropriate. As we have seen in Chapter 2, franchising is not immune to business failure and this fact should be considered. Once again, the franchisor's own data may offer some useful evidence, at least on outlet mortality rates. To the extent that some of its franchised outlets have failed in the past, these records can be used to estimate the probability of failure under various sets of circumstances. Of course, incorporating the possibility that the wrongfully terminated franchisee might have failed at some point within the remaining contract period will reduce the estimate of damages sustained due to the wrongful termination.

10.5.2 Alternative Business Valuation Methods

A variety of business valuation methods are available and used in a number of contexts. For the purposes of valuing the loss due to franchise termination, some of these alternatives are reasonable approximations of the present value of lost economic profits and may be relied upon, albeit with some caution. To the extent that any method deviates from the present value of the lost economic profits, that method is suspect from an economic perspective.

---

[338] Cal. Bus. & Prof. Code §20025; Conn. Gen. Stat. §42-133f; Del. Code Ann. tit. 6, §2552; Haw. Rev. Stat. §482E-6(2)(H); Mich. Comp. Laws §445.1527 (D); Minn. Stat. §80C.14, subd. 4; Neb. Rev. Stat. §87-404; N.J. Rev. Stat. §56:10-5; Wis. Stat. §135.03.

[339] As noted above, the non-renewal of gasoline franchises without good cause is proscribed by the federal Petroleum Marketing Practices Act while automobile manufacturers cannot refuse to renew a car dealership contract under most state laws.

[340] This issue is explored with some care by Garrod and Miklius (1987).

10.5.2.1 Capitalized Earnings

The concept of *capitalized earnings* is closest to the correct measure of damages. There are three basic approaches to capitalizing earnings. First is the so-called discounted cash flow approach, which is equivalent to what was explained as the present value of lost profits. While there may be some relatively minor differences, the spirit of the approach is the same.

A variant of this is the *income capitalization* method. In this case, the franchisee's net income for one year is calculated from the financial statements. Adjustments are made for non-cash items such as depreciation and amortization, which are influenced by tax rules rather than economic value. Adjustments for the value of the franchisee's time may also be necessary. Once the net income is determined, it is capitalized by dividing by the expected rate of return. For example, if a 20 percent return is expected and the net income for the year in question was $20,000, then the value would be $20,000 \div 0.20 =$ $100,000. In this case, the expected rate of return acts like the discount rate. For this approach to be reliable, the expected rate of return must be a good approximation of the appropriate discount rate. An implicit assumption of this approach is that the franchised outlet has an infinite life.[341] This implicit assumption may or may not be correct depending upon the circumstances.

The third capitalization method relies on excess earnings as a measure of *goodwill*. In essence, this approach reduces the franchisee's cash flow to account for opportunity costs, such as the required return on similar investments, as well as economic depreciation of capital assets and amortization of intangible assets. The net result is excess earnings, that is, earnings above those necessary to keep resources invested in this enterprise. This is precisely what economists call profits. The capitalized value of the excess earnings represents goodwill. Properly computed, this approach could provide a reasonably good approximation to the franchised outlet's value. Its major shortcoming is that the franchisee's effort, which is clearly a cost, may not be accounted for properly. Specifically, this method will yield a good estimate of the outlet's value only if the franchisee includes for himself a salary commensurate with the cost of his time in the calculation of his cash flows.

10.5.2.2 Market Determined Values

There are two valuation methods that rely upon market data. First, the value of a business can be established through stock market transactions, which

---

[341] This follows from the mathematical fact that the geometric series, $S = \frac{1}{1+i} + \frac{1}{(1+i)^2} + \ldots + \frac{1}{(1+i)^t} + \ldots$, converges to $1/i$ in the limit as t approaches infinity.

is referred to as the *market cap*. For a publicly traded company, this is a fairly simple procedure. For each class of stock, one simply multiplies the stock market value by the number of shares outstanding. Generally, this will not work for a franchise because franchised outlets typically are closely held corporations whose stocks are not publicly traded.[342]

A potentially fruitful approach resides in comparable sales. Similarly to what is done in evaluating housing market values, an analyst would obtain information on the sales of comparable franchised outlets and use those values to estimate the value of the terminated franchise. The problem, of course, lies in identifying truly comparable sales. In most instances, the franchisor's records can be used to identify sales of franchisees. Using economic and demographic data on the franchised outlets, one can identify the sales of fairly comparable properties. The purchase prices of comparable outlets may be quite reliable proxies for the market value of the terminated franchise.[343] Of course, if the terminated franchisee really were able to sell his franchise at a full comparable price, regardless of the wrongful termination, then the calculated damages under this method would be zero. But this simply highlights the reality that a franchisee who can sell his franchise in the market does not incur losses but instead captures the expected returns from this asset in the sales process. The only remaining claims a franchisee could make for the wrongful termination under such a scenario, where the franchisee is able to sell his franchise at market value despite the termination, would be related to the cost of transitioning to a new job or business. We discuss the issue of damage mitigation in more detail in the next section.

10.5.3 The Mitigation of Lost Profits

As we have seen, wrongful termination of a franchise relationship usually results in injury to the terminated franchisee in the form of lost profits. The extent of this injury can be estimated according to the principles outlined above. Before awarding damages, however, the injury must be defined to reflect actual or potential mitigation. The purpose of a damage award is to return the wrongfully terminated franchisee to the financial position it would have enjoyed had the wrongful termination not occurred. Generally,

---

[342] There is also a conceptual problem with this method. Stock prices reflect the cost of acquiring a minority interest in a company. They do not reflect the cost of acquiring a controlling interest in a company. Usually, this cost is much higher as can be seen in the difference between a tender offer and a stock's previous trading price.

[343] See Kaufmann and Lafontaine (1994) for examples of analyses involving capitalized profits and comparable sales at McDonald's.

the franchisee has a duty to mitigate damages, that is, to reduce the adverse consequences of a wrongful termination. Thus, the law may expect Fran to seek other employment rather than remain idle after her termination. In doing so, the law is requiring again that the award only cover lost economic profit; the effort of the franchisee after termination can be directed toward a different productive activity that will generate some level of compensation. To the extent that Fran's damages are (or can be) mitigated, for example, by taking on a new job, her award must take this into account or she will be overcompensated for the net injury suffered.

As another example of the need to recognize mitigating factors, consider the fact that Fran may be entitled to remain at her Gulf Harbour location, and only be required to surrender her identification as a Blair Burger franchisee. This is possible in many cases where the outlet does not have a distinctive appearance – the former franchisee may only have to change its sign and any other trade dress that identifies it as a Blair Burger franchisee. If the franchise contract does not contain a non-compete clause, Fran may continue in the same business, but as an independent rather than as a Blair Burger franchisee. To the extent that an independent earns less profit than a member of the franchise system, Fran will suffer some injury. The extent of that injury is the difference between the profit streams suitably discounted. In other words, the injury is equal to the impairment in the profits that Fran earns. If the damage award fails to account for the fact that Fran can continue in business as an independent, she will be overcompensated for any losses incurred as a result of the wrongful termination.

As another example, Fran may be permitted to sell her franchised location to someone else. As noted previously, in that case Fran should be able to recover most of the present value of the lost profits through the sale of her business. To the extent that the sales price incompletely capitalizes the future profits because of the distress nature of the sale, there may be some difference between the going concern value of the business as a franchise and the market value. This would be an appropriate measure of Fran's injury.

As a last example, consider the case where the franchisor buys out the terminated franchisee. In this instance, when the location will be managed by the franchisor or sold to another franchisee, Fran will suffer a loss only to the extent that the purchase price again does not reflect the present value of the future profits. If the price does reflect this value, then there has been no injury suffered and no damages should be awarded to Fran even though the termination was wrongful. No damage award is necessary because the franchisor has paid the full value of the asset that has been taken away from Fran.

10.6 Conclusion

In this chapter, we have shown that franchise contracts are typically quite long-term, and that franchise relationships usually extend beyond the term of the original contract. We also described available information on termination, transfer, and non-renewal rates. We then outlined the importance of contract duration and renewal in determining franchisees' willingness to invest both capital and effort in their franchised unit. We also discussed the role that contract termination plays in the private enforcement mechanism that franchisors use to entice profit maximizing franchisees to work within the confines of the business format. Moreover, we summarized how the law treats termination and non-renewal of franchise contracts in the U.S. Franchise relationship laws enacted in a number of states are meant to protect franchisees from franchisor opportunism. We have argued that while such opportunism can arise in some cases, most cases of termination seem to reflect the franchisors' need to enforce quality standards or a desire to exercise an option that was part of the initial contractual agreement. We also noted that the available empirical evidence does not support the notion that termination is usually a manifestation of franchisor opportunism: Franchisor opportunism would suggest that franchisors would terminate those units that are performing well, but the evidence suggests instead that they terminate outlets whose performance is below average. Finally, we reviewed the economics behind damages calculations in wrongful termination cases and pointed out that most of the principles described in this process would apply to damage calculations in many other settings.

11

Concluding Remarks

11.1 Introduction

Franchising entails a symbiotic relationship between what are, in reality, legally independently owned businesses. Franchisees can only succeed when the system as a whole succeeds. At the same time, the franchisor's profits derive from the success of its franchisees. Their mutual interdependence is, therefore, readily apparent. But while the interests of franchisors and franchisees often coincide, it remains true that they are not entirely compatible. This, of course, gives rise to conflict.

Broadly conceived, there are two major sources of conflict between franchisors and franchisees. First, some franchisees are simply ill-suited to being part of a chain where uniformity is essential. These people are just too independent. They want to modify the menu, select a different location, have different hours of operation, and so on. Because franchise systems thrive on uniformity of quality, appearance, hours of operation, and the like, there is a tension between the franchisor and some of its franchisees who chafe under the franchisor's insistence on compliance with the business model. There is no obvious way to resolve this problem except to note that those individuals who seek significant independence should not invest in a franchise, and franchisors also need to develop franchise sales and franchisee selection procedures that will prevent the sale of franchises to such individuals. Not surprisingly, the franchising trade and management consulting literatures discuss this problem at length.

The second major source of conflict is the one that we focus on in this book. It arises from the fact that the interests of franchisors and franchisees are not perfectly aligned. Franchisors and franchisees alike are interested in maximizing their own profits. Most franchise contracts, however, involve royalties on the basis of sales revenue. The literature often attributes conflict to the fact that the franchisor is interested in sales revenue maximization by the franchisee while the franchisee is interested in its profits, not in sales revenue *per se*. While this can contribute to the misalignment of incentives, we have noted on several occasions that even if the contract specified royalties on franchisee profits rather than sales, most of the conflict between franchisors and franchisees would remain. In other words, even with profit-based royalties, franchisor and franchisee incentives would still not be aligned.[344] As we saw, for example, in Chapters 5, 7 and 8, franchisors care about the sum of outlet outcomes (revenues or profits) while franchisees care about the profit in their own unit(s). Externalities, or spillover effects, necessarily arise among outlets that operate under a common brand. Such externalities imply that the whole is not simply the sum of its parts. In other words, because profits at a given location are influenced by the pricing and quality decisions made in other units in the chain, the prices and quality levels that maximize profits in each outlet do not maximize overall profits in the chain. This inevitably results in tension between the franchisor and its franchisees.

It is important to recognize that part of the problem with franchising, however, also arises from misconception as to what franchising is. Traditionally, franchisors have advertised franchises as opportunities for individuals to "be your own boss." In reality, owning a franchise is not at all the same as independent small business ownership. Franchisees buy the right to use a trademark in a particular location for a particular time period. The notion that this right should be perpetual, fully transferable to one's heirs, and so on, arises because of the tendency to view the franchise as a completely independent business rather than as a contractual agreement. One does not expect, upon signing a lease, for example, that the lease will necessarily be renewed under the same terms in perpetuity. The same should be true for a franchise. If franchisees come into franchising knowing that they are not buying a business but rather are entering into a contractual agreement of fixed duration, they will not feel betrayed when their franchisor makes further demands at the time of renewal or even does not renew their contract. Of course, franchisees would not behave like business owners either, but rather focus on what is best for them to do knowing that their relationship with their franchisor is not a permanent one. And franchisors would need to take this

---

[344] Writing contracts that base royalties on franchisee profit rather than revenues must not work well as there are few of them. See Chapter 3 for a detailed look at contract terms, and Chapter 4 for some discussion.

into account in designing their contracts and choosing clauses on territorial protection, duration, transfers, and so on.

Our goal in this book then was to do two main things. First, we wanted to describe franchising: what it is and how it works exactly. We did this throughout the book by relying on an extensive data set on the characteristics and contracting practices of U.S. based franchisors over time. We also relied on other sources whenever possible, and reviewed the main theoretical frameworks from economics that help us shed light on this form of business relationship and organization. Second, we wanted to describe and develop a better understanding of the main sources of conflict between franchisors and franchisees. Chapters 5 through 10 were dedicated to this endeavor. In each of these, we discuss what is the fundamental source of the conflict, present information concerning the contractual and management practices that give rise to or try to address this source of conflict, and finally summarize how the legal disputes in each area have been treated by the U.S. court system. Our hope is that those involved in franchising or related activities will find that our description puts into perspective certain aspects of this relationship, while scholars with an interest in franchising, whether they be economists like us or not, will find here enough details about this organizational form to foster further research on franchising and organization of the firm more generally. With this in mind, in what follows we summarize some of the main conclusions from our analyses.

11.2 A Summary

The first four chapters of this book were devoted to a description of franchising using our data and other sources, and to a discussion of the economic theories that help us understand the nature of the franchise relationship. We started in Chapter 1 by defining franchising, tracing some of the milestones in the history of franchising in the United States and elsewhere, and showing its current importance in the U.S. economy. We noted that in order to reach geographically dispersed consumers, firms in the retail and service industries have established networks of local outlets. They do this because large chains benefit from greater access to economies of scale in marketing and often can obtain supplies at lower prices. A firm that has developed efficient retail or inventory processes is better able to capitalize on these if it spreads the costs of these activities across numerous markets and the globe. Once it is clear that a firm will benefit from establishing a large number of geographically dispersed outlets, the next question that arises is how best to organize the firm's relationship with these outlets. Franchising is one mode of organization that a large subset of these firms has adopted. In those cases, the franchisor maintains ownership over the trade name and marks and, in the case of business-format franchising, develops a complete "recipe" to run each outlet. It then licenses the right to operate under the central trade name and business format in a given market for a certain period of time to individuals or small firms in exchange for various fees. The ownership stake of the franchisee in current and future profits leads him to put significant effort into the outlet. At the same time, the ongoing fees he pays to the franchisor ensure that the latter has incentives to maintain the value of the brand by, among other things, screening and monitoring franchisees and keeping abreast of market trends.

In Chapter 2, we reviewed a series of myths about franchising. Contrary to popular belief, we showed that franchising is not a low-risk form of business enterprise, for franchisors or franchisees. We also discussed exaggerated claims of growth in franchising, and showed that while franchising is an important part of the U.S. economy, it has not grown at the exponential rates often advertised. Finally, we discussed the size distribution of franchisors, showing that while most franchisees are associated with large networks, most franchisors are in fact relatively small businesses themselves. We also showed that contrary to received wisdom, franchisees are not always small "mom and pop" businesses.

In Chapter 3, we described in some detail the fees charged by franchisors, namely franchise fees, royalty rates, and advertising fees, showing that there is significant variation in these fees across firms and industry sectors. In Chapter 4, we reviewed the extent of dual distribution in franchised chains, that is, the tendency for these firms to operate some units directly and franchise others. We showed that there is also much variation in the extent of company ownership across franchising firms, and sought to explain this partly by discussing the equivalence of various forms of vertical restraints, and partly by introducing the type of incentive issues that the economics literature has relied upon to explain both the level of fees and the extent of dual distribution in franchised chains.

Next, we examined a number of situations where incentive incompatibility "rears its ugly head" in the franchise relationship. In Chapter 5, we focused on product quality issues. Quality must be as uniform as possible across all franchisees within a chain: McDonald's wants its Big Mac in Atlanta to taste just like one sold in San Francisco. A mobile customer base expects and demands such uniformity. But each individual franchisee can earn additional profit by reducing its quality and thereby reducing its costs. A franchisor cannot condone such behavior because it damages the entire system. We saw that quality control mechanisms in franchising appear to work since the empirical evidence indicates little quality variation between company-owned and franchised locations.

For a variety of reasons, including quality control, franchisors occasionally require that their franchisees buy a variety of inputs from the franchisor or its designated supplier. If franchisees perceive that they are paying a premium for those tied inputs, they will naturally complain since their profits will be lower. We discussed in Chapter 6 how the resultant conflict may lead to antitrust challenges under U.S. law. We also noted, however, that these have been unsuccessful generally because franchisors have been deemed to have insufficient market power to endanger competition.

As we saw in Chapter 7, in some instances a franchisor may want to limit the franchisee's pricing discretion. In particular, a franchisor may wish to impose *maximum* resale prices to prevent a successive monopoly problem from materializing or to internalize the effect of each outlet's price on the decisions that consumers make to frequent other outlets in the chain. The economic rationale is straightforward: by holding down the retail price, the franchisees' sales will be larger, which benefits the franchisor. Prior to the U.S. Supreme Court's decision in *Khan*, which overruled *Albrecht*, such vertical price controls were illegal *per se* under Section 1 of the Sherman Act. Now, however, maximum price controls will be evaluated under the rule of reason and almost surely will be deemed permissible. These resale price controls will be a source of conflict as the franchisor earns more profit while the franchisee earns less. In this case, our sympathies lie with the franchisor because those price controls confer a decided benefit on consumers in the form of lower prices. Interestingly, even though particular franchisees may resent the price controls, franchising as a business organization is promoted by this new outlook on maximum price controls because it reduces the likelihood that franchisors will turn to the alternative of complete vertical ownership integration.

In Chapter 8, we discussed how, as franchise chains mature and/or population patterns shift, incumbent franchisees may face what they perceive as encroachment. The incumbent franchisee considers a certain territory as his and does not expect to face any competition from intrabrand rivals, that is, from other franchisees or company units from the same chain in this perceived territory. Thus, the incumbent franchisee characterizes the establishment of a new franchised or company-owned unit as encroaching on his market. To a large extent, this is understandable. If the newcomer is close enough to cause a noticeable loss of sales for the incumbent, profits will fall and the incumbent franchisee will be unhappy. In many cases, the encroached upon franchisee believes or argues that this is the product of franchisor opportunism. In fact, franchisees have sought legislation that limits the franchisor's ability to open new outlets "too close" to existing outlets. Through a simple example, we have shown, however, that the consequences of protectionist legislation are predictable: the incumbent franchisees benefit at the expense of everyone else. The franchisor earns less profit, would-be franchisees are denied entry, and consumers pay more. In our view, conflict, and the need for protectionist legislation, can be reduced by providing complete information to franchisees before they sign their contracts. This should alter their expectations and make clear to them that each may face more intra-brand competition in the future. When the competition arrives, incumbents will not be happy about the resulting reduction in profitability, but they will not feel betrayed by their franchisor.

The terms of most franchise contracts require the franchisee to help pay for advertising. There is no doubt that franchisees recognize the value of advertising as well as other forms of promotion. There is also no doubt that they recognize their obligation under the franchise agreement to help pay for it. The conflict that we focus on in Chapter 9 arises when franchisees object to the effectiveness of the advertising – the message, the frequency, the placement, and so on. When the franchisee believes that he or she is not getting enough bang for the buck, complaints surface. If the franchisor continues to place ads as it sees fit, conflict develops and, in some instances, erupts into legal challenges. For the most part, the judicial results are predictable. If the franchise agreement provides the franchisor with full discretion regarding the expenditure of the advertising funds, the complaints of the franchisees will fall on deaf ears. It is only when the contract imposes an obligation on the franchisor to involve the franchisees in some way that the disgruntled franchisees will be heard. Again, it is clear that this sort of conflict can be minimized through ongoing communication. This is not to say that the franchisor should abdicate its prerogatives, but keeping franchisees informed about promotional strategies will be useful. In most cases, the franchisor will know better what is in the system's best interest, but individual franchisees are understandably concerned primarily with their own markets. Disagreements are unavoidable, but the consequences may be reduced through better explanations of current and future plans.

Finally, in Chapter 10, we described issues surrounding contract duration, termination, and non-renewals. Many franchisees view their franchise as their property. The longer the contract, the more permanent the relationship would appear to be. As a result, termination during the term of the contract or nonrenewal at the end of a contract will be a wrenching experience for the franchisee. In many cases, this is the ultimate conflict. But termination and contract duration provisions play a useful role in the franchisor–franchisee relationship. A franchisor's ability to terminate or not renew a franchisee provides an important threat that may be used to compel a franchisee's adherence to the terms of the franchise agreement or, more importantly, to the spirit of the franchise agreement. For example, when opportunities arise that might lead a franchisee to reduce quality at his location(s), the threat of termination may serve as a powerful deterrent. As in other areas of the relationship, franchisees suspect that termination or non-renewal results from franchisor opportunism. The data, however, do not support this suspicion in general. Termination usually involves poorly performing units rather than the superior locations that a franchisor might want to reclaim.

11.3 International Franchising

In our description of franchising practices, we have discussed what we know about franchising outside the U.S. whenever possible. We have not examined international franchising separately in this book, however, for two main reasons. First, the legal environment can vary significantly across countries. As a result, it is difficult, if not impossible, to draw general conclusions regarding how contract law, distribution law, and antitrust (or competition) policy interact and affect franchising around the globe. Of course, dealing with the legal treatment of franchising in a large number of countries in any level of detail is not only beyond our capabilities, it would also turn this book into a gargantuan series of treatises.[345] Second, and most important in our view, the economic forces at work in franchise relationships do not respect geo-political boundaries. In other words, the need for cooperation and the conflicts that we have examined between franchisors and franchisees arise, say, in Europe, China, Australia, and Japan, just as they do in the United States. The available information on franchising contracting outside the U.S. generally confirms our view that economic outcomes and issues in the international arena are similar to those found in the U.S. Still, much more work needs to be done if we are to truly understand how and why franchising works in various jurisdictions. Our hope is that the economic analyses herein will provide fertile ground and hence foster some of that work.

---

[345] However, see Mendelsohn (2003).

11.4 The Future

Despite the sources of conflict that we have identified throughout this book, franchising has withstood the test of time. From its modest beginnings in the late 1800s, in industries such as soft-drink bottling, car dealerships, and beauty salons, through the franchising boom of the 1950s in the U.S. – most of which occurred in the fast-food and in the hotel and motel industries – franchising has proven to be an efficient method of doing business in a large number of industries. Similarly, research on this organizational form has provided new insights not only about what works for franchising, but also about other forms of inter- and intra-firm contracting and organization of the firm issues generally. We believe that there is much more research to do in the fertile field of franchising to refine the answers to some of the questions raised in this book, but also to address new questions and phenomena arising in the field.

For one thing, franchising is not just one form of organization – a vast array of forms coexist within the franchising arena, from the simplest licensed distributorship to complete turn-key operations, from systems providing little support to those with completely detailed and regularly updated guidelines. McDonald's can be viewed as an example of a franchisor providing a complete turn-key package, as the original Harper system also did. Other franchisors are much less strict in terms of details and control: Dairy Queen, for example, for a long time had a very different reputation from McDonald's. According to Brown (1981), Dairy Queen's management "permitted an excess of free enterprise. The 19 (sic) year patent rights to D.Q., the trademark on the formula and territorial franchises were sold to operators who were left to develop their own regional stores. There was no strong centralized management to ensure standardized menus or similar buildings." In the last few years, the founders of the Great Harvest Bread Company have embraced the concept of what they call a "freedom franchise," a franchise that by design gives franchisees much freedom in running their business.[346] The company even allows its franchisees to choose the products they want to sell, thereby going against the notion that product offerings need to be standardized for franchising success. The philosophy of franchisors with respect to their focus on direct operations versus franchising, territorial exclusivity, input controls, and so on also varies tremendously across systems. This is not surprising really. After all, franchising is used in a variety of business sectors, and some practices are more suited to particular types of businesses than to others. Moreover, to this

---

[346] See McMakin (2001).

day the majority of franchisors are private companies where the personality of the founder or of the founding team, and their "tastes," can affect how the business is organized and its inner workings.

Experimentation also is part and parcel of the evolution of any mode of organization, and franchising is no exception. As a business organization, franchising is evolving over time. Presumably, what works well is retained and refined and what does not work well is discarded. As franchising changes in form, substance, scope, and character, new issues develop that demand analysis.

For example, franchisors in recent times have developed contracting practices allowing them to combine brands under a single roof.[347] Co-branding, as this is called, allows for more efficient usage of real estate resources and better spreading of other overhead costs; in other words, it makes further economies of scope possible. Though early experiments with co-branding have been fairly positive, just how the brands – especially if not owned by the same franchisor – should share the costs and benefits thereby generated is as yet to be determined. In other words, while a handful of franchisors are moving ahead with these types of agreements, there are no clear templates yet as to how these relationships should or will be organized.

Another important trend in franchising is reflected in the increased reliance on highly capitalized and experienced franchisees under area development agreements. In some sense, this represents a return toward what was fairly standard practice in the early days of franchising. According to Love (1986), many fast-food franchisors sold large territories to developers at the time Ray Kroc decided to orient his effort toward owner operators only. The success of the McDonald's system then led others to focus on small owner operators. But now the new area developers usually take on the task of opening numerous outlets in large territories on a very tight schedule. When successful, this strategy allows a franchisor to expand geographically very rapidly.[348] This increased tendency to rely on large area developers has two important implications. First, franchising may no longer be so available to operators wanting to start and develop a small business. Second, this new breed of franchisees often will rival their franchisors in experience and even in financial strength. Vogel (1996) gives an example:

> The background of Church's Chicken area developer Ben Feinswog, as is typical of area developers, isn't the grease pit. Feinswog, whose Miami-based Restaurant

---

[347] See Young et al. (1997) and Justis and Judd (1998), Ch. 7.
[348] But see Kalnius (2004a) on the low success rate of international master franchise arrangements.

Development Corp. employs 350 at its 16 Church's in Broward and Dade coun-
ties, worked for Johnson & Johnson and Citicorp in fields such as information
management and systems planning. Before getting into franchising, he was in
banking. He started with the Hardee's system and now is in Church's thanks in
part to financing that Church's provided.

The presence of such developers in any franchise system will inevitably alter
the nature of the franchisor–franchisee relationship as well as the relationship
among franchisees.[349]

Finally, the legal landscape not only varies across jurisdictions but it also
constantly evolves over time. In the U.S., new state and federal legislation can
alter the rights and responsibilities of franchisors and franchisees. Similarly,
judicial decisions can cause significant changes in the relationship. Thus, as
described in Chapter 6, the strategy initially adopted by Chicken Delight, to
earn income not by charging a royalty but instead by requiring franchisees
to purchase inputs exclusively from the franchisor, was found in violation of
U.S. antitrust laws. As a result of this decision, business-format franchisors
generally moved away from input purchase requirements toward approved
supplier clauses and toward adopting approaches where the franchisor is available as a potential, but not required, source of supplies. This same decision
also implied that business-format franchisors would move toward franchise
fees and royalties on sales as their main sources of income. Similarly, as noted
in Chapter 8, disputes over territorial rights in the quick-service restaurant
sector and in hotel chains have led many of the firms in these industries to include much more detailed territorial definitions in their contracts. They have
also led franchisors to develop more systematic review processes for new sites
and to develop policies for allocating new units to owners of nearby outlets,
thereby resolving at least part of the conflict. In industries where encroachment through alternative channels has been more problematic, a number of
franchisors have worked on ways to channel part of the sales or profits to
the local franchisee. Others have opted to stay out of the alternative channels. In all cases, the franchise contract and hence the franchisor–franchisee
relationship has been modified accordingly.

11.5 Conclusion

As mentioned above, our goal in this book has been to provide a thorough
description of franchising as an organizational form and economic phenomenon. We have used a unique data set and other sources to quantify,

---

[349] See also Maddocks (2001) on this issue.

as much as possible, various aspects of the franchise relationship, and we have analyzed in detail sources of friction in this relationship. Our hope is that this work will prove useful to many different types of readers, including those involved in franchising or related activities, as well as those who teach or study related subjects, and researchers interested generally in how firms organize various activities.

Articles, Books, and Other Publications

Achabal, Dale D., Wilpen L. Gorr, and Vijay Mahajan. 1982. MULTILOC: A Multiple Store Location Decision Model. *Journal of Retailing* 58 (Summer):5–25.

Ackerberg, Daniel A. and Maristella Botticini. 2002. Endogenous Matching and the Empirical Determinants of Contractual Form. *Journal of Political Economy* 110:564–591.

Agrawal, Deepak and Rajiv Lal. 1995. Contractual Arrangements in Franchising: An Empirical Investigation. *Journal of Marketing Research* 32:213–221.

Akerlof, George A. 1970. The Market For 'Lemons': Quality Uncertainty and the Market Mechanism. *Quarterly Journal of Economics* 84:488–500.

Akerlof, George A. and Janet L. Yellen. 1986. *Efficiency Wage Models of the Labor Market*. New York: Cambridge University Press.

Alchian, Armen A. and Harold Demsetz. 1972. Production, Information Costs, and Economic Organization. *American Economic Review* 62:777–795.

Allen, Douglas W. and Dean Lueck. 1992. Contract Choice in Modern Agriculture: Cropshare versus Cash Rent. *Journal of Law and Economics* 35:397–426.

Allen, Douglas W. and Dean Lueck. 1995. Risk Preferences and the Economics of Contracts. *American Economic Review* 85:447–451.

American Heritage Dictionary of the English Language, Fourth Edition. 2000. Boston: Houghton Mifflin Company.

Anderson, Erin and David C. Schmittlein. 1984. Integration of the Sales Force: An Empirical Examination. *RAND Journal of Economics* 15:385–395.

Anderson, Erin and Richard L. Oliver. 1987. Perspectives on Behavior-Based versus Outcome-Based Salesforce-Control Systems. *Journal of Marketing* 51:76–88.

Areeda, Phillip. 1991. *Antitrust Law*, vol. IX. Boston: Little, Brown.

Areeda, Phillip and Herbert Hovenkamp. 1993. *Antitrust Law* (Supp.), at ¶340.3 and ¶1640. Boston: Little, Brown.

Areeda, Phillip and Donald Turner. 1978. *Antitrust Law*, vol. II. Boston: Little, Brown.

Arthur Andersen & Co. 1995. *Worldwide Franchising Statistics: A Study of Worldwide Franchise Associations*.

Athey, Susan and Scott Stern. 1998. An Empirical Framework for Testing Theories about Complementarities in Organizational Design. NBER Working Paper 6600.

Atkins, D. 1990. Affidavit in the Matter of *Canterbury et al. v. Commissioner of Internal Revenue*, 160 Tax Decisions and Rulings K-2 (U.S. Tax Ct. 1992).

Azevedo, Paulo Furquim and Vivian Lara Dos Santos Silva. 2001. Contractual Mix Analysis in the Brazilian Franchising. *Mimeo*. São Carlos, Brazil: Federal University of São Carlos, Spain.

Azoulay, Pierre and Scott Shane. 2001. Entrepreneurs, Contracts, and the Failure of Young Firms. *Management Science* 47:337–358.

Bai, Chong-en and Zhigang Tao. 2000. Contract Mix in Franchising. *Journal of Economics & Management Strategy* 9(1):85–113.

Barkoff, Rupert M. and W. Michael Garner. 1994a. Encroachment: Franchising's Enigma. *Franchise Update* (2nd quarter):7–10.

Barkoff, Rupert M. and W. Michael Garner. 1994b. Encroachment: The Thorn in Every Successful Franchisor's Side. *Annual Forum on Franchising*. American Bar Association.

Barron, John M. and John R. Umbeck. 1984. The Effects of Different Contractual Arrangements: The Case of Retail Gasoline. *Journal of Law and Economics* 27:313–328.

Bassuk, Howard. 2000. Never Mind Encroachment, We Need More Franchisees! Brave New World or Brazen New World . . . It's Hard to Know. *ExploreBiz.net* (http://explorebiz.net/articles/hb21.html).

Bates, Timothy. 1995a. A Comparison of Franchise and Independent Small Business Survival Rates. *Small Business Economics* 7(5):377–388.

Bates, Timothy. 1995b. Analysis of Survival Rates Among Franchise and Independent Small Business Startups. *Journal of Small Business Management* 33(2):25–36.

Bates, Timothy. 1998. Survival Patterns Among Newcomers to Franchising. *Journal of Business Venturing* 13:113–130.

Baye, Michael R., Keith J. Crocker, and Jiandong Ju. 1996. Divisionalization, Franchising, and Divestiture Incentives in Oligopoly. *American Economic Review* 86:223–236.

Beales, Howard and Timothy J. Muris. 1995. The Foundation of Franchise Regulation: Issues and Evidence. *Journal of Corporate Finance: Contracting, Governance and Organization* 2:157–197.

Becker, Gary S. and Murphy. 1993. A Simple Theory of Advertising as a Good or Bad. *The Quarterly Journal of Economics* 108: 941–964.

Becker, Gary S. and George J. Stigler. 1974. Law Enforcement, Malfeasance, and Compensation of Enforcers. *Journal of Legal Studies* 3:1–20.

Beheler, R. L. 1991. Control in Various Organizational Forms: An Empirical Study of Company-Owned and Franchisee-Owned Units' Health Inspections. In J. R. Nevin, ed., *Fifth Annual Proceedings of the Society of Franchising*.

Bercovitz, Janet E. L. 1998a. An Analysis of Contractual Provisions in Business-Format Franchise Agreements. *Mimeo*, Durham, NC: Fuqua School of Business, Duke University.

Bercovitz, Janet E. L. 1998b. Franchising vs. Company Ownership. *Mimeo*, Durham, NC: Fuqua School of Business, Duke University.

Bhattacharyya, Sugato and Francine Lafontaine. 1995. Double-Sided Moral Hazard and the Nature of Share Contracts. *RAND Journal of Economics* 26:761–781.

Birkeland, Peter M. 2002. *Franchising Dreams*. Chicago: University of Chicago Press.

Blair, Roger D. 1988. Measuring Damages for Lost Profits in Franchise Termination Cases. *Franchise Law Journal* 8 (Fall):3–6, 23–27.

Blair, Roger D. and Amanda K. Esquibel. 1996. Maximum Resale Price Restraints in Franchising. *Antitrust Law Journal* 65:157–180.

Blair, Roger D. and J. M. Fesmire. 1986. Maximum Price Fixing and the Goals of Antitrust. *Syracuse Law Review* 37:43.

Blair, Roger D. and Jeffrey L. Harrison. 1989. Rethinking Antitrust Injury. *Vanderbilt Law Review* 42:1559–1573.

Blair, Roger D. and Jill Boylston Herndon. 1996. Restraints of Trade by Durable Good Producers. *Review of Industrial Organization* 11:339–353.

Blair, Roger D. and Jill Boylston Herndon. 1999. The Misapplication of *Kodak* in Franchise Tying Suits. *Journal of Business Venturing* 14:397–415.

Blair, Roger D. and David L. Kaserman. 1978. Vertical Integration, Tying, and Antitrust Policy. *American Economic Review* 68:397–402.

Blair, Roger D. and David L. Kaserman. 1980. Vertical Control with Variable Proportions: Ownership Integration and Contractual Equivalents. *Southern Economic Journal* 47:1118–1128.

Blair, Roger D. and David L. Kaserman. 1981. The Albrecht Rule and Consumer Welfare: An Economic Analysis. *University of Florida Law Review* 33:461.

Blair, Roger D. and David L. Kaserman. 1982. Optimal Franchising. *Southern Economic Journal* 494–504.

Blair, Roger D. and David L. Kaserman. 1983. *Law and Economics of Vertical Integration and Control*. Orlando, FL: Academic Press, Inc.

Blair, Roger D. and David L. Kaserman. 1985 *Antitrust Economics*. Homewood, IL: Richard D. Irwin Publishing.

Blair, Roger D. and David L. Kaserman. 1994. A Note on Incentive Incompatibility under Franchising. *Review of Industrial Organization* 9:323–330.

Blair, Roger D. and Lawrence W. Kenny. 1982. *Microeconomics for Managerial Decision Making*. New York: McGraw-Hill.

Blair, Roger D. and Francine Lafontaine. 1999. Will *Khan* Foster or Hinder Franchising? An Economic Analysis of Maximum Resale Price Maintenance. *Journal of Public Policy in Marketing* 18:25–36.

Blair, Roger D. and Gordon L. Lang. 1991. *Albrecht* After *ARCO*; Maximum Resale Price Fixing Moves Toward the Rule of Reason. *Vanderbilt Law Review* 44:1007–1039.

Blair, Roger D. and John E. Lopatka. 1998. *Albrecht* Overruled – At Last. *Antitrust Law Journal* 66:537–566.

Bond, Robert E. Various years. *Bond's Franchise Guide*. Oakland, CA: Source Book Publications.

Bond, Robert E. Various years. *The Source Book of Franchise Opportunities*. Richard D. Irwin Publishing.

Bradach, Jeffrey L. 1995. Chains Within Chains: The Role of Multi-Unit Franchisees. *Journal of Marketing Channels* 4:65–81.

Bradach, Jeffrey L. 1997. Using the Plural Form in the Management of Restaurant Chains. *Administrative Science Quarterly* 42:276–303.

Bradach, Jeffrey L. 1998. *Franchise Organizations*. Boston: Harvard Business School Press.

Bradach, Jeffrey L. and Patrick J. Kaufmann. 1988. "Franchisee or Independent Businessperson: Some Observations on the Decision Process." In *Research at the Marketing/Entrepreneurship Interface*, G. E. Hills and W. Laforge, eds. 38–48. Chicago: University of Illinois at Chicago.

Brickley, James A. 1999. Incentive Conflicts and Contracting: Evidence from Franchising. *Journal of Law and Economics* 42:745–774.

Brickley, James A. 2001. Evidence of Life-Cycle Pricing in Franchise Contracts. *Mimeo*. Rochester, NY: Simon School of Business, University of Rochester.

Brickley, James A. 2002. Royalty Rates and Franchise Fees in Share Contracts: Evidence from Franchising. *Journal of Law, Economics, and Organization*. 18:511–535.

Brickley, James A., Sanjog Misra, and R. Lawrence Van Horn. 2003. Contract Duration: Evidence from Franchise Contracts. *Mimeo*. Rochester, NY: Simon School of Business, University of Rochester.

Brickley, James A. and Frederick H. Dark. 1987. The Choice of Organizational Form: The Case of Franchising. *Journal of Financial Economics* 18:401–420.

Brickley, James A., Frederick H. Dark, and Michael S. Weisbach. 1991a. An Agency Perspective on Franchising. *Financial Management* 20:27–35.

Brickley, James A., Frederick H. Dark, and Michael S. Weisbach. 1991b. The Economic Effects of Franchise Termination Laws. *Journal of Law and Economics* 34:101–132.

Brown, H. 1971. Franchising – A Fiduciary Relationship. *Texas Law Review* 49:650–675.

Brown, Paul R. 1981. Mom-and-Pop Don't Read Memos. *Forbes* September 28:94–96.

Bureau of Economic Analysis, National Economic Accounts (http://www.bea.doc.gov/bea/dn1.htm).

Bureau of Labor Statistics, U.S. Department of Labor, Consumer Price Index, All Urban Consumers – CPI-U, U.S. City Average, All Items (ftp://ftp.bls.gov/pub/special.requests/cpi/cpiai.txt).

Burnstein, M. L. 1960. The Economics of Tie-In Sales. *Review of Economics and Statistics* 42:68–73.

Carlton, Dennis W. and Jeffrey M. Perloff. 2000. *Modern Industrial Organization*. Addison Wesley, 3rd edition.

Carmichael, H. Lorne. 1983. The Agent-Agent's Problem: Payment by Relative Output. *Journal of Labor Economics* 1:50–65.

Carney, Mick and Eric Gedajlovic. 1991. Vertical Integration in Franchise Systems: Agency Theory and Resource Explanations. *Strategic Management Journal* 12:607–629.

Caves, Richard E. and William F. Murphy. 1976. Franchising: Firms, Markets, and Intangible Assets. *Southern Economic Journal* 42:572–586.

Coase, Ronald H. 1937. The Nature of the Firm. *Economica* 4:386–405.

Coase, Ronald H. 1972. Durability and Monopoly. *Journal of Law and Economics* 15:143–149.

Cohen, Jane and Ryan Fehlig. 2001. Encroachment: The Hannibal Lecter of Franchising. *St. Louis Bar Journal* (March).

Cohn, Stuart R. 1998. Deception Condoned: Pre-Contract Misrepresentations and the Parole Evidence Rule, in Francine Lafontaine, ed., *Twelfth Annual Proceedings of the International Society of Franchising*.

Coughlan, Anne T. 1985. Competition and Cooperation in Marketing Channel Choice: Theory and Application. *Marketing Science* 4:110–129.

Dant, Rajiv P. and Paul D. Berger. 1996. Modeling Cooperative Advertising Decisions in Franchising. *The Journal of the Operational Research Society* 47:1120–1136.

Dant, Rajiv P., Patrick J. Kaufmann, and Audhesh K. Paswan. 1992. Ownership Redirection in Franchised Channels. *Journal of Public Policy and Marketing* 11:33–44.

David B. Green, McDonald's Senior Vice President for Marketing, 1993 testimony, http://www.mcspotlight.org/people/witnesses/advertising/green.html.

David McKinnon. Chairman and CEO, Service Brands International. 2002. Panel discussion, *Entrepalooza 2002*, University of Michigan Business School.

Dicke, Thomas S. 1992. *Franchising in the America: The Development of a Business Method, 1840–1980*. Chapel Hill, NC: University of North Carolina Press.

Dienelt, John F. 1998. Fourth Circuit Reverses $390 Million Meineke Judgment. *The Franchise Lawyer*, 1–3.

Dixit, Avinash K. and Victor Norman. 1978. Advertising and Welfare, *Bell Journal of Economics* 9:1–11.

Dnes, Antony W. 1992a. *Franchising: A Case-Study Approach*. Aldershot, England: Ashgate Publishing Ltd.

Dnes, Antony W. 1992b. 'Unfair' Contractual Practices and Hostages in Franchise Contracts. *Journal of Institutional and Theoretical Economics* 148:484–504.

Dnes, Antony W. 1993. A Case Study Analysis of Franchise Contracts. *Journal of Legal Studies* 22:367–393.

Dnes, Antony W. 1996. The Economic Analysis of Franchise Contracts. *Journal of Institutional and Theoretical Economics* 152:297–324.

Dnes, Anthony and Nuno Garoupa. 2005. Externality and Organizational Choice in Franchising. *Journal of Economics and Business* forthcoming.

Doctor's Associate "Subway Franchise Agreement." *Uniform Franchise Offering Circular*, 2002.

Dorfman, Robert and Peter O. Steiner. 1954. Optimal Advertising and Optimal Quality. *American Economics Review* 44:826–836.

Easterbrook, F. 1981. Maximum Price Fixing. *University of Chicago Law Review* 48:886.

Eaton, B. Curtis and Richard G. Lipsey. 1979. The Theory of Market Pre-emption: The Persistence of Excess Capacity and Monopoly in Growing Spatial Markets. *Economica* 46:149–158.

Eaton, Richard. 1980. State Regulation of Franchise and Dealership Terminations: An Overview. *Antitrust Law Journal* 49:1331–1350.

Eckard, E. W. Jr. 1985. The Effects of State Automobile Dealer Entry Regulation on New Car Prices. *Economic Inquiry* 24:226.

Elango, B. and V. H. Fried. 1997. Franchising Research: A Literature Review and Synthesis. *Journal of Small Business Management* 35:68–82.

Engel, Eduardo MRA, Ronald D. Fisher, and Alexander Galetovic. 2001. Least-Present-Value-of-Revenue Auctions and Highway Franchising. *Journal of Political Economy* 109:993–1020.

Entrepreneur. Franchise 500. Various years.

Eswaran, Mukesh and Ashok Kotwal. 1985. A Theory of Contractual Structure in Agriculture. *American Economic Review* 75:352–367.

European Commission. 2002. *Competition Policy in Europe: The Competition Rules for Supply and Distribution Agreements.* Luxembourg: Office for Official Publications of the European Communities.

Fédération Française de la Franchise. 2003. *Toute la Franchise: Les Textes, les Chiffres, les Réseaux.* Paris: Fédération Française de la Franchise.

Fieldstone, Ronald R. 1998. Franchise Encroachment Law. *Franchise Law Journal* (Winter).

Flaherty, Julie. 2001. By the Book: Individuality vs. Franchising. *New York Times* (Feb. 17).

Flohr, Eckhard. 2000. Franchise Law – The Concrete Effects of the New European Regulation on Contract Design and Contract Practice in Franchising. Düsseldorf. http://www.cgla.org/canada/documents/franchlaw.htm.

Franchise Annual. Various Years. Lewiston NY: Info Franchise News Inc.

Franchise Times. 1996. Growth Forecast for 1996. Vol. 2 no. 2 p. 3 Chicago, IL: Crain Communications Inc.

Franchise Times. Various Years. Monitor 200. Roseville, MN: Franchise Times Corporation.

Frazer, Lorelle. 1998. Motivations for Franchisors to Use Flat Continuing Franchise Fees. *The Journal of Consumer Marketing* 15:587–596.

Frazer, Lorelle. 2001. Why Franchisors Discontinue Franchising but Continue Operating. *International Small Business Journal* 19:29–38.

Gagné, Robert, Simon Pierre Sigué, and Georges Zaccour. 1998. Droit d'Entrée et Taux de Redevance dans les Franchises d'Exploitation au Québec. *L'Actualité Economique* 74:651–668.

Gallini, Nancy T. and Nancy A. Lutz. 1992. Dual Distribution and Royalty Fees in Franchising. *Journal of Law, Economics, & Organization* 8:471–501.

Gal-Or, Esther. 1991. Optimal Franchising in Oligopolistic Markets with Uncertain Demand. *International Journal of Industrial Organization* 9:343–364.

Gal-Or, Esther. 1995. Maintaining Quality Standards in Franchise Chains. *Management Science* 41:1774–1792.

Garner, W. Michael. 2002. *Franchise and Distribution Law and Practice.* Thompson West.

Garrod, Peter and Walter Miklius. 1987. Accounting for Mortality of Business Firms in the Estimation of Lost Profits. *Mimeo.*

Gertner, Robert H. and Robert S. Stillman. 2001. Vertical Integration and Internet Strategies in the Apparel Industry. *Journal of Industrial Economics* 49:417–440.

Gibson, Richard. 1998. McDonald's Problems in Kitchen Don't Dim the Lure of Franchises. *Wall Street Journal*, June 3:A1.

Ghosh, Avijit and C. Samuel Craig. 1991. FRANSYS: A Franchise Distribution Location Model. *Journal of Retailing* 67:466–495.

Goldberg, Jeffrey D. 1983. *A Transaction Costs Analysis of Franchising with Empirical Applications to the Restaurant Industry.* Ph.D. Dissertation, University of Pennsylvania.

Goldstein Law Group. 2003. Arbitration Panel Finds That Block Franchisees Harmed by Block's Internet Tax Preparation Activities May Have Claims for Damages Against Block. *Goldstein Law Group Press Release*, January 16. www.goldlawgroup.com/release/pr011603.html.

Graddy, Kathryn. 1997. Do Fast-Food Chains Price Discriminate on the Race and Income Characteristics of an Area. *Journal of Business and Economic Statistics* 15:391–401.

Greenhut, M. L. and H. Ohta. 1979. Vertical Integration of Successive Oligopolies. *American Economic Review* 69:137–141.

Grimes, Warren S. 1996. When Do Franchisors Have Market Power? Antitrust Remedies For Franchisor Opportunism. *Antitrust Law Journal* 65:105–155.

Grossman, Sanford J. and Oliver D. Hart. 1986. The Costs and Benefits of Ownership: A Theory of Vertical and Lateral Integration. *Journal of Political Economy* 94:691–719.

Gupta, Srabana and Richard Romano. 1998. Monitoring the Principal with Multiple Agents. *RAND Journal of Economics* 29:427–442.

Hadfield, Gillian K. 1990. Problematic Relations: Franchising and the Law of Incomplete Contracts. *Stanford Law Review* 42:927–992.

Hadfield, Gillian K. 1991. Credible Spatial Preemption Through Franchising. *RAND Journal of Economics* 22:531–543.

Harman, Kathryn Lea. 1998. Comment, The Good Faith Gamble in Franchise Agreements: Does Your Implied Covenant Trump My Express Term? *Cumberland Law Review* 28:473.

Hellriegel, John E. Sr. and William Slater Vincent. 2000. The Encroachment Handbook: The Problem, the History, the Solution, in Audhesh K. Paswan, ed., *Fourteenth Annual Proceedings of the International Society of Franchising.*

Holmberg, C. and K. Boe Morgan. 1996. The Franchise Failure Continuum in Ann Dugan, ed., *Tenth Annual Proceedings of the Society of Franchising.*

Holmstrom, Bengt. 1979. Moral Hazard and Observability. *Bell Journal of Economics* 10:74–91.

Holmstrom, Bengt. 1982. Moral Hazard in Teams. *Bell Journal of Economics* 13:324–340.

Holmstrom, Bengt and Paul Milgrom. 1987. Aggregation and Linearity in the Provision of Intertemporal Incentives. *Econometrica* 55:303–328.

Holmstrom, Bengt and Paul Milgrom 1991. Multitask Principal-Agent Analyses: Incentive Contracts, Asset Ownership, and Job Design. *Journal of Law, Economics, and Organization* 7:24–51.

Holmstrom, Bengt and Paul Milgrom. 1994. The Firm as an Incentive System. *American Economic Review* 84:972–991.

Hotelling, Harold. 1929. Stability in Competition. *Economic Journal* 39:41–57.

Hovenkamp, Herbert. 1999. *Federal Antitrust Policy: The Law of Competition and Its Practice* St. Paul, MN: West Publishing Group.

Hoy, Frank and John Stanworth, Eds. 2002. *Franchising: An International Perspective.* London: Routledge.

Hunt, Shelby D. 1972. The Socioeconomic Consequences of the Franchise System of Distribution. *Journal of Marketing* 36:32–38.

Hunt, Shelby D. 1973. The Trend Toward Company-Operated Units in Franchise Chains. *Journal of Retailing* 49:3–12.

Hunt, Shelby D. and John R. Nevin. 1974. Power in a Channel of Distribution: Sources and Consequences. *Journal of Marketing Research* 11:186–193.

Hunt, Shelby D. and John R. Nevin. 1975. Tying Agreements in Franchising. *Journal of Marketing* 39:20–26.

IFA. Various years. *Franchise Opportunities Guide.* Washington, DC: IFA.

IFA Educational Foundation. 2002. *Multi Unit Owner Study.* Washington, DC: IFA.

IFA Educational Foundation and Arthur Andersen. 1992. *Franchising in the Economy, 1989–1992.* Washington, DC: IFA.

IFA Educational Foundation and Frandata Corp. 1998–2000. *The Profile of Franchising, Volumes I, II and III.* Washington, DC: IFA.

IFA Educational Foundation and Price Waterhouse Coopers 2004. *Economic Impact of Franchised Businesses.*

John, George and Barton A. Weitz. 1988. Forward Integration into Distribution: An Empirical Test of Transaction Cost Analysis. *Journal of Law, Economics, and Organization* 4:337–355.

Johnson, Tim. 1998. Revitalization of the Mom & Pop's. *Franchise Times* 5(2) (February):16–17.

Joskow, Paul. 1988. Asset Specificity and the Structure of Vertical Relationships: Empirical Evidence. *Journal of Law, Economics, and Organization* 4:95–117.

Justis, Robert T. and Richard J. Judd. 1998. *Franchising.* Houston, TX: Dame Publications.

Kalnins, Arturs. 2003. Hamburger Prices and Spatial Econometrics. *Journal of Economics and Management Strategy* 12:591–616.

Kalnins, Arturs. 2004a. Development Commitments, Overestimation and Venture Performance: Evidence from International Master Franchising Contract Announcements. *Mimeo,* Marshall School of Business, University of Southern California.

Kalnins, Arturs. 2004b. An Empirical Analysis of Territorial Encroachment within Franchised and Company-owned Branded Chains. *Marketing Science* 23:476–489.

Kalnins, Arturs and Francine Lafontaine. 2004. Multi-Unit Ownership in Franchising: Evidence from the Fast-Food Industry in Texas. *RAND Journal of Economics,* 35:

Kanouse, K. 2000. Collective Negotiation of Franchise Agreements. http://www.kanouse.com/collneg.htm.

Katz, Michael L. 1989. Vertical Contractual Relations. In R. Schmalensee and R. Willig, eds., *Handbook of Industrial Organization*. New York: Elsevier Science Publishers.

Kaufmann, David J. 1992. An Introduction to Franchising and Franchise Law. In *Franchising 1992, Business and Legal Issues*, Commercial Law and Practice Course Handbook Series, no. 603, Practicing Law Institute, New York, NY.

Kaufmann, Patrick J. and Rajiv P. Dant. 1996. Multi-Unit Franchising: Growth and Management Issues. *Journal of Business Venturing* 11:343–358.

Kaufmann, Patrick J. and Rajiv P. Dant. 2001. The Pricing of Franchise Rights. *Journal of Retailing* 77:537–545.

Kaufmann, Patrick J., Naveen Donthu, and Charles M. Brooks. 2000. Multi-Unit Retail Site Selection Processes: Incorporating Opening Delays and Unidentified Competition. *Journal of Retailing* 76(1):113–127.

Kaufmann, Patrick J. and Sevgin Eroglu. 1998. Standardization and Adaptation in Business Format Franchising. *Journal of Business Venturing* 14:69–95.

Kaufmann, Patrick J. and Sang Hyeon Kim. 1995. Master Franchising and System Growth Rates. *Journal of Marketing Channels* 4:49–64.

Kaufmann, Patrick J. and Francine Lafontaine. 1994. Costs of Control: The Source of Economic Rents for McDonald's Franchisees. *Journal of Law and Economics* 37:417–454.

Kaufmann, Patrick J. and V. Kasturi Rangan. 1990. A Model for Managing System Conflict During Franchising Expansion. *Journal of Retailing* 66:155–173.

Kaufmann, Patrick J. and John Stanworth. 1995. The Decision to Purchase a Franchise: A Study of Prospective Franchisees. *Journal of Small Business Management* 33:22–33.

Kehoe, Michael R. 1996. Franchising, Agency Problems, and the Cost of Capital. *Applied Economics* 28:1485–1493.

Kennedy, Peter. 2003. *A Guide to Econometrics* fifth edition. Cambridge, MA: MIT Press.

Killion, William and Brian B. Schnell. 1997. Franchisors as Fiduciaries in Handling Marketing Dollars: Whose Money Is It Anyway? *Franchise Law Journal* 17:37, 52–60.

Kirby, D. A. and A. Watson. 1999. Franchising as a Strategy for Growth: The Case of the Construction Industry. In Stanworth J. and D. Purdy, eds., *Thirteenth Annual Proceedings of the International Society of Franchising*.

Klein, Benjamin. 1980. Transaction Cost Determinants of 'Unfair' Contractual Arrangements. *American Economic Review* 70:356–362.

Klein, Benjamin. 1995. The Economics of Franchise Contracts. *Journal of Corporate Finance* 2:9–37.

Klein, Benjamin. 1999. Market Power in Franchise Cases in the Wake of Kodak: Applying Post Contract Hold-Up Analysis to Vertical Relationships. *Antitrust Law Journal* 67:283–326.

Klein, Benjamin, Robert G. Crawford, and Armen A. Alchian. 1978. Vertical Integration, Appropriable Rents, and the Competitive Contracting Process. *Journal of Law and Economics* 21:297–326.

Klein, Benjamin and Keith Leffler. 1981. The Role of Market Forces in Assuring Contractual Performance. *Journal of Political Economy* 89:615–641.

Klein, Benjamin and Kevin M. Murphy. 1988. Vertical Restraints as Contract Enforcement Mechanisms. *Journal of Law and Economics* 31:265–297.

Klein, Benjamin and Lester F. Saft. 1985. The Law and Economics of Franchise Tying Contracts. *Journal of Law and Economics* 28:345–361.

Kmenta, Jan. 1986. *Elements of Econometrics* (2nd ed.). New York: Macmillan.

Knight, Frank. 1921. *Risk, Uncertainty, and Profit.* Chicago: Houghton Mifflin.

Knox, D. M. 1958. The Development of the Tied House System in London. *Oxford Economic Papers* 10:66–83.

Knight, Russell M. 1986. Franchising from the Franchisor and Franchisee Points of View. *Journal of Small Business Management* 24:8–15.

Kolton, Jeffrey E. 1992. The FranData Franchise Termination Report. *Info Franchise Newsletter* (August).

Krattenmaker, Thomas G., Robert H. Lande, and Steven C. Salop. 1987. Monopoly Power and Market Power in Antitrust Law. *Georgetown Law Journal* 76:241–269.

Kroc, Ray. 1977. *Grinding It Out: The Making of McDonald's.* New York: St. Martin's Press.

Krueger, Alan B. 1991. Ownership, Agency and Wages: An Examination of the Fast Food Industry. *Quarterly Journal of Economics* 106:75–101.

Lafontaine, Francine. 1992a. Agency Theory and Franchising: Some Empirical Results. *RAND Journal of Economics* 23:263–283.

Lafontaine, Francine. 1992b. How and Why do Franchisors do What They do: A Survey Report. In P. J. Kaufmann, ed., *Sixth Annual Proceedings of the Society of Franchising.*

Lafontaine, Francine. 1993. Contractual Arrangements as Signaling Devices: Evidence from Franchising. *Journal of Law, Economics, and Organization* 9:256–289.

Lafontaine, Francine. 1995a. A Critical Look at Data Sources in Franchising. *Journal of Marketing Channels* 4:5–25.

Lafontaine, Francine. 1995b. "Pricing Decisions in Franchised Chains: A Look at the Fast-Food Industry." NBER Working Paper #5247.

Lafontaine, Francine. 1999. Franchising vs. Corporate Ownership: The Effect on Price Dispersion. *Journal of Business Venturing* 14:17–34.

Lafontaine, Francine and Sugato Bhattacharyya. 1995. The Role of Risk in Franchising. *Journal of Corporate Finance* 2:39–74.

Lafontaine, Francine and Patrick J. Kaufmann. 1994. The Evolution of Ownership Patterns in Franchise Systems. *Journal of Retailing* 70:97–113.

Lafontaine, Francine and Joanne Oxley. 2004. International Franchising Practices in Mexico: Do Franchisors Customize their Contracts? *Journal of Economics and Management Strategy* 13:95–124.

Lafontaine, Francine and Emmanuel Raynaud. 2002. Residual Claims and Self Enforcement as Incentive Mechanisms in Franchise Contracts: Substitute or Complements. In *The Economics of Contracts: Theory and Applications,* Eric

Brousseau and Jean Michel Glachant, Eds. Cambridge: Cambridge University Press.

Lafontaine, Francine and Kathryn L. Shaw. 1998. Franchising Growth and Franchisor Entry and Exit in the U.S. Market: Myth and Reality. *Journal of Business Venturing* 13:95–112.

Lafontaine, Francine and Kathryn L. Shaw. 1999. The Dynamics of Franchise Contracting: Evidence from Panel Data. *Journal of Political Economy* 107:1041–1080.

Lafontaine, Francine and Kathryn L. Shaw. Forthcoming. Targetting Managerial Control: Evidence from Franchising. *RAND Journal of Economics.*

Lafontaine, Francine and Margaret E. Slade. 1996. Retail Contracting and Costly Monitoring: Theory and Evidence. *European Economic Review* 40:923–932.

Lafontaine, Francine and Margaret E. Slade. 1997. Retail Contracting: Theory and Practice. *Journal of Industrial Economics* 45:1–25.

Lafontaine, Francine and Margaret E. Slade. 2001. Incentive Contracting and the Franchise Decision. In K. Chatterjee and W. Samuelson, Eds. *Game Theory and Business Applications of Game Theory*, Boston, MA: Kluwer Academic Press.

Lal, Rajiv 1990. Improving Channel Coordination through Franchising. *Marketing Science* 9:299–318.

Landes, William and Richard Posner. 1981. Market Power in Antitrust Cases. *Harvard Law Review* 94:937–996.

Lazear, Edward P. 2000. Performance Pay and Productivity. *American Economic Review* 90:1346–1361.

Lerner, Abba. 1934. The Concept of Monopoly and the Measurement of Monopoly Power. *Review of Economic Studies* 1:157–175.

Lewin, Shira. 1998. Autonomy, Contractibility, and the Franchise Relationship. *Mimeo*, University of Cambridge.

Lewis, Matt. 2003. Asymmetric Price Adjustment and Consumer Search: An Examination of the Retail Gasoline Market. *Mimeo*. University of California, Berkeley, Dept. of Economics.

Lillis, Charles M., Chem L. Narayan, and John L. Gilman. 1976. Competitive Advantage Variation Over the Life Cycle of a Franchise. *Journal of Marketing* 40:77–80.

LNA/Media Watch, Various Years, *Ad $ Summary*, New York: Competitive Media Reporting (CMR).

Love, John F. 1986. *McDonald's: Behind the Arches.* New York: Bantam Books, Inc.

Lowell, H. B. 1991. *Multiple-Unit Franchising: The Key to Rapid System Growth*, Brownstein Zeidman and Schomer, Washington, D.C.

Lutz, Nancy A. 1995. Ownership Rights and Incentives in Franchising. *Journal of Corporate Finance* 2:103–130.

Luxenberg, Stan. 1985. *Roadside Empires: How the Chains Franchised America.* New York: Penguin Books.

Lyons, Bruce R. 1996. Empirical Relevance of Efficient Contract Theory: Inter-Firm Contracts. *Oxford Review of Economic Policy* 12:27–52.

Machlup, Fritz and Martha Taber. 1960. Bilateral Monopoly, Successive Monopoly, and Vertical Integration. *Economica* 27:101–119.

Maddocks, Tom. 2001. Buying in Bulk. *Entrepreneur* (September).

Makar, Scott. 1988. In Defense of Franchisors: The Law and Economics of Franchise Quality Assurance Mechanisms. *Villanova Law Review* 33:721–766.

Maness, Robert. 1996. Incomplete Contracts and the Choice Between Vertical Integration and Franchising. *Journal of Economic Behavior and Organization* 31:101–115.

Martin, Robert E. 1988. Franchising and Risk Management. *American Economic Review* 78:954–968.

Marvel, Howard. 1995. Tying, Franchising, and Gasoline Service Stations. *Journal of Corporate Finance* 2:199–225.

Marx, Thomas G. 1985. The Development of the Franchise Distribution System in the U.S. Automobile Industry. *Business History Review* 59:465–474.

Masten, Scott E. 1998. Contractual Choice. *Encyclopaedia of Law & Economics*. B. Boukaert and G. De Geest, Eds., Edward Elgar Publishing.

Mathewson, Frank and Ralph Winter. 1985. The Economics of Franchise Contracts. *Journal of Law and Economics* 28:503–526.

Mathewson, Frank and Ralph Winter. 1994. Territorial Restrictions in Franchise Contracts. *Economic Inquiry* 32:181–192.

Mazzeo, Michael J. 2002. Product Choice and Oligopoly Market Structure. *RAND Journal of Economics* 33:1–22.

Mazzeo, Michael, J. 2004. Retail Contracting and Organizational Form: Alternatives to Chain Affiliation in the Motel Industry. *Journal of Economics and Management Strategy* 13:599–616.

McAfee, R. Preston and Marius Schwartz. 1994. Opportunism in Multilateral Vertical Contracting: Nondiscrimination, Exclusivity, and Uniformity. *American Economic Review* 84:210–230.

McDonald's Corporation. 2003. Franchise Agreement. *Uniform Franchise Offering Circular.*

McMakin, Tom. 2001. *Bread and Butter.* New York: St. Martin's Press.

Mendelsohn, Martin, ed. 2003. *International Encyclopaedia of Franchising Law.* Richmond: Richmond Law & Tax.

Michael, Steven C. 1999. Do Franchised Chains Advertise Enough? *Journal of Retailing* 75:461–478.

Michael, Steven C. 2000a. The Effect of Organizational Form on Quality: The Case of Franchising. *Journal of Economic Behavior & Organization* 43:295–318.

Michael, Steven. C. 2000b. The Extent, Motivation, and Effect of Tying in Franchise Contracts. *Managerial and Decision Economics* 21:191–201.

Michael, Steven C. and Hollie J. Moore. 1995. Returns to Franchising. *Journal of Corporate Finance* 2:133–156.

Milgrom, Paul and John Roberts. 1992. *Economics, Organization and Management.* Englewoods Cliffs, NJ: Prentice-Hall.

Minkler, Alanson. 1990. An Empirical Analysis of a Firm's Decision to Franchise. *Economics Letters* 34:77–82.

Minkler, Alanson and Timothy A. Park. 1994. Asset Specificity and Vertical Integration. *Review of Industrial Organization* 9:409–423.

Muris, Timothy J., David T. Scheffman, and Pablo T. Spiller. 1992. Strategy and Transaction Costs: The Organization of Distribution in the Carbonated Soft Drink Industry. *Journal of Economics & Management Strategy* 1:83–128.

Murphy, Lee H. 2000. Close Quarters Irk Franchisees. *Crain's Chicago Business* 23(25).

Naisbitt Group, The. 1989. *The Future of Franchising- Looking 25 Years Ahead to the Year 2010.* Washington, DC: International Franchise Association.

Noll, Roger G. and Andrew Zimbalist. 1997. *Sports, Jobs, and Taxes: The Economic Impact of Sports Teams and Stadiums.* Washington, DC: Brookings Institution Press.

Noren, D. L. 1990. The Economics of the Golden Arches: A Case Study of the McDonald's System. *The American Economist* 34:60–64.

Norton, Seth W. 1988. An Empirical Look at Franchising as an Organizational Form. *Journal of Business* 61:197–217.

O'Donnell, Thomas. 1984. No Entrepreneurs Need Apply. *Forbes* 134(13):124–130.

Oxenfeldt, Alfred R. and Anthony O. Kelly. 1969. Will Successful Franchise Systems Ultimately Become Wholly-Owned Chains? *Journal of Retailing* 44:69–87.

Ozanne, Urban B. and Shelby D. Hunt. 1971. *The Economic Effect of Franchising.* Washington, DC: GPO Select Committee on Small Business (U.S. Senate, 92nd Congress).

Pashigian, B. Peter. 1961. *The Distribution of Automobiles: An Economic Analysis of the Franchising System.* Englewoods Cliffs, NJ: Prentice-Hall.

Pashigian, B. Peter and Eric D. Gould. 1998. Internalizing Externalities: The Pricing of Space in Shopping Malls. *Journal of Law and Economics* 41:115–142.

Pénard, Thierry, Emmanuel Raynaud, and Stéphane Saussier. 2003. Dual Distribution and Royalty Rates in Franchised Chains: An Empirical Exploration Using French Data. *Journal of Marketing Channels* 10:5–31.

Perrigot, Rozenn. 2004. Le choix des réseaux de points de vente: Une approche par l'écologie des populations et les analyses de survie. Thèse doctorale, Université de Rennes 1, France.

Pindyck, Robert S. and Daniel Rubinfield. 2001. *Microeconomics,* 5th ed. Upper Saddle River, NJ: Prentice-Hall.

Pitegoff, Thomas M. 1989. Franchise Relationship Laws: A Minefield for Franchisors. *Business Law* 45:289.

Plitt, Jane R. 2000. *Martha Mathilda Harper and the American Dream.* New York: Syracuse University Press.

Prager, Robin A. 1990. Firm Behavior in Franchise Monopoly Markets. *RAND Journal of Economics* 21:211–225.

Prendergast, Canice. 2002. The Tenuous Trade-Off Between Risk and Incentives. *Journal of Political Economy* 110:1071–1102.

Prewitt, Milford. 1998. Ruby Tuesday Franchise Plan Offers Buy-Back Guarantee. *Nation's Restaurant News* 32(9):10, 130.

Prewitt, Milford. 2003. Encroachment 'Battlefield' Now More Peaceful. *Nation's Restaurant News* 37:1, 43+.

Purdy, D., J. Stanworth, and M. Hatcliffe. 1996. Franchising in Figures. *Lloyds Bank Plc/IFRC Franchising in Britain Report* 1(2).

Rao, Ram C. and Shubashri Srinivasan. 1995. Why are Royalty Rates Higher in Service-Type Franchises. *Journal of Economics & Management Strategy* 4:7–31.

Reid, Joseph D. Jr. 1973. Sharecropping as an Understandable Market Response: The Post-Bellum South. *Journal of Economic History* 33:106–130.

Rey, Patrick and Joseph E. Stiglitz. 1995. The Role of Exclusive Territories in Producers' Competition. *RAND Journal of Economics* 26:431–451.

Rey, Patrick and Jean Tirole. A Primer on Foreclosure. *Handbook of Industrial Organization.* Forthcoming.

Romano, Richard E. 1994. Double Moral Hazard and Resale Price Maintenance. *RAND Journal of Economics* 25:455–466.

Rubin, Paul. 1978. The Theory of the Firm and the Structure of the Franchise Contract. *Journal of Law and Economics* 21:223–233.

Rysman, Marc. 2001. How Many Franchises in a Market? *International Journal of Industrial Organization,* 519–542.

Salvaneschi, Luigi. 1996. *Location, Location, Location: How to Select the Best Site for Your Business.* Portland, OR: Psi Successful Business Library, Oasis Press.

Sass, Tim R. and David S. Saurman. 1993. Mandated Exclusive Territories and Economic Efficiency: An Empirical Analysis of the Malt-Beverage Industry. *Journal of Law and Economics* 36:153.

Sass, Tim R. and David S. Saurman. 1996. Efficiency Effects of Exclusive Territories: Evidence from the Indiana Beer Market. *Economic Inquiry* 34:597.

Sasser, W. Earl and Samuel H. Pettway. 1974. Case of Big Mac's Pay Plans. *Harvard Business Review* 52:30–46, 156–158.

Schmalensee, Richard. 1982. Product Differentiation Advantages of Pioneering Brands. *American Economic Review* 72:349.

Schmidt, Torsten. 1994. An Analysis of Intrabrand Competition in the Franchise Industry. *Review of Industrial Organization* 9:293–310.

Scott, Frank A. 1995. Franchising vs. Company Ownership as a Decision Variable of the Firm. *Review of Industrial Organization* 10:69–81.

Seaton, Jonathan S. 2003. An Analysis of UK Franchise Contracting 1989–1999. *Managerial and Decision Economics* 24:25–34.

Seid, Michael H. 1988. Letter. *The Info Franchise Newsletter.* 12(9):2–3.

Seltz, David D. 1981. *The Complete Handbook of Franchising.* New York: Addison-Wesley Publishing Co.

Sen, Kabir C. 1993. The Use of Initial Fees and Royalties in Business Format Franchising. *Managerial and Decision Economics* 14:175–190.

Sen, Kabir C. 1995. Advertising Fees in the Franchised Channel. *Journal of Marketing Channels* 4(1–2):83–101.

Shane, Scott A. 1996. Hybrid Organizational Arrangements and Their Implications for Firm Growth and Survival: A Study of New Franchisors. *Academy of Management Journal* 39:216–234.

Shane, Scott A. 2001. Organizational Incentives and Organizational Mortality. *Organization Science* 12:136–160.

Shapiro, Carl and Joseph E. Stiglitz. 1984. Equilibrium Unemployment as a Worker Discipline Device. *American Economic Review* 74:433–444.

Shelton, John P. 1967. Allocative Efficiency vs. 'X-Efficiency': Comment. *American Economic Review* 57:1252–1258.

Shepard, Andrea. 1993. Contractual Form, Retail Price, and Asset Characteristics. *RAND Journal of Economics* 24:58–77.

Silberman, Alan H. 1996. The Myth of Franchise 'Market Power.' *Antitrust Law Journal* 65:181–221.

Silvester, T., J. Stanworth, D. Purdy, and M. Hatcliffe. 1996. Secrets of Success. *Lloyds Bank Plc/IFRC Franchising in Britain Report*: 1(3).

Slade, Margaret E. 1996. Multitask Agency and Contract Choice: An Empirical Assessment. *International Economic Review* 37:465–486.

Slade, Margaret E. 1998a. Beer and the Tie: Did Divestiture of Brewer-Owned Public Houses Lead to Higher Beer Prices? *Economic Journal* 108:1–38.

Slade, Margaret E. 1998b. Strategic Motives for Vertical Separation: Evidence from Retail Gasoline. *Journal of Law, Economics, & Organization* 14:84–113.

Smith II, Richard L. 1982. Franchise Regulation: An Economic Analysis of State Restrictions on Automobile Distribution. *Journal of Law and Economics* 25:125–157.

Spengler, Joseph J. 1950. Vertical Integration and Antitrust Policy. *Journal of Political Economy* 58:347–352.

Stanworth, John. 1977. *A Study of Franchising in Britain: A Research Report.* London: Social Science Research Council.

Stanworth, John. 1996. Dispelling the Myths Surrounding Franchise Failure Rates – Some Recent Evidence from Britain. *Franchising Research: An International Journal* 1:25–28.

Stanworth, John and James Curran. 1999. Colas, Burgers, Shakes and Shirkers: Towards a Sociological Model of Franchising in the Market Economy. *Journal of Business Venturing* 14:323–344.

Stanworth, John and Patrick J. Kaufmann. 1996. Similarities and Differences in UK and U.S. Franchise Research Data: Towards a Dynamic Model of Franchisee Motivation. *International Small Business Journal* 14:57–70.

Stanworth, John, David Purdy, and Stuart Price. 1997. Franchise Growth and Failure in the USA and the UK: A Troubled Dreamworld Revisited. *Franchising Research: An International Journal* 2:75–94.

Stanworth, John, David Purdy, Stuart Price, and Nicos Zafiris. 1998. Franchise Versus Conventional Small Business Failure Rates in the U.S. and UK: More Similarities than Differences. *International Small Business Journal* 16:56–69.

Stassen, Robert and R. A. Mittelstaedt. 1991. A Successive Monopolies Examination of Conflict in Franchise Channels. In John Nevin, Ed. Fifth *Annual Proceedings of the Society of Franchising.*

Stassen, Robert E. and Robert A. Mittelstaedt. 1995. Territory Encroachment in Maturing Franchise Systems. *Journal of Marketing Channels* 4:27–48.

Stassen, Robert E. and Robert A. Mittelstaedt. 2002. Do Franchise Systems Advertise Enough? U.S. Restaurant Expenditures and Performance 1989 to 1998. *Journal of Marketing Channels* 10(2):3–18.

Stigler, George J. 1961. The Economics of Information. *Journal of Political Economy* 69:213–225.

Stigler, George J. 1968a. Economies of Scale. *Journal of Law and Economics* 1:54–71.

Stigler, George J. 1968b. Price and Nonprice Competition. *Journal of Political Economy* 72:149–154.

Stiglitz, Joseph E. 1974. Incentives and Risk-Sharing in Sharecropping. *Review of Economic Studies* 41:219–255.

Tannenbaum, Jeffrey A. 1997. Franchisors Push Local Marketing Efforts by Franchisees. *Wall Street Journal* (April 1):B2.

Tannenbaum, Jeffrey A. and Stephanie N. Mehta. 1997. Bias at Single Store Can Taint Franchise Chain's Image. *Wall Street Journal* (March 6):B2.

Terry, Andrew. 2001. The E-Business Challenge to Franchising, in Lorelle Frazer Ed., *Fifteenth Annual Proceedings of the International Society of Franchising.*

Trutko, James, John Trutko, and Andrew Kostecka. 1993. *Franchising's Growing Role in the U.S. Economy, 1975–2000.* U.S. Department of Commerce, National Technical Information Service, Springfield VA.

Thomadsen, Raphael. 2005. The Effect of Ownership Structure on Prices in Geographically Differentiated Industries. *RAND Journal of Economics,* forthcoming.

Thompson, R. Steve. 1994. The Franchise Life Cycle and the Penrose Effect. *Journal of Economic Behavior and Organization* 24:207–218.

United States General Accounting Office. 2001. *Federal Trade Commission Enforcement of the Franchise Rule.* Washington, DC: GAO 01–776.

U.S. Census Bureau. Various years. Annual Survey of Manufacturers.

U.S. Census Bureau. Monthly Retail Trade Survey.

U.S. Census Bureau. 1992 Characteristics of Business Owners Survey.

U.S. Census Bureau. Various years. Historical Retail Trade Services.

U.S. Department of Commerce (USDOC). Various years. *Franchise Opportunities Handbook,* compiled by Andrew Kostecka. Washington, DC.

U.S. Department of Commerce (USDOC). Various years. *Franchising in the Economy,* prepared by Andrew Kostecka. Washington, DC.

Udell, G. 1972. Anatomy of a Franchise Contract. *Cornell Hotel and Restaurant Administration Quarterly* 13:13–21.

Vernon, John and Daniel Graham. 1971. Profitability of Monopolization by Vertical Integration. *Journal of Political Economy* 79:924–925.

Vincent, William S. 1998. Encroachment: Franchising's Nightmare (Neutralizing the Black Widow Spider). In Francine Lafontaine Ed. *Twelfth Annual Proceedings of the International Society of Franchising.*

Vines, Leonard D. 1996. *Mergers & Acquisitions of Franchise Companies.* Chicago: American Bar Association.

Vogel, Mike. 1996. Little Guy Needn't Apply. *Miami Daily Business Review* Aug. 9, 71(44).

Walkup, Carolyn. 2001. Embers Sparks 'Individuality': New Franchisees May Keep Old Names. *Nations Restaurant News* (March 13).

Warren-Boulton, Frederick R. 1974. Vertical Control with Variable Proportions. *Journal of Political Economy* 82:783–802.

Warren-Boulton, Frederick R. 1978. *Vertical Control of Markets: Business and Labor Practices.* Cambridge, MA: Ballinger Publishing Co.

Wheaton, William C. 2000. Percentage Rent in Retail Leasing: The Alignment of Landlord-Tenant Interests. *Real Estate Economics* 28:185–204.

Whinston, Michael D. 1990. Tying, Foreclosure and Exclusion. *American Economic Review* 80:837–859.

Williams, Darrell L. 1996a. "Franchise Contract Termination: Is there Evidence of Franchisor Abuse?" In Ann Dugan Ed., *Tenth Annual Proceedings of the International Society of Franchising*.

Williams, Darrell L. 1996b. Incomplete Contracting and Ex-Post Opportunism: Evidence from Franchise Contract Terminations. *Mimeo*. UCLA, Dept. of Economics.

Williams, Darrell. 1999. Why do Entrepreneurs Become Franchisees? An Empirical Analysis of Organizational Choice. *Journal of Business Venturing* 14:103–124.

Williamson, Oliver E. 1971. The Vertical Integration of Production: Market Failure Considerations. *American Economic Review* 61:112–123.

Williamson, Oliver E. 1979. Transaction Cost Economics: The Governance of Contractual Relations. *Journal of Law and Economics* 22:233–262.

Williamson, Oliver E. 1983. Credible Commitments: Using Hostages to Support Exchange. *American Economic Review* 73:519–540.

Williamson, Oliver E. 1985. *The Economic Institutions of Capitalism*. New York: Free Press.

Wimmer, Bradley S. and John E. Garen. 1997. Moral Hazard, Asset Specificity, Implicit Bonding, and Compensation: The Case of Franchising. *Economic Inquiry* 35:544–554.

Windsperger, Josef. 2002. *The Dual Structure of Franchising Firms*, in Joyce Young, ed., 16th Annual Proceedings of the International Society of Franchising.

Young, Joyce, Audhesh K. Paswan, John M. Buch, Lori Ashby, 1997. Fast-Food Franchises and Supercenters: A Tale of Two Alliances and Beyond. In Mark Spriggs (ed.) Proceedings of the 11th Annual International Society of Franchising Conference.

Zarco, R. and J. Dienelt, 1994. Point Counterpoint. *Franchise Update* (2nd quarter): 22–25.

Zeidman, Philip F. 1989. *Survey of Foreign Laws and Regulations Affecting International Franchising*. Chicago: American Bar Association.

Zellner, Richard E., Dale D. Achabal, and Laurence A. Brown. 1980. Market Penetration and Locational Conflict in Franchise Systems. *Decision Sciences* 11:58–90.

Zupan, Mark A. 1989a. Cable Franchise Renewals: Do Incumbent Firms Behave Opportunistically? *RAND Journal of Economics* 20:473–482.

Zupan, Mark A. 1989b. The Efficacy of Franchise Bidding Schemes in the Case of Cable Television: Some Systematic Evidence. *Journal of Law and Economics* 32:401–456.

Cases, Codes, and Statutes

Ala. Code § 8-20-5.

Albrecht v. Herald Company, 390 U.S. 145 (1968).

Amerada Hess Corporation v. Quinn, 143 N.J. Super 237, 362 A 2d 1258 (Law Div. 1976).

Arthur Wishart Act, Ontario, Canada.

Atlantic Richfield Co. v. USA Petroleum Co., 495 U.S. 328 (1990).

Barnes v. Burger King Corp., 932 F. Supp. 1420, 1437–38 SD FLA (1996).

Bigelow v. RKO Radio Pictures, 327 U.S. 251, 265 (1946).

Broussard v. Meineke Discount Muffler Shops, Inc., 155 F.3d 331 (4th Cir. 1998).

Broussard v. Meineke Discount Muffler Shops, Inc., 958 F. Supp. 1087 (W.D.N.C. 1997).

Burger King Corp. v. CR Weaver, 169 F.3d 1310 (11th Cir. 1999).

Business Electronics Corp. v. Sharp Electronics Corp, 485 U.S. 717 (1988).

Cal. Bus. & Prof. Code § 20025.

Cal. Veh. Code § 3060.

Camp Creek Hospitality Inns, Inc. v. Sheraton Franchise Corp., 139 F.3d 1396 (11th Cir. 1998).

Canterbury, Charles D. et al. v. Commissioner of Internal Revenue (1992), Tax Decisions and Rulings, no. 160, Washington D.C., The Bureau of National Affairs, Inc., K2–K24.

Caribe BMW, Inc. v. Bayerische Motoren Werke Aktiengesellschaft, 19 F.3d 745 (1st Cir. 1994).

Carlock v. Pillsbury Co., 719 F. Supp. 791 (D. Minn. 1989).

Clark v. America's Favorite Chicken Co., 110 F.3d 295 (5th Cir. 1997).

Clayton Act, 15 U.S.C. §§ 12–27.

Cohn v. Taco Bell Corp, WL 13771 (N.D. Ill. 1994).

Collins v. International Dairy Queen, 1997 WL 627504 (M.D. Ga. Oct. 1997).

Collins v. International Dairy Queen, 939 F. Supp. 875 (M.D. Ga. 1996).

Conn. Gen. Stat. § 42–133f.

Conn. Gen. Stat. § 42–133v.

Continental T.V. v. GTE Sylvania, Inc., 433 U.S. 36 (1977).

Cook v. Little Caesar Enterprises, Inc., 972 F. Supp. 400, 409 (E.D. Mich. 1997).

Curry v. Steve's Franchise Co., 1985–2, CCH Trade Cases, par. 66877.

Del. Code Ann. tit. 6, § 2552.

Domed Stadium Hotel, Inc. v. Holiday Inns, Inc., 732 F. 2d 480 (5th Cir. 1984).

Dr. Miles Medical Co. v. John D. Park & Sons Co., 220 U.S. 373 (1911).

Eastman Kodak Company v. Image Technical Service, 504 U.S. 451 (1992).

EEC Block Exemption for Vertical Restraints.

Emporium Drug Mart Inc. v. Drug Emporium Inc. of Denton, No. 71 114 00126 00 (Am. Arbitration Assoc., Dallas, Texas, Sept. 2, 2000).

Far Horizons Pty Ltd v. McDonald's Australia Ltd, VSC 310 (August 18, 2000).

Federal Trade Commission. 1979. *Disclosure Requirements and Prohibitions Concerning Franchising and Business Opportunity Ventures*, 16 CFR § 436.1 et seq.

Federal Trade Commission v. Sinclair Refining Co., 261 U.S. 463 (1923).

Fla. State. § 320.64(1)(a).

Foodmaker, Inc. v. Quershi, Bus. Franchise Guide (CCH) ¶11780 (Cal. Super. Ct., Dec. 1, 1999).

Fortner Enterprises v. United States Steel Corporation, 394 U.S. 495 (1969).

Franchising Code of Conduct, 1998, Commonwealth of Australia.

Glover v. Henderson, 120 Mo 367, 25 SW 175 (1894).

Haw. Rev. Stat. § 482E-6(2)(H).

Haw. Rev. Stat. § 482E-6(2).

Ill. Rev. Stat. ch. 121 1/2¶754(d)(6).

Indiana Code §§ 23-2-2.7–1(2) & 23-2-2.7–2(4).

Iowa Code 2001 Supplement, Section 537A.10.

Iowa Code 523H, 1995 & 1992.

Jack Walters and Sons Corporation v. Morton Building, Inc., 737 F. 2d 698 (7th Cir.), *cert. denied*, 469 U.S. 1018 (1984).

Jefferson Parish Hospital District No. 2 v. Hyde, 104 S.Ct. 1551 (1984).

Kentucky Fried Chicken Corporation v. Diversified Packaging Corporation, 549 F. 2d 368 (1977).

Kiefer-Stewart Co. v. Joseph E. Seagram & Sons, 340 U.S. 211 (1951).

Krehl v. Baskin-Robbins Ice Cream Company, 664 F. 2d 1348 (9th Cir. 1982).

Kypta v. McDonald's Corporation, 671 F. 2d 1282 (11th Cir. 1982).

Little Caesar Enterprises, Inc. v. Smith, 34 F. Supp. 2d 459 (E.D. Mich. 1998).

Mass. Gen. L. ch. 93B, § 4(3)(e), § 9.

Metrix Warehouse, Inc. v. Daimler Benz, 828 F. 2d 1033 (4th Cir. 1987).

Mich. Comp. Laws § 445.1527 (D).

Miller v. Western Men, Inc., 20 Utah 2d 352, 437 P.2d 892 (1968).

Minn. Stat. § 80C.14, subd. 4.

Monsanto Co. v. Spray-Rite Service Corp., 465 U.S. 752 (1984).

N.J. Rev. Stat. § 56:10–5.

Neb. Rev. Stat. § 87–404.

In re *Nissan Antitrust Litigation*, 577 F. 2d 910 (5th Cir. 1978), *cert. denied*, 439 U.S. 1072 (1979).

Northern Pacific Railway v. United States, 356 U.S. 1 (1958).

Payne v. McDonald's Corp., 957 F. Supp. 749, 754–60 (D. Md. 1997).

Petroleum Marketing Practices Act.

Phillips v. Crown Central Petroleum Corp., 395 F. Supp. 435 (E.D. Mich. 1975).

Photovest Corp. v. Fotomat Corp., 606 F.2d 704 (7th Cir. 1979), *cert. denied,* 445 U.S. 917 (1980).

Principe v. McDonald's Corporation, 631 F. 2d 303 (1980).

Queen City Pizza, Inc. v. Domino's Pizza, Inc., 124 F.3d 430, reh'g denied, 129 F.3d 724 (3d Cir. 1997).

Queen City Pizza, Inc. v. Domino's Pizza, Inc., 922 F. Supp. 1055 (E.D. Pa. 1996).

Robinson Patman Act, 15 U.S.C. § 13.

Redd v. Shell Oil Co., 524 F. 2d 1054 (10th Cir. 1975).

Restatement of Contracts § 205 (1977).

Rosenberg v. Pillsbury Co., 718 F. Supp. 1146 (S.D.N.Y. 1989).

Scheck v. Burger King Corp., 756 F. Supp. 543 (S.D. Fla. 1991) ("Scheck I").

Scheck v. Burger King Corp., 798 F. Supp. 692, 696 (S.D. Fla. 1992) ("Scheck II").

Schubot v. McDonald's. Corp., 963 F.2d 385 (11th Cir. 1992).

Sherman Antitrust Act, 15 U.S.C. §§ 1–11.

Siegal v. Chicken Delight, 448 F. 2d 43 (9th Cir. 1971).

Small Business Franchise Act (1999).

State Oil Co. v. Khan, US Sup. CT, No. 96–871.

Subsolutions, Inc. v. Doctor's Associates, Inc. 62 F. Supp. 2d 616 (D. Conn. 1999).

Tex. Rev. Civ. Stat. Ann. art. 4413(36) § 5.02(3).

Uniform Commercial Code (UCC § 2–309[2]).

United States Steel Corporation v. Fortner Enterprises, 429 U.S. 610 (1977).

United States v. Socony-Vacuum Oil Co., 310 U.S. 150 (1940).

USA Petroleum Co. v. Atlantic Richfield Co., 13 F. 3d 1276 (9th Cir. 1994).

Vicorp Restaurants, Inc. v. Village Inn Pancake House of Albuquerque, Inc., Bus. Franchise Guide (CCH) ¶10994 (D.N. Mex. 1996).

Vylene Enterprises, Inc. v. Naugles, Inc., 90 F. 3d 1472 (9th Cir. 1996).

Wilson v. Mobil Oil Corporation, 940 F. Supp. 944 (E.D. La. 1996).

Wilson v. Mobil Oil Corporation, 984 F. Supp. 450 (E.D. La. 1997).

Wis. Stat. § 135.03.

Wisconsin Fair Dealership Law.

Index